# PUBLIC PROCUREMENT

## A Practical Guide to the U.K. Regulations and Associated Community Rules

AUSTRALIA
The Law Book Company
Brisbane - Sydney - Melbourne - Perth


CANADA
Carswell
Ottawa - Toronto - Calgary - Montreal - Vancouver



**Agents**
Steimatzky's Agency Ltd., Tel Aviv
N.M. Tripathi (Private) Ltd., Bombay
Eastern Law House (Private) Ltd., Calcutta
M.P.P. House, Bangalore
Universal Book Traders, Delhi
Aditya Books, Delhi
MacMillan Shuppan KK, Tokyo
Pakistan Law House, Karachi, Lahore

# Public Procurement

## A Practical Guide to the U.K. Regulations and Associated Community Rules

*by*

## Andrew Geddes

M.A., *Barrister*

London
Sweet & Maxwell
1993

Published in 1993 by
Sweet & Maxwell Limited of
South Quay Plaza
183 Marsh Wall
London E14 9FT
Computerset by Mendip Communications Limited, Frome
Printed by Butler & Tanner Limited, Frome, Somerset

No natural forests were destroyed to make this product;
only farmed timber was used and replanted

A CIP catalogue record for this book is
available from the British Library

ISBN 0-421-48970-7

# Preface

The liberalisation of public procurement is seen by the Member States and the E.C. Commission as a centrepiece of the Internal European Market programme and as having great importance from an industrial policy point of view. (This principle is now enshrined in Article 130 F(2) of the E.C. Treaty as amended by the Single European Act 1987.) The European economy – as the Commission have pointed out on several occasions – will not move closer together unless the tendency to favour "national champions" when awarding public contracts is abandoned once and for all. In order to achieve these objectives the Community has adopted a number of directives which supplement the Treaty provisions on which they are based and which will in future regulate the advertising and award of virtually all public authority and utility contracts over a certain value threshold. In addition provision has been made for contractors and suppliers who suffer, or risk suffering, damage as a result of a breach of the new rules, with a right to obtain redress (including damages) by way of court action. These directives have been implemented into U.K. law by way of three sets of Regulations: The Public Works Contracts Regulations (1991), The Public Supply Contracts Regulations 1991 (both in force December 21, 1991) and the Utilities Supply and Works Contracts Regulations 1992 (in force January 13, 1993). Further Regulations are being prepared to implement the directives bringing service contracts within the new regime. These Regulations should come into force, on July 1, 1993 in relation to public service contracts, and July 1, 1994 in relation to utilities service contracts. It is intended that these will be the subject of updates to this Guide once they have been adopted by Parliament.

This Guide sets out in detail what the new rules are and how in the light of decisions of the European Court of Justice and Commission guidance they, and the associated Community rules relating to the free movement of goods and services, will probably be interpreted.

The Guide is intended to assist those who will have to wrestle with the complexities of the new regime as much as those whose job it will be to advise in regard to them.

In writing the Guide I have been greatly helped by the Treasury team who have been responsible for drafting the Regulations. They have referred me to a number of relevant Commission documents which would not otherwise have come to my attention and have read through the text and made a number of helpful suggestions. It goes without saying however that any errors contained in the text are my responsibility alone.

The Guide refers to the law as it stood at May 1, 1993.

A. C. GEDDES

EUROPEAN LAW GROUP
2 Essex Court
Temple
London
EC4

# CONTENTS

APPENDICES

# TABLE OF CASES

ix

# TABLE OF UNITED KINGDOM STATUTES

# TABLE OF UNITED KINGDOM STATUTORY INSTRUMENTS

(References in **bold** denote where the text of the Statutory Instrument is printed)

xiv

# TABLE OF EUROPEAN COMMUNITY SECONDARY LEGISLATION

(References in **bold** denote where the text of the Legislation is printed)

## Recommendations

## Regulations

## Treaties

# Chapter One

## INTRODUCTION

### The Procurement Directives

The opening up of procurement by government bodies and by the utilities to **1–01** E.C.-wide competition has been recognised by the Member States as a key component in the creation of the internal European market. This huge sector of the economy is estimated by the E.C. Commission as representing some 15 per cent. (592 milliard ECUs at 1989 prices) of Community G.D.P. of which some seven to ten per cent. (260–380 milliard ECUs) takes the form of contracts falling within the new public procurement regime. Of that total, building and construction represents 28.5 per cent.[1] Although there are a number of directly effective Treaty provisions which must be taken into account in the award of public authority contracts (see *Chapter Two*) these are insufficient to ensure that such contracts are opened up to Community-wide tendering. The E.C. has consequently adopted a number of specific measures whose purpose is to supplement the Treaty provisions by applying detailed rules to the award of public and utility procurement contracts over a certain value. The two principal measures are the Public Works Directive 71/305/EEC and the Public Supplies Directive 77/62/EEC which have been in force in the United Kingdom (by way of ministry circular) since 1973 and 1978 respectively. The "Works" Directive, which has been substantially amended on a number of occasions has now been consolidated with minor amendments into the draft directive at *Appendix* A which at the time of writing was only awaiting the formal approval of the European Parliament before adoption. It is confidently anticipated that the text as published will be adopted in June 1993.[2] It has been incorporated into U.K. law by the Public Works Contracts Regulations (as amended) (*Appendix* B) which came into force on December 21, 1991. The "Supplies" Directive has also been substantially amended and is to be consolidated into the proposed directive at *Appendix* C.[3] The opportunity has been taken in the consolidating directive to carry out certain further amendments to the Supplies Directive, primarily in order to bring it into line with the Works Directive with regard to the public authorities affected. Further amendments of a minor nature may be made before adoption which it is anticipated will take place in the autumn of 1993. The Supplies Directive has been incorporated into law in the United Kingdom by the

---

[1] Public Procurement Regional and Social Aspects Com (89) 400 final July 29, 1989.
[2] For reasons of space the annexes to the draft Directive have not been included.
[3] *Ibid.*

Public Supply Contracts Regulations 1991 (as amended) (*Appendix* D) which also came into force on December 21, 1991. As a result of the amendments contained in the consolidating directive, these Regulations will have to be amended again, probably by the end of 1994. The Works and Supplies Regulations are dealt with in detail in *Chapter Three* (paras. 3–01 to 3–25 and 3–26 to 3–49 respectively).

**1–02**    The contracts covered by the Works and Supplies Directives exclude contracts for works and supplies awarded by certain entities operating in the water, energy, transport and telecommunications sectors because of particular problems in relation to some of those entities being governed by public and some by private law. The award of those contracts is now covered by virtue of a separate Directive 90/531/EEC adopted on September 17, 1990 and known as the "Excluded Sectors" or "Utilities" Directive (*Appendix* E).[4] That Directive, which was required to be implemented in the United Kingdom by July 1, 1992 and to be in force not later than January 1, 1993, has been implemented in the United Kingdom by the Utilities Supply and Works Contracts Regulations 1992 which came into force on January 13, 1993. (*Appendix* F). The Directive will nevertheless have direct effect in respect of some utilities during that short period of delay (see para. 5–20). Those Regulations are dealt with in detail in *Chapter Four* of this Guide.

**1–03**    Despite the introduction of the Works and Supplies Directives, the Commission were dissatisfied with the extent to which Member States complied with them (it is estimated, for example that only about 20 per cent. of public contracts falling within the provisions of the directives were being properly advertised). This was brought about in part by the inadequacy, or in some cases the total absence, of any remedies available to potential contractors or suppliers for their breach. The Community have therefore introduced two measures designed to overcome this problem. The first, known as the "Compliance" Directive 89/665/EEC, sets out the remedies which must be made available for breach of the Works and Supplies Directives and relevant Treaty provisions to those injured by such a breach. The relevant provisions of this Directive have been implemented in the United Kingdom by their incorporation into the Works and Supplies Regulations. The second measure, known as the "Remedies" Directive 92/13/EEC, provides similar remedies for breach of the Utilities Directive and has been implemented in the Utilities Regulations referred to above. Both Remedies Directives are set out at *Appendix* G. The nature and effect of the provisions in the Works, Supplies and Utilities Regulations implementing both Directives together with other relevant provisions relating to their enforcement are set out at *Chapter Five.*

**1–04**    The final plank of the Community's public procurement rules is the bringing of public and utility service contracts within the new regime. This has been achieved in so far as public service contracts are concerned by means of Directive 92/50/EEC (*Appendix* H) which is required to be in force by July 1, 1993 and which amends the Compliance Directive so as to apply its provisions to contracts for services. It will be achieved so far as service contracts awarded in

---

[4] For reasons of space the annexes to the Directive have not been included.

the utilities sector are concerned by a new amended Utilities Directive. A common position on the amended directive was reached on December 21, 1992.[5] It is anticipated that the amended directive will be adopted in the summer of 1993 and will be implemented in July 1994. Particular note should be given to Article 13 of the draft amended directive which if adopted will permit certain intra group contracts for services to be exempted from its provisions. The utilities which wish to take advantage of this concession will have to reorganise their activities so as to bring them into line with the requirements of the provision before the Regulations implementing the amended directive come into effect.

## The Purpose of the Community Procurement Regime

The aim of these directives is not to harmonise all national rules on public procurement. In the United Kingdom, for example, purely national rules such as those contained in the Local Government Act 1988 remain unaffected. Their aim is to coordinate national contract award procedures by introducing a minimum body of common rules for contracts above a given value threshold. These common rules can be summarised as follows:  **1–05**

(a) rules defining the type of procurement agency and the scope of the contracts subject to the directives.

(b) rules defining the type of contract award procedure which procurement agencies should normally use.

(c) rules on technical specifications, whereby preference is to be given to Community standards and discriminatory technical requirements are excluded from the contract documents.

(d) advertising rules whereby tender notices must be published in the *Official Journal of the European Communities* (the "Official Journal" or "O.J."), must comply with specific requirements concerning time limits and must be drawn up in accordance with pre-established models.

(e) common rules on participation comprising objective criteria for qualitative selection and for the award of contracts on the basis of either the lowest price or the most economically advantageous tender.

(f) obligations as regards statistical reporting.

In addition the directives introduce common rules as to the remedies to be made available to contractors and suppliers who suffer or risk suffering loss as a result of a breach of the Regulations implementing the directives or of any related Community obligation.

It must be emphasised that subject to any margin of discretion which the directives permit to Member States, and subject to a concession in favour of  **1–06**

---

[5] Not yet published (March 1993).

Spain, Portugal and Greece in relation to the implementation of the Utilities Directive, these common rules apply throughout the Community (and will soon apply to most EFTA States as well). A U.K. contractor or supplier can therefore as much take advantage of them when tendering for a contract in another Member State as he can when tendering for such a contract in the United Kingdom. In order to assist in this respect the Commission are publishing official guides to the public procurement rules of each Member State. These guides will be available in all the official languages.

Spain is required to implement the Utilities Directive and the associated Remedies Directive by January 1, 1996 and Portugal and Greece by January 1, 1998 (Article 37).

## The Primacy of the Provisions of the Directives over the Regulations which implement them

**1–07**    Each of the directives has binding force in relation to the result to be achieved for each Member State to which it is addressed but it leaves each Member State free to choose the form and method of implementing it.[6] As a matter of Community law the national courts when applying the Regulations must interpret them in the light of the wording and purpose of the directive in order to ensure the directive is fully effective in accordance with the objective which it pursues.[7] In construing the Regulations it will therefore frequently be necessary to construe the underlying directive in order to establish its objective. This must be done, not only by considering its relevant provisions in the light of its preamble and any preparatory material, but also by considering the directive in the context of the totality of the Community public procurement regime.[8] In this respect it is important to appreciate that the directives are mutually exclusive in relation to the contracts to which they apply but together create a comprehensive and interlocking whole. Thus, for example where it is necessary to decide whether a given contract is a contract for the supply of goods and therefore falls within the provisions of the Supply Regulations or is a contract for the supply of services and therefore is not at present (May 1993) caught by the Regulations, it will be necessary to consider *inter alia* the provisions of the Services Directive (*Appendix* H) and in particular Article 1 and Annexes 1A and 1B thereto, together with the related UN Central Product Classification (C.P.C.) documentation referred to therein. The C.P.C. will soon be replaced by a Community document of a similar nature.

The correct construction of the directive (and therefore of the Regulations) is ultimately a matter for the European Court of Justice and not the national courts

---

[6] See Art. 189 of the EEC Treaty.
[7] Case 14/83, *Van Colson & Kamann v. Land Nordrhein-Westfalen:* [1984] E.C.R. 1891.
[8] Case 283/81, C.I.L.F.I.T.: [1982] E.C.R. 3415.

and it must be expected that as the first cases go through the courts there will be a number of references under Article 177 of the Treaty for clarification of the directives' meaning and effect. These will be less frequent than might otherwise be the case as the Regulations have, it is submitted, been exceptionally well drafted and substantially give effect to the purpose of the directives which they implement.[9]

## Future Developments

The Commission have indicated that they intend in due course to consolidate **1–08** the Works, Supplies, and Services Directives into one directive which will possibly include the provisions of the Remedies Directives as well. The process of consolidating the Utilities Directive is already in hand. In relation to the Regulations, additional amendments can be anticipated to take account of the transitional provisions contained in the European Economic Area (EEA) Agreement. The EEA Bill currently before Parliament will extend the benefits of the Regulations to the EFTA States which ratify the agreement but the Regulations will need to make clear which EFTA States will benefit and which will not as a result of those transitional provisions. Finally, as an indication of possible developments in the future it should be noted that at paragraph 27 of its report entitled "The Internal Market after 1992" (the Sutherland Report, October 1992) the high level group recommend that:

"Alleged infringements by authorities in the award of public contracts need to be firmly and rapidly dealt with. To enable Community legislation on remedies in this field to be really effective, consideration should be given to the appointment of a mediator in each member State who would be independent of the complainant and the awarding authority."

---

[9] Compare, *e.g.* the implementation of the Product Liability Directive 85/374/EEC by Pt. 1 of the Consumer Protection Act 1987 which has been the subject of formal complaint by the Commission.

# Chapter Two

## TREATY PROVISIONS AFFECTING PROCUREMENT CONTRACTS

The origin of all Community rules relating to public procurement is the EEC **2–01** Treaty itself, where directly effective provisions have been given effect in the United Kingdom by the European Communities Act 1972 and particularly section 2(1) thereof.

Those provisions (as well as the secondary legislation made under them) take precedence over any conflicting measure of national law.[1]

The principal Treaty provisions which affect public procurement contracts are: **2–02** Article 7, which prohibits discrimination on the grounds of nationality; Articles 30 *et seq.* which prohibit as between Member States all quantitative restrictions on imports and all measures having equivalent effect; Articles 52 *et seq.* which prohibits restrictions on the freedom of establishment of nationals of a Member State in the territory of another Member State, whether this is done in person or by means of an agency, branch or subsidiary; Article 59, which prohibits restrictions on the provision of services within the Community and Article 92 *et seq.* which, save as otherwise provided in the Treaty, prohibit in so far as it affects trade between Member States any aid granted by a Member State or through State resources which distorts or threatens to distort competition by favouring certain undertakings or the production of certain goods.

The final arbiter of the meaning and extent of these Treaty provisions (as well **2–03** as the secondary legislation made under them) is the European Court of Justice, which has given a number of decisions of particular importance to public procurement contracts. Thus the Court has held that the requirement in a works contract specifying that tenderers use only a product manufactured to a national standard and only obtainable in that Member State has the effect of impeding imports in *intra* Community trade and is therefore contrary to Article 30. There would be no objection however if the words "or equivalent" were used after the specification concerned.[2] Similarly the Court has held that national legislation which obliged local authorities to obtain a minimum proportion of their supplies from a particular region or country was in breach of Community law.[3] In relation to Articles 52 and 59, the European Court has held that national laws which constitute a barrier to the freedom of establishment or the freedom to supply services are contrary to those Articles. Thus a national rule providing that

---

[1] Case 106/77, *Amministrazione delle Finanze dello Stato v. Simmenthal SpA*: |1978| E.C.R. 629.
[2] Case 45/87, *Commission v. Ireland*: |1988| E.C.R. 4929.
[3] Case 21/88, *Du Pont de Nemours Italiana SpA v. Unita Sanitaria Locale, no. 2 di Carrara*: |1990| I E.C.R. 889.

only companies in which a majority of shares are held directly or indirectly by the State may tender for certain government contracts is in breach of those provisions.[4] On the other hand there is nothing in those Articles which prohibits the fixing by a Member State of the maximum value of works which may be carried out at any one time by a particular contractor as this does not affect access by contractors in the Community to public works contracts.[5]

**2–04**  The remedies available to those who have suffered or may suffer damage as a result of breaches of the Community rules relating to public procurement are set out in *Chapter Five.*

**2–05**  It should be emphasised that the Treaty provisions described above (as well as the decisions of the European Court referred to) affect all public procurement contracts entered into by public authorities within the United Kingdom irrespective of whether they are also governed by the more specific Community legislation described below.

**2–06**  In respect of the Channel Islands and the Isle of Man it would appear that only those Community rules relating to quantitative restrictions apply (*i.e.* Articles 30 *et seq.* and related secondary legislation).[6] Consequently Community rules relating to public works contracts and public service contracts have no effect in those territories.

[4] Case 3/88, *Commission* v. *Italy:* |1989| E.C.R. 4035.
[5] Cases 27–29, C.E.I. *and others* v. *Association Intercommunale pour les Autoroutes des Ardennes:* |1987| E.C.R. 3347.
[6] See Art. 227(5)(c) of the Treaty and Art. 1(1) of Protocol 3 to the Act of Succession.

# Chapter Three

## U.K. NATIONAL MEASURES IMPLEMENTING THE WORKS AND SUPPLIES DIRECTIVES

### The Public Works Contracts Regulations 1991

The Regulations, like the directive they implement, have three principal aims **3–01** in respect of the contracts to which they apply:

(a) E.C.-wide advertising of contracts above a certain value threshold so that contractors in every Member State have an equal opportunity of expressing their interest in tendering and/or in tendering for them.
(b) The prohibition of technical specifications in the contract documents which favour particular contractors.
(c) The application of objective criteria in procedures leading to the award, and in the award itself.

### Contracts to which the Regulations apply

The Regulations apply whenever a contracting authority seeks offers in **3–02** relation to a proposed public works contract other than a public works contract expressly excluded from the operation of the Regulations regardless of whether a contract is awarded or not (reg. 5). There are certain exceptions to the general application of the Regulations where the public works contract is also a "public works concession contract", which is defined as "a public works contract under which the consideration given by the contracting authority consists of or includes the grant of a right to exploit the work or works to be carried out under the contract" (reg. 2(1), and see below at para. 3–05).

1. *Meaning of "Contracting Authority"*

A contracting authority is defined by regulation 3(1) as: **3–03**

(a) a Minister of the Crown,
(b) a government department,
(c) the House of Commons,
(d) the House of Lords,
(e) the Northern Ireland Assembly,
(f) a Local Authority,

(g) a Fire Authority constituted by a combination scheme under the Fire Services Act 1947,

(h) the Fire Authority for Northern Ireland,

(i) a Police Authority constituted under section 3 of the Police Act 1964 or a combined police authority established by an amalgamation scheme under that Act,

(j) the Police Authority for Northern Ireland,

(k) an authority established under section 10 of the Local Government Act 1985,

(l) a joint authority established by Part IV of that Act,

(m) any body established pursuant to an order under section 67 of that Act,

(n) the Boards Authority,

(o) any joint board the constituent members of which consist of any of the bodies specified in paras. (f), (g), (i), (k), (l), (m) and (n) above,

(p) a joint or special planning board constituted for a National Park by an order under paras. 1 or 3 of Schedule 17 to the Local Government Act 1972, and

(q) a joint education board constituted under the provisions of Part I of the First Schedule to the Education Act 1944,

(r) a corporation established, or a group of individuals appointed to act together, for the specific purpose of meeting needs in the general interest, not having an industrial or commercial character, and
  (i) financed wholly or mainly by another contracting authority, or
  (ii) subject to management supervision by another contracting authority, or
  (iii) more than half of the board of directors or members of which, or, in the case of a group of individuals, being appointed by another contracting authority, and

(s) associations of or formed by one or more of the above.

A list of bodies or categories of bodies in each Member State which fulfil the criteria set out at (r) above (which implements Article 1(b) of the Directive) are set out at Annex I to the Directive. The most recent amendment to Annex I dated September 3, 1992 ([1992] O.J. L257/33) contains the following in relation to the United Kingdom:

BODIES

— Central Blood Laboratories Authority,
— Design Council,
— Health and Safety Executive,
— National Research Development Corporation,
— Public Health Laboratory Services Board,
— Advisory, Conciliation and Arbitration Service,
— Commission for the New Towns,

— Development Board for Rural Wales,
— English Industrial Estates Corporation,
— National Rivers Authority,
— Northern Ireland Housing Executive,
— Scottish Enterprise,
— Scottish Homes,
— Welsh Development Agency.

### CATEGORIES

— Universities and polytechnics, maintained schools and colleges,
— National Museums and Galleries,
— Research Councils,
— Fire Authorities,
— National Health Service Authorities,
— Police Authorities,
— New Town Development Corporations,
— Urban Development Corporations.

The list is not definitive but is as "exhaustive as possible."

Further, "local authority" is defined in the Regulations in relation to England and Wales as:

"(a) a county council, a district council, a London borough council, a parish council, a community council, or the Council of the Isles of Scilly;
(b) the Common Council of the City of London in its capacity as local authority or policy authority,"

in relation to Scotland as:

"a regional, island or district council or any joint board or joint committee within the meaning of sec 235 of the Local Government (Scotland) Act 1973,"

and in relation to Northern Ireland as:

"a district council within the meaning of the Local Government Act (Northern Ireland) 1972."

Where an entity specified in regulation 3(1) does not have the capacity to enter into a contract, the contracting authority in relation to that entity means a person whose function it is to enter into contracts for that entity.

2. *Meaning of "Public Works Contract"*

A public works contract is defined by regulation 2(1) as:                    **3–04**

"a contract in writing for consideration (whatever the nature of the consideration)—

11

> (a) for the carrying out [i.e. the construction or the design and construction of a work or works for a contracting authority, or
>
> (b) under which a contracting authority engages a person to produce by any means the carrying out for the contracting authority of a work corresponding to specified requirements."

A "work" is defined in the same regulation as:

> "the outcome of any works which is sufficient of itself to fulfil an economic and technical function,"

and "works" are defined as:

> "any of the activities specified in Schedule 1, being activities contained in the general industrial classification of economic activities within the Communities."

Schedule 1 to the Regulations sets out a variety of building and civil engineering activities (e.g. "construction of flats, office blocks, hospitals and other buildings both residential and non-residential") broken down into tasks (e.g. "erection and dismantling of scaffolding") carried out in the course of those activities.

BORDERLINE CASES

Where it is not clear whether or not the contract is in substance a works contract and it is in consequence difficult to decide which directive (and therefore which set of Regulations) applies, the general rule is that if the value of the goods to be supplied excluding those to be used for the purposes of the construction work exceeds that of the works to be performed then it is a supply contract. If on the other hand the value of the works falling within the Regulations exceeds that of the goods it is a public works contract.[1] Where both works and services are required then if the works can be separated from the services into a separate contract then the fact that the services are the main element of the requirement will not exempt the works element from the provisions of the Regulations if they would otherwise be affected[2] (and see para. 3–30 below in relation to public supply contracts).

## The Public Works Contracts excluded from the operation of the Regulations

1. *Contracts related to certain utilities*

**3–05**     For the reasons already given at para. 1–02 the Regulations do not apply to the seeking of offers in relation to a proposed public works contract:

> "(a) for the purpose of carrying out an activity specified in the second

---

[1] Guide to the Community Rules on Open Government procurement ([1987] O.J. C358/1, p. 16).
[2] See Chap. 2, n. 4.

column of Schedule 1 to the |Utilities Regulations| other than an activity specified in paragraphs 2 or 3 thereof;

(b) where a contracting authority exercises the activity specified in paragraph 1 of Schedule 1 to the |Utilities Regulations| for the purpose of carrying out an activity specified in paragraphs 2 or 3 thereof."
(reg. 6 as amended)

The effect of this provision, which was first introduced by the Utilities Regulations, is to ensure that such public works contracts are dealt with, if at all, under the Utilities and not the Works Regulations. The activities listed in the second column of Schedule 1 broadly concern the operation or provision of public networks or facilities in the water, energy, transport and telecommunications fields and the supply to such networks, together with certain mining activities in relation to gas, oil, coal and other solid fuels. The exceptions contained in (a) and (b) above have the effect of requiring that a public works contract continues to be dealt with under the Works Regulations where the contract is for the purpose of carrying out hydraulic engineering, irrigation, or land drainage, or the disposal or treatment of sewage, but where the contracting authority provides or operates a fixed network providing a service to the public in connection with the production, transport or distribution of drinking water those exceptions will not apply provided that in relation to hydraulic engineering, irrigation or land drainage activities the volume of water intended for the supply of drinking water represents not less than 20 per cent. of the total volume of water made available by those activities.

It will be noted that only the provision of airport and port facilities and the operation of railway and bus and similar services are included in the transport section of the second column of Schedule 1 to the Utilities Regulations. Public works contracts for the carrying out of other transport activities by public authorities (e.g. ferry services) will continue to be covered by the Works Regulations unless otherwise excluded.

*2. Secret contracts, contracts involving State security and contracts carried out pursuant to international agreement*

In addition the Regulations do not apply to a public works contract:

"(d) which is classified as secret or where the carrying out of the work or works under it must be accompanied by special security measures in accordance with the laws regulations or administrative provisions of any part of the United Kingdom or where the protection of the basic interests of the security of the United Kingdom require it

(e) certain contracts carried out pursuant to international agreements."
(reg. 6(e))

*3. Contracts below certain value thresholds*

The Regulations do not apply to the seeking of offers in relation to a proposed

13

public works contract "where the estimated value of the contract (net of VAT) at the relevant time is less than 5,000,000 ECU" (reg. 7(1)). The "relevant time" is the date on which a contract notice would be sent to the Official Journal if the requirement to send such a notice applied to that contract in accordance with the Regulations (i.e. generally when the contracting authority forms the intention to seek offers in relation to the contract) (reg. 7(7)).

The value in sterling of 5,000,000 ECUs must be calculated by reference to the exchange rate for the time being applying for the purposes of Council Directive 71/305/EEC as published from time to time in the Official Journal. For the period January 1, 1992 to December 31, 1993 the sterling equivalent of 5,000,000 ECUs is £3,535,775.[3]

The "estimated value" for the purposes of regulation 7(1) is the value of the consideration which the contracting authority expects to give under the contract. However, where the public works contract is one of a number of contracts entered into or to be entered into for the carrying out of "a work" the "estimated value" is the aggregate of the value of the consideration which the contracting authority has paid or expects to give under all the contracts for the carrying out of the work (reg. 7(3)). Thus, for example where a contracting authority seeks offers in relation to the provision of scaffolding at an estimated cost of 1,000,000 ECUs for the construction of a hospital at an estimated cost (inclusive of the scaffolding) of 20 million ECUs then the Regulations will apply to both the scaffolding contract and to the contract for the construction of the hospital. Where, however, the part contract has an estimated value of less than 1,000,000 ECUs and where that contract and any other part contract in respect of which the contracting authority chooses to take advantage of the disapplication provisions provided by regulation 7(4) amounts in aggregate to less than 20 per cent. of the total cost of the whole "work" the Regulations will not apply to the part contract. In the example given, therefore, if the estimated cost of the scaffolding was 900,000 ECUs then (assuming there were no other part contracts aggregating to 4,000,000 ECUs or more) the Regulations would not apply to that part contract.

Where a contracting authority intends to provide any goods to the person awarded a public works contract for the purpose of carrying out that contract the value of these must be taken into account when calculating the estimated value of the contract.

In relation to public works concession contracts the "estimated value" is the value of the consideration which the contracting authority would expect to give for the carrying out of the work (taking into account any goods supplied by them) if it did not propose to grant a concession.

A contracting authority must not enter into separate contracts with the intention of avoiding the application of the Regulations to those contracts (reg. 7(8)).

---

[3] See Appendix I.

## Rules governing technical specifications

Detailed rules as to the technical specifications which are permitted in public **3–06** works contracts which are subject to the Regulations are set out in regulation 8. The purpose behind these rules is to avoid any discrimination against contractors who might be disadvantaged if technical specifications were required which could only be met or more easily met by a national contractor.

Technical specifications (which are defined in reg. 8(1)), whether relating to the works themselves or the goods to be used in them, must be specified in the contract documents, and subject to certain exceptions must be defined by reference to any "European specifications" which are relevant. "European specification" means a common technical specification, a British standard implementing a European standard or a European technical approval. The Commission have issued policy guidelines on the interpretation of the obligation to refer to European Standards (See Appendix A: Part 2). These apply to both works and supply contracts.

Under regulation 8(4) and (5) a contracting authority may define a technical specification other than by reference to a relevant European specification if:

"(4) (a) the contracting authority is under an obligation to define the technical specifications by reference to technical requirements which are mandatory in the United Kingdom for the work or works to be carried out under the contract or for the materials or goods to be used in or for it or them, (but only to the extent that such an obligation is compatible with Community obligations);

(b) the relevant European specifications do not include provision for establishing conformity to, or it is technically impossible to establish satisfactorily that the work or works or the materials or goods do conform to, the relevant European specifications;

(c) subject to paragraph (5) below, application of the relevant European specifications would oblige the contracting authority to acquire a work, works, material or goods incompatible with equipment already in use or would entail disproportionate costs or disproportionate technical difficulties; or

(d) the work or works are of a genuinely innovative nature for which use of existing relevant European specifications would be inappropriate.

(5) A contracting authority may only define the technical specifications other than by reference to relevant European specifications on the grounds specified in paragraph (4)(c) above where the contracting authority has a clearly defined and recorded strategy for changing over, within a set period, to European specifications."

Where a contracting authority relies on one of the above exceptions it must state in the contract notice which exception it relies on or if it is impossible to include this information in the contract notice it must be specified in the contract documents.

In the absence of a relevant European specification the technical specifications in the contract documents:

> "(a) shall be defined by reference to the British technical specifications recognised as complying with the basic requirements specified in any Council Directives on technical harmonisation in accordance with the procedures laid down in those directives and, in particular, in accordance with the procedure laid down in Council Directive 89/1106/EEC on the approximation of laws, regulations and administrative procedures in the member States relating to construction products,[4]
>
> (b) may be defined by reference to British technical specifications relating to design and method of calculation and execution of a work or works and use of materials and goods;
>
> (c) may be defined by reference to the following standards (and, if they are so defined, preference shall be given to the following standards in the order in which they are listed)—
>
>   (i) British standards implementing international standards;
>   (ii) other British standards and technical approvals; or
>   (iii) any other standards."

Subject to two exceptions technical specifications must not refer to materials or goods of a specific make or source or to a particular process which have the effect of favouring or eliminating particular contractors. In particular references to trademarks, patents, types, origin or means of production must not be used. Exceptionally such references may be made where:

> (a) such references are justified by the subject of the contract, or
>
> (b) the work or works to be carried out under the contract cannot otherwise be described by reference to technical specifications which are sufficiently precise and intelligible to all contractors, provided that the references are accompanied by the words "or equivalent."

### Rules governing the procedures leading to the award of a Public Works Contract

*1. The procedures to be used in awarding the contract*

**3–07**    The principal requirement of the Regulations is that in seeking offers in relation to a public works contract from contractors or potential contractors who are nationals of and established in a Member State a contracting authority must use one of the following procedures:

---

[4] |1989| O.J. L40/12.

— **the open procedure**, whereby any person who is interested may submit a tender;
— **the restricted procedure** whereby only those persons selected by the contracting authority may submit tenders; and
— **the negotiated procedure** whereby the contracting authority negotiates the terms of the contract with one or more persons selected by it.

The Regulations lay down provisions for making the choice of procedure. The negotiated procedure may only be used in certain limited circumstances. Special rules apply in relation to a public housing scheme works contract (see para. 3–22 below).

*2. Advertising the intention to seek offers by means of a prior information notice*

The contracting authority must publicise its intention to seek offers in relation to a public works contract in the Official Journal as soon as the decision approving the planning of works is taken (the "prior information notice") (reg. 9). It must do this again at the start of the procedure leading to the award, once this has been selected (the "contract notice") although the latter requirement is dispensed with in certain circumstances when the negotiated procedure is used. The form of the advertisement and the information which it must contain in relation to the proposed contract is specified in Schedule 2. If the notice is also to be published in the U.K. Press it must be limited to the information published in the Official Journal.

**3–08**

*3. Selection of contract award procedure*

A contracting authority may only use the negotiated procedure in the following circumstances:

**3–09**

(a) in the event that the procedure leading to the award of a public works contract by the contracting authority using the open or restricted procedure was discontinued,
  (i) because of irregular tenders, or
  (ii) following an evaluation of offers made in accordance with the regulations relating to open and restricted procedures.
  However, the negotiated procedure may only then be used if the proposed terms of the contract are substantially unaltered from the proposed terms of the contract in relation to which offers were sought using the open or restricted procedure. Without prejudice to the generality of the term a tender may be considered irregular if the contractor fails to meet the requirements, or the tender offers variations on the requirements specified in the contract documents where this is not permitted under the terms of the invitation to tender, or the work, works, materials or goods offered do not meet the technical specifications of the contracting authority;
(b) when the work or works are to be carried out under the contract purely for

the purpose of research, experiment or development but not where the works are to be carried out to establish commercial viability or to recover research and development costs.

Once the experiment or trial has proved successful this exception will cease to apply and if the contracting authority then decides to go ahead with the works it must comply with the Regulations if the contract concerned is one which falls within their provisions;

(c) exceptionally, when the nature of the work or works to be carried out under the contract is such, or the risks attaching thereto are such, as not to permit overall pricing;

(d) in the absence of tenders or of appropriate tenders in response to an invitation to tender by the contracting authority using the open or restricted procedure. However, again this exception may not be relied upon unless the proposed terms of the contract are substantially unaltered from the proposed terms of the contract in relation to which offers were sought using the open or restricted procedure;

(e) when for technical or artistic reasons, or for reasons connected with the protection of exclusive rights, the work or works to be carried out under the contract may only be carried out by a particular person.

It might be argued by a disappointed contractor who had been excluded for technical reasons that given enough time he could have acquired the expertise and/or machinery to qualify technically but the exception can probably be relied upon where for technical reasons only one contractor can carry out the works within the reasonable time required by the contracting authority for their completion;

(f) when (but only if it is strictly necessary) for reasons of extreme urgency brought about by events unforeseeable by and not attributable to the contracting authority, the time limits specified in the Regulations relating to the various contract award procedures cannot be met;

(g) when a contracting authority wants a person who has entered into a public works contract with the contracting authority to carry out additional works which through unforeseen circumstances were not included in the project initially considered or in the original public works contract and,

(i) such works cannot for technical or economic reasons be carried out separately from the works carried out under the original public works contract without great inconvenience to the contracting authority, or

(ii) such works can be carried out separately from the works carried out under the original public works contract but are strictly necessary to the later stages of the contract. However, this exception may not be relied upon where the aggregate value of the consideration to be given under contracts for the additional works exceeds 50 per cent. of the value of the consideration payable under the original contract

The value of the consideration must be taken to include the estimated value of any goods which the contracting authority provided to the person awarded the contract for the purposes of carrying out the contract;

(h) when a contracting authority wishes a person who has entered into a public works contract with that contracting authority to carry out new works which are a repetition of works carried out under the original contract and which are in accordance with the project for the purpose of which the first contract was entered into. However, that exception may only be relied upon if the contract notice relating to the original contract stated that a public works contract for new works which would be a repetition of the works carried out under the original contract may be awarded using the negotiated procedure and unless the procedure for the award of the new contract is commenced within three years of the original contract being entered into.

In accordance with principles of Community law each of the above exceptions must be strictly construed. Unless such an exception applies the contracting authority must use the open procedure or the restricted procedure.

### 4. The open procedure

As has already been noted the contracting authority must publicise its **3–10** intention to seek offers in relation to the public works contract by sending to the Official Journal a notice (the "contract notice") inviting tenders and containing specified information in relation to the contract (reg. 11(2)). The form and contents of that notice are set out in Part B of Schedule 2.

The Commission has now recommended[5] that contracting authorities use standard notices and standardised nomenclature from January 1, 1992 when advertising public works and public supplies contracts in the Official Journal. The use of such notices and nomenclature may eventually be made compulsory under the terms of a new directive. The standard forms together with an explanatory note as to how they should be used have been published in the supplement to the Official Journal dated November 16, 1991.[6] The U.K. Government has recommended that all contracting authorities as defined by the Works Regulations and Supply Regulations comply with the recommendations. There are as yet no standard forms for either public works prior information notices or public works concession contract notices.

The date fixed as the last date for the receipt of tenders must be specified in the notice and must not be less than 52 days from the date of dispatch of the notice. This period must be extended where the contract documents are too bulky to be supplied within that time or where it is necessary for contractors to be given an opportunity to inspect the site. The period of 52 days may be reduced

---

[5] Commission Recommendation 91/561/EEC. [1991] O.J. L305/19.
[6] [1991] O.J. S217 N/1.

to a period of not less than 36 days where the contracting authority has published a "prior information notice". The contract documents must be sent within six days of the receipt of a request from any contractor provided that the documents are requested in good time and any fee specified in the contract notice has accompanied the request. Further information reasonably required relating to the contract documents must be supplied provided that the request is made in sufficient time to enable the contracting authority to supply the information no later than six days before the date specified in the contract notice as the final date for the receipt of tenders.

The contracting authority may only exclude a tender from the evaluation of offers if the contractor may be treated as ineligible on a ground specified in the Regulations or if the contractor fails to satisfy minimum standards of economic and financial standing and technical capacity required of contractors by the contracting authority when assessed according to the requirements of the Regulations (see paras. 3–13 and 3–14 below).

5. *The restricted procedure*

SELECTING THOSE INVITED TO TENDER

**3–11**    When using the restricted procedure the contracting authority must, as with the open procedure, publish a contract notice as soon as possible after forming the intention to seek offers. The contract notice must be in a form and contain the information substantially corresponding to that set out in Part C of Schedule 2 inviting requests to be selected to tender.

The date fixed as the last date for receipt of requests to be selected for tender must be specified in the contract notice and must be not less than 37 days from the date of the dispatch of the notice. Where compliance with the 37 day period is rendered impracticable by reasons of urgency the contracting authority may substitute a period of not less than 15 days.

The contracting authority may exclude a contractor from those persons from whom it will make the selection of persons to be invited to tender only if the contractor may be treated as ineligible on a ground permitted by the Regulations or if the contractor fails to satisfy the minimum standards of economic and financial standing and technical capacity required of contractors by the contracting authority as assessed according to the requirements of the Regulations (see below at para. 3–13).

Having excluded any contractors as above, the contracting authority must select the contractors they intend to invite to tender solely on the basis of the information obtained regarding the contractor's past record, his economic standing and his technical capacity as permitted by the Regulations (see below at paras. 3–14 to 3–16) and in making the selection and in issuing invitations the contracting authority must not discriminate between contractors on the grounds of their nationality or the Member State in which they are established.

The contracting authority may prescribe the range within which the number of undertakings which they intend to invite will fall. The number invited must be not less than five nor more than twenty. If a range is to be specified it must be specified in the contract notice and in any event the number must be sufficient to ensure genuine competition (reg. 12(7)).

THE INVITATION TO TENDER

The invitation to tender must be sent in writing simultaneously to each contractor selected to tender, and must be accompanied by the contract documents or contain the address from which they may be requested. The invitation to tender must include the following information:

(a) the address to which requests for the contract documents (if not accompanying the invitation) and further information relating to those documents should be sent, the final date for making such a request and the amount and terms of the fee which may be charged for supplying that material;

(b) the final date for the receipt of tenders, the address to which they must be sent and the language or languages in which they must be drawn up;

(c) a reference to the published contract notice;

(d) an indication of the information to be included with the tender which the contracting authority may require to be provided in accordance with the Regulations and

(e) the criteria for the award of the contract if this information was not specified in the contract notice.

The last date for the receipt of tenders must normally not be less than 40 days from the date of the dispatch of the invitation (26 days where a "prior information notice" has been published) but if it is necessary that contractors should be given the opportunity to inspect the premises on which the works under the contract are to be carried out or documents relating to the contract documents then that minimum period must be extended to allow for such inspection.

Where compliance with the minimum periods referred to is rendered impracticable for reasons of urgency a period of not less than 10 days may be substituted and in those circumstances the contracting authority must send the invitation to tender by the most rapid means possible.

The contracting authority must supply such further information relating to the contract documents as may reasonably be requested provided that the request is received in sufficient time to enable the contracting authority to supply it not less than six days (four in situations of urgency) before the date specified in the invitation to tender as the final date for the receipt of tenders.

A contracting authority shall not refuse to consider an application to be invited to tender if it is made by letter, telegram, telex, facsimile or telephone provided that in the last four cases it is confirmed by letter before the date fixed by the contracting authority as the last date for the receipt of requests to be selected to tender.

### 6. *The negotiated procedure*

**3–12**     A contracting authority using the negotiated procedure pursuant to sub-para. (*d*), (*e*), (*f*), (*g*) or (*h*) in para. 3–09 above or pursuant to sub-para. (*a*) of that paragraph who invites to negotiate every contractor who submitted a tender following an invitation made during the course of the discontinued open or restricted procedure (not being an "excluded" tender) is not subject to any procedural rules other than those relating to exclusion on the grounds of ineligibility, and selection of contractors invited to negotiate already referred to in relation to those invited to tender under the restricted procedure. In all other cases the following rules in addition apply:

(*a*)  The contracting authority must publicise its intention to seek offers in relation to the public works contract by publishing a contract notice in the Official Journal in the form prescribed in Part D of Schedule 2 inviting requests to be selected to negotiate and containing the information specified.

(*b*)  The date fixed as the last date for the receipt of requests to be selected to negotiate must be specified in the contract notice and must be not less than 37 days (15 days in cases of urgency) from the date of dispatch of the notice.

(*c*)  Where there is a sufficient number of persons who are suitable to be selected to negotiate the contract the number must be not less than three.

(*d*)  Similar rules apply in relation to applications to be selected to negotiate made by letter, telegram, telex, facsimile or telephone as they do to applications made under the restricted procedure.

## Selection of contractors

### 1. *Criteria for rejection of contractors*

**3–13**     Detailed rules are laid down in the Regulations as to the only criteria on which applicants to tender and tenderers may be excluded as ineligible from the tendering process. These are that the contractor:

(*a*)  being an individual is bankrupt or has had a receiving order or administration order made against him or has made any composition or arrangement with or for the benefit of his creditors or has made any conveyance or assignment for the benefit of his creditors or appears unable to pay a debt within the meaning of section 268 of the Insolvency Act 1968, or Article 242 of the Insolvency (Northern Ireland) Order 1989, or in Scotland has granted a trust deed for creditors or become otherwise apparently insolvent, or is the subject of a petition presented for sequestration of his estate, or is the subject of any similar procedure under the law of any other State;

(b) being a partnership constituted under Scots law has granted a trust deed or become otherwise apparently insolvent, or is the subject of a petition presented for sequestration of its estate;

(c) being a company has passed a resolution or is the subject of an order by the court for the company's winding up otherwise than for the purposes of bona fide reconstruction or amalgamation, or has had a receiver, manager or administrator on behalf of a creditor appointed in respect of the company's business or any part thereof or is the subject of proceedings for any of the above procedures or is the subject of similar procedures under the law of any other State;

(d) has been convicted of a criminal offence relating to the conduct of his business or profession;

(e) has committed an act of grave misconduct in the course of his business or profession;

(f) has not fulfilled obligations relating to the payment of social security contributions under the law of any part of the United Kingdom or of the Member State in which the contractor is established;

(g) has not fulfilled obligations relating to the payment of taxes under the law of any part of the United Kingdom (in the Consolidated Directive this is extended to the Member State of the contracting authority);

(h) is guilty of serious misrepresentation in providing any information required of him under the Regulations;

(i) is not registered on the professional or trade register of the Member State in which the contractor is established under the conditions laid down by that State. The relevant registers or their equivalent are listed in the Regulations (reg. 14(1)).

Further, the Regulations prescribe the manner in which contractors may furnish proof that they satisfy those criteria. The contracting authority may require a contractor to provide such information as it considers it needs to make a decision in respect of any of the abovementioned criteria but it must accept as conclusive evidence that a contractor does not fall within the grounds specified in sub-para. (a), (b), (c), (d), (f) or (g) above if that contractor provides to the contracting authority:

(1) in relation to the grounds specified in paras. (a), (b), (c) or (d) above,
    (i) an extract from the judicial record, or
    (ii) in a Member State which does not maintain such a judicial record, a document issued by the relevant judicial or administrative authority;

(2) in relation to the grounds specified in paras. (f) or (g) above, a certificate issued by the relevant competent authority;

(3) in a Member State where the documentary evidence specified in the above two paragraphs is not issued in relation to one of the grounds specified in paras. (a), (b), (c), (d), (f) or (g) above, a declaration on oath made by the

contractor before the relevant judicial, administrative or competent authority or a relevant notary public or commissioner for oaths.

"Relevant" in relation to a judicial, administrative or competent authority, notary public or commissioner for oaths means an authority designated by, or a notary public or commissioner for oaths in, the Member State in which the contractor is established.

However, where a contractor is registered on the official list of recognised contractors in a Member State which maintains such a list and in which the contractor is established and the contractor submits to the contracting authority a certificate of registration issued by the authority administrating the official list and which specifies the information submitted to that authority which enabled the contractor to be registered, and states the classification given, the contracting authority, to the extent that the certificate deals with the grounds referred to in (a) to (e), (h) and (i) above, shall accept the certificate as evidence that the contractor does not fall within those grounds and shall not be entitled to require the contractor to submit further information relating to those grounds (reg. 18).

*2. Information as to economic and financial standing*

**3–14**    Subject to a similar provision relating to the situation where the contractor is registered on an official list of recognised contractors, under the Regulations the contracting authority in assessing whether a contractor meets any minimum standards of economic and financial standing may apparently "only" take into account any of the following information and it may require a contractor to provide such of that information as it considers it needs to make the assessment or selection:

(a) appropriate statements from the contractor's bankers.

(b) statements of accounts or extracts therefrom relating to the business of the contractor where publication of the statement is required under the law of the Member State where the contractor is established.

(c) a statement of the overall turnover of the business of the contractor and the turnover in respect of works in the three previous financial years of the contractor.

Where the information specified above is not appropriate in a particular case a contracting authority may require a contractor to provide other information to demonstrate the contractor's economic and financial standing.

Where a contractor is unable for a valid reason to provide the information which the contracting authority has required, the contracting authority must accept such other information provided by the contractor as the contracting authority considers appropriate.

The information required must be specified in the contract notice (reg. 15).

### 3. Information as to technical capacity

Again subject to a similar provision relating to the situation where the **3–15** contractor is registered on an official list of recognised contractors, the contracting authority, in assessing whether a contractor meets any minimum standards of technical capacity, may under the Regulations "only" take into account the following information and it may require a contractor to provide such of that information as it considers it needs to make the assessment or selection:

(a) a list of the contractor's educational and professional qualifications where the contractor is an individual and a list of such qualifications of the contractor's managerial staff if any and those of the person or persons who would be responsible for carrying out the works under the contract;

(b) a list of works carried out over the past five years together with (unless the contracting authority specifies that the following certificates should be submitted direct to the contracting authority by the person certifying) certificates of satisfactory completion for the most important of those works indicating in each case the value of the consideration received, when and where the works were carried out and specifying whether they were carried out according to the rules of the trade or profession and properly completed;

(c) a statement of the tools, plant and technical equipment available to the contractor for carrying out the work under the contract;

(d) a statement of the contractor's average annual manpower and the number of managerial staff over the previous three years;

(e) a statement of the technicians or technical services which the contractor may call upon for the carrying out of the work under the contract, whether or not the technicians or persons providing the technical services are independent of the contractor.

The contract notice must specify which of the above items of information the contractor must provide (reg. 16).

It has been held by an English court that the evaluation of technical capacity includes an assessment of a contractor's compliance with health and safety legislation.[7]

### 4. Limits on the information which may be required or taken into account.

The mandatory nature of regulations 15 and 16 as regards information which **3–16** may be required and/or taken into account by the contracting authority when assessing economic and financial standing and technical capacity is not reflected in the Directive (see Article 26 and 27 of the Consolidating Directive). In joined cases 27–29/86 C.E.I. v. *Association pour les Autoroutes des Ardennes*, the European Court of Justice held in relation to Article 26 (Article 25 of the original

---

[7] *General Building and Maintenance* v. *Greenwich Borough Council, The Times*, March 3, 1993.

directive) that "it can be seen from the very wording of that Article and, in particular the second paragraph thereof, that the List of references mentioned therein is not exhaustive"[8] and that consequently a contracting authority is entitled to require a contractor to furnish a statement of the total value of the works he has in hand as a reference within the meaning of that Article. Further the Court held that neither Article 26 of the directive nor any other precludes a Member State from fixing the value of the works which may be carried out at one time. Accordingly it is submitted that despite the apparent wording of regulation 15 a Court should construe that regulation as permitting a contracting authority (whether under regulation 15(2) or otherwise) to require and/or take into account evidence of a contractor's economic and financial standing not specified in that regulation but that where such evidence is required it must be specified in the contract notice or the invitation to tender.

The wording of Article 27 (which is implemented by regulation 16), as construed by the European Court in case 76/81 *Transporoute* v. *Minister of Public Works*[9] makes it clear that the list of references which may be *required* under that Article on the other hand is exhaustive. However it is submitted that there is nothing in that Article or that decision which would preclude a contracting authority from *taking into account* other evidence which it had not required the contractor to furnish but which it had obtained by other means. It would be remarkable, for example if a contracting authority could not take into account its own experience of a contractor's competence acquired on previous contracts carried out by that contractor. It is submitted therefor that regulation 16 should be construed so as to permit a contracting authority to take into account evidence relating to a contractor's technical capacity (but not other matters) other than that specified in the regulation. That appears to have been the view taken by the Court in GBM v. *Greenwich*[10] where it was held that a contracting authority was entitled to take into account any independent knowledge it might have regarding a contractor's compliance with health and safety legislation when carrying out other contracts. Although a contracting authority may require a contractor to supplement or to clarify the above information (but not in relation to a certificate of registration on an official list) it may not require the contractor to furnish such additional evidence unless it falls within the limits specified in regulations 14, 15 and 16 (reg. 17).

A contracting authority may require a contractor from another Member State to furnish proof that his undertaking has the financial and economic standing and technical capacity required by national law even when the contractor is recognised in the official list of the Member State in which he is established in a class equivalent to that required by that national law by reason of the value of the contract to be awarded, unless the classification of undertakings in both Member States is based on equivalent criteria in regard to the capacities

---

[8] |1987| E.C.R. 3347, para. 9.
[9] |1982| E.C.R. 417, see particularly para. 9 of the judgment.
[10] *General Building and Maintenance* v. *Greenwich Borough Council*, *The Times*, March 3, 1993.

required.[11] It is important to appreciate that the directive and therefore the Regulations do not delimit the contracting authorities' discretion to fix the level of financial and economic standing and technical knowledge required; they merely determine the evidence that may be furnished in order to establish whether those levels are met. Accordingly for the purposes of the directive and the Regulations the criterion of specific experience for the work to be carried out is a legitimate criterion of technical ability and knowledge for ascertaining the suitability of a contractor.[12]

### 5. Consortia

The Regulations lay down special rules in relation to consortia. A consortium **3—17** is defined as two or more persons at least one of whom is a contractor (*i.e.* a national of and established in a Member State) acting jointly for the purpose of being awarded a public works contract.

It is not a legitimate ground for excluding a consortium from the tendering process that it has not formed a legal entity, but before entering into or as a term of a contract the contracting authority may require it to do so.

In the Regulations references to a contractor or to a concessionaire where the contractor or concessionaire is a consortium includes a reference to each person who is a member of that consortium (reg. 19).

It is by forming a consortium with a contractor who is a national of and established in a Member State that third country contractors will most readily obtain the advantages of the Community public procurement regime.

## The award of the Public Works Contract

### 1. The basis for the award

The contracting authority must award the public works contract on the basis **3—18** either of the tender (including in-house bids) which offers the lowest price or the one which is the most "economically advantageous" (reg. 20).

The criteria which a contracting authority may use to determine that an offer is the most economically advantageous include price, period for completion, running costs, profitability and technical merit.

The list is not exhaustive, but it is clear from the examples given that only objective criteria may be used which are relevant to the particular project, and uniformly applicable to all bidders.

All the criteria the contracting authority intends to apply in determining the most economically advantageous offer must be stated in the contract notice or contract documents preferably in descending order of importance. No criteria not mentioned in the notice or the contract documents may be used. A

---

[11] Cases 27–29/86, C.E.I. *and others* v. *Association Intercommunale pour les Autoroutes des Ardennes:* |1987| E.C.R. 3347.
[12] Case 31/87, *Gebroeders Beentjes BV* v. *State of the Netherlands:* |1988| E.C.R. 4865.

distinction, however, must be made between a contractual condition requiring the successful contractor to co-operate with some policy objective of the contracting authority and the criteria for the selection of contractors or for the award of the contract. Thus a condition attached to the award of a public works contract, under which the contractor is required to engage a given member of long-term unemployed, is compatible with the directive and therefore the Regulations. It is not relevant to the assessment of the contractor's economic, financial or technical capacity to carry out the work, nor does it form part of the criteria applied by the contracting authority to decide to whom to award the contract.[13] Such conditions must, however, be compatible with the Treaty, particularly with those provisions on freedom to provide services, freedom of establishment and non-discrimination on the grounds of nationality. They must also be mentioned in the contract notice. Thus it would be a breach of the Treaty if it appeared on the facts that the condition could only be fulfilled by national firms or if it would be more difficult for tenderers coming from other Member States to fulfil that condition. Even a request for information from tenderers (as opposed to the insertion of a contractual term) can in certain circumstances be in breach of the rules if such request would reasonably lead the tenderer to believe that discrimination on local or national grounds is likely to occur. In this context the U.K. Department of the Environment, basing itself on Treasury guidance, has published a circular to assist local authorities in complying with the rules governing public procurement.[14] The circular clarifies the Commission's view that requiring the tenderer to give information on whether local labour and local experience will be used may imply that a tenderer using local labour would be more likely to win the contract. Local authorities are advised therefore not to put such requirements into contract notices.

When a contracting authority awards a public works contract on the basis of the offer which is most economically advantageous it may take account of offers which offer variations on the requirements specified in the contract documents if the offer meets the minimum requirements of the contracting authority and it has indicated in the contract notice that offers offering variations will be considered, and has stated in the contract documents the minimum requirements which the offer must meet and any specific requirements for the presentation of an offer offering variations (reg. 20(4)).

### 2. Abnormally low tenders

**3–19**     If an offer for a public works contract is or appears to be abnormally low the contracting authority may reject that offer but only if it has requested in writing an explanation of the offer or of those parts which it considers contribute to the offer being abnormally low and has:

(a)  if awarding the contract on the basis of lowest price, examined the details

[13] Case 31/87, *Gebroeders Beentjes* BV v. *State of the Netherlands:* |1988| E.C.R. 4635.
[14] Circular 21/89, Department of the Environment, September 14, 1989.

of all the offers made taking into account any explanation given to it of the abnormally low tender, before awarding the contract, or

(b) if awarding the contract on the basis of the offer which is the most economically advantageous taken any such explanation into account in assessing which is the most economically advantageous offer (reg. 20(6)).

Thus a contracting authority may not automatically reject a tender because it fails to satisfy some predetermined mathematical criterion adopted in relation to the public works contract concerned. In every case the contractor must be given an opportunity for explanation and thereafter the examination procedure specified must be followed.[15]

If a contracting authority which rejects an abnormally low tender is awarding the contract on the basis of the offer which offers the lowest price, it shall send a report justifying the rejection to the Government for onward transmission to the Commission.

### 3. Contracting authority's obligations once contract has been awarded

It may be a matter of considerable importance to disappointed tenderers to **3–20** know the outcome of a contract award procedure, not least to establish whether there may be grounds on which to challenge the award (as to which see *Chapter 5* below). The Regulations impose upon contracting authorities the following obligations in this respect:

(a) the authority must not later than 48 days after the award, send to the Official Journal a notice substantially corresponding to the form set out in Part E of Schedule 2 and containing the information therein specified. The information required may be omitted in a particular case where to publish such information would impede law enforcement, would otherwise be contrary to the public interest, would prejudice the legitimate commercial interests of any person or might prejudice fair competition between contractors (reg. 21);

(b) the authority must within 15 days of the date on which it receives a request from any unsuccessful contractor inform that contractor why he was unsuccessful and if the contractor was unsuccessful as a result of the evaluation of offers it must also tell him the name of the person awarded the contract (reg. 22).

A contracting authority must in addition prepare a record in respect of each public works contract awarded containing specified information which must be available for transmission to the Commission if requested. Where a contracting authority decides not to award a public works contract which has been advertised nor to seek offers in relation to another public works contract for the same purpose it must inform the Official Journal of that decision and must, if so requested by any

[15] Case 103/88, *Fratelli Costanzo SpA v. Commission de Milano:* [1989] E.C.R. 1839.

contractor who submitted an offer or who applied to be included amongst the persons to be selected to tender for or negotiate the contract, give the reasons for its decision (reg. 22(4)).

## Miscellaneous

### 1. Subsidised Works Contracts

**3–21**    Where a contracting authority undertakes to contribute more than half of the consideration expected to be paid under certain public works contracts which will be or have been entered into by the thus subsidised body (other than another contracting authority) the contracting authority must make it a condition of making such contribution that the subsidised body complies with the Regulations in relation to the contract as if it were a contracting authority, and must ensure that the subsidised body does so comply or recover the contribution. The contracts to which this provision applies are those which are for carrying out any of the activities specified in Group 502 of Schedule 1 (Civil Engineering, construction of roads, bridges, railways, etc.) or for the carrying out of building works for hospitals, facilities intended for sports recreation and leisure, school and university buildings or buildings for administrative purposes (reg. 23).

### 2. Public Housing Scheme Works Contracts

**3–22**    A public housing scheme works contract is defined as "a public works contract relating to the design and construction of a public housing scheme" (reg. 2(1). For the purpose of seeking offers in relation to a public housing scheme works contract where the size and complexity of the scheme and the estimated duration of the works involved require that the planning of the scheme be based from the outset on a close collaboration of a team comprising representatives of the contracting authority, experts and the contractor, the contracting authority may, subject as below, depart from the provisions of the Regulations in so far as it is necessary to do so to select the contractor who is most suitable for integration into the team. The contracting authority must in any event comply with the provisions relating to the restricted procedure up to the selection of contractors to be invited to tender (see para. 3–11 above). The contracting authority must in addition include in the contract notice a job description which is as accurate as possible so as to enable contractors to form a valid idea of the scheme and of the minimum standards relating to the business or professional status, the economic and financial standing and the technical capacity which the person awarded the contract will be expected to fill (reg. 24).

### 3. Public Works Concession Contracts

**3–23**    A Public Works Concession Contract is defined in the Regulations as "a public works contract under which the consideration given by the contracting authority consists of or includes the grant of a right to exploit the work or works to be carried out under the contract" (reg. 2(1)).

A contracting authority seeking offers in relation to a public works concession contract must as soon as possible after forming that intention publicise its intention by means of a contract notice in the Official Journal. The contract notice must be in a form substantially corresponding to that set out in Part F of Schedule 2 and containing the information therein specified in relation to the concession contract. The last date for the receipt of tenders or of requests to be selected to tender or negotiate the contract must be not less than 52 days from the date of dispatch of the notice (reg. 25).

A contracting authority seeking offers in relation to a public works concession contract must either:

(a) include in the invitation to tender or to apply to be selected to tender or to negotiate, a request that the applicant specify whether he would intend, if awarded the contract, to sub-contract to persons who are not affiliated to him (as defined) any of the work or works and if so how much as a proportion of the value of such work or works would be so contracted or,

(b) require as a term of the concession contract
(i) that the concessionaire sub-contract to persons who are not affiliated to the concessionaire some or all of the work or works to be carried out under the concession contract and
(ii) that the amount of the works so contracted be not less than 30 per cent., or such higher percentage as may be specified in the contract at the option of the contracting authority or the concessionaire, of the contract value if no concession had been granted.

Where the concessionaire is itself a contracting authority it must comply with the Regulations in respect of public works contracts it seeks offers in relation to for the purpose of sub-contracting the work or works to be carried out under its public works concession contract.

Where the concessionaire is not a contracting authority it must in relation to contracts to which the provisions apply:

(a) publicise its intention to seek offers by sending to the Official Journal as soon as possible after forming the intention a notice in a form substantially corresponding to that set out in Part G of Schedule 2 and containing the information therein specified in relation to the contract;

(b) comply with the provisions as to publication of notices in relation to that notice as if the concessionaire were a contracting authority;

(c) if that notice invites tenders, fix as the last date for the receipt by the concessionaire of tenders a date of not less than 40 days from the date of the dispatch of the notice and specify that date in the notice; and

(d) if the notice invites applications to be selected to tender for or negotiate the contract,
(i) fix as the last date for the receipt of such applications a date not less

31

than 37 days from the date of dispatch of the notice and specify that date in the notice; and

(ii) fix as the last date for the receipt of tenders following selection of the persons to be invited to tender a date of not less than 40 days from the date of dispatch of the invitation and specify that date in the invitation.

Those provisions apply to a contract

(a) in relation to which the concessionaire is seeking offers for the purpose of sub-contracting any of the work or works to be carried out under its public works concession contract.
(b) which the concessionaire does not intend to enter into with a person affiliated to him.
(c) which would, if the concessionaire were a contracting authority, be a public works contract other than a public works contract in respect of which a contracting authority would be entitled to use the negotiated procedure (reg. 26) (see para. 3–12 above).

### 4. *Obligations relating to employment protection and working conditions*

**3–24**    A contracting authority which includes in the contract documents relating to a public works contract information as to where a contractor may obtain information about obligations relating to employment protection and working conditions which will apply to the works to be carried out under the contract, must ask contractors to indicate that they have taken account of those obligations in preparing their tender, or in negotiating the contract.

### 5. *Contracting authorities' obligations as regards reports*

**3–25**    The Regulations require that each contracting authority shall, not later than July 31, 1993 and July 31 in each alternate year thereafter, send to the Treasury a report containing the information specified in relation to each public works contract awarded by it in the year preceding the year in which the report is made. In addition the Treasury may require contracting authorities to provide specific reports relating to particular public works contracts for the purpose of informing the Commission (reg. 28).

Where a contracting authority is not a Minister of the Crown or a government department any report which is required by the Regulations to be sent to the Treasury shall be sent instead to the Minister responsible for that contracting authority and that Minister shall be responsible for sending the report to the Treasury (reg. 29).

# The Public Supply Contracts Regulations 1991

The Supply Regulations implement the Public Supplies Directive 77/62/EEC, **3–26** which has been amended many times,[16] together with the relevant part of the Remedies Directive 89/665/EEC (*Appendix* G). In the interests of intelligibility it has been thought appropriate to include only the proposed consolidating directive at *Appendix* C but it should be borne in mind that this directive introduces a number of amendments which are not yet included in the Regulations. These amendments, which are designed to align the Supplies Directive with the Works Consolidating Directive (*Appendix* A) and the Services Directive (*Appendix* H), relate in particular to the following:

(a) the definition of a contracting authority (Article 1(*b*)).
(b) the option to have recourse to the open or restricted procedure (Article 6(4)).
(c) the requirement to justify the refusal of candidates or tenderers (Article 7(1)).
(d) the rules for drawing up reports on the execution of the different award procedures (Article 7(3)).
(e) the conditions for referring to the common rules in the technical field (Article 8).
(f) the introduction of the Advisory Committee procedure (Article 29).

Pending the implementation of the consolidating directive (estimated for the end of 1993) the Regulations must therefore be construed in the light of Directive 77/62/EEC as amended.

The Supply Regulations, like the Directive they implement, apply to public **3–27** supply contracts similar rules to those set out in the Works Regulations (see paras. 3–01 to 3–25 above). It is not necessary therefore to repeat those rules in detail but only to point out where the two Regulations differ.

### Contracts to which the Regulations apply

The Regulations apply whenever a contracting authority seeks offers in **3–28** relation to a proposed public supply contract other than a public supply contract which is excluded under the Regulations (reg. 5).

1. *Meaning of "Contracting Authority" (reg. 3(1))*

The contracting authorities for the purposes of the Regulations as presently **3–29** drafted are identical with those set out in the Works Regulations (see para. 3–03

---

[16] In particular by:
  80/767/EEC ([1980] O.J. L215).
  88/295/EEC ([1988] O.J. L127).
  90/531/EEC (*Appendix* E).
  92/50/EEC (*Appendix* H at Art. 42(1)).

above) save that in the case of "a corporation established or a group of individuals appointed to act together for the specific purpose of meeting needs in the general interest not having an industrial or commercial character" (reg. 3(1)(r) under the Supply Regulations) the needs are limited to those met through the national health service or with respect to education or urban development, and "GATT contracting authorities" are included to the extent not already covered by sub-paras. (a) to (q) of regulation 3(1). A GATT contracting authority is defined as:

"one of the entities specified in Schedule 1 being entities in respect of which special provision is made by these Regulations in pursuance of the obligations of the Economic Community under the Agreement on Government Procurement between certain parties to the General Agreement on Tariffs and Trade (GATT) signed in Geneva on 12 April 1979."
(reg. 2(1)).

2. *Meaning of "Public Supply Contract"*

**3–30**      A public supply contract is defined by regulation 2(1) as:

"a contract in writing for consideration (whatever the nature of the consideration)—

> (a) for the purchase of goods by a contracting authority (whether or not the consideration is given in instalments and whether or not the purchase is conditional upon the occurrence of a particular event), or
> (b) for the hire of goods by a contracting authority (both where the contracting authority becomes the owner of the goods after the end of the period of hire and where it does not),

and for any siting or installation of those goods, but where under such a contract services are also to be provided, the contract shall only be a public supply contract—

> (i) where the value of the consideration attributable to the goods and any siting or installation of the goods is equal to or greater than the value attributable to the services or
> (ii) where the value of the consideration attributable to the services is greater than the value attributable to the goods and of any siting or installation of the goods, if the goods could have been provided separately from the services."
> (reg. 2(1)).

See also Article 2 of the Services Directive 92/50/EEC (*Appendix* H).

"Goods" includes substances, growing crops and things attached to or forming part of land which are agreed to be severed before the purchase or hire under the supply contract and any ship, aircraft or vehicle. "Ship" includes any boat and other description of a vessel used in navigation. It does not include electricity.

"Substance" means any natural or artificial substance whether in solid, liquid or gaseous form, or in the form of vapour (reg. 2(1)).

Those provisions are complimented by the provisions of the Services Directive at Article 1 (*Appendix* H) which expressly exclude from its ambit contracts for services which would fall within the definition of a "public supply contract" or a "public works contract" contained in the Supplies Directive or the Works Directive as implemented by the Regulations concerned. Further Article 2 of the Services Directive provides that:

> "If a public contract is intended to cover both products within the meaning of |the Supplies Directive| and services within the meaning of Annexes 1A and 1B to this Directive. It shall fall within the scope of this Directive if the value of the services in question exceeds that of the products covered by the contract."

It will be appreciated that the procurement Directives and therefore the Regulations which implement them are intended to be mutually exclusive as regards the contracts to which they apply. It will be important therefore to establish at the outset the correct category into which a given contract must be placed. The problem can probably best be illustrated by a number of examples:

A.—A local authority wishes to enter into a contract for the general maintenance of its housing stock. Under the proposed contract the contractor will be required to carry out regular inspections of the buildings, execute any necessary repairs or redecoration works and supply all necessary materials for this purpose. The contract is to be for an indefinite period but it is estimated that it will cost £4 million in its first year of which the cost of materials will be £1 million.

The contract is a "public works contract" because although general building maintenance is not specifically mentioned in Schedule 1 to the Works Regulations it is included in the term "general building and civil engineering work" in group 500. Where, however, maintenance is part of a building management contract this would not alter the status of the management contract as a service for the purposes of the public procurement regime.

B.—The Royal Botanic Gardens at Kew (a GATT authority listed in Schedule 1 to the Supply Regulations) wishes to award a contract for the conversion of all its records on to computer disks. The estimated value of the contract is £2.5 million.

The contract is not a "public supply contract" because although it will result in the production and supply of "goods" (computer disks) the contract is essentially a data processing contract and thus falls within C.P.C. ref. 84 and Category 7 ("Computer and Related Services") of Schedule 1A to the Services Directive. It is clear that the Services Directive contemplates that many contracts falling within Annex 1A or 1B (and which are therefore to be treated as "service contracts" for the purposes of that directive) may incidentally result in the supply of a "good". Thus category 9, "Accountancy and Auditing Services" may result in the supply of a company's annual balance sheet and profit and loss accounts; category 12 "Architectural Services" in architectural drawings;

category 15, "Publishing and Printing Services on a fee or contract basis" may result in the production of letter-heads or leaflets.[17] In each case the directive defines such contracts as service contracts. Further support that this is the correct approach to the distinction to be made between a supply and a service contract can be found in the Utilities Directive at Article 1(3)(a) which expressly provides that a contract for "software services" for use in a telecommunications network is to be deemed a "supply" contract for the purposes of that directive *but not otherwise* (emphasis added). In addition the Treasury points out that in the Commission working documents preparatory to the drafting of the Services Directive it was agreed that "off the shelf" software would be treated as a product but that customised software where the cost of customisation exceeded 50 per cent. of the total cost would be treated as a service. Thus if in the example given Kew Gardens wished to place a contract for the supply of copies of the disks referred to, to a value in excess of £89,000, such a contract would be a "public supply contract" and would therefore fall within the Regulations.

C.—The Metropolitan Police Authority wish to purchase equipment necessary for the establishment of a data processing system. The cost attributable to the creation of software, the planning, maintenance and technical commissioning of the system is greater than the cost of the hardware and its installation. The hardware could have been provided separately from the services and would otherwise fall within the provisions of the Regulations.

The contract is a public supply contract[18] (see para. 3–04 "Borderline cases" above).

CONDITIONAL PURCHASE CONTRACTS

As has been seen the Regulations include in the definition of a public supply contract a contract for the purchase of goods "whether or not the purchase is conditional upon the occurrence of a particular event." The directive makes no express mention of conditional purchase contracts being included in the definition of a public supply contract but it is submitted that the words used by the directive, namely "contracts involving the purchase of products" are wide enough to include such conditional purchase contracts. Thus, for example, where a contracting authority agrees to purchase goods on condition that at the end of the trial period it finds them satisfactory, that agreement will be a public supply contract. The same will be true where the contracting authority agrees to take goods on trial (whether free or otherwise) on condition that if the trial is successful it will then enter into a separate contract of purchase for those and/or other goods. In both cases the contracting authority will be contractually bound to purchase the goods conditionally upon the occurrence of a particular event

---

[17] Clarification is awaited from the Commission as to whether the printing of books, magazines and newspapers, etc., is to be treated as a supply of services under this category or whether it should properly be treated as a supply of goods. It is submitted that the latter is probably correct.

[18] See Chap. 2, n. 4.

(*i.e.* a successful outcome to the trial). Further, in neither case will the contracting authority be able to rely on the provision contained in regulation 10(3)(*c*) which permits a contracting authority to use the negotiated procedure "when the goods to be purchased or hired under the contract are to be manufactured [*i.e.* used] purely for the purpose of research experiment study or development" because by definition the trial would be over by the time the goods were purchased or hired. In the second example given above the actual contract of purchase would also be a public supply contract but it would of course be unnecessary to comply with the public procurement procedure in respect of that contract (assuming it applied) if that procedure had already been complied with in respect of the conditional purchase agreement of which it formed part. It would be otherwise if the contracting authority had failed to comply with the required procedure in respect of the conditional purchase agreement.

## The Public Supply Contracts excluded from the operation of the Regulations

1. *Contracts related to certain utilities*

The Supply Regulations do not apply to the seeking of offers in relation to a **3–31** proposed public supply contract by a contracting authority for the purpose of carrying out certain activities in the water, transport, energy, or telecommunications sectors, in precisely the same way as such contracts in those sectors are excluded under the Works Regulations (see para. 3–05(1.) above). Such contracts will fall to be dealt with if at all under the Utilities Regulations (*Appendix* F) (reg. 6(*a*) and (*b*)) of the Supply Regulations as amended).

2. *Secret contracts, contracts involving State security and contracts carried out pursuant to international agreement*

In addition the Supply Regulations, like the Works Regulations, do not apply to a public supply contract:

(*a*) which is classified as secret or where the delivery of the goods under it must be accompanied by special security measures in accordance with the laws, regulations or administrative provisions of any part of the United Kingdom or when the basic interests of the security of the United Kingdom require it;

(*b*) where goods to be purchased or hired under the contract are goods to which the provisions of Article 223.1(*b*) of the EEC Treaty apply [arms, munitions and war material]; or

(*c*) certain contracts carried out pursuant to international agreements (reg. 6(*f*)).

### 3. Contracts below certain value thresholds

Again, like the Works Regulations the Supply Regulations, do not apply to the seeking of offers in relation to a proposed public supply contract "where the estimated value of the contract (net of value added tax) at the relevant time is less than the relevant threshold" (reg. 7(1)).

The relevant threshold is:

(a)  in relation to a public supply contract in respect of which offers are sought by a GATT contracting authority (but in the case of such a contract in relation to which offers are sought by the Secretary of State for Defence only if it is for the purchase or hire of the goods specified in Schedule 2) is the amount for the time being to be treated as the ECU equivalent of 130,000 special drawing rights for the purposes of Council Directive 77/62/EEC as published from time to time in the Official Journal. For the period January 1, 1992 to December 31, 1993 the amount to be treated as the ECU equivalent of 130,000 special drawing rights is 125,576 ECUs (£88,802).[19] The GATT contracting authorities are listed in Schedule 1.

(b)  in relation to all other public supply contracts, is 200,000 ECUs (£141,431)[20] (reg. 7(2)).

The "estimated value" for the purposes of a public supply contract is normally the value of the consideration which the contracting authority expects to give under the contract (reg. 7(3)).

Exceptionally the "estimated value" is to be calculated in accordance with what has become known as the "aggregation provisions" and is as follows:

1.  In the case of a public supply contract for the hire, leasing or hire-purchase of goods for an indefinite period or for a period which is uncertain at the time the contract is entered into, the estimated value is the value of the consideration which the contracting authority expects to give in respect of each month of the hire multiplied by 48 (reg. 7(4)).

2.  In a case where the contracting authority proposes to enter into two or more public supply contracts at the same time in order to purchase or hire goods "of a particular type", the "estimated value" of each of those contracts is the aggregate of the value of the consideration which the contracting authority expects to give under each of those contracts (reg. 7(5)).

3.  In a case where a contracting authority has "a recurrent need" to purchase or hire goods of the type to be purchased or hired under the contract and for that purpose enters into separate public supply contracts at different times or into a public supply contract which under its terms is renewable or into a public supply contract for the purchase or hire of goods over an indefinite period, the "estimated value" of the contract is the amount calculated by applying one of the following two valuation methods:

[19] See Appendix I.
[20] See Appendix I.

(a) by taking the aggregate of the value of the consideration given by the contracting authority under such contracts for the purchase or hire of goods of the type to be purchased or hired under the contract during the last financial year of the contracting authority ending before, or the period of 12 months ending immediately before, the relevant time, and by adjusting that amount to take account of any expected changes in quantity and cost of the goods of that type to be purchased or hired in the period of 12 months commencing with the relevant time, or

(b) by estimating the aggregate of the value of the consideration which the contracting authority expects to give under such contracts for the purchase or hire of goods of the type to be purchased or hired under the contract during the period of 12 months from the first date of delivery of the goods to be purchased or hired under the contract or, where the contract is for a definite term of more than 12 months, during the term of the contract, except that when the goods to be purchased or hired under the contract are required for the sole purposes of a "discrete operational unit" within the organisation of the contracting authority and,

    (i)  the decision whether to purchase or hire goods of that type has been devolved to such a unit, and

    (ii)  that decision is taken independently of any other part of the contracting authority, the valuation methods described in sub-paras. (a) and (b) above shall be adapted by aggregating only the value of the consideration which the contracting authority has given or expects to give, as the case may be, for goods of the type to be purchased or hired under the contract which were or are required for the sole purposes of that unit. (reg. 7(6)).

It will be noted that the directive makes no such exception as is provided by regulation 7(6)(b) above (see Art. 5(3)). However, the Regulation interprets the Article in a way which is consistent with its origins in the 1977 GATT Government Procurement Agreement and has been accepted by the Commission in informal discussions with the Treasury. It is submitted that it accurately reflects the purposes of the directive and therefore there is no inconsistency between the Regulations and the directive in this respect. The Commission have, in relation to Utility Supply contracts, issued draft policy guidelines on the application of the aggregation provisions where discrete operational units are or may be involved. It is submitted that those guidelines provide useful guidance in relation to public supply contracts also (see *Appendix E: Part 2*).

The term "recurrent need" ("regular contracts" in Article 5(3) of the Consolidated Supplies Directive) is not defined in the

Regulations. However, it is submitted that the term should be given the same meaning as is given in the parallel provision in the Utilities Regulations, namely "requirement over a period" (reg. 9(6)). Further, the additional objective test provided by regulation 9(7) of the Utilities Regulations, namely that only contracts with "similar characteristics" for the same type of goods need be aggregated should, it is submitted, be read into regulation 7(6) of the Supply Regulations. It is implicit in the regulation that a contracting authority will only have a "recurrent need" where this is known to that authority at the time the relevant contract is entered into. So, for example, where at the time of entering the contract it is not anticipated that the contracting authority will require further goods of that type in the next 12 months then the aggregation provisions will not apply to that contract even though there has been a recurrent need for such goods in the past.

(c) In the case of a contract which is to be treated as a public supply contract by virtue of the fact that it is a contract for both goods and services and the services have a greater value than but are separate from the goods (reg. 2(1)), the "estimated value" is that proportion of the value of the consideration which the contracting authority expects to give under the contract which is attributable to the purchase or hire of the goods and to any siting or installation of the goods (reg. 7(7)).

(d) In a case where the public supply contract includes one or more options the "estimated value" of the contract is the highest possible amount payable under the contract.

The "relevant time" is the date on which a contract notice would be sent to the Official Journal if the requirement to send such a notice applied to that contract.

A contracting authority is not permitted to enter into separate public supply contracts nor select nor exercise a choice of valuation method (where this is authorised) with the intention of avoiding the application of the Regulations.

### 4. Framework Agreements

**3–32**   It will be appreciated from the above that where a contracting authority has a "recurrent need" for a particular product it must comply with the Regulations on every occasion that it seeks offers in respect of a contract for the supply of that product so long as the estimated value of that contract after applying the aggregation provisions exceeds the threshold and is not otherwise excluded.

A contracting authority may, however, enter into a single supply contract which is subject to the Regulations which contains provisions for regular call-offs. Such call-offs, not being themselves contracts, will not be subject to the Regulations. No express provision is made in the Supplies Directive (as is made in the Utilities Regulations at regulation 10), and hence the Regulations, for framework arrangements which, while not in themselves public supply contracts, set out the terms (particularly as to price and quantity) under which a supplier will enter into supply contracts with a contracting authority in the period during which the framework arrangements apply, and which permits the framework arrangement to be submitted to the provisions of the Regulations while exempting the supply contracts made under it. However, the Treasury have stated that an agreement has been reached between the E.C. Commission and the Member States permitting such framework arrangements to be treated as though they were supply contracts subject to the provisions of the directive and that where they are so treated the contracts made under them will be exempted from the need to be advertised again, although there are questions to be resolved on the need for contract award notices in those circumstances. It is submitted that national courts can and should construe the Regulations in the light of that agreement.

## Rules governing technical specifications

Making allowance for the difference in nature between public contracts for works and public contracts for supplies, the rules relating to technical specifications in public supply contracts are virtually identical to those relating to public works contracts (see para. 3–06 above). There are, however, two additions; in the Supply Regulations it is provided that: **3–33**

(a) A contracting authority may additionally define the technical specifications in the contract documents relating to a public supply contract other than by reference to relevant European specifications if definition by reference to the relevant European specifications would conflict with the application of Council Directive 86/361/EEC[21] (now superseded by 91/263/EEC[22]) on the initial stage of mutual recognition of type approval for telecommunications terminal equipment or Council Decision 87/95/EEC on standardisation in the field of information technology and telecommunications[23] or other Community obligations in specific service or goods areas (reg. 8(4)(c)), and

(b) where the goods to be purchased or hired under a public supply contract are to be the subject of a design competition, or where the supplier is permitted under the terms of the invitation to tender to submit tenders based on different technical specifications, the contracting authority must not reject a tender on the ground that it has been drawn up by reference to different calculations from those used in the United Kingdom if the tender otherwise accords with the terms and conditions of the contract documents and the supplier submits with the tender the evidence

[21] |1986| O.J. L217/21.
[22] |1991| O.J. L128/1.
[23] |1987| O.J. L36/31.

necessary for examining the tender and provides such additional explanations as the contracting authority considers necessary (reg. 8(11).

## Rules governing the procedures leading to the award of a Public Supply Contract

*1. The procedures to be used in awarding the contract*

**3–34**     Like the Works Regulations, the Supply Regulations require that, in seeking offers in relation to a public supply contract, a contracting authority must use the "open procedure", the "restricted procedure" or the "negotiated procedure", which have the same definitions in relation to public supply contracts as they do in relation to public works contracts (see para. 3–07 above). Again, the Supply Regulations lay down rules for deciding which of those procedures may be used.

*2. Advertising the intention to seek offers by means of a prior information notice*

**3–35**     A GATT contracting authority (see para. 3–29 above) must at the beginning of each financial year send to the Official Journal a notice in the prescribed form setting out certain public supply contracts in relation to which it expects to seek offers leading to an award during that financial year. The public supply contracts concerned are those for the purchase or hire of goods of a particular type whose value exceeds the relevant threshold (due regard having been given to the aggregation provisions) and which in aggregate is estimated at or more than 750,000 ECUs (£530,366)[24] (reg. 9).

*3. Selection of contract award procedure*

**3–36**     Unlike the position under the Works Regulations where there is no such restraint, a contracting authority may only use the restricted procedure when to do so is justified by the circumstances, such as:

(a)   where the cost of using the open procedure would be disproportionate to the value of the goods to be purchased or hired under the contract;

(b)   the nature of the goods to be purchased or hired under the contract (reg. 10(2)).

The circumstances in which a contracting authority may exceptionally use the negotiated procedure are virtually identical to those applicable to the Works Regulations (see para. 3–09 above). However, the following differences should be noted:

(a)   there is no equivalent under the Supply Regulations to para. 10(2)(c) of the Works Regulations that the negotiated procedure may be used when "the nature of the work or works to be carried out under the contract is such or the risks attaching thereto are such as not to permit overall pricing."

---

[24] See Appendix I.

(b) paragraphs 10(2)(g) and (h) under the Works Regulations are replaced under the Supply Regulations by a provision that the negotiated procedure may be used when the goods to be purchased or hired under the contract are required by the contracting authority as a partial replacement for, or addition to, existing goods or an installation, and when to obtain the goods from a person other than the person who supplied the existing goods or the installation would oblige the contracting authority to acquire goods having different technical characteristics which would result in,

(i) incompatibility between the existing goods or the installation and the goods to be purchased or hired under the contract, or

(ii) disproportionate technical difficulties in the operation and maintenance of the existing goods or the installation (reg. 10(3)(f)).

However, a contracting authority must not use the negotiated procedure in those circumstances if the term of the proposed contract or the term of that contract and of any other contract entered into for the same purpose is more than three years, unless there are reasons why it is unavoidable that that period should be exceeded. In all other circumstances the contracting authority must use the open procedure.

4. *The open procedure*

The open procedure under the Supply Regulations is the same as that under the Works Regulations (see para. 3–10 above) save that:    **3–37**

(a) the last date for the receipt of tenders (not less than 52 days from the date of dispatch of the contract notice) cannot under the Supply Regulations be reduced to 36 days in the circumstances permitted by the Works Regulations, and

(b) the contract documents must, under the Supply Regulations, be sent within four days (as opposed to six) of the receipt of a request from any supplier.

5. *The restricted procedure*

The restricted procedure under the Supply Regulations is the same as that under the Works Regulations (see para. 3–11 above) save that:    **3–38**

(a) there is no restriction on the number of suppliers who may be invited to tender under the Supply Regulations

(b) the invitation to tender may be sent by letter, telegram, telex, facsimile or telephone but in the last four cases it must be confirmed in writing. There are no specific rules relating to the information which the invitation to tender must contain other than that it must be accompanied by the contract documents.

(c) the last date for the receipt of tenders is not less than 40 days from the dispatch of the invitation to tender and there are no exceptions as provided by the Works Regulations.

### 6. The negotiated procedure

**3–39**     As with the Works Regulations a contracting authority which uses the negotiated procedure in reliance on the exceptions contained in regulation 10(3)(b) (absence of tenders), 10(3)(c) (goods purchased or hired for the purpose of research experiment study or development), 10(3)(d) (technical or artistic reasons or reasons connected with exclusive rights limiting supplier to one person only) or 10(3)(f) (goods required for partial replacement of or in addition to existing goods) is not subject to any procedural rules other than those relating to the exclusion of suppliers on the grounds of ineligibility and their selection to negotiate already referred to (see para. 3–12 above). The same applies to a contracting authority using the negotiated procedure in reliance on the exception contained in regulation 10(3)(a) (discontinued procedure) so long as the authority invites to negotiate every supplier who submitted a tender (not being a tender which has been excluded in accordance with the Regulations).

In all other cases identical rules apply to those applicable in relation to public works contracts subject to the negotiated procedure (see para. 3–12 above) save that in relation to public supply contracts there is no lower limit placed on the number selected to negotiate.

## Selection of suppliers

### 1. Criteria for rejection of suppliers

**3–40**     The criteria on which applications to tender and tenderers may be excluded as ineligible from the tendering process are virtually identical to those applicable to public works contracts (see para. 3–13 above) save that no provision is made under the Supply Regulations for an exception to the obligation on the supplier to provide information to the contracting authority to enable it to make the necessary evaluation on the grounds that the supplier is registered on an official list of recognised suppliers.

### 2. Information as to economic and financial standing

**3–41**     The information for which a contracting authority may ask and which it may take into account when assessing whether a supplier meets any minimum standards of economic and financial standing is identical to that set out in the Works Regulations (see para. 3–14 and 3–16 above) save that no exception is made in the Supply Regulations in respect of the situation where a supplier is registered on an official list of recognised suppliers (reg. 15).

### 3. Information as to technical capacity

The only information for which a contracting authority may ask and which it **3–42** may apparently take into account when assessing whether a supplier meets any minimum standards of technical capacity is set out at regulation 16(1) and are as follows:

(a) a list of deliveries by the supplier of goods of a similar type to the goods to be purchased or hired under the public supply contract in the past three years, specifying in each case the date of delivery, the consideration received and the identity of the purchaser, accompanied by a certificate issued or countersigned by the purchaser confirming the details of the sale or, but only where the purchaser was not a contracting authority, a declaration by the supplier attesting the details of the purchase;

(b) a description of the supplier's technical facilities, measures for ensuring quality and study and research facilities in relation to the goods to be purchased or hired under the public supply contract;

(c) an indication of the technicians or technical bodies who would be involved with the production of the goods to be purchased or hired under the public supply contract, particularly those responsible for quality control, whether or not they are independent of the supplier;

(d) samples, descriptions and photographs of the goods to be purchased or hired under the public supply contract and certification of the authenticity of such samples, descriptions or photographs;

(e) certification by official quality control institutes or agencies of recognised competence attesting that the goods to be purchased or hired under the public supply contract conform to standards and technical specifications (within the meaning of the regulations) identified by the contracting authority. There would in addition appear to be no impediment to the contracting authority requiring a quality assurance as regards the candidates' management system (cf. Article 33 of the Public Services Directive);

(f) where the goods to be sold or hired under the public supply contract are complex or are required for a special purpose, a check, carried out by the contracting authority or on its behalf by a competent official body of the Member State in which the supplier is established, on the production capacity of the supplier in respect of the goods to be purchased or hired under the contract and, if relevant, on the supplier's study and research facilities and quality control measures.

The contracting authority must specify in the contract notice which part of the information specified in para. 16(1) it requires to be provided.

### 4. Limits on the information which may be required or taken into account

The observations made at paras. 3–16 above with regard to the information **3–43** which a contracting authority may require and/or take into account when assessing a contractor's economic and financial standing and technical capacity apply with equal force it is submitted to regulations 15 and 16 of the Supply Regulations. Those regulations implement what are now Articles 22 and 23 of the Consolidated Supplies Directive (*Appendix* C) which are in similar form to Articles 26 and 27 of the Works Directive. Accordingly those regulations should be construed in a similar manner (*i.e.* more flexibly than the wording might at first glance indicate) to regulations 15 and 16 of the Works Regulations. In addition under the Supply Regulations a contracting authority must comply with such requirements as to confidentiality of information provided to it by a supplier as the supplier may reasonably request (reg. 18).

5. *Consortia*

**3–44**     Identical provisions relating to consortia apply under the Supply Regulations as they do under the Works Regulations (reg. 19) (see para. 3–17 above).

## The award of a Public Supply Contract

1. *The basis for the award*

**3–45**     The contracting authority must award a public supply contract on the same criteria as it awards a public works contract, namely on the basis of either the tender (including in-house bids) which offers the lowest price or the one which is the most economically advantageous (reg. 20).

The criteria which a contracting authority may use to determine that an offer is the most economically advantageous include price, delivery date, running costs, cost effectiveness, quality, aesthetic and functional characteristics, technical merit, after-sales service and technical assistance (reg. 20(2)). All the criteria the contracting authority intends to apply in determining the most economically advantageous offer must be stated in the contract notice or contract documents preferably in descending order of importance. A distinction, however, must be made between on the one hand a contractual condition requiring the successful supplier to co-operate with some policy objective of the contracting authority, and the criteria for the selection of suppliers or for the award of the supply contract on the other (see para. 3–18 above and cases referred to therein).

2. *Abnormally low tenders*

**3–46**     If an offer for a public supply contract is obviously abnormally low the contracting authority must request an explanation of the offer, or of those parts which it considers contribute to the offer being abnormally low, and must,

(a) if awarding the contract on the basis of the offer which offers the lowest price, examine the details of all the offers made, taking into account any explanation given to it of the abnormally low tender, before awarding the contract, or

(*b*) if awarding the contract on the basis of the offer which is the most economically advantageous, take any such explanation into account in assessing which is the most economically advantageous offer.

A contracting authority may, if it is not satisfied with the explanation of any supplier given in respect of an abnormally low offer, reject that offer but, if a contracting authority which rejects an offer for this reason is awarding the contract on the basis of the offer which offers the lowest price, it must send a report justifying the rejection to the Treasury for onward transmission to the Commission.

*3. Contracting authority's obligations once contract has been awarded*

A contracting authority's obligations with regard to publicity once the supply **3–47** contract has been awarded are more limited than under the Works Regulations. It must within 48 days after the award send to the Official Journal a notice substantially corresponding to the form set out in Part E of Schedule 3 and containing the information specified. The information required may be omitted in the same circumstances as apply in the Works Regulations (see para. 3–20 above).

## Miscellaneous

*1. Public service bodies*

Where a contracting authority (other than one which is a contracting authority **3–48** only by reason of being a GATT contracting authority) grants to a person other than a contracting authority special or exclusive rights to carry on a service for the benefit of the public it must impose an express duty on that person not to discriminate in seeking offers in relation to, or in awarding, a contract for the purchase or hire of goods on the grounds of nationality against a person who is a national of and established in a Member State or on the grounds that the goods to be supplied under the contract originate in another Member State (reg. 22).

*2. Contracting authority's obligations as regards reports*

Special reporting obligations with regard to public supply contracts awarded **3–49** by them are placed by the Regulations on contracting authorities (reg. 23). These vary according to whether the contracting authority is a GATT contracting authority or not but in both cases involve the authorities submitting to the Treasury either annually or bi-annually reports containing specified information similar to that required under the Works Regulations. The principal purpose of these reports is to enable the Commission to monitor both the application and effectiveness of the directives.

# Chapter Four

## THE UTILITIES SUPPLY AND WORKS CONTRACTS REGULATIONS 1992

### Introduction

These Regulations which are made by the Treasury under section 2(2) of the **4–01** European Communities Act 1972 implement in its entirety the Utilities Directive 90/531/EEC (*Appendix* E) "concerning the coordination of procedures for the award of supply and works contracts by certain entities operating in the water, energy, transport and telecommunications sectors." The entities affected are specified in Schedule 1 and in the Regulations are called utilities (reg. 3) (see para. 4–13 below).

The Regulations like the Works and Supply Regulations, apply when utilities **4–02** are seeking offers in relation to certain contracts for the purchase or hire of goods called in the Regulations "supply contracts" (regs. 2(1) and 5) and when they are seeking offers in relation to certain contracts providing for, or engaging a person to procure the carrying out or the design and carrying out of certain building and engineering works called in the Regulations "works contracts" (regs. 2(1) and 5). They deal in particular with the treatment to be accorded to suppliers or contractors (or potential suppliers or contractors) who are nationals of and established in Member States (reg. 4).

Certain contracts are excluded from the applications of the Regulations, **4–03** principally where the contract is not for the purpose of carrying out an activity specified in the Part of Schedule 1 in which the utility concerned is specified but also where the contract is for the purpose of carrying out an activity outside the territory of the Communities, contracts for resale, secret contracts, contracts connected with international agreements (reg. 6), certain contracts awarded by utilities operating in the telecommunications sector (reg. 7 and Schedule 2) and those contracts where the value of the contract is beneath the threshold for coverage (reg. 9). Certain contracts awarded by utilities operating in the energy sector may be exempt from the detailed rules of the Regulations, in which case the utility must comply with the principles of non-discrimination and competitive procurement in seeking offers in relation to them (reg. 8).

Like the Works and Supply Regulations the principal requirement of the **4–04** Utilities Regulations is that in seeking offers in relation to a supply or a works contract, a utility must use either the open procedure, the restricted procedure or the negotiated procedure (see para. 3–07 above) however the Utilities Regulations in accordance with the Utilities Directive has adopted a more flexible approach to the choice of procedure than is contained in the earlier Regulations; so long as the utility makes a "call for competition" as defined in the Regulations any of the three procedures may be used and in certain specified circumstances no call for competition need be made (regs. 14 and 15).

**4–05**     As with the Works Regulations, (see para. 3–08) and the Supply Regulations in relation to GATT authorities, (see para. 3–35), a utility is required to publicise the supply or works contracts which it expects to award in the Official Journal at least once a year (reg. 13) and again when it starts the procedure leading to the award (reg. 14) although the latter requirement is dispensed with in certain cases (regs. 14 and 15).

**4–06**     Unlike the earlier Regulations the Utilities Regulations permit the operation of a system of qualification of suppliers or contractors, from which a utility may select suppliers or contractors to tender for or to negotiate a contract without advertisement at the start of the award procedure. In this case the existence of the qualification system must be advertised (reg. 17).

**4–07**     The form of the different advertisements and the information which it has to contain in relation to the proposed contract is specified in Schedule 3. If the notice is also to be published in the press it must be limited to the information in the Official Journal (reg. 28).

**4–08**     Similar to the Works and Supply Regulations, the Utilities Regulations lay down minimum time limits in relation to responses by potential suppliers or contractors to invitations to tender, to be selected to tender for or to negotiate the contract, and for obtaining the relevant documents (reg. 16). The Regulations also indicate the matters to which the utility may have regard in excluding tenders from suppliers or contractors who are regarded as ineligible or in selecting suppliers or contractors to tender for or to negotiate the contract (reg. 18), and as before they require that the utility award a supply or works contract on the basis either of the offer (including in-house bids) which offers the lowest price or the one which is the most economically advantageous (reg. 20). In addition the Regulations lay down similar rules in relation to technical specifications (reg. 11) to publicising their awards (reg. 22) and to the keeping of records and to reporting (regs. 25 and 26).

**4–09**     The Regulations introduce a number of innovations into the public procurement regime. A utility is permitted to advertise an arrangement which establishes the terms under which suppliers or contractors will enter supply or works contracts with it over a period of time (called in the Regulations "framework agreements") in which case it need not advertise the supply and works contracts made under it (reg. 10) (see para. 3–32 above). Secondly a utility may, and in other limited circumstances must, reject an offer for a supply contract if more than 50 per cent. of the value of the goods are goods which originate in States with which the Communities have not concluded an agreement ensuring comparable and effective access to markets for undertakings in Member States (reg. 21).

**4–10**     The Regulations also implement the Utilities Remedies Directive 92/13/EEC (Appendix G) which is in similar form to the Works and Supply Compliance

Directive 89/665/EEC but which introduces two innovations of its own. First, the Directive and therefore the Regulations (reg. 30(7)) expressly empowers the Court to award a supplier or a contractor his tendering costs where it is satisfied he would have had a "real chance" of being awarded the contract had the contracting authority not been in breach of the Regulations. Secondly, the Directive and therefore the Regulations (reg. 31) introduces the concept of conciliation at the Community level with the agreement of the utility concerned (see paras. 5–12 and 5–13 below).

Finally, the Regulations amend the Works and Supply Regulations to ensure   **4–11** that not more than one set of Regulations applies to any contract. The Works and Supply Regulations in *Appendix* B and *Appendix* D are printed as thus amended.

## The Application of the Utilities Regulations

The Regulations apply whenever a "utility" seeks offers in relation to a   **4–12** proposed supply contract or a proposed works contract other than a contract excluded from the operation of the Regulations (reg. 5).

### Meaning of a "Utility"

For the purposes of the Regulations a utility is "a person specified in the first   **4–13** column of Schedule 1" (reg. 3). These are broadly public authorities and public as well as private undertakings which operate as suppliers to, and operators or providers of, fixed networks or certain facilities in the water, energy, transport and telecommunications sectors. The second column in Schedule 1 sets out certain activities carried out by those utilities. Both columns are divided horizontally into parts. The Regulations only apply where a utility seeks offers in relation to a contract for the purpose of carrying out an activity which is set out in the part in which the utility is specified (reg. 6(a)). Because a number of exceptions have to be made (for example where a supplier to a relevant network does so to a minor degree and only incidentally to some other non relevant activity) the Regulations are necessarily complex. Their comprehension is probably made easier therefore if the contents of the Schedule are taken sector by sector so that each of the utilities can be identified, and each sector is then subdivided into its constituent parts in order to define in relation to which activities of those utilities the Regulations (unless otherwise excluded) will apply. This is the procedure which has been adopted in this Guide.

**1.** Water

PART A

Utilities

(a)  A company holding an appointment as a water undertaker under the Water Industry Act 1991.
(b)  A water authority as defined in section 3(1) of the Water (Scotland) Act 1980.
(c)  The Department of the Environment of Northern Ireland.

Relevant Activities

(**1**)—The provision or operation of a fixed network which provides or will provide a service to the public in connection with the production, transport or distribution of drinking water.

(**2**)—Hydraulic engineering, irrigation, or land drainage, but only if more than 20 per cent. of the total value of water made available by such authority is intended for the supply of drinking water.

(**3**)—The disposal or treatment of sewage.

PART B

Utilities

(a)  A "relevant person" not specified in Part C.
(b)  Any other person not specified in Part C who supplies drinking water to a network which is referred to in para. (1) above and which is provided or operated by a person specified in Part A.

Relevant Activities

(**4**)—The supply of drinking water to a network referred to in para. (**1**) above.
  A "relevant person" is defined in the Schedule as:

(a)  a public authority, (i.e. a contracting authority within the meaning of regulation 3(1) of the Works Regulations (see para. 3–03 above),
(b)  a public undertaking (i.e. a person over whom one or more public authorities are able to exercise directly or indirectly a "dominant" influence as defined in the Schedule) or,
(c)  a person who is not a public authority or a public undertaking but who (i) has as one of its activities an activity specified in the second column of Schedule 1 (other than an activity specified in paras. (**2**) and (**3**)) and (ii) carries out that activity on the basis of a "special and exclusive right". A "special and exclusive right" is defined in the Schedule as "a right deriving from authorizations granted by a competent authority when the requirement for the authorization has the effect of reserving for one or

more persons the exploitation of an activity specified in the second column of this Schedule, and in particular a person shall be considered to enjoy a special or exclusive right where for the purpose of constructing a network or facilities referred to in the second column of this Schedule it may take advantage of a procedure for the appropriation or use of property or may place network equipment on, under or over a highway."

PART C

Utilities

(a) A relevant person, other than a public authority, who produces drinking water because its consumption is necessary for the purpose of carrying on an activity not specified in the second column of the Schedule and who supplies only the excess to a network which is referred to in para. (1) above.
(b) Any other person who is not a public authority, who produces drinking water for a similar purpose and similarly supplies only the excess to a public network provided or operated by a person in Part A.

Relevant Activities

5)—The supply of drinking water to a network referred to in para. (1) above but only if the drinking water supplied in the period of 36 months ending at the relevant time as defined in regulation 9(16) (see below) has exceeded 30 per cent. of the total produced by the utility in that period.

In other words the effect of Part C is that "relevant" and other persons who are not public authorities will not be caught by the Regulations if they only supply drinking water to the public network incidentally to some other non qualifying activity and the amount of such supply is below the 30 per cent. threshold over the relevant period (and see Article 2(5)(a) of the Utilities Directive).

Prima facie it would appear from the above that a utility which engages in any of the activities listed in Parts A, B or C above would be caught by the Regulations when contracting to purchase water. However such contracts are expressly excluded from the ambit of the Regulations by regulation 6(f).

2. Electricity

PART D

Utilities

(a) A person licensed under section 6 of the Electricity Act 1989
(b) A person licensed under article 10(1) of the Electricity (Northern Ireland) Order 1992.

Relevant Activities

6)—The provision or operation of a fixed network which provides or will provide a service to the public in connection with the production, transport or distribution of electricity.

PART E

*Utilities*

(a) A "relevant person" not specified in Part F.
(b) Any other person not specified in Part F who supplies electricity to a network which is referred to in para. (**6**) above and which is provided or operated by a person specified in Part N.

*Relevant Activities*

(**7**)—The supply of electricity to a network referred to in para. (**6**) above.

PART F

*Utilities*

(a) A "relevant person" other than a public authority who produces electricity because its use is necessary for the purpose of carrying out an activity not specified in the second column of the Schedule and who supplies only the excess to a network referred to in para. (**6**) above.
(b) Any other person, who is not a public authority, who produces electricity because its use is necessary for the purpose of carrying out an activity not specified in the second column to this Schedule and who supplies only the excess to a network which is referred to in para. (**6**) above and which is provided or operated by a person specified in Part N.

*Relevant Activities*

(**8**)—The supply of electricity to a network referred to in para. (**6**) above but only if the electricity supplied in the period of 36 months ending at the relevant time as defined in regulation 9(16), has exceeded 30 per cent. of the total produced by the utility in that period.

Again, as in the case of incidental suppliers of water to the public network, utilities who are not public authorities will escape the Regulations altogether if the amount of electricity supplied by them is below the 30 per cent. threshold over the relevant period.

**3.** *Gas*

PART G

*Utilities*

(a) A public gas supplier as defined in section 7(1) of the Gas Act 1986.
(b) A person declared to be an undertaker for the supply of gas under article 14(1) of the Gas (Northern Ireland) Order 1977.

*Relevant Activities*

(**9**)—The provision or operation of a fixed network which provides or will provide a service to the public in connection with the production, transport, or distribution of gas.

*Utilities*

(*a*)  A "relevant person" not specified in Part I.
(*b*)  Any other person not specified in Part I who supplies gas to a network which is referred to in para. (**9**) above and which is provided or operated by a person specified in Part G.

*Relevant Activities*

(**10**)—The supply of gas to a network referred to in para. (**9**) above.

## PART I

*Utilities*

(*a*)  A "relevant person" other than a public authority who produces gas only as the unavoidable consequence of carrying out an activity not specified in the second column of the Schedule and who supplies gas for the sole purpose of the economic exploitation of the production to a network referred to in para. (**9**) above.
(*b*)  Any other person who is not a public authority who produces gas only as the unavoidable consequence of carrying out an activity not specified in the second column of the Schedule and who supplies gas for the sole purpose of the economic exploitation of the production to a network which is referred to in para. (**9**) above and which is provided or operated by a person specified in Part G.

*Relevant Activities*

(**11**)—The supply of gas to a network referred to in para. (**9**) above but only if the total consideration payable in the period of 36 months ending at the relevant time as defined in regulation 9(16) on account of such supply has exceeded 20 per cent. of the total turnover of the utility in that period.

It will be noted that the conditions which an incidental supplier of gas to the public network must meet before it can avoid the effect of the Regulations are somewhat more stringent than is the case of a similar supplier of drinking water or electricity. First the production of gas must be the "unavoidable consequence" of carrying out an activity not specified in the Schedule. If gas is an optional by-product therefore the utility will not be exempted even if the supply falls below the threshold requirements set out in para. (**11**). Secondly the utility's principal activity must not be one falling *anywhere* within the second column, therefore if, for example, the principal activity is the extraction of oil (para. 15 in the Schedule) and the production of gas is an unavoidable consequence of this the utility would not be exempted. Thirdly, the supply of gas to the public network must not exceed the threshold requirements set out in para. (**11**) (and see reg. 2(5)(*b*) of the Utilities Directive).

**4.** *Heat*

PART J

*Utilities*

(*a*)  A local authority (defined as in paras. 2–4 of regulation 3 of the Works Regulations).
(*b*)  A person licensed under section 6(1)(*a*) of the Electricity Act 1989 whose licence includes the provisions referred to in section 10(3) of that Act.
(*c*)  The Northern Ireland Housing Executive.

*Relevant Activities*

(**12**)—The provision or operation of a fixed network which provides or will provide a service to the public in connection with the production, transport or distribution of heat.

PART K

*Utilities*

(*a*)  A "relevant person" not specified in Part L.
(*b*)  Any other person not specified in Part L who supplies heat to a network which is referred to in para. (**12**) above and which is provided or operated by a person specified in Part J.

*Relevant Activities*

(**13**)—The supply of heat to a network referred to in para. (**12**) above.

PART L

*Utilities*

(*a*)  A relevant person other than a public authority who produces heat as an unavoidable consequence of carrying out an activity not specified in the second column of the Schedule and who supplies heat for the sole purpose of the economic exploitation of the production to a network referred to in para. (**12**) above.
(*b*)  Any other person who is not a public authority who produces heat only as the unavoidable consequence of carrying out an activity not specified in the second column of the Schedule and who supplies heat for the sole purpose of the economic exploitation of the production to a network

which is referred to in para. (**12**) above and which is provided or operated by a person specified in Part J.

*Relevant Activities*

(**14**)—The supply of heat to a network referred to in para. (**12**) above but only if the total consideration payable in the 36 months ending at the relevant time as defined in regulation 9(16) on account of such supply has exceeded 20 per cent. of the total turnover of the utility in that period.

It will be appreciated that as the gas and heat sectors are treated identically, the observations made above in respect of the gas sector apply with equal force to the heat sector.

## 5. *Extraction of oil and gas*

PART M

*Utilities*

(*a*)  A person licensed under the Petroleum (Production) Act 1934.
(*b*)  A person licensed under the Petroleum (Production) Act (Northern Ireland).

*Relevant Activities*

(**15**)—The exploitation of a geographical area for the purpose of exploring for or extracting oil or gas.

## 6. *Extraction of coal and other solid fuels*

PART N

*Utilities*

(*a*)  The British Coal Corporation.
(*b*)  A person licensed by the British Coal Corporation under the Coal Industry (Nationalisation) Act 1946.
(*c*)  The Department of Economic Development (Northern Ireland).
(*d*)  A person who holds a prospective licence, a mining lease, a mining licence or a mining permission as defined by section 57(1) of the Mineral Development Act (Northern Ireland) 1969.

*Relevant Activities*

(**16**)—The exploitation of a geographical area for the purposes of exploring for or extracting coal or other solid fuels.

Again, as in the water sector, it might appear from the above that a utility in the energy sector (*i.e.* Parts D–N above) would be caught by the Regulations when contracting to purchase energy, or fuel for the production of energy (*e.g.*

coal or gas for the generation of electricity); however such contracts are expressly excluded from the scope of the Regulations by regulation 6(g).

By virtue of regulation 8 which implements Article 3 of the Directive, utilities concerned with the extraction of oil, gas, coal or other solid fuels (activities listed in Parts M and N) may, in certain circumstances be exempted from certain provisions of the Regulations, both in relation to their extraction activities and, when this is relevant, to their activities supplying to the fixed public network (see para. 4–15(6.) below).

## 7. Transport

PART O

*Utilities*

(a) A local authority.
(b) An airport operator within the meaning of the Airports Act 1986 who has the management of an airport subject to economic regulations under Part IV of that Act.
(c) Highland and Islands Airports Ltd.
(d) A subsidiary of the Northern Ireland Transport Holding Company within the meaning of the Aerodromes Act (Northern Ireland) 1971.
(e) An aerodrome undertaking within the meaning of the Aerodromes Act (Northern Ireland) 1971.
(f) Any other relevant person.

*Relevant Activities*

(17)—The exploitation of a geographical area for the purpose of providing airport or other terminal facilities to carriers by air.

The Utilities Directive and therefore the Regulations do not apply to air transport services as such, as competition in this sector is governed by a separate E.C. regime. However the directive makes clear in its preamble that "the situation ought to be reviewed at a later stage in the light of progress made as regards competition."

PART P

*Utilities*

(a) A harbour authority within the meaning of section 57 of the Harbours Act 1964.
(b) British Waterways Board.
(c) A local authority.
(d) A harbour authority as defined by section 38(1) of the Harbours Act (Northern Ireland) 1970.
(e) Any other "relevant person."

## Relevant Activities

**(18)**—The exploitation of a geographical area for the purpose of providing maritime or inland port or other terminal facilities to carriers by sea or inland waterway.

Shipping transport services are not covered by the directive and therefore the Regulations, although the directive points out in its preamble that "shippers operating sea-going ferries should be kept under review." Certain inshore and river ferry services operated by public authorities are covered by the Works Regulations in relation to public works contracts and by the Supply Regulations in relation to public supply contracts.

### PART Q

### Utilities

(a)  British Railways Board.
(b)  A subsidiary of British Railways Board within the meaning of section 25 of the Transport Act 1962.
(c)  Eurotunnel plc.
(d)  Northern Ireland Transport Holding Company.
(e)  London Regional Transport.
(f)  London Underground Ltd.
(g)  Docklands Light Railway Ltd.
(h)  Strathclyde Passenger Transport Executive.
(i)  Greater Manchester Passenger Transport Executive.
(j)  Greater Manchester Metro Ltd.
(k)  Tyne and Wear Passenger Transport Executive.
(l)  Brighton Borough Council.
(m) South Yorkshire Passenger Transport Executive.
(n)  South Yorkshire Supertram (No. 2) Ltd.
(o)  Any other "relevant person."

### Relevant Activities

**(19)**—The operation of a "network" providing a service to the public in the field of transport by railway.

"Network" in relation to a service in the fields of transport (Parts Q–S) is defined in the Schedule as "a system operated in accordance with conditions laid down by or under the law in any part of the United Kingdom including such conditions as the routes to be served, the capacity to be made available and the frequency of the service."

### PART R

### Utilities

(a)  Greater Manchester Passenger Transport Executive.

(b) Greater Manchester Metro Ltd.
(c) Blackpool Transport Services Ltd.
(d) Aberconwy Borough Council.
(e) South Yorkshire Passenger Transport Executive.
(f) South Yorkshire Supertram (No. 2) Ltd.
(g) Any other "relevant person."

*Relevant Activities*

**(20)**—The operation of a "network" providing a service to the public in the field of transport by automated systems, tramway, trolleybus, or cable.

PART S

*Utilities*

(a) London Regional Transport.
(b) A subsidiary of London Regional Transport within the meaning of section 36 of the Transport Act 1985.
(c) A person who provides a London bus service as defined in section 34(2)(b) of the Transport Act 1985 in pursuance of an agreement entered into by London Regional Transport by virtue of section 3(2) of the London Regional Transport Act 1984.
(d) Northern Ireland Transport Holding Company.
(e) A person who holds a road service licence under section 4(1) of the Transport Act (Northern Ireland) 1967 which authorises him to provide a regular service within the meaning of that licence.
(f) Any other "relevant person."

*Relevant Activities*

**(21)**—The operation of a network providing a service to the public in the field of transport by bus in a geographical area in which other persons are not free to provide the service under the same conditions as the utility.

The directive is not concerned to regulate the procurement activities of entities whose activities are directly exposed to competitive forces in markets to which entry is unrestricted. In relation to the provision of bus services, the Regulations do not therefore apply where other persons are free to provide the same service in the area under the same conditions as the utility.

**8.** *Telecommunications*

PART T

*Utility*

(a) A public telecommunications operator under the Telecommunications Act 1984.

*Relevant Activities*

**(22)**—The provision or operation of a public telecommunications network.

**(23)**—The provision of one or more telecommunications services.

A "public telecommunications network" is defined in regulation 2(1) as "an infrastructure for the use of the public which enables signals to be conveyed by wire, microwave, optical means or other electromagnetic means between physical connections which are necessary for access to and efficient communication through the network", and "public telecommunications services" is defined in the same regulation as "services which consist in whole or in part in the transmission and routing of signals on a public telecommunications network by means of telecommunications processes other than radio broadcasting and television."

By regulation 7 certain telecommunications operations are exempted from the provisions of the Regulations in relation to contracts for the exclusive purpose of enabling them to provide certain specified public telecommunications services (see para. 4–15(5.) below).

Annexes I to X of the directive list the bodies or types of bodies to which the directive when it was adopted in September 1990 was expected to apply. They are now significantly out of date and will be amended to bring them into line with Schedule 1 of the Regulations. The Annexes until amended should be approached with caution when they are being relied upon in relation to other Member States.

## Contracts to which the Regulations apply

1. *Supply Contracts*

A supply contract is defined similarly to a public supply contract in the Supply **4–14** Regulations (see para. 3–30), as "a contract in writing for consideration (whatever the nature of the consideration),

    (a) for the purchase of goods by a utility (whether or not the consideration is given in instalments and whether or not the purchase is conditional upon the occurrence of a particular event), or

    (b) for the hire of goods by a utility (both where the utility becomes the owner of the goods after the end of the period of time and where it does not),

and for any siting and installation of those goods, but where, under such a contract services are also to be provided, the contract shall only be a supply contract if the value of the consideration attributable to the goods and to any siting installation of the goods is greater than the value attributable to the services."
(reg. 2(1)).

"Goods" as in the Supply Regulations includes substances (similarly defined) growing crops and things attached to or forming part of the land which are agreed to be severed before the purchase or hire under a supply contract and any ship (similarly defined) aircraft or vehicle. In addition "goods" in the Utilities Regulations are deemed to include "telecommunications software services" when the utility is an entity specified in Part T of Schedule 1. A telecommunications software service is defined as "software services (*i.e.* the design or adaptation of software) for use in the operation of a public telecommunications network or which are intended to be used in a public telecommunications service as such" (reg. 2(1)). As with the earlier Regulations the definition is not exhaustive. It does not include electricity however.

### 2. Works Contracts

A Works Contract like a Public Works Contract is defined as "a contract in writing for consideration (whatever the nature of the consideration),

(*a*)  for the carrying out (*i.e.* the construction or the design and construction) of a work or works for a utility, or

(*b*)  under which a utility engages a person to produce by any means the carrying out for the utility of a work corresponding to specified requirements" (reg. 2(1)).

A "Work" is defined in the same regulation as:

"the outcome of any works which is sufficient of itself to fulfil an economic function."

and "Works" are defined as "any of the activities specified in Schedule 3, being activities contained in the general industrial classification of economic activities within the Communities."

Schedule 3 is identical to Schedule 1 in the Works Regulations.

Subject to the general exclusions the Regulations will in addition apply to any supply or works contract which is awarded by a person in (*b*) above acting as the utility's agent. They do not apply, however, to contracts which a works contractor or management contractor awards as a principal.

## Works and Supply Contracts excluded from the operation of the Regulations

### 1. Non-relevant activities

**4–15**   As has already been noted the Regulations do not apply to the seeking of offers in relation to a contract for the purpose of carrying out an activity which is not listed in the same Part of Schedule 1 in which the utility concerned is specified (reg. 6(*a*)).

### 2. Activities outside the Community

The Regulations do not apply to contracts for the purpose of carrying out any activity outside the territory of the Communities, but only if the carrying out of that activity does not involve the physical use of a network or geographical area within the Communities (reg. 6(*b*)).

### 3. Contracts for resale or hire to others

The Regulations do not apply to the seeking of offers in relation to contracts for the purpose of acquiring goods or works in order to sell or hire them to another person, unless the utility has a special or exclusive right to sell or hire such goods or works, or other persons are not free to sell them under the same conditions (reg. 6(*c*)).

### 4. Secret Contracts and Contracts awarded pursuant to certain International Agreements

The Regulations do not apply to the seeking of offers in relation to a contract which is classified as secret by the Minister, or when the performance of the contract must be accompanied by special security measures in accordance with the laws, regulations or administrative provisions of any part of the United Kingdom, or when protection of the basic interests of the security of the United Kingdom require it. Similarly they do not apply to certain contracts awarded pursuant to International agreement (reg. 6(*e*)).

### 5. Certain Contracts awarded by utilities operating in the telecommunications sector

The Regulations do not apply to the seeking of offers in relation to a contract by a utility specified in Schedule 2 for the exclusive purpose of enabling it to provide one or more of the public telecommunications services specified in the Part of Schedule 2 in which the utility is specified (reg. 7(1)).

The utilities and the relevant services specified under Schedule 2 are as follows:

PART A

*Utilities*

Public telecommunications operators under the Telecommunications Act 1984 other than British Telecommunications plc and Kingston Communications (Hull) plc.

*Relevant Services*

(**1**)—All public telecommunications services.

PART B

*Utilities*

British Telecommunications plc.
Kingston Communications (Hull) plc.

63

## Relevant Services

(**2**)—All public telecommunications services (as defined in para. 4–13, section 8 above) other than the following services when they are provided within the geographical area for which the provider is licensed as a public telecommunications operator:

(*a*) basic voice telephone services, defined as telecommunications services consisting of the conveyance of messages in the form of two-way live speech telephone calls, including only such switching, processing, data storage or protocol conversion as is necessary for the conveyance of these messages in real time.

(*b*) basic data transmission services, defined as telecommunications services consisting of the conveyance of messages other than two-way live speech telephone calls, including only such switching, processing, data storage or protocol conversion as is necessary for the conveyance of these messages in real time.

(*c*) the provision of private leased circuits, defined as,
"a communication facility which is—

(i) provided by one or more public telecommunications networks (as defined in para. 4–13, section 8 above).

(ii) for the conveyance of messages between points, all of which are points of connection between public telecommunications networks and other telecommunications networks.

(iii) made available to a particular person or particular persons.

(iv) such that all the messages transmitted at any of the points referred to in (ii) above are received at every other such point, and

(v) such that the points mentioned in (i) above are fixed by the way in which the facility is installed and cannot otherwise be selected by persons or telecommunications apparatus sending messages by means of the facility."

(vi) maritime services, defined as "two way telecommunications services including voice telephony and data transmission services consisting of the transmission and reception of messages conveyed between seagoing vessels and hovercraft."

Not surprisingly this is a highly controversial provision which at first sight appears to discriminate arbitrarily between telecommunications operators by exempting some, while subjecting others to its provisions in respect of the majority of their services. However the provision implements Article 8 of the directive which, as with bus service operators, makes clear that the directive is not intended to apply where sufficient competition exists within a given sector. Article 8 provides that: "This directive shall not apply to contracts which [telcommunications operators] award for purchases intended exclusively to enable them to provide one or more telecommunications services where other entities are free to offer the same services in the same geographical area and under substantially the same conditions."

Regulation 7(2) and (3) contain reporting obligations which are designed to ensure that the exemption is not abused, while protecting business confidentiality.

## 6. Exemption in respect of certain utilities operating in the energy sector

Regulation 8 which implements the relevant provisions of Article 3 of the directive provides that the Commission may on application by a Member State decide that an activity specified in Parts M and N of Schedule 1 (exploring for, or extracting oil, gas, coal or other solid fuel) is not to be considered a relevant activity and further that the entities undertaking that activity shall not be considered as operating under "special or exclusive rights" under Article 2(3)(b) of the directive where they supply gas or heat to the public network. Article 2(3)(b) deems any entity which carries out such supply to be acting under such special or exclusive rights. Before making such a decision the Commission must satisfy itself that the conditions set out in Article 3 are met with respect to the relevant national provisions concerning such activities. Once a favourable decision has been made by the Commission the utility is exempted from complying with Parts II to V of the Regulations and Regulations 23, 24, 25, 26 other than para. 2(a), and 28 in seeking offers in relation to a contract to be awarded for the purpose of carrying out any activity referred to in that decision.

A utility which relies on the exemption so granted must still observe the principles of non-discrimination and competitive procurement and in particular must:

(a) hold a competition unless it can objectively justify not doing so; and

(b) in making information about its procurement intentions available to suppliers and contractors, in specifying its requirements to them, in establishing and using a qualification system, in selecting suppliers or contractors to tender for or to negotiate the contract and in awarding the contract, make decisions objectively on the basis of relevant criteria (reg. 8(2)).

The U.K. Government has made an application to the Commission under Article 3 in respect of the oil and gas sector and although at the time of writing (January 1993) no decision has been made, it is confidently anticipated a favourable decision will be given shortly.

## 7. Contracts below certain thresholds

Similarly to the Works and Supply Regulations the Utilities Regulations do not apply to the seeking of offers in relation to a proposed contract where the estimated value of the contract (net of V.A.T.) at the relevant time:

(a) in relation to a supply contract to be awarded to a utility which is not a telecommunications operator under Part T of Schedule 1, is less than 400,000 ECUs.

(b) in relation to a supply contract to be awarded by a telecommunications operator specified in Part T of the Schedule is less than 600,000 ECUs.

(c) in relation to Works contracts, is less than 5,000,000 ECUs.

The value in the currency of any Member State of the above ECU sums is to be determined by reference to the rate for the time being applicable for the purposes of the Utilities Directive, as published from time to time in the Official Journal (reg. 2(2)). For the period January 1, 1993 to December 31, 1993 the sterling equivalent of 400,000 ECUs is £282,862, of 600,000 ECUs is £424,293 and of 5,000 000 ECUs is £3,535,775.[1]

The "estimated value" will normally be the value of the consideration which the utility expects to give under the contract. Exceptionally the "estimated value" is to be calculated according to aggregation provisions similar to, but not identical with, those contained in the Works Regulations, in relation to works contracts (see para. 3–05(3.) above) and in the Supply Regulations, in relation to supply contracts (see para. 3–31(3.) above). The differences between the aggregation provisions in the Utilities Regulations and the similar provisions in the Works and Supply Regulations are as follows:

WORKS CONTRACTS

(a) Where a utility intends to provide any goods or services to the person awarded a works contract for the purpose of carrying out that contract, the value of the consideration must include the estimated value at the relevant time of those goods and services (reg. 9(12)).

(b) Where the "estimated value" of a works contract is less than the relevant threshold and where goods which are not necessary for its execution are to be purchased or hired under it, the "estimated value" of the contract is the value of the consideration which the utility expects to give for the goods and the relevant threshold is the one that would be applicable if the contract were a supply contract (i.e. either 400,000 ECUs or 600,000 ECUs depending on whether the utility is a telecommunications operator under Part T of the Schedule or not) (reg. 9(13)).

(c) Special thresholds apply to framework agreements (see para. 4–26 below).

SUPPLY CONTRACTS

(a) The "discrete operational unit" provisions, which in the Supply Regulations apply only to situations where the contracting authority has a "recurrent need" for the same type of goods (see reg. 7(6) and para. 3–31(3.) above) apply additionally in the Utilities Regulations where the utility proposes to enter into two or more supply contracts at the same time in order to purchase or hire goods of a particular type (reg. 9(5)). The Commission have prepared draft policy guidelines on the application of

[1] Appendix 1.

the aggregation provisions where discrete operational units are or may be involved (see *Appendix* E Part 2). Those guidelines do not have any legal status but will be useful when deciding in any given situation whether the discrete operational unit provisions apply.

(*b*) Regulation 7(6) of the Supply Regulations has been redrafted in the Utilities Regulations to provide an additional objective test for the application of the aggregation rules to the valuation of each of a group of contracts (reg. 9(6)). In addition to the contract having to be for the same type of goods, it also has to have "similar characteristics" if the rules are to apply (reg. 9(7)). In addition "recurrent need" is replaced by "requirement over a period" to reflect more closely the wording of the directive at Article 12(4). These changes should result in a slight relaxation of the aggregation rules in that they will permit contracts which are for the same type of goods but which are subject to significantly different terms and conditions to be treated as not being part of the series subject to aggregation.

In all other respects the aggregation rules in the Utilities Regulations are the same as the parallel provisions in the Works and Supply Regulations.

The "relevant time" for the purposes of the Utilities Regulations is when the decision is taken that the contract award procedure is to begin and is defined as:

(*a*) Where the utility selects suppliers or contractors to tender for or to negotiate the contract in accordance with a qualification system established in accordance with regulation 17 (see para. 4–23 below), the date on which the selection commences, or

(*b*) Where the utility satisfies the requirement that there be a call for competition by indicating the intention to award the contract in a periodic indicative notice in accordance with regulation 14(2)(*a*)(1) (see para. 4–20(*a*) below), the date on which the notice is sent to the Official Journal; or

(*c*) In any other case, the date on which a contract notice would be sent to the Official Journal if the requirement that there be a call for competition applied and the utility decided to satisfy that requirement by sending such a notice (reg. 9(6).

### 8. *Framework Agreements*

As has been noted at para. 3–32 above, the Utilities Regulations introduce a **4–16** new concept not found in the Works or Supply Regulations of "framework agreements." These are defined in the Regulations as: "a contract or other arrangement which is not in itself a supply or works contract but which establishes the terms (in particular the terms as to price and, where appropriate, quantity) under which the supplier or contractor will enter into supply or works contracts with a utility in the period during which the framework agreement applies" (reg. 2(1)).

A utility which is proposing to enter a framework agreement may choose to treat that agreement as a contract to which the Regulations apply; where it does so the framework agreement is treated as the contract for the purposes of the Regulations and the individual contracts made under it will not in addition be caught (reg. 10). For the purposes of the threshold provisions the estimated value of a framework agreement is the aggregate of the "estimated" values of all the contracts which could be entered into under it (reg. 9(14)).

A utility which chooses to treat a framework agreement as a contract for the purposes of the Regulations must not use the framework agreement to hinder, limit or distort competition (reg. 10(2)).

Problems may arise where a framework agreement entered into before the Regulations came into effect is intended to apply after that time. None of the Regulations contain any transitional provisions or in any other way deal with this situation. It is submitted that such a framework agreement having been entered into before the Regulations came into force cannot itself be treated as "a contract to which the Regulations apply" under the above provision and that consequently each of the contracts made under it fall for separate consideration. Further, a framework agreement which has not been treated as a contract for the purposes of the Regulations and which for example requires that the utility enter into contracts (which will include contracts for services after July 1994) to a minimum value each year would, it is submitted, be unenforceable to the extent that any of those contracts are caught by the Regulations. The nearest parallel can perhaps be found in those cases where there was a statutory requirement to obtain a licence for work above a stipulated financial limit but up to that limit no licence was required and where the Courts have enforced the contract up to that limit.[2]

It is submitted that any agreement entered into prior to the implementation of the Utilities Directive or any other directive (*e.g.* the Services Directives) with the purpose of circumventing the provisions of that directive would in so far as it purported to achieve that purpose be void and of no effect. Any utility or contracting authority attempting to rely on such a contract as a reason for not complying with the Regulations would be unlikely to succeed if challenged. An agreement, for example to provide specified services to a utility for a 10-year period from January 1, 1993 would be void as regards contracts for services entered into after the Regulations implementing the amended Utilities Directive came into force during 1994 unless such an agreement could be justified on objective commercial grounds. Parties who are contemplating such an agreement would be wise to seek expert advice first.

### Rules governing technical specifications

**4–17**     The rules applicable to the use of technical specifications in works and supply contracts under the Utilities Regulations are virtually identical to those

---

[2] See, *e.g. Frank W. Clifford Ltd.* v. *Garth:* [1956] 3 W.L.R. 570.

pplicable in respect of such contracts under the Works and Supply Regulations espectively (see para. 3–06 in relation to Works contracts and para. 3–33 in elation to Supply contracts). Although marginally different wording is occasionally employed in the Utilities Regulations two additions only need be noted:

(a) A utility may additionally define the technical specifications other than by reference to relevant European specifications if definition by reference to European specifications would conflict with the application of Council Directive 91/263/EEC[3] on the initial stage of the mutual recognition of type approval for telecommunications terminal equipment or Council Decision 87/95/EEC[4] on standardisation in the field of information technology and telecommunications (reg. 11(4)(c)).

(b) The requirement to state in any contract notice which of the permitted circumstances was the ground for defining the technical specifications other than by reference to European specifications is extended in the case of utilities to periodic indicative notices used as a call for competition (see para. 4–20 below) (reg. 11(7)).

Regulation 11 has been drafted in accordance with the Commission Policy Guidelines on Article 13(3) of the directive concerning the meaning of "standards having currency in the Community"; reference should be made to those guidelines when any question as to the meaning of that term arises (see Appendix E Part 2).

Regulation 11(13) and (14) require a utility to provide to any supplier or contractor who requests it certain information as to technical specifications which it regularly uses or intends to use.

## Rules governing the procedures leading to the award of a contract

The rules governing the procedures leading to the award of a contract under the Utilities Regulations are more flexible than those applying under the Works and Supply Regulations. Although as before, for the purposes of seeking offers in relation to a proposed contract, a utility must use the "open", "the restricted" or "the negotiated procedure" (reg. 12) the choice of procedure is unrestricted. In every case however, unless exempted from doing so, a utility must make a "call for competition." In addition a utility must normally advertise its intention to seek offers by means of a "periodic indicative notice." (cf. a similar requirement on GATT authorities under the Supply Regulations at para. 3–35 above).   **4–18**

1. *Advertising the intention to seek offers by means of a periodic indicative notice* (reg. 13)

A utility must at least once every 12 months send to the Official Journal a   **4–19**

---

[3] [1991] O.J. L128/1.
[4] [1982] O.J. L36/31.

notice, in a form substantially corresponding to that set out in Part A of Schedule 4 and containing the information therein specified, in respect of:

(a) certain supply contracts which the utility expects to award during the period of 12 months beginning with the date of the notice; and
(b) certain works contracts which the utility expects to award.

The supply contracts referred to in (a) are those whose "estimated" value (as defined above) at the date of dispatch of the notice is not less than the relevant threshold and which are for the purchase or hire of goods of a type which the utility expects at the date of dispatch of the notice to purchase or hire under supply contracts which have an "estimated" value which in aggregate for that type of goods is, or is more than, 750,000 ECUs (£530,366 until December 31, 1993).[5]

Regulation 13 implements Article 17 of the directive where it is provided that the contracts which are to be aggregated for the purpose of that provision are those for products which fall within the same "product area." As has been noted the regulation employs the term "contracts ... for that type of goods" in the same context. The Commission have prepared draft guidelines as to what products are to be considered as falling within the "same product area" (see Appendix E Part 2) but the status of those guidelines can at best only be advisory at this stage.

The Works Contracts referred to in (b) are those whose estimated value at the date of dispatch of the notice is not less than the relevant threshold.

A notice sent to the Official Journal under this provision need not repeat information about contracts included in a previous periodic indicative notice provided that the notice clearly states that it is an additional notice (reg. 13).

2. *Call for competition*

**4–20**     A "call for competition" must be satisfied in one of the following ways:

(a) Where the contract is to be awarded using the restricted or negotiated procedure,
   (i) By indicating the intention to award the contract in a periodic indicative notice which refers specifically to the goods or works which are to be the subject of the proposed contracts and which states that offers are to be sought using the restricted or negotiated procedure without further publication of a notice calling for competition, and invites suppliers or contractors to express their interest in writing.

     The utility must then send to all suppliers or contractors who express such an interest detailed information on the contract concerned and before beginning the selection of suppliers or contractors invite them to confirm their wish to be selected to tender for or to negotiate the contract. The notice concerned must not be

---

[5] See Appendix I.

published more than 12 months before the date on which the invitation referred to above is sent; or

(ii) Where a notice indicating the existence of a "qualification system" for suppliers or contractors has been sent to the Official Journal in accordance with regulation 17(12) (see para. 4–23 below), the suppliers selected to tender for or to negotiate the contract are selected from candidates who qualify in accordance with the system.

(b) In any case, by sending to the Official Journal a contract notice in a form substantially corresponding to that set out in,

(i) Part B of Schedule 4, in the case of a contract to be awarded using the open procedure

(ii) Part C of Schedule 4, in a case of a contract to be awarded using the restricted procedure, and

(iii) Part D of Schedule 4, in the case of a contract to be awarded using the negotiated procedure,

and in every case containing the information specified in the relevant Part in respect of the contract. (reg 14).

As with the Works and Supply Regulations (see para. 3–10 above) the use of standard notices and standardised nomenclature is recommended by the Commission when utilities advertise Works and Supply contracts in the Official Journal. Standard forms have been prepared and are in the process of being considered by the Treasury with a view to recommending their use in the United Kingdom.[6]

### 3. Award without a call for competition (reg. 15)

A utility may only seek offers in relation to a proposed contract without a call **4–21** for competition, in circumstances similar to those specified in the Works and Supply Regulations in relation to the use of the negotiated procedure. However, because the Utilities Regulations differ in a number of respects from the provisions contained in the earlier Regulations (in particular in the addition of the circumstances specified in (h) to (k) below) it has been thought appropriate to set them out in full:

"(1) (a) in the absence of tenders or suitable tenders in response to a procedure with a call for competition but only if the original terms of the proposed contract have not been substantially altered;

(b) when the contract is to be awarded purely for the purposes of research, experiment, study or development but not where it has the purpose of ensuring profit or of recovering research and development costs;

(c) when for technical or artistic reasons, or for reasons connected with the protection of exclusive rights, the contract may only be performed by a particular person;

(d) when (but only if it is strictly necessary) for reasons of extreme urgency

---

[6] See [1992] O.J. S252A.

brought about by events unforeseeable by the utility, the time limits specified below cannot be met;

(e) when the contract to be awarded is a supply contract and the goods to be purchased or hired under the contract are required by the utility as a partial replacement for, or addition to, existing goods or an installation when to obtain the goods from a person other than the person who supplied the existing goods or the installation would oblige the utility to acquire goods having different technical characteristics which would result in,

    (i) incompatibility between the existing goods or installation and the goods to be purchased or hired under the contract, or

    (ii) disproportionate technical difficulties in the operation and maintenance of the goods or installation;

(f) when the contract to be awarded is a works contract and the utility wants a person who has entered into a works contract with the utility to carry out additional works which through unforeseen circumstances were not included in the project initially considered or in the original works contract and,

    (i) such works cannot for technical or economic reasons be carried out separately from the works carried out under the original works contract without great inconvenience to the utility, or

    (ii) such works can be carried out separately from the works carried out under the original works contract but are strictly necessary to the later stages of that contract;

(g) subject to para. (2) below when the contract to be awarded is a works contract and the utility wishes a person who has entered into a works contract with it following a call for competition which satisfies the requirement of regulation 14(1) to carry out new works which are a repetition of works carried out under the original contract and which are in accordance with the project for the purpose of which the first contract was entered into;

(h) in respect of a supply contract for the purchase or hire of goods quoted and purchased on a commodity market;

(i) when the contract to be awarded is to be awarded under a framework agreement which has been awarded in accordance with these Regulations and to which the provisions of regulation 10 apply;

(j) when the contract to be awarded is a supply contract, to take advantage of a particularly advantageous bargain available for a very short period of time at a price considerably lower than normal market prices; and

(k) when the contract to be awarded is a supply contract, to take advantage of particularly advantageous conditions for the purchase of goods in a closing down sale or in a sale brought about by insolvency.

(2) A utility shall not seek offers without a call for competition pursuant to paragraph (1)(g) above unless,

(a) the original contract was awarded after a call for competition,

(b) when the utility invited contractors to tender for or to negotiate the contract it gave notice that a works contract for new works which would be a repetition of the works carried out under the original contract might be awarded without a call for competition pursuant to paragraph (1)(g) above, and

(c) in determining the estimated value of the original contract for the purposes of regulation 9 above the utility took into account the value of the consideration which it expected to pay for the new works."

In relation to Article 15 of the directive (which is implemented by regulation 15 above) the Council and the Commission have stated that:

"in open and restricted procedures all negotiations with candidates or tenderers on fundamental aspects of contracts, variations in which are likely to distort competition, and in particular on prices, shall be ruled out; however discussions with candidates or tenderers may be held but only for the purpose of clarifying or supplementing the content of their tenders or the requirements of the contracting entities and provided this does not involve discrimination".[7]

This represented a compromise between those wanting the directive to include a prohibition on any form of negotiation in open and restricted procedures and those wanting the freedom for contracting entities to enter into full post-tender negotiations where appropriate. The statement is understood to mean that in open and restricted procedures post-tender negotiations are considered to be unacceptable if they have the effect of distorting competition, for example by changing a requirement in a way that other suppliers and contractors might have been able to meet had they been given the opportunity.

The legal status of such statements (which are becoming increasingly common) is uncertain but a national Court and certainly the European Court is likely to attach considerable weight to them.

### 4. *Time Limits*

Time limits are similar to those applicable in the Works and Supply Regulations. They vary according to the procedure adopted and are as follows: **4–22**

#### (1) OPEN PROCEDURE

(a) In response to a contract notice the last day for receipt of tenders must be specified in the notice and must not be less than 52 days from the date of dispatch of the notice.

(b) In response to a periodic indicative notice 36 days may be substituted for the period of 52 days referred to above.

---

[7] [1990] O.J. L297/48.

## (2) NEGOTIATED OR RESTRICTED PROCEDURE

Where there has been a call for competition the last date for receipt of requests to be selected to tender for or to negotiate the contract must be specified in the contract notice, or where the call for competition is made by means of a periodic indicative notice in the invitation to suppliers or contractors made in accordance with regulation 4(3)(c) (see para. 4–20(a)(i) above) and must in general be at least five weeks from the date of the dispatch of the notice or invitation and must in any case be not less than 22 days from that date.

The last date for the receipt of tenders made in response to an invitation to tender by a utility using the restricted or negotiated procedure with a call for competition must be agreed between the utility and the suppliers or contractors invited to tender, and must be the same for all suppliers and contractors. In the absence of such agreement the date must be fixed by the utility and must as a general rule be at least three weeks and in any event not less than 10 days from the date of dispatch of the invitation to tender.

In fixing time limits a utility must take into account the time required to allow for any examination of voluminous documentation such as lengthy technical specifications, or any inspection of the site, or documents relating to the contract documents, which is necessary.

A utility using the open system must send the contract documents as a general rule within six days of the receipt of a request from any supplier or contractor provided that the documents are requested in good time and any fee specified in the contract notice has accompanied the request.

A utility using the restricted or the negotiated procedure with or without a call for competition must send invitations in writing and simultaneously to each of the suppliers or contractors selected to tender for or to negotiate the contract and the invitation must be accompanied by the contract documents.

The following information must be included in the invitation,

(a) the address to which requests for any further information should be sent, the final date for making such a request and the amount and method of payment of any fee which may be charged for supplying that information;

(b) the final date for the receipt of tenders, the address to which they must be sent and the language or languages in which they must be drawn up;

(c) a reference to any contract notice;

(d) an indication of the information to be included with the tender;

(e) the criteria for the award of the contract if this information was not specified in the contract notice; and

(f) any other special contract condition.

A utility using the open, the restricted or the negotiated procedure with or without a call for competition must provide not less than six days before the final date for the receipt of tenders such further information relating to the contract documents as may reasonably be requested by a supplier or contractor provided the information is requested in good time and any fee specified in the contract notice or in the invitation to tender has accompanied the request.

A utility must not refuse to consider an application to be invited to tender for or to negotiate the contract if it is made by letter, telegram, telex, facsimile, telephone or any electronic means provided that, in the last five cases, it is confirmed by letter dispatched before the date fixed by the utility as the last date for the receipt of applications to be invited to tender for or negotiate the contract. (reg. 16)

## Qualification and selection of suppliers and contractors

A utility may establish and operate a system of qualification of suppliers or contractors if that system satisfies certain conditions laid down in the Regulations (reg. 17). As has been seen at para. 4–20 above a "call for competition" will be satisfied where the utility intends to award a contract using the restricted or negotiated procedure, if a notice indicating the existence of such a system has been sent to the Official Journal in accordance with regulation 17(12) and suppliers and contractors selected to tender for or to negotiate the contract are selected from the candidates who qualify in accordance with the system. **4–23**

The system may involve different stages of qualification and must be based on objective rules and criteria to be established by the utility. European standards must be used as a reference where they are appropriate (reg. 17(2)). The growing practice among utilities of charging firms a fee for inclusion in their list of qualifiers is of doubtful legality. It is difficult to see how such a rule could properly be characterised as "objective." The European Commission is currently considering creating a single qualification system for the entire Community and favours asking European standardisation bodies to come up with a European standard for classifying suppliers and contractors that would remove the need for disparate criteria and such charges.

The rules and criteria for qualification at the different stages must be made available to suppliers and contractors on request and if so requested any amendment to those rules and criteria must be sent to them as the amendment is incorporated into the system. A utility may establish a system of qualification pursuant to which a supplier or contractor may qualify under the system of or be certified by another person and in those circumstances the utility must inform suppliers and contractors who apply to qualify of the name of that person.

The utility must inform applicants for qualification of the success or failure of their application within a reasonable period and, if the decision will take longer than six months from the presentation of an application, the utility must inform the applicant, within two months of the application, of the reasons justifying a longer period and of the date by which his application will be accepted or refused.

In determining what rules and criteria are to be met by applicants to qualify under the system and in determining whether a particular applicant does qualify under the system a utility must not impose conditions of an administrative, technical or financial nature on some suppliers or contractors which are not imposed upon others and must not require the application of tests or th submission of evidence which duplicates objective evidence already available

A utility must inform any applicant whose application to qualify is refused c the decision and the reasons for refusal.

An application may only be refused if the applicant fails to meet th requirements for qualification laid down in accordance with regulation 17(2).

The utility must keep a written record of qualified suppliers and contractor which may be divided into categories according to the type of contract for whic the qualification is valid.

The utility may cancel the qualification of a supplier or contractor who ha qualified under the qualification system only if he does not continue to meet th rules and criteria laid down in accordance with regulation 17(2). It must nc cancel a qualification however unless it notifies the supplier or contractor i writing beforehand of its intention and of the reason or reasons justifying th proposed cancellation.

The utility must send a notice substantially corresponding to the form set ou in Part E of Schedule 4 and containing the information relating to th qualification system therein specified to the Official Journal when the system i first established and, if the utility expects to operate the system for more tha three years, or if it has operated the system for more than three years, it mus send additional notices annually.

### 1. Selection of suppliers and contractors in the restricted or negotiated procedures

**4–24**     A utility using the restricted or the negotiated procedure with or without a cal for competition must make the selection of the suppliers or contractors to b invited to tender for or to negotiate the contract on the basis of objective criteri and rules which it determines and which it makes available to suppliers o contractors who request them (reg. 18(1)).

Similarly to the Works and Supply Regulations a utility may decide to exclud a supplier or contractor from the selection process on certain objective criteri set out in reg. 18(2). The list, which is identical (save as to non-registration) t that contained in the Works Regulations at regulation 14(1) (see para. 3–1 above), is not exhaustive.

The criteria on which selection is made may be based on the need of the utilit to reduce the number of suppliers or contractors selected to tender for or t negotiate the contract to a level which is justified by the characteristics of th award procedure and the resources required to complete it. This probably give scope for tenderers costs to be considered. The utility must in every cas however take account of the need to ensure adequate competition i determining the number of persons selected to tender for or to negotiate th contract.

Unlike the situation under the Works and Supply Regulations the Utilitie Regulations place no restriction on the grounds on which tenders may b excluded from the evaluation of offers, although the requirements of objectivit and non discrimination will apply. Thus in the open procedure, and in the negotiated and restricted procedures after the selection of contractors or suppliers to be invited to tender for or to negotiate the contract has taken place, the utility will not be restricted in the information it may require in order that it may be satisfied as to a contractor's or a supplier's economic or financial standing or as to its technical capacity. The minimum standards required by the utility in these respects must however be set out in the contract notice.

## 2. Consortia

Virtually identical provisions apply to Consortia in the Utilities Regulations as apply in the Works and Supply Regulations (reg. 19) (see para. 3–17 above). **4–25**

## The award of a contract

As in the earlier Regulations, save in the case of what are known as "third country offers" (see para. 4–27 below), a utility must award the contract on the basis of the offer (including in-house bids) which offers either the lowest price or is the most "economically advantageous" to the utility (reg. 20). The criteria for determining which is the most "economically advantageous" offer are the same as in the Works and Supply Regulations although in the Utilities Regulations "commitments with regard to spare parts" and "security of supply" are additionally referred to (reg. 20(2)). Those two criteria would however be equally relevant in relation to a public supply contract. The obligations with regard to advertising the criteria which will be relied upon, the circumstances in which offers which offer variations on the contract requirements may be taken into account, and the prohibition on rejecting a tenderer on the grounds that it is based on certain technical specifications are the same as in the earlier Regulations (see para. 3–18 above). **4–26**

Similarly the provisions relating to abnormally low tenders are virtually identical (reg. 20(6) to (18)) (see paras. 3–19 and 3–46 above). An additional ground is however set out at regulation 20(7) which provides that: "A utility may reject a tender for a contract which is abnormally low owing to the receipt of state aid within the meaning of article 92 of the Treaty but only if it has consulted the supplier or contractor and the supplier or contractor has not been able to show that the aid in question has been notified to the Commission pursuant to article 93(3) of the Treaty or has received the Commission's approval." A utility which rejects a tender in accordance with regulation 20(1) must send a report to the Minister for onward transmission to the Commission. It is probable that that ground would be a sufficient reason for rejecting a tender which is abnormally low under the Works and Supply Regulations as well.

## 1. Rejection of third country offers

The directive (at Article 29) and therefore the Regulations (at reg. 21) permits an offer of goods to be rejected even if it is the best offer, where more than 50 per **4–27** cent. of the value of the goods originate (as determined in accordance with E.C. origin rules[8]) in States with which the Communities have not concluded an agreement ensuring comparable access for undertakings in Member States to the markets of those States or in States to which the benefit of the provisions of the Utilities Directive has not been extended (defined as "third country offers"). This will apply even where the supplier is Community based (there is of course no E.C. obligation to consider an offer from a third country supplier or contractor, irrespective of the origin of the goods).

Further in the limited circumstances that a "third country offer" and an offer of goods mainly of E.C. (or associated) origin are equivalent, the latter offer must normally be preferred. Such offers will be equivalent if:

(a) in the case of a contract to be awarded on the basis of the lowest price, where the price of the goods of mainly E.C. (or associated) origin is the same as or up to three per cent. more than the price of the offer of goods mainly of third country origin.

(b) in the case of a contract to be awarded on the basis of the offer which is most economically advantageous, if the goods mainly of E.C. (or associated) origin is at least as economically advantageous as the offer of goods of mainly third country origin *and* the prices are to be treated as equivalent because the price of the offer of goods mainly of E.C. (or associated) origin is the same as or up to three per cent. more than the price of the offer of goods mainly originating from third countries.

This latter provision has not surprisingly been met with vigorous protests from third countries, most notably the U.S.A., who consider that it will result in unfair discrimination against their own industries particularly in the telecommunications and power generating sectors. The U.S.A. has threatened retaliatory action against E.C. imports but at the time of writing this issue was unresolved.

A utility may exceptionally accept an "equivalent" offer of goods of mainly third country origin if its rejection would oblige the utility to acquire goods having technical characteristics different from those of existing goods or an installation resulting in incompatibility, technical difficulties in operation and maintenance, or disproportionate costs (reg. 21(3)).

The Treasury point out in their note of November 1992 on the implementation of the Regulations that:

"Separate measures will be needed if E.C. status is to be afforded to any third country following a bilateral or multilateral agreement. The first of these is likely to be ratification of the European Economic Area (E.E.A.) Agreement. The E.E.A. bill currently before Parliament will extend the benefits of the Regulations to the E.F.T.A. countries but, as the E.E.A. agreement involves

---

[8] See Council Regulation (EEC) No. 802/68 (|1968| O.J. L148/1), as amended by Council Regulation (EEC) No. 3860/87 (|1987| O.J. L363/30).

transitional arrangements for certain E.F.T.A. countries, we may need to make further Regulations to clarify which will benefit and which will not. We will in any case take the earliest opportunity to amend all the public procurement Regulations to clarify the position on E.F.T.A. countries once the E.E.A. agreement is ratified. This may be some time away following the Swiss referendum." [rejecting the Agreement]

Any such amendment will be the subject of any updates to this Guide in due course.

### 2. Contract award notice

A utility which has awarded a supply or a works contract (other than one **4–28** excluded from the Regulations) must, not later than two months after the award, send to the Official Journal a notice, substantially corresponding to the form set out at Part F of Schedule 4 and including the information specified therein. The utility may indicate that any of the information included in paras. 6 and 9 of the notice is of a sensitive commercial nature and request that it not be published (reg. 22).

## Miscellaneous

### 1. Obligations relating to employment protection and working conditions

A utility which includes in the contract documents relating to a works contract **4–29** information as to where a contractor may obtain information about the obligations relating to employment protection and working conditions which will apply to the works to be carried out under the contract must request contractors to indicate that they have taken account of those obligations in preparing their tender or in negotiating the contract (reg. 23).

### 2. Sub-contracting

A utility may require a supplier or contractor to indicate in his tender what part **4–30** of the contract if any he intends to sub-contract to another person (reg. 24). Such an indication cannot affect the principal contractor's legal liability to the contracting authorities (Article 21 of the directive).

### 3. Requirement to preserve records

Utilities are required to keep appropriate information on every contract **4–31** affected by the Regulations including those which are expressly excluded. The information must be sufficient to justify decisions taken in connection with,

(a) the qualification and selection of suppliers or contractors and the award of contracts;

(b) the recourse to derogations from the requirement that European specifications be referred to pursuant to regulation 11(4);

79

(c) the use of a procedure without a call for competition pursuant to regulation 15.

Further where a utility decides not to apply the Regulations to a proposed contract on a ground permitted by the Regulations it must keep appropriate information on such a contract sufficient to justify that decision (reg. 25).

### 4. Obligations as regards reporting

**4–32**    A utility must each year by the date notified to it by the Minister (as defined in reg. 27) send to the Minister a report specifying the aggregate value (estimated if necessary) of the consideration payable under the contracts awarded in the previous year and excluded from the operation of the Regulations by regulation 9 (i.e. those below the relevant threshold (see para. 4–15(7.) above). The contracts must be broken down into the categories of activity listed in the regulation (reg. 26). The requirement on a utility to send any report under the Regulations is enforceable by the Minister by mandamus or in Scotland by an Order for specific performance (reg. 27(3)).

### 5. Official Journal notices

**4–33**    Any notice required by the Regulations to be sent to the Official Journal must be sent by the most appropriate means to the Office for Official Publications of the European Communities at 2 Rue Mercier, L2985, Luxembourg. The utility must retain evidence of the date of dispatch of the notice. A utility may publish the information contained in a contract notice in such other way as it thinks fit but it must not do so until the notice has been dispatched and must not publish any information other than that contained in the notice (reg. 28).

### 6. Confidentiality of information

**4–34**    A utility which makes information available to a supplier or contractor pursuant to the Regulations may impose requirements on him for the purpose of protecting the confidentiality of that requirement (reg. 29). This is a new provision.

# Chapter Five

## ENFORCEMENT OF COMMUNITY OBLIGATIONS RELATING TO PUBLIC AND UTILITY, WORKS AND SUPPLY CONTRACTS

### Under the Works, Supply and Utilities Regulations

All three sets of Regulations provide a "supplier" or "contractor" (*i.e.* one who is     **5–01**
national of and established in a Member State) who suffers or risks suffering
oss or damage as a result of a breach of the Regulations or the breach of any
Community obligation in respect of a contract to which the Regulations apply,
with a right to obtain redress by way of court action. The remedies available and
the procedures by which they are obtained are very similar in respect of each of
the Regulations. In this respect the Works and Supply Regulations give effect to
the Compliance Directive 89/665/EEC and the Utilities Regulations to Directive
2/13/EEC already referred to (see para. 1–03 above).

The obligation on contracting authorities and utilities to comply with the     **5–02**
provisions of the Regulations (other than certain provisions relating to reporting
and the supply of information) and with enforceable Community obligations in
respect of a supply or works contract falling within the Regulations, is conceived
under the Regulations as a duty owed to suppliers and contractors the breach
thereof gives rise to an action for breach of statutory duty.

A similar duty is placed upon a public works concessionaire to comply with     **5–03**
the obligations placed upon it by Regulation 26(3) of the Works Regulations (see
para. 3–23 above) and where such a duty is imposed the term "contractor"
includes any person who sought or who seeks or who would have wished to be
the person to whom a contract to which regulation 26(3) applies is awarded and
who is a national of and established in a Member State.

A breach of the duty referred to is not a criminal offence but is actionable by     **5–04**
any contractor or supplier who in consequence "suffers or risks suffering loss or
damage."

Proceedings brought in England and Wales and in Northern Ireland must be     **5–05**
brought in the High Court, and in Scotland, before the Court of Session.

However, proceedings under the Regulations may not be brought unless,     **5–06**

(a) the supplier or contractor bringing the proceedings has informed the
    contracting authority (including a concessionaire), or utility of the breach
    or apprehended breach of the duty referred to and of his intention to bring
    proceedings under the Regulations in respect of it; and

(b) they are brought promptly and in any event within three months from the date when grounds for the bringing of the proceedings first arose unless the Court considers that there is good reason for extending the period within which proceedings may be brought.

**5–07** In proceedings brought under each of the Regulations the Court may, without prejudice to any other powers it may have:

(a) by interim order (whether or not the defendant is the Crown) suspend the procedure leading to the award of the relevant contract, or suspend the implementation of any decision or action taken by the contracting authority or utility in the course of following such a procedure; and
(b) if satisfied that a decision or action taken by a contracting authority or utility was in breach of the duty referred to,
   (i) order the setting aside of that decision or action or order the contracting authority or utility to amend any document,
   (ii) award damages to a contractor or supplier who has suffered loss or damage as a consequence of the breach, or
   (iii) do both of those things.

**5–08** However, in proceedings brought under each of the Regulations the Court can only award damages, if the contract in relation to which the breach occurred has been entered into. The Court cannot therefore set aside a contract which has been entered into in breach of the Regulations. It is uncertain however whether such a contract in English law is unenforceable as between the parties to it or the grounds of public policy. It is submitted that where both parties are aware of the breach at the time of entering the contract (e.g. where the proposed contract was not advertised) public policy requires that the contract should be unenforceable by both parties.[1] Where only one party is in breach without the other party's knowledge (e.g. where a contracting authority without justification selects a contractor who has not submitted the lowest tender) then the contract should only be unenforceable by the party in breach.[2]

**5–09** In the English Courts any interim order under (a) above will be by way of interlocutory injunction which it is anticipated will be granted or refused on the familiar principles laid down by the House of Lords in *American Cyanamid Co. v. Ethicon Ltd.*[3] These principles may be summarised as follows:

(i) The Plaintiff must establish that he has a good arguable claim to the right he seeks to protect;
(ii) The Court must not attempt to decide the claim on the affidavits; it is enough if the Plaintiff shows that there is a serious question to be tried
(iii) If the Plaintiff satisfies these tests the grant or refusal of an injunction is a matter for the Court's discretion on the balance of convenience including that of the public where this is affected.

[1] See, *e.g. Apthorp* v. *Neville* (1907) 23 T.L.R. 575.
[2] See, *e.g. Edler* v. *Auerbach*: |1950| 1 K.B. 359.
[3] |1975| A.C. 396.

Although the factors relevant to the exercise of the discretion are many and varied (of which the question whether damages would be a sufficient remedy is arguably the most important) in public procurement cases the question of the public interest is often likely to be decisive against the grant of the injunction. This fact is expressly recognised by both Remedies Directives which provide that:

'The Member States may provide that when considering whether to order interim measures the body responsible may take into account the probable consequences of the measures for all interests likely to be harmed, as well as the public interest, and may decide not to grant such measures where their negative consequences could exceed their benefits. A decision not to grant interim measures shall not prejudice any other claim of the person seeking these measures."
(Article 2(4) of both directives).

No such provision appears in the Regulations no doubt because it was considered that the practice of the Courts when granting or refusing interlocutory injunctions was entirely consistent with the discretion given by the Remedies Directives in this respect.

Even where the public interest element is not decisive the usual requirement that the Plaintiff undertake to pay the defendants damages caused by the injunction should it prove to have been wrongly granted will often dissuade a Plaintiff from pursuing this remedy in public procurement cases where such damages are likely to be heavy.

A contractor or supplier may wish under (b) above to have set aside a decision **5–10** to reject his bid made on the basis of criteria not permitted by the Regulations, or a decision to exclude his bid as abnormally low where he has not been given an opportunity to give an explanation. Equally a contractor or supplier may require that a contract document be amended so as to exclude a specification not permitted by the Regulations.

It will be noted that each of the Regulations while providing contractors and **5–11** suppliers with a remedy in damages do not specify how those damages are to be assessed. In Community law it is left to national laws to provide the remedies required in order to ensure that Community rights are protected. However, that principle, as the European Court has made clear on a number of occasions is subject to two qualifications; first, the remedy provided must be at least as favourable as any comparable rule of domestic law (the principle of non discrimination) and secondly the remedy must be effective in ensuring that Community rights and obligations are observed.[4] That second qualification includes a requirement that national procedural conditions must not make it impossible in practice (*e.g.* because of difficulties of proof) to exercise the rights which the national courts have a duty to protect.[5]

Generally speaking under national law the ordinary tortious measure of

---

[4] Case 14/83, *Von Colson & Kamann* v. *Land Nordrhein-Westfalen*: |1984| E.C.R. 1891.
[5] Case 199/82, *Amministrazione delle Finanze dello Stato* v. *San Giorgio*: |1983| E.C.R. 3595.

damages will apply to claims made under the Regulations; that is to say the Plaintiff will only recover such sum as on the balance of probabilities he can show that he has lost as a result of the defendants' breach. In the context of the Regulations this would mean that a contractor or supplier could only recover damages if he could show that his bid would have been successful. Where, for example the contractor or supplier has submitted the lowest tender which has been improperly rejected, that task should not be unduly difficult, and the ordinary tortious measure of damages would no doubt apply. Where on the other hand no bid had been made, for example because the contractor or supplier was denied an opportunity to tender owing to a failure by the contracting authority or utility to advertise the project in the Official Journal the task may well be virtually impossible. In those circumstances the contractor or supplier under domestic law would have to prove (a) that he would have tendered (and what that tender would have been) (b) that he would have been successful, and (c) that as a result of the breach he has suffered a quantifiable loss of benefit.

In those and similar circumstances it would be arguable that national procedural rules make it impossible in practice to exercise the Community rights which the national courts have a duty to protect and that therefore a different approach should be adopted. One such approach which would appear to satisfy the Community requirement of effectiveness is provided by the case of *Chaplin* v. *Hicks*[6] where the court simply assessed the Plaintiff's chance of winning the contract and then awarded that proportion of the benefit which the Plaintiff would on the balance of probabilities have received had he been successful. Whether this principle may generally be applied in tort cases was expressly left open by the House of Lords in *Hotson* v. *East Berkshire Health Authority*.[7]

**5–12**      In the case of the Utilities Regulations alone the task of recovering certain damage is eased by regulation 30(7) which provides that:

"Where in proceedings under this regulation the Court is satisfied that a supplier or contractor would have had a real chance of being awarded a contract if that chance had not been adversely affected by a breach of the duty owed to him by the utility pursuant to |the Regulations| the supplier or contractor shall be entitled to damages amounting to his costs in preparing his tender and in participating in the procedure leading to the award of the contract."

Regulation 30(8) makes it clear that that remedy is without prejudice to a claim by a supplier or contractor that he has suffered other loss or damage or that he is entitled to relief other than damages and further that subsection 7 is without prejudice to the matters on which a supplier or contractor may be required to satisfy the Court in respect of any other such claim.

To what standard the Plaintiff will have to prove that he had a "real chance"

---

[6] |1911| 2 K.B. 786.
[7] |1987| 2 All E.R. 909 and see on this topic Arrowsmith "Enforcing the E.C. Public Procurement Rules: The Remedies System in England and Wales." Public Procurement Law Review, March 1992.

(identical words are used in Article 2(3) of the directive) of being awarded the contract is as yet unclear but it is submitted that this will be something less than on the balance of probabilities.

Article 2(7) of the directive on which the regulation is based is clearly a development in the Community's thinking in relation to the enforcement of its procurement regime and there is no reason in principle why it should not also be applied in suitable cases brought under the Works and Supply Regulations. It is submitted that the national courts should apply the principle in those circumstances and that this would be consistent with the Community requirement of effectiveness.

A contractor or supplier can of course only rely on the provision where he has incurred tendering costs and/or costs in participating in the award procedure and in relation to such a claim. In all other circumstances (e.g. where there has been a failure to advertise or where he is claiming for loss of profit) he will have to prove his case on the usual basis of the balance of probabilities.

It will readily be appreciated from the above that more than one contractor or supplier may be able to establish a successful claim against a contracting authority or utility in respect of the same contract. For example a number of contractors or suppliers may be able to recover their tendering costs by showing that each of them had a "real chance" of being awarded the contract which was adversely affected by a breach of duty owed to them. Similarly more than one contractor or supplier may be able to recover a proportion of their lost profits under the principle enunciated in *Chaplin* v. *Hicks, supra* should the Court approach the award of damages in that way. It would seem improbable however that more than one contractor or supplier could establish on the balance of probability that it would have been awarded the contract had it not been for the breach, although where separate proceedings are brought the risk of inconsistent judgments in this respect cannot be ruled out.

A further innovation introduced for the first time by the Utilities Directive, and **5–13** therefor by the Utilities Regulations (reg. 31), is the possibility of resolving disputes by conciliation at a Community level. This is a purely voluntary procedure on the part of both the aggrieved contractor or supplier and the utility concerned and it is expressly provided that neither the request for conciliation nor any action taken pursuant to it is to affect the rights or liabilities of any party (reg. 3(2)). The regulation provides for the procedure to be initiated by a request to the Treasury for onward transmission to the Commission but it can equally well be made to the Commission direct. The purpose of the procedure is to enable the parties to settle their differences by agreement as quickly as possible in accordance with Community law. The details of the procedure are set out at Articles 10 and 11 of the directive but of particular importance is (a) the opportunity to be given to other candidates or tenderers participating in the relevant contract award procedure to make representations (Article 10(3)), and (b) the right of conciliators to terminate proceedings where such a party who is pursuing a claim through the Courts declines to join the conciliation process and whose participation they consider is necessary to resolve the dispute (Article 11(1)).

**5–14**    Despite the apparently mandatory requirements of Article 3 of Directive 92/13/EEC which requires that Member States shall give utilities the possibility of having recourse to an "attestation system" in accordance with Articles 4 to 7, the Utilities Regulations have not yet done so. The attestation system envisaged would enable utilities whose contract award procedures fall within the Utilities Directive to have them periodically reviewed "with a view to obtaining an attestation that, at that time those procedures and practices are in conformity with Community law concerning the award of contracts and the national rules implementing the law" (Article 4).

## Enforcement by way of Judicial Review

**5–15**    As the Regulations make clear the remedies provided under them are to be "without prejudice to any other powers of the Court." An action against a contracting authority and certain public bodies which are also "utilities" for breach of purely domestic rules relating to public procurement might in an appropriate case be by way of judicial review where one of the five remedies of certiorari, prohibition, mandamus injunction and declaration may be sought. However complaints regarding the contracting authority's behaviour relating to public procurement will generally lack a sufficient public law element to open it to challenge by way of judicial review.[7a] Nevertheless where that public law element is present, judicial review may exceptionally be available in addition to, or as an alternative to, an action under the Regulation.

Judicial review may be the only procedure, for enforcing Community public procurement obligations against public bodies where these arise in award procedures which are not subject to the Regulations (*e.g.* in relation to contracts falling below the thresholds or excluded for some other reason). Directly effective Treaty provisions (*e.g.* Articles 30, 52 and 59 (see para 2–02 above) may be enforced in this way. Further in the light of the decision of the European Court in *Francovitch v. Republic of Italy*[8] damages will probably now be recoverable in such an action. The House of Lords has observed in the recent case of *Kirklees Borough Council v. Wickes Building Supplies Ltd.*[9] that as a result of the decision in *Francovitch* the decision of the Court of Appeal in *Bourgoin SA v. M.A.F.F.*[10] (where it was held that damages were not recoverable for a breach of Article 30), is "probably no longer good law."

---

[7a] R. v. *The Lord Chancellor, ex p. Hibbit and Saunders (a firm), The Times*, March 12, 1993.
[8] [1992] I.R.L.R. 84.
[9] [1992] 2 C.M.L.R. 765.
[10] [1986] Q.B. 716.

## Claims for Damages for Misfeasance in Public Office

When a contracting authority knowingly acts in an unlawful manner an affected party may claim damages for any loss suffered under the tort of misfeasance in public office.[11] Such a claim might be more favourable than a claim under the Regulations. For example, it is arguable that in those circumstances the Court should assume that an authority would have exercised its discretion in the Plaintiff's favour if it had acted lawfully.

**5–16**

## Proceedings under Article 169 of the EEC Treaty

Article 169 EEC provides that if the Commission considers that a Member State has failed to fulfil an obligation under the Treaty it may, after taking certain procedural steps designed to give the Member State an opportunity to comply with its obligations, bring the matter before the European Court of Justice. There will be such a failure to fulfil an obligation under the Treaty where a public procurement directive has not been implemented in due time or where it has not been implemented correctly. A breach may also arise where the actions of individual awarding authorities for which the State is responsible, fail to comply with the procurement rules. It is now clear that States may be responsible for the conduct of authorities which are independent of them such as local authorities[12] but it is doubtful whether they could be held responsible for bodies which are outside government control altogether such as private companies subject to the Utilities Regulations. It is submitted that the correct test is probably that laid down by the European Court in *Foster v. British Gas*[13] in relation to State controlled bodies against whom the direct effect doctrine will apply, but whether this is in fact so will have to await a ruling of the European Court.

**5–17**

Once proceedings have been commenced it is open to the Commission to seek interim measures from the Court under Article 186 of the Treaty. These can include an application for the suspension of the contract award procedure in question. At present it would appear that the Court only has power, in a final judgment, to declare the Member State to be in breach. However as a result of a recent decision[14] it may be prepared to go further than this. In that case in proceedings under Article 169 against the Italian Republic for awarding a supply contract in breach of Treaty articles and the provisions of the Supplies Directive, the Court ordered by way of interim measures under Article 186 of the Treaty, that the Italian Republic suspend, until final judgment, the legal effects of a concession contract it had entered into with the Lotto-matica consortium for the

---

[11] *Bourgoin SA v. Ministry of Agriculture, Fisheries and Food:* |1986| Q.B. 716.
[12] See, *e.g.* Case 45/87, *Commission v. Ireland:* |1988| E.C.R. 4929.
[13] Case C89/89, *Foster v. British Gas:* |1990| 2 C.M.L.R. 833, and see para. 5–19 below.
[14] Case C–272/91R, *Commission v. Italy*, Order of January 31, 1992 (unreported).

automation of its national lottery system. The fact that the Court was willing to order suspension of a concluded contract as an interim measure indicates that it might be willing to find that a State must set aside a concluded contract if it is declared in Article 169 proceedings to be in breach of the procurement rules. In this way the restrictions placed on the national courts which prevent them from setting aside a concluded contract (see para. 5–08 above) may be circumvented.

An aggrieved contractor may therefore make a complaint to the Commission where there has been a breach of the Regulations or any related Community obligation, both in addition to or instead of bringing proceedings in the national court. Complaints can be handled confidentially and there is no administrative fee. Only the Commission can bring proceedings under Article 169 and whether it does so or not is entirely at its discretion.


## Enforcement of the Community Procurement rules in another Member State

**5–18**     Where a contractor or supplier suffers, or risks suffering loss or damage as a result of a breach of the Works, Supplies, or Utilities Directives, or related Community rules, in another Member State he must normally seek his remedy under the national measure implementing the relevant directive in the State concerned. Exceptionally, where the relevant directive has not been implemented in due time or has not been implemented correctly he may be able to rely on the "direct effect" doctrine in an action against the State or a State controlled body (see para 5–19 below). The Remedies Directives give the Member States considerable discretion as to the measures they must adopt in order to ensure that the decisions of contracting authorities and utilities may be reviewed effectively where they have infringed Community law in the field of public procurement, or national rules implementing that law. However in every case the measures taken must include provision for the enforcement authority to:

(a) take at the earliest opportunity and by way of interlocutory procedures, interim measures with the aim of correcting the alleged infringement or preventing further damage to the interests concerned including measures to suspend or to ensure the suspension of the procedure for the award of a contract or the implementation of any decision taken by the contracting authority or utility,

(b) either set aside or ensure the setting aside of decisions taken unlawfully, including the removal of discriminatory technical, economic or financial specifications in documents relating to the contract award procedure in question,

(c) award damages to persons injured by an infringement.

In the case of breaches of the Utilities Directive Member States may, as an alternative to (a) and (b) above, give their review body power to order "dissuasive payments" against some or all utilities (Article 2(1)(c) of Directive 92/13/EEC). This option, which has not been adopted by the United Kingdom, was inserted to accommodate the constitutional provisions in some Member States which apparently prevent a court from using injunctions to interfere in decisions taken by private sector bodies. Instead any Member State may empower a court to order payments in the nature of penalties, payable only if a utility fails to correct or avoid a breach of the rules. The aim is the correction or avoidance of the breach. Such payments could be payable either to the Court or the complainant, but in either case, as Article 2(5) makes clear, the sum to be paid must be set at a level high enough to dissuade the utility from committing or persisting in the infringement.

Both Remedies Directives provide that Member States may require that where damages are claimed on the grounds that a decision was taken unlawfully the contested decision must first be set aside (Article 2(5)). Further, except where that option has been adopted, Member States may provide that after the conclusion of a contract following its award the powers of the body responsible for the review procedures shall be limited to awarding damages to any person harmed by the infringement (Article 2(6)) of both Remedies Directives. As has been seen this latter option has been adopted by the United Kingdom.

As has been pointed out (see para. 5–18) an aggrieved contractor or supplier **5–19** may rely on a directly effective treaty Article in actions brought against State authorities or State controlled bodies irrespective of whether the contract concerned falls within the provisions of the procurement directives. In addition such a Plaintiff may rely on the provisions of the relevant directive against such a Defendant under the "direct effect doctrine" where the Member State has failed to implement the directive in due time or has done so incorrectly. This could be a matter of considerable importance to U.K. contractors and suppliers who have suffered actual or prospective loss by reason of a breach of the procurement rules by a contracting authority in another Member State as the implementation of the directives has been, to say the least, patchy. The "direct effect" doctrine which has been evolved by the European Court in such cases as *Becker*[15] and *Tullio Ratti*[16] provides that individuals may rely on the terms of a directive only:

(a) where the date for the implementation of that directive has expired,
(b) where the terms of the directive relied upon are clear, precise and unconditional, and
(c) where the person against whom the directive is pleaded is the "State".

It has been held by the European Court in several cases that the rules in the procurement directives relating to advertising and award procedures generally

---

[15] Case 8/81, *Becker* v. *Finanzmt Munster-Innenstadt*: |1982| E.C.R. 53.
[16] Case 148/78, *Pubblico Ministero* v. *Tullio Ratti*: |1979| E.C.R. 1629.

(and possibly other provisions) do have direct effect.[17] Guidance as to who or what is the "State" for the purposes of the direct effect doctrine has been provided by the European Court in *Foster* v. *British Gas*[18] where it was held that a provision of a directive which has direct effect:

> "may be relied upon in a claim for damages against a body, whatever its legal form, which has been made responsible pursuant to a measure adopted by the State for providing a public service under the control of the State, and has for that purpose special powers beyond those which result from the normal rules applicable in relations between individuals."
> (para. 22 of the judgment).

It is probable that all the contracting authorities which fall within the Works and Supplies Directives will satisfy that definition (which is not exhaustive) and that some but by no means all of the contracting entities falling within the scope of the Utilities Directive will also qualify.

Even where the direct effect doctrine cannot be relied upon (*e.g.* because the defendant is not a State body) a Plaintiff may be able to recover damages from the Member State concerned for being in breach of its Community obligations under the principles set out in the case of *Francovitch, supra.*

**5–20**    Although a contractor or supplier would normally bring his proceedings in the Member State in which the offending contracting authority or utility was domiciled this is not necessarily the case. The jurisdiction of a national court to hear such proceedings is governed by the provisions of the Brussels Convention 1968 to which all the Member States are signatories. That Convention provides that subject to certain exceptions, persons domiciled in a Contracting State must be sued in the courts of that State (Article 2). However by Article 5(3) a person domiciled in a Contracting State may in addition be sued in another Contracting State "in matters relating to tort delict or quasi delict in the courts of the place where the harmful event occurred." Whether a claim relates to "tort delict or quasi delict" is a matter of Community, and not national law. It includes any action relating to a defendant's liability which does not fall within the meaning of "matters relating to contract" in Article 5(1) of the Convention.[19] Claims under the public procurement rules would therefore fall within Article 5(3). The European Court has given the words "harmful event" in that Article a very wide meaning and has held that it is to be construed as referring both to the place where the damage occurred and the place of the event giving rise to it.[20] In a subsequent case[21] the Court has to some extent clarified what is meant by "where the damage occurred" when it stated that the concept:

---

[17] See, *e.g.* Case 31/87, *Gebroeders Beentjes BV v. The Netherlands*: |1988| E.C.R. 4635, and Case 103/88, *Fratelli Costanzo SpA v. Commune di Milano*: |1989| E.C.R. 1839.
[18] |1990| 2 C.M.L.R. 833.
[19] Case 189/87, *Kalfelis v. Schroder Munchmeyer Hengst & Co. and Others*: |1988| E.C.R. 5565.
[20] Case 21/76, *Bier v. Mines de Potasse*: |1976| E.C.R. 1735.
[21] Case 220/88, *Dumez France v. Hessiche Landesbank*: |1990| E.C.R. 49.

"can be understood only as indicating the place where the event giving rise to the damage, and entailing tortious delictual or quasi delictual liability, directly produced its harmful effects upon the person who is the immediate victim of that event."
(para. 20 of the judgment).

In relation to a claim under the public procurement rules the event giving rise to the damage is the breach of those rules and this will normally occur in the Member State where the contracting authority or utility is situated. That breach it is submitted directly produces its harmful effects on the contractor or supplier (in the form of actual or potential loss of profits or tendering costs thrown away) in the Member State where the contractor or supplier is established.

A U.K. contractor or supplier can therefore it is submitted, bring proceedings in the United Kingdom in relation to an alleged breach of the Community procurement rules occurring within another Contracting State (*e.g.* when that Contracting State's authorities fail to advertise a relevant contract or where they improperly discriminate in favour of their own nationals in the awarding of contracts). It may choose to do so not only for reasons of ease of access to the national courts and familiarity with their language and procedure but also because the remedies available in the U.K. procurement Regulations may be more favourable than those available in the alternative jurisdiction of the contracting state in which the relevant contracting authority or utility is domiciled. Any judgment or order granted by the U.K. Court (with the exception of certain *ex parte* orders—see below) would under the terms of the Brussels Convention normally be automatically enforceable by the Courts of the Contracting State affected. Similarly an aggrieved contractor or supplier domiciled in another Contracting State could bring proceedings in that Contracting State against a U.K. contracting authority or utility and any order of that State's Courts (*e.g.* ordering a suspension of the procedure leading to the award of a contract pending trial) would similarly normally be automatically enforceable in the United Kingdom.

Even in a situation where the U.K. courts do not have jurisdiction a contractor **5–21** or supplier can seek *interim* relief in his national court under Article 24 of the Brussels Convention which provides that:

"Application may be made to the Courts of a Contracting State for such provisional including protective measures as may be available under the law of that State even if under this Convention the Courts of another Contracting State have jurisdiction as to the substance of the matter."

In relation to public procurement matters the interim relief available in the U.K. would be that provided for in regulation 26(5)(*a*) of the Supply Regulations. regulation 31(6)(*a*) of the Works Regulations, and regulation 30(5)(*a*) of the Utilities Regulations (see para. 5–07 above).

For the national courts to have jurisdiction to grant interim relief under Article

24 it is not necessary for the Plaintiff to have commenced proceedings either in the national courts or in the courts of another Contracting State.

An order made under Article 24 is in general susceptible to recognition and enforcement in other Contracting States under Article 25 in the same way as any other judgment. However any order made *ex parte* (*i.e.* without notice of the application having been given to the defendant) is not enforceable in another Contracting State until the defendant has been given notice of the Order and a reasonable time has elapsed to enable him to apply for the order to be revoked or discharged.[22]

## Action by the Commission

**5–22**    The Remedies Directives provide that in certain circumstances the Commission may take action to ensure that the Community procurement rules are complied with. This residual power is particularly important where an infringement has taken place but no contractor or supplier seeks a review. This may frequently prove to be the case, because as the House of Lords Select Committee pointed out in its report on "Compliance with Public Procurement Directives"[23]:

> "a tenderer contemplating taking legal proceedings in a national Court against a public authority claiming breach of the Community's procurement rules faces fundamental problems. It is likely that the tenderer still hopes subsequently to do business with the procuring authority, he will not want to bite the hand that feeds him. The situation is not comparable to suing competitors for breach of the rules on competition. It is therefor unrealistic to expect that tenderers will collectively police the Community rules. Most tenderers will prefer to cut their immediate losses in the hope of establishing a longer term relationship of trust and confidence."

The circumstances in which the Commission may act arise when prior to a contract being concluded the Commission considers that "a clear and manifest infringement of Community provisions in the field of procurement has been committed during a contract award procedure" falling within the scope of the Works, Supplies or Utilities Directives "or in relation to Article 3(2)(a) of the Utilities Directive in the case of the contracting entities to which that provision applies" (Article 3(1) of 89/665/EEC and Article 8(1) of 92/13/EEC). The Commission must notify the Member State and the contracting entity that such an infringement has been committed and request its correction. Within 21 days (30 days in the case of a utility) of receipt of that notification the Member State concerned must communicate to the Commission:

[22] Case 125/79, *Denilauer* v. *Couchet Freres*: [1980] E.C.R. 1553.
[23] 12th Report of the Select Committee on the European Communities of the House of Lords 1987–88.

(a) its confirmation that the infringement has been corrected; or

(b) a reasoned submission as to why no correction has been made; or

(c) a notice to the effect that a contract award procedure has been suspended either by the contracting entity on its own initiative or as the result of interim measures granted by a Court to that effect.

A reasoned submission in accordance with para. (b) above may rely among other matters on the fact that the alleged infringement is already the subject of judicial or other review proceedings. In such a case, the Member State must inform the Commission of the result of those proceedings as soon as it becomes known.

Where notice has been given that a contract award procedure has been suspended in accordance with para. (c) above, the Member State must notify the Commission when the suspension is lifted or another contract procedure relating in whole or in part to the same subject matter is begun. That notification must confirm that the alleged infringement has been corrected or include a reasoned submission as to why no correction has been made.

The powers given to the Commission under the Remedies Directives are in addition to those it may exercise under Article 169 of the Treaty. As has already been noted, when acting under Article 169 the Commission is not constrained by the fact that a contract has already been concluded (see para. 5–17 above).

# Monitoring compliance with the Public Procurement rules in the case of contracts financed with the aid of Community funds

The Commission, aided by the national authorities monitors compliance with Community public procurement rules in particular in relation to contracts that benefit from Community assistance. In relation to contracts which may receive Community financing the Commission addresses a detailed questionnaire to the applicant regarding its compliance with the public procurement rules which it is required to answer. Failure to return a duly completed questionnaire verified by the national authorities after the contracts have been awarded will result in the suspension of payments once notice to the interested party has been given to submit its comments.     **5–23**

In addition the Commission has made it clear that failure to comply with Community public procurement rules in such cases may result not only in the initiation of proceedings against the Member State concerned under Article 169 of the Treaty but also in the rejection of requests for assistance, or suspension, (and in some cases even the recovery) of assistance already paid.[24]

[24] Commission Notice C(88) 2510 (|1989| O.J. C22/3).

# Appendix A

## PART 1

## DRAFT CONSOLIDATED WORKS DIRECTIVE

**Council Directive concerning the coordination of procedures for the award of public works contracts**

*(as submitted to the European Parliament in February 1993)*

(93/—/EEC)

THE COUNCIL OF THE EUROPEAN COMMUNITIES,

Having regard to the Treaty establishing the European Economic Community, and in particular Articles 57(2), 66 and 100A thereof,   **A–01**

Having regard to the proposal from the Commission,[1]

In cooperation with the European Parliament,[2]

Having regard to the opinion of the Economic and Social Committee,[3]

Whereas Council Directive 71/305/EEC of 26 July 1971, concerning the coordination of procedures for the award of public works contracts,[4] as last amended by Directive 90/531/EEC,[5] has been amended substantially and on numerous occasions; whereas for reasons of clarity and rationality the said Directive should be consolidated;

Whereas the simultaneous attainment of freedom of establishment and freedom to provide services in respect of public works contracts awarded in Member States on behalf of the State, or regional or local authorities or other legal persons governed by public law entails not only the abolition of restrictions but also the coordination of national procedures for the award of public works contracts;

Whereas such coordination should take into account as far as possible the procedures and administrative practices in force in each Member State;

Whereas works contracts awarded by entities operating in the water, energy, transport and telecommunication sectors are covered by Directive 90/531/EEC;

Whereas, in view of the increasing importance of concession contracts in the public works area and of their specific nature, rules concerning advertising should be included in this Directive;

Whereas works contracts of less than ECU 5 000 000 may be exempted from competition as provided for under this Directive; whereas it is appropriate to provide for their exemption from coordination measures;

Whereas provision must be made for exceptional cases where measures concerning the coordination of procedures may not necessarily be applied, but such cases must be expressly limited;

Whereas the negotiated procedure should be considered to be exceptional and therefore only applicable in certain limited cases;

---

[1] OJ No C 46 20.2.1992, p. 79.
[2] Opinion delivered on 8 April 1992 (not yet published in the Official Journal) and decision of (date not yet available) (not yet published in the Official Journal).
[3] OJ No C 106, 27.4.1992, p. 11.
[4] OJ No L 185, 16.8.1971, p. 5.
[5] OJ No L 297, 29.10.1990, p. 1.

Whereas it is necessary to provide common rules in the technical field which take account of the Community policy on standards and specifications;

Whereas to ensure development of effective competition in the field of public contracts it is necessary that contract notices drawn up by the authorities of Member States awarding contracts be advertised throughout the Community; whereas the information contained in these notices must enable contractors established in the Community to determine whether the proposed contracts are of interest to them; whereas, for this purpose, it is appropriate to give them adequate information about the services to be provided and the conditions attached thereto; whereas, more particularly, in restricted procedures advertisement is intended to enable contractors of Member States to express their interest in contracts by seeking from the authorities awarding contracts invitations to tender under the required conditions;

Whereas it is necessary to provide common rules for participation in public works contracts which must include both qualitative selection criteria and criteria for the award of the contract;

Whereas this Directive must not affect the obligations of the Member States concerning the deadlines for transposal of the Directives set out in Annex VII.

HAS ADOPTED THIS DIRECTIVE:

## TABLE OF CONTENTS

*(The following Annexes are not reproduced in this Text)*

TITLE I

## GENERAL PROVISIONS

*Article 1*

For the purpose of this Directive:                                             **A–02**

(a) "public works contracts" are contracts for pecuniary interest concluded in writing between a contractor and a contracting authority as defined in (b), which have as their object either the execution, or both the execution and design, of works related to one of the activities referred to in Annex II or a work defined in (c) below, or the execution, by whatever means, of a work corresponding to the requirements specified by the contracting authority;

(b) "contracting authorities" shall be the State, regional or local authorities, bodies governed by public law, associations formed by one or several of such authorities or bodies governed by public law.

A body governed by public law means any body:

— established for the specific purpose of meeting needs in the general interest, not having an industrial or commercial character, and

— having legal personality, and

— financed, for the most part, by the State, or regional or local authorities, or other bodies governed by public law; or subject to management supervision by those bodies; or having an administrative, managerial or supervisory board, more than half of whose members are appointed by the State, regional or local authorities or by other bodies governed by public law.

The list of bodies or of categories of such bodies governed by public law which fulfil the criteria referred to in the second subparagraph are set out in Annex I. These lists shall be as exhaustive as possible and may be reviewed in accordance with the procedure laid down in Article 35. To this end, Member States shall periodically notify the Commission of any changes to their lists of bodies and categories of bodies;

(c) a "work" means the outcome of building or civil engineering works taken as a whole that is sufficient of itself to fulfil an economic and technical function;

(d) "public works concession" is a contract of the same type as that indicated in (a) except for the fact that the consideration for the works to be carried out consists either solely in the right to exploit the construction or in this right together with payment;

(e) "open procedures" are those national procedures whereby all interested contractors may submit tenders;

(f) "restricted procedures" are those national procedures whereby only those contractors invited by the contracting authority may submit tenders;

(g) "negotiated procedures" are those national procedures whereby contracting authorities consult contractors of their choice and negotiate the terms of the contract with one or more of them;

(h) a contractor who submits a tender shall be designated by the term "tenderer" and one who has sought an invitation to take part in a restricted and negotiated procedure by the term "candidate".

*Article 2*

**1.** Member States shall take the necessary measures to ensure that the contracting authorities comply or ensure compliance with this Directive where they subsidize directly by more than 50% a works contract awarded by an entity other than themselves.

97

**2.** Paragraph 1 shall concern only contracts covered by Class 50, Group 502, of the general industrial classification of economic activities within the European Communities (NACE) nomenclature and contracts relating to building work for hospitals, facilities intended for sports, recreation and leisure, school and university buildings and buildings used for administrative purposes.

## Article 3

**1.** Should contracting authorities conclude a public works concession contract the advertising rules as described in Article 11(3), (6), (7) and (9) to (13), and in Article 15, shall apply to that contract when its value is not less than ECU 5 000 000.

**2.** The contracting authority may:

— either require the concessionaire to award contracts representing a minimum of 30% of the total value of the work for which the concession contract is to be awarded, to third parties, at the same time providing the option for candidates to increase this percentage. This minimum percentage shall be specified in the concession contract,
— or request the candidates for concession contracts to specify in their tenders the percentage, if any, of the total value of the work for which the concession contract is to be awarded which they intend to assign to third parties.

**3.** When the concessionaire is himself a contracting authority, as referred to in Article 1 (*b*) he shall comply with the provisions of this Directive in the case of works to be carried out by third parties.

**4.** Member States shall take the necessary steps to ensure that a concessionaire other than a contractional authority awarding contracts shall apply the advertising rules listed in Article 11(4), (6), (7), and (9) to (13), and in Article 16, in respect of the contracts which it awards to third parties when the value of the contracts is not less than ECU 5 000 000. Advertising rules shall not be applied where works contracts meet the conditions laid down in Article 7(3).

Undertakings which have formed a group in order to obtain the concession contract, or undertakings affiliated to them, shall not be regarded as third parties.

An "affiliated undertaking" means any undertaking over which the concessionaire may exercise, directly or indirectly, a dominant influence or which may exercise a dominant influence over the concessionaire or which, in common with the concessionaire, is subject to the dominant influence of another undertaking by virtue of ownership, financial participation or the rules which govern it. A dominant influence on the part of an undertaking shall be presumed when, directly or indirectly in relation to another undertaking, it:

— holds the major part of the undertaking's subscribed capital, or
— controls the majority of the votes attaching to shares issued by the undertakings, or
— can appoint more than half of the members of the undertaking's administrative managerial or supervisory body.

A comprehensive list of these undertakings shall be enclosed with the candidature for the concession. This list shall be brought up to date following any subsequent changes in the relationship between the undertakings.

## Article 4

This Directive shall not apply to:

(a) contracts awarded in the fields referred to in Articles 2, 7, 8 and 9 of Directive 90/531/EEC or fulfilling the conditions in Article 6(2) of that Directive;

(b) works contracts which are declared secret or the execution of which must be accompanied by special security measures in accordance with the laws, regulations or administrative provisions in force in the Member States concerned or when the protection of the basic interests of that State's security so requires.

### Article 5

This Directive shall not apply to public contracts governed by different procedural rules and awarded:

(a) in pursuance of an international agreement, concluded in conformity with the Treaty, between a Member State and one or more non-member countries and covering works intended for the joint implementation or exploitation of a project by the signatory States; all agreements shall be communicated to the Commission which may consult the Advisory Committee for Public Contracts set up by Council Decision 71/306/EEC[6];

(b) to undertakings in a Member State or a non-member country in pursuance of an international agreement relating to the stationing of troops;

(c) pursuant to the particular procedure of an international organization.

### Article 6

**1.** The provisions of this Directive shall apply to public works contracts whose estimated value net of VAT is not less than ECU 5 000 000.

**2.**(a) The value of the threshold in national currencies shall normally be revised every two years with effect from 1 January 1992. The calculation of this value shall be based on the average daily values of these currencies in terms of the ecu over the 24 months terminating on the last day of October immediately preceding the 1 January revision. The values shall be published in the *Official Journal of the European Communities* at the beginning of November.

(b) The method of calculation laid down in subparagraph (a) shall be reviewed on a proposal from the Commission, by the Advisory Committee for Public Contracts in principle two years after its initial application.

**3.** Where a work is subdivided into several lots, each one the subject of a contract, the value of each lot must be taken into account for the purpose of calculating the amounts referred to in paragraph 1. Where the aggregate value of the lots is not less than the amount referred to in paragraph 1, the provisions of that paragraph shall apply to all lots. Contracting authorities shall be permitted to depart from this provision for lots whose estimated value net of VAT is less than ECU 1 000 000, provided that the total estimated value of all the lots exempted does not, in consequence, exceed 20% of the total estimated value of all lots.

**4.** No work or contract may be split up with the intention of avoiding the application of the preceding paragraphs.

**5.** When calculating the amounts referred to in paragraph 1 and in Article 7, account shall be taken not only of the amount of the public works contracts but also of the estimated value of the supplies needed to carry out the works which are made available to the contractor by the contracting authorities.

[6] OJ No L 185, 16.8.1971, p. 15.

## Article 7

**1.** In awarding public works contracts the contracting authorities shall apply the procedures defined in Article 1(e), (f) and (g).

**2.** The contracting authorities may award their public works contracts by negotiated procedure, with prior publication of a tender notice and after having selected the candidates according to qualitative public criteria, in the following cases:

(a) in the event of irregular tenders in response to an open or restricted procedure or in the event of tenders which are unacceptable under national provisions that are in accordance with the provisions of Title IV, in so far as the original terms of the contract are not substantially altered. The contracting authorities shall not, in these cases, publish a tender notice where they include in such negotiated procedure all the enterprises satisfying the criteria of Articles 24 to 29 which, during the prior open or restricted procedure, have submitted offers in accordance with the formal requirements of the tendering procedure;

(b) when the works involved are carried out purely for the purpose of research, experiment or development, and not to establish commercial viability or to recover research and development costs;

(c) in exceptional cases, when the nature of the works or the risks attaching thereto do not permit prior overall pricing.

**3.** The contracting authorities may award their public works contracts by negotiated procedure without prior publication of a tender notice, in the following cases:

(a) in the absence of tenders or of appropriate tenders in response to an open or restricted procedure in so far as the original terms of the contract are not substantially altered and provided that a report is communicated to the Commission at its request;

(b) when, for technical or artistic reasons or for reasons connected with the protection of exclusive rights, the works may only be carried out by a particular contractor;

(c) in so far as is strictly necessary when, for reasons of extreme urgency brought about by events unforeseen by the contracting authorities in question, the time limit laid down for the open, restricted or negotiated procedures referred to in paragraph 2 above cannot be kept. The circumstances invoked to justify extreme urgency must not in any event be attributable to the contracting authorities;

(d) for additional works not included in the project initially considered or in the contract first concluded but which have, through unforeseen circumstances, become necessary for the carrying out of the work described therein, on condition that the award is made to the contractor carrying out such work:
— when such works cannot be technically or economically separated from the main contract without great inconvenience to the contracting authorities, or
— when such works, although separable from the execution of the original contract, are strictly necessary to its later stages,
however, the aggregate value of contracts awarded for additional works may not exceed 50% of the amount of the main contract;

(e) for new works consisting of the repetition of similar works entrusted to the undertaking to which the same contracting authorities awarded an earlier contract, provided that such works conform to a basic project for which a first contract was awarded according to the procedures referred to in paragraph 4.
As soon as the first project is put up for tender, notice must be given that this procedure might be adopted and the total estimated cost of subsequent works shall be taken into consideration by the contracting authorities when they apply

the provisions of Article 6. This procedure may only be applied during the three years following the conclusion of the original contract.

**4.** In all other cases, the contracting authorities shall award their public works contracts by the open procedure or by the restricted procedure.

### Article 8

**1.** The contracting authority shall, within 15 days of the date on which the request is received, inform any eliminated candidate or tenderer who so requests of the reasons for rejection of his application or his tender, and, in the case of a tender, the name of the successful tenderer.

**2.** The contracting authority shall inform candidates or tenderers who so request of the grounds on which it decided not to award a contract in respect of which a prior call for competition was made, or to recommence the procedure. It shall also inform the Office for Official Publications of the European Communities of that decision.

**3.** For each contract awarded the contracting authorities shall draw up a written report which shall include at least the following:

— the name and address of the contracting authority, the subject and value of the contract,
— the names of the candidates or tenderers admitted and the reasons for their selection,
— the names of the candidates or tenderers rejected and the reasons for their rejection,
— the name of the successful tenderer and the reasons for his tender having been selected and, if known, any share of the contract the successful tenderer may intend to subcontract to a third party,
— for negotiated procedures, the circumstances referred to in Article 7 which justify the use of these procedures.

This report, or the main features of it, shall be communicated to the Commission at its request.

### Article 9

In the case of contracts relating to the design and construction of a public housing scheme whose size and complexity, and the estimated duration of the work involved, require that planning be based from the outset on close collaboration within a team comprising representatives of the authorities awarding contracts, experts and the contractor to be responsible for carrying out the works, a special award procedure may be adopted for selecting the contractor most suitable for integration into the team.

In particular, authorities awarding contracts shall include in the contract notice as accurate as possible a description of the works to be carried out so as to enable interested contractors to form a valid idea of the project. Furthermore, authorities awarding contracts shall, in accordance with the provisions of Articles 24 to 29, set out in such contract notice the personal, technical and financial conditions to be fulfilled by candidates.

Where such procedure is adopted, authorities awarding contracts shall apply the common advertising rules relating to restricted procedure and to the criteria for qualitative selection.

## TITLE II

### COMMON RULES IN THE TECHNICAL FIELD

*Article 10*

**A–03**   1. The technical specifications defined in Annex III shall be given in the general or contractual documents relating to each contract.

2. Without prejudice to the legally binding national technical rules and in so far as these are compatible with Community law, such technical specifications shall be defined by the contracting authorities by reference to national standards implementing European standards, or by reference to European technical approvals or by reference to common technical specifications.

3. A contracting authority may depart from paragraph 2 if:

(a)   the standards, European technical approvals or common technical specifications do not include any provision for establishing conformity, or technical means do not exist for establishing satisfactorily the conformity of a product to these standards, European technical approvals or common technical specifications;

(b)   use of these standards, European technical approvals or common technical specifications would oblige the contracting authority to acquire products or materials incompatible with equipment already in use or would entail disproportionate costs or disproportionate technical difficulties, but only as part of a clearly defined and recorded strategy with a view to change-over, within a given period, to European standards, European technical approvals or common technical specifications;

(c)   the project concerned is of a genuinely innovative nature for which use of existing European standards, European technical approvals or common technical specifications would not be appropriate.

4. Contracting authorities invoking paragraph 3 shall record, wherever possible, the reasons for doing so in the tender notice published in the *Official Journal of the European Communities* or in the contract documents and in all cases shall record these reasons in their internal documentation and shall supply such information on request to Member States and to the Commission.

5. In the absence of European standards or European technical approvals or common technical specifications, the technical specifications:

(a)   shall be defined by reference to the national technical specifications recognized as complying with the basic requirements listed in the Community directives on technical harmonization, in accordance with the procedures laid down in those directives, and in particular in accordance with the procedures laid down in Council Directive 89/106/EEC of 21 December 1988 on construction products[7];

(b)   may be defined by reference to national technical specifications relating to design and method of calculation and execution of works and use of materials;

(c)   may be defined by reference to other documents.
In this case, it is appropriate to make reference in order of preference to:

   (i)   national standards implementing international standards accepted by the country of the contracting authority;

   (ii)   other national standards and national technical approvals of the country of the contracting authority;

   (iii)   any other standard.

[7] OJ No L 40, 11.2.1989, p. 12.

**6.** Unless it is justified by the subject of the contract, Member States shall prohibit the introduction into the contractual clauses relating to a given contract of technical specifications which mention products of a specific make or source or of a particular process and which therefore favour or eliminate certain undertakings. In particular, the indication of trade marks, patents, types, or of a specific origin or production shall be prohibited. However, if such indication is accompanied by the words "or equivalent", it shall be authorized in cases where the authorities awarding contracts are unable to give a description of the subject of the contract using specifications which are sufficiently precise and intelligible to all parties concerned.

TITLE III

## COMMON ADVERTISING RULES

*Article 11*

**1.** Contracting authorities shall make known, by means of an indicative notice, the    **A–04**
essential characteristics of the works contracts which they intend to award and the estimated value of which is not less than the threshold laid down in Article 6(1).

**2.** Contracting authorities who wish to award a public works contract by open, restricted or negotiated procedure referred to in Article 7(2), shall make known their intention by means of a notice.

**3.** Contracting authorities who wish to award a works concession contract shall make known their intention by means of a notice.

**4.** Works concessionaires, other than a contracting authority, who wish to award a work contract to a third party as defined in Article 3(4), shall make known their intention by means of a notice.

**5.** Contracting authorities who have awarded a contract shall make known the result by means of a notice. However, certain information on contract award may, in certain cases, not be published where release of such information would impede law enforcement or otherwise be contrary to the public interest, would prejudice the legitimate commercial interests of particular enterprises, public or private, or might prejudice fair competition between contractors.

**6.** The contracting authorities shall send the notices referred to in the preceding paragraphs as rapidly as possible and by the most appropriate channels to the Office for Official Publications of the European Communities. In the case of the accelerated procedure referred to in Article 14, the notice shall be sent by telex, telegram or telefax.

(a) The notice referred to in paragraph 1 shall be sent as soon as possible after the decision approving the planning of the works contracts that the contracting authorities intend to award:

(b) the notice referred to in paragraph 5 shall be sent at the latest 48 days after the award of the contract in question.

**7.** The notices referred to in paragraphs 1, 2, 3, 4 and 5 shall be drawn up in accordance with the models given in Annexes IV, V and VI, and shall specify the information requested in those Annexes.

In open, restricted and negotiated procedures, the contracting authorities may not require any conditions but those specified in Articles 26 and 27 when requesting information concerning the economic and technical standards which they require of contractors for their selection (point 11 of Annex IV B, point 10 of Annex IV C and point 9 of Annex IV D).

**8.** The notices referred to in paragraphs 1 and 5 shall be published in full in the *Official*

*Journal of the European Communities* and in the TED data bank in the official languages of the Communities, the original text alone being authentic.

**9.** The notices referred to in paragraphs 2, 3 and 4 shall be published in full in the *Official Journal of the European Communities* and in the TED data bank in their original language. A summary of the important elements of each notice shall be published in the other official languages of the Community, the original text alone being authentic.

**10.** The Office for Official Publications of the European Communities shall publish the notices not later than 12 days after their dispatch. In the case of the accelerated procedure referred to in Article 14, this period shall be reduced to five days.

**11.** The notice shall not be published in the official journals or in the press of the country of the contracting authority before the date of dispatch, and it shall mention this date. It shall not contain information other than that published in the *Official Journal of th European Communities.*

**12.** The contracting authorities must be able to supply proof of the date of dispatch

**13.** The cost of publication of the notices in the *Official Journal of the European Communitie* shall be borne by the Communities. The length of the notice shall not be greater than one page of the Journal, or approximately 650 words. Each edition of the Journal containing one or more notices shall reproduce the model notice or notices on which the published notice or notices are based.

## Article 12

**1.** In open procedures the time limit for the receipt of tenders shall be fixed by the contracting authorities at not less than 52 days from the date of sending the notice.

**2.** The time limit for the receipt of tenders laid down in paragraph 1 may be reduced to 36 days where the contracting authorities have published the notice, provided for in Article 11(1), drafted in accordance with the specimen in Annex IV A, in the *Official Journal of the European Communities.*

**3.** Provided they have been requested in good time, the contract documents and supporting documents must be sent to the contractors by the contracting authorities or competent departments within six days of receiving their application.

**4.** Provided it has been requested in good time, additional information relating to the contract documents shall be supplied by the contracting authorities not later than six days before the final date fixed for receipt of tenders.

**5.** Where the contract documents, supporting documents or additional information are too bulky to be supplied within the time limits laid down in paragraph 3 or 4 or where tenders can only be made after a visit to the site or after on-the-spot inspection of the documents supporting the contract documents, the time limits laid down in paragraphs 1 and 2 shall be extended accordingly.

## Article 13

**1.** In restricted procedures and negotiated procedures as described in Article 7(2), the time limit for receipt of requests to participate fixed by the contracting authorities shall be not less than 37 days from the date of dispatch of the notice.

**2.** The contracting authorities shall simultaneously and in writing invite the selected candidates to submit their tenders. The letter of invitation shall be accompanied by the contract documents and supporting documents. It shall include at least the following information:

(a) where appropriate, the address of the service from which the contract documents and supporting documents can be requested and the final date for making such a request, also the amount and terms of payment of any sum to be paid for such documents;

(b) the final date for receipt of tenders, the address to which they must be sent and the language or languages in which they must be drawn up;

(c) a reference to the contract notice published;

(d) an indication of any documents to be annexed, either to support the verifiable statements furnished by the candidate in accordance with Article 11(7), or to supplement the information provided for in that Article under the same conditions as those laid down in Articles 26 and 27;

(e) the criteria for the award of the contract if these are not given in the notice.

**3.** In restricted procedures, the time limit for receipt of tenders fixed by the contracting authorities may not be less than 40 days from the date of dispatch of the written invitation.

**4.** The time limit for receipt of tenders laid down in paragraph 3 may be reduced to 26 days where the contracting authorities have published the notice, provided for in Article 11(1), drafted according to the specimen in Annex IV A, in the *Official Journal of the European Communities.*

**5.** Requests to participate in procedures for the award of contracts may be made by letter, by telegram, telex, telefax or by telephone. If by one of the last four, they must be confirmed by letter dispatched before the end of the period laid down in paragraph 1.

**6.** Provided it has been requested in good time, additional information relating to the contract documents must be supplied by the contracting authorities not later than six days before the final date fixed for the receipt of tenders.

**7.** Where tenders can be made only after a visit to the site or after on-the-spot inspection of the documents supporting the contract documents, the time limit laid down in paragraphs 3 and 4 shall be extended accordingly.

*Article 14*

**1.** In cases where urgency renders impracticable the time limits laid down in Article 13, the contracting authorities may fix the following time limits:

(a) a time limit for receipt of requests to participate which shall be not less than 15 days from the date of dispatch of the notice;

(b) a time limit for the receipt of tenders which shall be not less than 10 days from the date of the invitation to tender.

**2.** Provided it has been requested in good time, additional information relating to the contract documents must be supplied by the contracting authorities not later than four days before the final date fixed for the receipt of tenders.

**3.** Requests for participation in contracts and invitations to tender must be made by the most rapid means of communication possible. When requests to participate are made by telegram, telex, telefax or telephone, they must be confirmed by letter dispatched before the expiry of the time limit referred to in paragraph 1.

*Article 15*

Contracting authorities who wish to award a works concession contract shall fix a time limit for receipt of candidatures for the concession, which shall not be less than 52 days from the date of dispatch of the notice.

*Article 16*

In works contracts awarded by a concessionaire of works other than an authority awarding contracts, the time limit for the receipt of requests to participate shall be fixed by the concessionaire at not less than 37 days from the date of dispatch of the notice, and the time limit for the receipt of tenders at not less than 40 days from the date of dispatch of the notice or the invitation to tender.

*Article 17*

Contracting authorities may arrange for the publication in the *Official Journal of the European Communities* of notices announcing public works contracts which are not subject to the publication requirement laid down in this Directive.

TITLE IV

**COMMON RULES ON PARTICIPATION**

*Article 18*

**A–05**  Contracts shall be awarded on the basis of the criteria laid down in Chapter 2 of this Title, taking into account Article 19, after the suitability of the contractors not excluded under Article 24 has been checked by the contracting authorities in accordance with the criteria of economic and financial standing and of technical knowledge or ability referred to in Articles 26 to 29.

*Article 19*

Where the criterion for the award of the contract is that of the most economically advantageous tender, contracting authorities may take account of variants which are submitted by a tenderer and meet the minimum specification required by the contracting authorities.

The contracting authorities shall· state in the contract documents the minimum specifications to be respected by the variants and any specific requirements for their presentation. They shall indicate in the tender notice if variants are not permitted.

Contracting authorities may not reject the submission of a variant on the sole grounds that it has been drawn up with technical specifications defined by reference to national standards transposing European standards, to European technical approvals or to common technical specifications referred to in Article 10(2) or again by reference to national technical specifications referred to in Article 10(5)(a) and (b).

*Article 20*

In the contract documents, the contracting authority may ask the tenderer to indicate in his tender any share of the contract he may intend to subcontract to third parties.

This indication shall be without prejudice to the question of the principal contractor's liability.

*Article 21*

Tenders may be submitted by groups of contractors. These groups may not be required to assume a specific legal form in order to submit the tender; however, the group selected may be required to do so when it has been awarded the contract.

### Article 22

**1.** In restricted and negotiated procedures the contracting authorities shall, on the basis of information given relating to the contractor's personal position as well as to the information and formalities necessary for the evaluation of the minimum conditions of an economic and technical nature to be fulfilled by him, select from among the candidates with the qualifications required by Articles 24 and 29 those whom they will invite to submit a tender or to negotiate.

**2.** Where the contracting authorities award a contract by restricted procedure, they may prescribe the range within which the number of undertakings which they intend to invite will fall. In this case the range shall be indicated in the contract notice. The range shall be determined in the light of the nature of the work to be carried out. The range must number at least 5 undertakings and may be up to 20.

In any event, the number of candidates invited to tender shall be sufficient to ensure genuine competition.

**3.** Where the contracting authorities award a contract by negotiated procedure as referred to in Article 7(2), the number of candidates admitted to negotiate may not be less than three provided that there is a sufficient number of suitable candidates.

**4.** Each Member State shall ensure that contracting authorities issue invitations without discrimination to those nationals of other Member States who satisfy the necessary requirements and under the same conditions as to its own nationals.

### Article 23

**1.** The contracting authority may state in the contract documents, or be obliged by a Member State so to do, the authority or authorities from which a tenderer may obtain the appropriate information on the obligations relating to the employment protection provisions and the working conditions which are in force in the Member State, region or locality in which the works are to be executed and which shall be applicable to the works carried out on site during the performance of the contract.

**2.** The contracting authority which supplies the information referred to in paragraph I shall request the tenderers or those participating in the contract procedure to indicate that they have taken account, when drawing up their tender, of the obligations relating to employment protection provisions and the working conditions which are in force in the place where the work is to be carried out. This shall be without prejudice to the application of the provisions of Article 30(4) concerning the examination of abnormally low tenders.

### Chapter I

#### Criteria for qualitative selection

### Article 24

Any contractor may be excluded from participation in the contract who:　　　　**A–06**

(a) is bankrupt or is being wound up, whose affairs are being administered by the court, who has entered into an arrangement with creditors, who has suspended business activities or who is in any analogous situation arising from a similar procedure under national laws and regulations;

(b) is the subject of proceedings for a declaration of bankruptcy, for an order for compulsory winding up or administration by the court or for an arrangement with creditors or of any other similar proceedings under national laws or regulations;

(c) has been convicted of an offence concerning his professional conduct by a judgment which has the force of *res judicata*;

(d) who has been guilty of grave professional misconduct proven by any means which the authorities awarding contracts can justify;

(e) has not fulfilled obligations relating to the payment of social security contributions in accordance with the legal provisions of the country in which he is established or with those of the country of the authority awarding contracts;

(f) has not fulfilled obligations relating to the payment of taxes in accordance with the legal provisions of the country in which he is established or those of the country of the contracting authority;

(g) is guilty of serious misrepresentation in supplying the information required under this Chapter.

Where the authority awarding contracts requires of the contractor proof that none of the cases quoted in (a), (b), (c), (e) or (f) applies to him, it shall accept as sufficient evidence:

— for points (a), (b) or (c), the production of an extract from the "judicial record" or, failing this, of an equivalent document issued by a competent judicial or administrative authority in the country of origin or in the country whence that person comes showing that these requirements have been met,

— for points (e) or (f), a certificate issued by the competent authority in the Member State concerned.

Where the country concerned does not issue such documents or certificates, they may be replaced by a declaration on oath (or, in Member States where there is no provision for declarations on oath, by a solemn declaration) made by the person concerned before a judicial or administrative authority, a notary or a competent professional or trade body, in the country of origin or in the country whence that person comes. Member States shall designate the authorities and bodies competent to issue these documents and shall forthwith inform the other Member States and the Commission thereof.

## Article 25

Any contractor wishing to take part in a public works contract may be requested to prove his enrolment in the professional or trade register under the conditions laid down by the laws of the Member State in which he is established:

— in Belgium the registre du commerce—Handelsregister,

— in Denmark, the Handelsregistret, Aktieselskabsregistret and Erhvervsregistret,

— in Germany, the Handelsregister and the Handwerksrolle,

— in Greece, the register of contractors' enterprises ("a Μητρώο Εργοληπτικών Επιχειρήσεων"—Μ.Ε.Ε.Π.) of the Ministry for Environment, Town and Country Planning and Public Works (Υ.ΠΕ.Χ.Ω.Δ.Ε.),

— in Spain, the Registro Oficial de Contratistas del Ministerio de Industria y Energia,

— in France, the registre du commerce and the répertoire des métiers,

— in Italy, the Registro della Camera di commercio, industria, agricoltura e artigianato,

— in Luxembourg, the registre aux firmes and the rôle de la Chambre des métiers,

— in the Netherlands, the Handelsregister,

— in Portugal, the Commissão de Alvarás de Empresas de Obras Públicas e Particulares (CAEOPP),

— in the United Kingdom and Ireland, the contractor may be requested to provide a certificate from the Registrar of Companies or the Registrar of Friendly Societies or, if this is not the case, a certificate stating that the person concerned has declared on oath that he is engaged in the profession in question in the country in which he is established, in a specific place and under a given business name.

### Article 26

Proof of the contractor's financial and economic standing may, as a general rule, be furnished by one or more of the following references:

(a) appropriate statements from bankers;
(b) the presentation of the firm's balance sheets or extracts from the balance sheets, where publication of the balance sheet is required under the law of the country in which the contractor is established;
(c) a statement of the firm's overall turnover and the turnover on construction works for the previous three financial years.

The contracting authorities awarding contracts shall specify in the notice or in the invitation to tender which reference or references they have chosen and what references other than those mentioned under (a), (b) or (c) are to be produced.

If, for any valid reason, the contractor is unable to supply the references requested by the authorities awarding contracts, he may prove his economic and financial standing by any other document which the authorities awarding contracts consider appropriate.

### Article 27

Proof of the contractor's technical knowledge or ability may be furnished by:

(a) the contractor's educational and professional qualifications and/or those of the firm's managerial staff and, in particular, those of the person or persons responsible for carrying out the works;
(b) a list of the works carried out over the past five years, accompanied by certificates of satisfactory execution for the most important works. These certificates shall indicate the value, date and site of the works and shall specify whether they were carried out according to the rules of the trade and properly completed. Where necessary, the competent authority shall submit these certificates to the authority awarding contracts direct;
(c) a statement of the tools, plant and technical equipment available to the contractor for carrying out the work;
(d) a statement of the firm's average annual manpower and the number of managerial staff for the last three years;
(e) a statement of the technicians or technical divisions which the contractor can call upon for carrying out the work, whether or not they belong to the firm.

The authorities awarding contracts shall specify in the notice or in the invitation to tender which of these references are to be produced.

### Article 28

The authority awarding contracts may, within the limits of Articles 24 to 27, invite the contractor to supplement the certificates and documents submitted or to clarify them.

### Article 29

1. Member States who have official lists of recognized contractors must, on the

implementation of this Directive, adapt them to the provisions of Article 24(a) to (d) and (g) and of Articles 25, 26 and 27.

**2.** Contractors registered in the official lists may, for each contract, submit to the authority awarding contracts a certificate of registration issued by the competent authority. This certificate shall state the references which enabled them to be registered in the list and the classification given in this list.

**3.** Certified registration in the official lists by the competent bodies shall, for the authorities of other Member States awarding contracts, constitute a presumption of suitability for works corresponding to the contractor's classification only as regards Articles 24(a) to (d) and (g), 25, 26(b) and (c) and 27(b) and (d).

Information which can be deduced from registration in official lists may not be questioned. However, with regard to the payment of social security contributions, an additional certificate may be required of any registered contractor whenever a contract is offered.

The authorities of other Member States awarding contracts shall apply the above provisions only in favour of contractors who are established in the country holding the official list.

**4.** For the registration of contractors of other Member States in an official list, no further proofs and statements may be required other than those requested of nationals, and in any event, only those provided for under Articles 24 to 27.

**5.** Member States holding an official list shall communicate to other Member States the address of the body to which requests for registration may be made.

Chapter II

**Criteria for the award of contracts**

*Article 30*

**A–07**  **1.** The criteria on which the authorities awarding contracts shall base the award of contracts shall be:

— either the lowest price only,
— or, when the award is made to the most economically advantageous tender, various criteria according to the contract: e.g. price, period for completion, running costs, profitability, technical merit.

**2.** In the case referred to in the second indent of paragraph 1, the contracting authorities awarding contracts shall state in the contract documents or in the contract notice all the criteria they intend to apply to the award, where possible in descending order of importance.

**3.** Paragraph 1 shall not apply when a Member State bases the award of contracts on other criteria, within the framework of rules in force at the time of the adoption of this Directive whose aim is to give preference to certain tenderers, on condition that the rules invoked are compatible with the Treaty.

**4.** If, for a given contract, tenders appear to be abnormally low in relation to the service, before it may reject those tenders the contracting authority shall request, in writing, details of the constituent elements of the tender which it considers relevant and shall verify those constituent elements taking account of the explanations received.

The contracting authority may take into consideration explanations which are justified on objective grounds including the economy of the construction method, or the technical solutions chosen, or the exceptionally favourable conditions available to the tenderer for the execution of the work, or the originality of the work proposed by the tenderer.

If the documents relating to the contract provide for its award as the lowest price tendered, the contracting authority must communicate to the Commission the rejection of tenders which it considers to be too low.

However, until the end of 1992, if current national law so permits, the contracting authority may exceptionally, without any discrimination on grounds of nationality, reject tenders which are abnormally low in relation to the service, without being obliged to comply with the procedure provided for in the first subparagraph if the number of such tenders for a particular contract is so high that implementation of this procedure would lead to a considerable delay and jeopardize the public interest attaching to the execution of the contract in question. Recourse to this exceptional procedure shall be mentioned in the notice referred to in Article 11(5).

### Article 31

**1.** Until 31 December 1992, this Directive shall not prevent the application of existing national provisions on the award of public works contracts which have as their objective the reduction of regional disparities and the promotion of job creation in regions whose development is lagging behind and in declining industrial regions, on condition that the provisions concerned are compatible with the Treaty, in particular with the principles of non-discrimination on grounds of nationality, freedom of establishment and freedom to provide services, and with the Community's international obligations.

**2.** Paragraph 1 shall be without prejudice to Article 30(3).

### Article 32

**1.** Member States shall inform the Commission of national provisions covered by Article 30(3) and Article 31 and of the rules for applying them.

**2.** Member States concerned shall forward to the Commission, every year, a report describing the practical application of these provisions. The reports shall be submitted to the Advisory Committee for Public Works Contracts.

### TITLE V

### FINAL PROVISIONS

### Article 33

The calculation of the time limit for receipt of tenders or requests to participate shall be **A–08** made in accordance with Council Regulation (EEC, Euratom) No 1182/71 of 3 June 1971 determining the rules applicable to periods, dates and time limits.[8]

### Article 34

**1.** In order to permit assessment of the results of applying the Directive, Member States shall forward to the Commission a statistical report on the contracts awarded by contracting authorities by 31 October 1993 at the latest for the preceding year and thereafter by 31 October of every second year.

Nevertheless, for Greece, Spain and Portugal, the date of 31 October 1993 shall be replaced by 31 October 1995.

[8] OJ No L 124, 8.6.1971, p. 1.

**2.** The statistical report shall detail at least the number and value of contracts awarded by each contracting authority or category of contracting authority above the threshold, subdivided as far as possible by procedure, category of work and the nationality of the contractor to whom the contract has been awarded, and in the case of negotiated procedures, subdivided in accordance with Article 7, listing the number and value of the contracts awarded to each Member State and to third countries.

**3.** The Commission shall determine the nature of any additional statistical information, which is requested in accordance with the Directive, in consultation with the Advisory Committee for Public Works Contracts.

## Article 35

**1.** Article 1 shall be amended by the Commission, in accordance with the procedure laid down in paragraph 3, when, in particular on the basis of the notifications from the Member States, it appears necessary:

(a) to remove from the said Annex bodies governed by public law which no longer fulfil the criteria laid down in Article 1 (b);

(b) to include in that Annex bodies governed by public law which meet those criteria.

**2.** The conditions for the drawing up, transmission, receipt, translation, collection and distribution of the notices referred to in Article 12 and of the statistical reports provided for in Article 30a, the nomenclature provided for in Annex II, as well as the reference in the notices to particular positions of the nomenclature, may be modified in accordance with the procedure laid down in paragraph 3.

**3.** The chairman of the Advisory Committee for Public Works Contracts shall submit to the Committee a draft of any measures to be taken. The Committee shall deliver its opinion on the draft, if necessary by taking a vote, within a time limit to be fixed by the chairman in the light of the urgency of the matter.

The opinion shall be recorded in the minutes; in addition, each Member State shall have the right to request that its position be recorded in the minutes.

The Commission shall take the fullest account of the opinion delivered by the Committee. It shall inform the Committee of the manner in which its opinion has been taken into account.

**4.** Amended versions of Annexes I and II and of the conditions set out in paragraph 2 shall be published in the *Official Journal of the European Communities.*

## Article 36

**1.** Directive 71/305/EEC[9] is hereby repealed, without prejudice to the obligations of the Member States concerning the deadlines for transposition into national law and for application indicated in Annex VII.

---

[9] Including the provisions which amended this Directive, namely:
—Directive 78/669/EEC (OJ No L 225, 16.8.1978. p. 41),
—Directive 89/440/EEC (OJ No L 210, 21.7.1989, p. 1),
—Commission Decision 90/380/EEC (OJ No L 187, 19.7.1990, p. 55) and
—Article 35(2) of Directive 90/531/EEC (OJ No L 297, 29.10.1991, p. 1).

**2.** References to the repealed Directive shall be construed as references to this Directive and should be read in accordance with the correlation table given in Annex VIII.

*Article 37*

This Directive is addressed to the Member States.

Done at Brussels,

*For the Council*
*The President*

# PART 2

### Policy Guidelines on the interpretation of the obligation to refer to European standards in the framework of the Public Procurement Directives

(*This document was favourably considered by the Advisory Committee on the opening-up Public Procurement at its 36th meeting on October 14, 1992 and by the Advisory Committee on Public Procurement at its 68th meeting on October 21, 1992.*)

**A–12**      Article 7 of Directive 77/62/EEC (as amended by Directive 88/295/EEC) and Article 10 of Directive 71/305/EEC (as amended by Directive 89/440/EEC) provide that "without prejudice to the legally binding national technical rules in so far as these are compatible with Community law, (...) technical specifications shall be defined by the contracting authorities by reference to national standards implementing European standards, or by reference to European technical approvals or by reference to common technical specifications".

Those provisions have to be understood in the sense that they oblige contracting authorities to define the technical specifications of the goods to be supplied by reference to national standards transposing European standards where they exist, except in certain exceptional circumstances.

This interpretation is the result of a deliberate Council policy decision adopted while amending the public procurement Directives whose main intentions are to limit the contracting authorities' margin of discretion, to avoid the possibilities of using national technical specifications in a discriminatory manner and to foster the practical realm of European standards in the field of public procurement. Possible restrictive effects on trade, discussed infra, that this interpretation may entail have been consciously taken into account by the Council, which in the field of public procurement and as regards contracting authorities has tended to depart from its previous statements concerning the non-compulsory character of standards.

Approved European standards are transposed by the national standardization bodies of Member States into their domestic systems, where they replace existing national standards applying to the same area. Therefore, as a matter of principle, no problems of incompatibility would emerge in so far as European standards become the applicable national standards.

There are, however, some scenarios where difficulties of interpretation appear; these situations are discussed below:

### (1) Compatibility with harmonised EEC legislation

A new approach Directive lays down the essential requirements to be fulfilled, and this is accompanied by the adoption of specific European standards. Since the latter are by definition non-obligatory, producers remain free to respond to those essential requirements either by making their goods in conformity with the adopted European standard, in which case they benefit from a presumption of conformity to Community legislation throughout the Community, or by any other means provided that evidence of compliance with the established essential requirements is supplied.[1] In this latter case, following the interpretation described above, the producer would be foreclosed from participating in a public contract as its goods do not conform with the specifications of the purchaser, based on the existing European standard.

In relation to this restriction imposed to the purchaser, it is submitted that the possible negative consequences have been taken into account by the Council when deciding its

---

[1] Council Resolution of 7 May 1985 (O.J. No. C 136, of 4.6.85).

policy in the field of public procurement. The possible negative effects on trade that could result from the requirement to refer to European standards would be more than compensated by the benefits expected from the homogeneous use of European standards by contracting authorities. It is noteworthy that the use of different sorts of standards constitutes one of the main obstacles in the opening-up of public procurement to competition, which is the ultimate objective of the Directives in the area.

It should also be noted that in practice the significance of such cases appears to be minimal due to the normal practice of public procurement whereby reference in the contract clauses to standards is very common and most firms operating in this area usually adapt their products to current standards. While Member States are bound by the principle of mutual recognition as regards the free circulation of goods, contracting authorities, as buyers, usually make a choice in their contract clauses amongst the different goods legally on the market. It is not up to them to determine equivalence of goods, but to select those which they deem suitable for their purposes. The Directives' modifications are therefore intended to ensure that this choice takes account of the consensus already achieved through European standardization, although, of course, contracting authorities remain free to specify their requirements as they wish for aspects that are not covered in the relevant European standards. Any interpretation other than the one proposed would certainly deprive the Directives' modifications of any useful effect.

## (2) Compatibility with national technical rules

A second case of conflict may appear when in a given area there exists a European standard but no Community measure harmonizing essential requirements. Member States are then entitled to maintain their national technical rules ensuring the achievement of legitimate policy objectives such as public health, safety or consumer protection, as they retain the ultimate responsibility for such domains. These national rules themselves may not make reference to any standard, but fix the technical specifications required to guarantee a proper degree of safety, public health, etc. Since standards are in principle not compulsory whereas technical rules are defined by Directive 83/189/EEC[2] are, it may be argued that contracting authorities confronted with this type of situation should be able to choose between referring to European standards or to national technical rules, provided these are compatible with Community law, as the Directives seem to require.

In practice, approved European standards are subject to thorough negotiations and a public enquiry and are designed to take into account legal requirements relating to safety, consumer protection, public health, etc. The inclusion of "A-type deviations"[3] when adopting European standards makes the possibility of conflict with national technical rules purely theoretical.

## (3) An "unsafe" standard

This brings us to the last scenario, the case where a Member State realizes that a European standard transposed into its national system does not ensure, due to particular domestic circumstances, the adequate attainment of essential requirements in the sense of Article 36 of the Treaty. In this situation, Member States are entitled to adopt national technical rules which overrule those standards. (In practice, when such case appears,

---

[2] "Technical regulation" means technical specifications, including the relevant administrative provisions, the observance of which is compulsory, de jure or de facto, in the case of marketing or use in a Member State or a major part thereof, except those laid down by local authorities.
[3] A-type deviation is a national deviation to a European standard or harmonized document due to national regulation.

European standards stop applying to the specific State until an appropriate new standard is devised or a "type-A deviation" is agreed). It is in these circumstances that the sentence "without prejudice to the national technical rules legally binding in so far as these are compatible with Community law..." contained in the public procurement Directives' modified Articles acquires its "raison d'être".

# Appendix B

## PUBLIC WORKS CONTRACTS REGULATIONS 1991

### (S.I. No. 2680)

*(In force from December 21, 1991)*

**ARRANGEMENT OF REGULATIONS**

PART I

*General*

PART II

*Technical Specifications*

PART III

*Procedures Leading to the Award of a Public Works Contract*

PART IV

*Selection of Contractors*

PART V

*The Award of a Public Works Contract*

The Treasury, being the Minister designated[1] for the purposes of section 2(2) of the European Communities Act 1972[2] in relation to public procurement, in exercise of the powers conferred upon them by the said section 2(2) and all other powers enabling them in that behalf, hereby make the following Regulations:–

PART I

**GENERAL**

**B–01**    **Title and commencement**

**1.** These Regulations may be cited as the Public Works Contracts Regulations 1991 and shall come into force on 21st December 1991.

**Interpretation**

**2.**—(1) In these Regulations—

"to award" means to accept an offer made in relation to a proposed contract;
"carrying out", in relation to a work or works, means the construction or the design and construction of that work or those works;
"the Commission" means the Commission of the Communities;
"concessionaire" means a person who has entered into a public works concession contract with a contracting authority;
"contract documents" means the invitation to tender for or negotiate the contract, the proposed conditions of contract, the specifications or description of the work or works required by the contracting authority and of the materials or goods to be used in or for it or them, and all documents supplementary thereto;

[1] S.I. 1991/755.
[2] 1972 c.68.

"contract notice" means a notice sent to the Official Journal in accordance with regulation 11(2), 12(2), 13(2), 25(2) or 26(3);

"contracting authority" has the meaning ascribed to it by regulation 3;

"contractor" has the meaning ascribed to it by regulation 4;

"ECU" means the European Currency Unit as defined in Council Regulation (EEC) No. 3180/78[3];

"established" means the same as it does for the purposes of the Community Treaties;

"financial year" means the period of 12 months ending on 31st March in any year or, in relation to any person whose accounts are prepared in respect of a different 12 month period, that period of 12 months;

"government department" includes a Northern Ireland department or the head of such department;

"Minister of the Crown" means the holder of an office in Her Majesty's Government in the United Kingdom, and includes the Treasury;

"national of a member State" means, in the case of a person who is not an individual, a person formed in accordance with the laws of a member State and which has its registered office, central administration or principal place of business in a member State;

"negotiated procedure" means a procedure leading to the award of a public works contract whereby the contracting authority negotiates the terms of the contract with one or more persons selected by it;

"Official Journal" means the Official Journal of the Communities;

"open procedure" means a procedure leading to the award of a public works contract whereby all interested persons may tender for the contract;

"public housing scheme works contract" means a public works contract relating to the design and construction of a public housing scheme;

"public works concession contract" means a public works contract under which the consideration given by the contracting authority consists of or includes the grant of a right to exploit the work or works to be carried out under the contract;

"public works contract" means a contract in writing for consideration (whatever the nature of the consideration)—

(a)  for the carrying out of a work or works for a contracting authority, or

(b)  under which a contracting authority engages a person to procure by any means the carrying out for the contracting authority of a work corresponding to specified requirements;

"restricted procedure" means a procedure leading to the award of a public works contract whereby only persons selected by the contracting authority may submit tenders for the contract;

"work" means the outcome of any works which is sufficient of itself to fulfil an economic and technical function;

"working day" means a day other than a Saturday, Sunday or Bank Holiday within the meaning of the Banking and Financial Dealings Act 1971[4];

"works" means any of the activities specified in Schedule 1, being activities contained in the general industrial classification of economic activities within the Communities; and

"year" means a calendar year.

(2) The value in the currency of any member State of any amount expressed in these

---

[3] OJ No L379, 30.12.78, p. 1, as amended by Council Regulation (EEC) No. 2626/84 (OJ No. L247, 16.9.84, p. 1).

[4] 1971 c. 80.

Regulations in ECU shall be calculated by reference to the exchange rate for the time being applying for the purposes of Council Directive 71/305/EEC[5] as published from time to time in the Official Journal.[6]

(3) Where a thing is required to be done under these Regulations—

(a) within a period after an action is taken, the day on which that action was taken shall not be counted in the calculation of that period;
(b) within a certain period, that period must include 2 working days;
(c) within a period and the last day of that period is not a working day, the period shall be extended to include the following working day.

(4) References in these Regulations to a regulation are references to a regulation in these Regulations and references to a Schedule are references to a Schedule to these Regulations.

## Contracting authorities

**3.**—(1) For the purposes of these Regulations each of the following is a "contracting authority"—

(a) a Minister of the Crown,
(b) a government department,
(c) the House of Commons,
(d) the House of Lords,
(e) the Northern Ireland Assembly,
(f) a local authority,
(g) a fire authority constituted by a combination scheme under the Fire Services Act 1947,[7]
(h) the Fire Authority for Northern Ireland,
(i) a police authority constituted under section 2 of the Police Act 1964[8] or a combined police authority established by an amalgamation scheme under that Act,
(j) the Police Authority for Northern Ireland,
(k) an authority established under section 10 of the Local Government Act 1985,[9]
(l) a joint authority established by Part IV of that Act,
(m) any body established pursuant to an order under section 67 of that Act,
(n) the Broads Authority,
(o) any joint board the constituent members of which consist of any of the bodies specified in paragraphs (f), (g), (i), (k), (l), (m) and (n) above,
(p) a joint or special planning board constituted for a National Park by an order under paragraphs 1 or 3 of Schedule 17 to the Local Government Act 1972,[10] and
(q) a joint education board constituted under the provisions of Part I of the First Schedule to the Education Act 1944,[11]
(r) a corporation established, or a group of individuals appointed to act together, for

---

[5] OJ No. L185, 16.8.71, p. 5, as amended by Council Directive 89/440/EEC (OJ No. L210, 21.7.89, p. 1).
[6] The rates are determined for each successive period of 2 years by calculating the average of the daily exchange rates between each currency and the ECU over a period of 24 months preceding the determination. The exchange rates applying at the time of coming into force of these Regulations are published in OJ No. C18, 25.1.90, p. 3.
[7] 1947 c. 41.
[8] 1964 c. 48.
[9] 1985 c. 51.
[10] 1972 c. 70.
[11] 1944 c. 31.

the specific purpose of meeting needs in the general interest, not having an industrial or commercial character, and

(i) financed wholly or mainly by another contracting authority, or

(ii) subject to management supervision by another contracting authority, or

(iii) more than half of the board of directors or members of which, or in the case of a group of individuals, more than half of those individuals, being appointed by another contracting authority, and

(s) associations of or formed by one or more of the above.

(2) In the application of these Regulations to England and Wales, "local authority" in paragraph (1) above means—

(a) a county council, a district council, a London borough council, a parish council, a community council, or the Council of the Isles of Scilly;

(b) the Common Council of the City of London in its capacity as local authority or police authority.

(3) In the application of these Regulations to Scotland, "local authority" in paragraph (1) above means a regional, islands or district council or any joint board or joint committee within the meaning of section 235 of the Local Government (Scotland) Act 1973.[12]

(4) In the application of these Regulations to Northern Ireland, "local authority" in paragraph (1) above means a district council within the meaning of the Local Government Act (Northern Ireland) 1972.[13]

(5) Where an entity specified in paragraph (1) above does not have the capacity to enter into a contract, the contracting authority in relation to that entity means a person whose function it is to enter into contracts for that entity.

## Contractors

**4.**—(1) For the purposes of these Regulations a "contractor" means a person—

(a) who sought, or who seeks, or would have wished, to be the person to whom a public works contract is awarded, and

(b) who is national of and established in a member State.

(2) When these Regulations apply a contracting authority shall not treat a person who is not a national of and established in a member State more favourably than one who is.

## Application of the Regulations

**5.** These Regulations apply whenever a contracting authority seeks offers in relation to a proposed public works contract other than public works contracts excluded from the operation of these Regulations by regulations 6 and 7; except that in Parts II, III, IV and V of these Regulations and in regulations 24, 27 and 28 references to a "public works contract" shall not include a public works concession contract.

## General exclusions

**6.** These Regulations shall not apply to the seeking of offers in relation to a proposed public works contract—

[(a) for the purpose of carrying out an activity specified in the second column of

---

[12] 1973 c. 65.
[13] 1972 c. 9 (N.I.).

Schedule 1 to the Utilities Supply and Works Contracts Regulations 1992, other than an activity specified in paragraphs 2 or 3 thereof;
(b) when a contracting authority exercises the activity specified in paragraph 1 of Schedule 1 to the Utilities Supply and Works Contracts Regulations 1992, for the purpose of carrying out an activity specified in paragraph 2 or 3 thereof;]*
(d) which is classified as secret or where the carrying out of the work or works under it must be accompanied by special security measures in accordance with the laws, regulations or administrative provisions of any part of the United Kingdom, or when the protection of the basic interests of the security of the United Kingdom require it;
(e) where different procedures govern the procedures leading to the award of the contract and it is to be entered into—
  (i) pursuant to an international agreement to which the United Kingdom and a State which is not a member State are parties and it provides for the carrying out of works intended for the joint implementation or exploitation of a project pursuant to that agreement;
  (ii) pursuant to an international agreement relating to the stationing of troops; or
  (iii) in accordance with the contract award procedures of an organisation of which only States are members (an "international organisation") or of which only States or international organisations are members.

**Thresholds**

**7.**—(1) These Regulations shall not apply to the seeking of offers in relation to a proposed public works contract where the estimated value of the contract (net of value added tax) at the relevant time is less than 5,000,000 ECU.

(2) Subject to paragraphs (3), (5) and (6) below, the estimated value for the purposes of paragraph (1) above of a public works contract shall be the value of the consideration which the contracting authority expects to give under the contract.

(3) Subject to paragraphs (4) and (6) below, the estimated value for the purposes of paragraph (1) above of a public works contract which is one of a number of contracts entered into or to be entered into for the carrying out of a work shall be the aggregate of the value of the consideration which the contracting authority has paid or expects to give under all the contracts for the carrying out of the work.

(4) Paragraph (3) above shall not apply to any public works contract (unless the contracting authority chooses to apply that paragraph to that contract) if that contract has an estimated value (calculated in accordance with paragraph (2) above) of less than 1,000,000 ECU, and the aggregate value of that contract and of any other public works contract for the carrying out of the work in respect of which the contracting authority takes advantage of the disapplication of paragraph (3) above by virtue of this paragraph is less than 20 per cent of the aggregate of the value of the consideration which the contracting authority has paid or expects to pay under all the contracts for the carrying out of the work.

(5) Subject to paragraph (6) below, the estimated value for the purposes of paragraph (1) above of a public works concession contract shall be the value of the consideration which the contracting authority would expect to give for the carrying out of the work or works if it did not propose to grant a concession.

(6) Where a contracting authority intends to provide any goods to the person awarded the public works contract for the purpose of carrying out that contract, the value of the

* Publisher's note: Passage in square brackets amended by regulation 32 of the Utilities Supply and Works Contracts Regulations 1992.

consideration for the purposes of paragraphs (2) and (3) above shall be taken to include the estimated value at the relevant time of those goods.

(7) The relevant time for the purposes of paragraphs (1) and (6) above means, in relation to a public works contract, the date on which a contract notice would be sent to the Official Journal if the requirement to send such a notice applied to that contract in accordance with those Regulations.

(8) A contracting authority shall not enter into separate public works contracts with the intention of avoiding the application of these Regulations to those contracts.

PART II

TECHNICAL SPECIFICATIONS

**Technical specifications in the contract documents**                                    **B–02**

**8.**—(1) In this regulation—

"common technical specification" means a technical specification drawn up in accordance with a procedure recognised by the member States with a view to uniform application in all member States and which has been published in the Official Journal;

"essential requirements" means requirements relating to safety, health and certain other aspects in the general interest which the works must meet;

"European specification" means a common technical specification, a British standard implementing a European standard or a European technical approval;

"European standard" means a standard approved by the European Committee for Standardisation ("CEN") or by the European Committee for Electrotechnical Standardisation ("CENELEC") as a "European Standard" ("EN") or a "Harmonisation Document" ("HD") according to the Common Rules of those organisations;

"European technical approval" means an approval of the fitness for use of a product, issued by an approval body designated for the purpose by a member State, following a technical assessment of whether the product fulfils the essential requirements for building works, having regard to the inherent characteristics of the product and the defined conditions of application and use;

"standard" means a technical specification approved by a recognised standardising body for repeated and continuous application, compliance with which is in principle not compulsory;

"technical specifications" means the technical requirements defining the characteristics required of the work or works and of the materials and goods used in or for it or them (such as quality, performance, safety or dimensions) so that the works, work, materials and goods are described objectively in a manner which will ensure that they fulfil the use for which they are intended by the contracting authority. In relation to materials and goods, "technical specifications" include requirements in respect of quality assurance, terminology, symbols, tests and testing methods, packaging, marking and labelling. In relation to a work or works, they include requirements relating to design and costing, the testing, inspection and acceptance of a work or works, and the methods or techniques of construction.

(2) If a contracting authority wishes to lay down technical specifications which the work or works to be carried out under a public works contract and which the materials and goods used in or for it or them must meet it shall specify all such technical specifications in the contract documents.

(3) Subject to paragraph (4) below, the technical specifications in the contract

123

documents relating to a public works contract shall be defined by reference to any European specifications which are relevant.

(4) A contracting authority may define the technical specifications referred to in paragraph (3) above other than by reference to relevant European specifications if—

(a) the contracting authority is under an obligation to define the technical specifications by reference to technical requirements which are mandatory in the United Kingdom for the work or works to be carried out under the contract or for the materials or goods to be used in or for it or them, (but only to the extent that such an obligation is compatible with Community obligations);

(b) the relevant European specifications do not include provision for establishing conformity to, or it is technically impossible to establish satisfactorily that the work or works or the materials or goods do conform to, the relevant European specifications;

(c) subject to paragraph (5) below, application of the relevant European specifications would oblige the contracting authority to acquire a work, works, material or goods incompatible with equipment already in use or would entail disproportionate costs or disproportionate technical difficulties; or

(d) the work or works are of a genuinely innovative nature for which use of existing relevant European specifications would be inappropriate.

(5) A contracting authority may only define the technical specifications other than by reference to relevant European specifications on the grounds specified in paragraph (4)(c) above where the contracting authority has a clearly defined and recorded strategy for changing over, within a set period, to European specifications.

(6) A contracting authority shall state in the contract notice which of the circumstances specified in paragraph (4) above was the ground for defining the technical specifications other than by reference to European specifications or, if it is impossible to include this information in the contract notice, the contracting authority shall specify it in the contract documents and shall in any event keep a record of this information which, if the Commission or any member State requests it, it shall send to the Treasury for onward transmission to the Commission or member State which requested it.

(7) In the absence of European specifications relevant to the work or works to be carried out under a public works contract or to the materials or goods to be used in or for it or them, the technical specifications in the contract documents—

(a) shall be defined by reference to the British technical specifications recognised as complying with the basic requirements specified in any Council Directives on technical harmonisation in accordance with the procedures laid down in those directives and, in particular, in accordance with the procedures laid down in Council Directive 89/106/EEC on the approximation of laws, regulations and administrative procedures in the member States relating to construction products[14];

(b) may be defined by reference to British technical specifications relating to design and method of calculation and execution of a work or works and use of materials and goods;

(c) may be defined by reference to the following standards (and, if they are so defined, preference shall be given to the following standards in the order in which they are listed)—

    (i) British standards implementing international standards;

    (ii) other British standards and technical approvals; or

[14] OJ No. L40, 11.2.89, p. 12.

124

(iii) any other standards.

(8) Subject to paragraph (10) below, the contract documents relating to a public works contract shall not include technical specifications which refer to materials or goods of a specific make or source or to a particular process and which have the effect of favouring or eliminating particular contractors.

(9) Without prejudice to the generality of paragraph (8) above, references to trademarks, patents, types, origin or means of production shall not be incorporated into the technical specifications in the contract documents.

(10) Notwithstanding paragraph (8) and (9) above, a contracting authority may incorporate the references referred to in paragraphs (8) and (9) above into the technical specifications in the contract documents if—

(a) such references are justified by the subject of the contract, or
(b) the work or works to be carried out under the contract cannot otherwise be described by reference to technical specifications which are sufficiently precise and intelligible to all contractors, provided that the references are accompanied by the words "or equivalent".

PART III

## PROCEDURES LEADING TO THE AWARD OF A PUBLIC WORKS CONTRACT

**Prior information notices**                                                                    B–03

**9.** A contracting authority intending to seek offers in relation to a public works contract shall, as soon as possible after the decision approving the planning of the work or works, send to the Official Journal a notice, in a form substantially corresponding to that set out in Part A of Schedule 2, and containing the information therein specified in relation to the contract.

### Selection of contract award procedure

**10.**—(1) For the purpose of seeking offers in relation to a proposed public works contract (but, in the case of a public housing scheme works contract, subject to regulation 24) a contracting authority shall use the open procedure, the restricted procedure or the negotiated procedure and shall decide which of those procedures to use in accordance with the following paragraphs of this regulation.

(2) A contracting authority may use the negotiated procedure in the following circumstances—

(a) subject to paragraph (3) below, in the event that the procedure leading to the award of a public works contract by the contracting authority using the open or restricted procedure was discontinued—
    (i) because of irregular tenders, or
    (ii) following an evaluation made in accordance with regulation 11(7) or 12(4); and without prejudice to the generality of the meaning of the words "irregular tenders" a tender may be considered irregular if the *contractor* fails to meet the requirements of, or the tender offers variations on the requirements specified in, the contract documents where this is not permitted under the terms of the invitation to tender, or the work, works, materials or goods offered do not meet the technical specifications (within the meaning of regulation 8(1)) of the contracting authority;
(b) when the work or works are to be carried out under the contract purely for the purpose of research, experiment or development but not where the works are to be

carried out to establish commercial viability or to recover research and development costs;

(c)  exceptionally, when the nature of the work or works to be carried out under the
contract is such, or the risks attaching thereto are such, as not to permit prior
overall pricing;

(d)  subject to paragraph (3) below, in the absence of tenders or of appropriate tenders
in response to an invitation to tender by the contracting authority using the open
or restricted procedure;

(e)  when, for technical or artistic reasons, or for reasons connected with the protection
of exclusive rights, the work or works to be carried out under the contract may only
be carried out by a particular person;

(f)  when (but only if it is strictly necessary) for reasons of extreme urgency brought
about by events unforeseeable by, and not attributable to, the contracting
authority, the time limits specified in regulations 11, 12 and 13 if the open or
restricted procedures or the negotiated procedure pursuant to paragraphs (2)(a) to
(c) are used cannot be met;

(g)  subject to paragraph (4) below, when a contracting authority wants a person who
has entered into a public works contract with the contracting authority to carry out
additional works which through unforeseen circumstances were not included in
the project initially considered or in the original public works contract and—

  (i)  such works cannot for technical or economic reasons be carried out
separately from the works carried out under the original public works contract
without great inconvenience to the contracting authority, or

  (ii)  such works can be carried out separately from the works carried out under the
original public works contract but are strictly necessary by the later stages of
that contract; and

(h)  subject to paragraph (5) below, when a contracting authority wishes a person who
has entered into a public works contract with that contracting authority to carry out
new works which are a repetition of works carried out under the original contract
and which are in accordance with the project for the purpose of which the first
contract was entered into.

(3) A contracting authority shall not use the negotiated procedure pursuant to
paragraphs (2)(a) or (d) above unless the proposed terms of the contract are substantially
unaltered from the proposed terms of the contract in relation to which offers were sought
using the open or restricted procedure.

(4) A contracting authority shall not use the negotiated procedure pursuant to
paragraph (2)(g) above where the aggregate value of the consideration to be given under
contracts for the additional works exceeds 50 per cent of the value of the consideration
payable under the original contract; and, for the purposes of this paragraph, the value of
the consideration shall be taken to include the estimated value of any goods which the
contracting authority provided to the person awarded the contract for the purpose of
carrying out the contract.

(5) A contracting authority shall not use the negotiated procedure pursuant to
paragraph (2)(h) above unless the contract notice relating to the original contract stated
that a public works contract for new works which would be a repetition of the works carried
out under the original contract may be awarded using the negotiated procedure pursuant
to paragraph (2)(h) above and unless the procedure for the award of the new contract is
commenced within three years of the original contract being entered into.

(6) In all other circumstances the contracting authority shall use the open procedure or
the restricted procedure.

(7) A contracting authority using the negotiated procedure pursuant to paragraph (2)(d) above shall, if the Commission requests it, submit a report recording the fact that it has done so to the Treasury for onward transmission to the Commission.

## The open procedure

**11.**—(1) A contracting authority using the open procedure shall comply with the following paragraphs of this regulation.

(2) The contracting authority shall publicise its intention to seek offers in relation to the public works contract by sending to the Official Journal as soon as possible after forming the intention a notice, in a form substantially corresponding to that set out in Part B of Schedule 2, inviting tenders and containing the information therein specified in relation to the contract.

(3) Subject to paragraph (4) below, the date which the contracting authority shall fix as the last date for the receipt by it of tenders made in response to the contract notice shall be specified in the notice and shall be not less than 52 days from the date of despatch of the notice but, if the contract documents are too bulky to be supplied within this time or it is necessary that contractors be given the opportunity to inspect the site on which the work or works under the contract is or are to be carried out or documents relating to the contract documents, then that minimum period shall be extended to allow for such supply or inspection.

(4) Where the contracting authority has published a notice in accordance with regulation 9 in relation to the public works contract it may substitute for the period of not less than 52 days specified in paragraph (3) above a period of not less than 36 days.

(5) The contracting authority shall send the contract documents within 6 days of the receipt of a request from any contractor provided that the documents are requested in good time and any fee specified in the contract notice has accompanied the request.

(6) The contracting authority shall supply such further information relating to the contract documents as may reasonably be requested by a contractor provided that the request is received in sufficient time to enable the contracting authority to supply the information no later than 6 days before the date specified in the contract notice as the final date for the receipt of tenders.

(7) The contracting authority may exclude a tender from the evaluation of offers made in accordance with regulation 20 only if the contractor may be treated as ineligible to tender on a ground specified in regulation 14 or if the contractor fails to satisfy the minimum standards of economic and financial standing and technical capacity required of contractors by the contracting authority; for this purpose the contracting authority shall make its evaluation in accordance with regulations 14, 15, 16 and 17.

## The restricted procedure

**12.**—(1) A contracting authority using the restricted procedure shall comply with the following paragraphs of this regulation.

(2) The contracting authority shall publicise its intention to seek offers in relation to the public works contract by sending to the Official Journal as soon as possible after forming the intention a notice, in a form substantially corresponding to that set out in Part C of Schedule 2, inviting requests to be selected to tender and containing the information therein specified in relation to the contract.

(3) Subject to paragraph (14) below, the date which the contract authority shall fix as the last date for the receipt by it of requests to be selected to tender shall be specified in

the contract notice and shall be not less than 37 days from the date of the despatch of the notice.

(4) The contracting authority may exclude a contractor from those persons from whom it will make the selection of persons to be invited to tender only if the contractor may be treated as ineligible on a ground specified in regulation 14 or if the contractor fails to satisfy the minimum standards of economic and financial standing and technical capacity required of contractors by the contracting authority; for this purpose the contracting authority shall make its evaluation in accordance with regulations 14, 15, 16 and 17.

(5) The contracting authority shall make the selection of the contractors to be invited to tender in accordance with regulations 14, 15, 16 and 17; and in making the selection and in issuing invitations the contracting authority shall not discriminate between contractors on the grounds of their nationality or the member State in which they are established.

(6) The contracting authority may predetermine the range within which the number of persons which it intends to invite to tender for the contract shall be fixed but only if—

(a) the lower number of the range is not less than 5 and the higher number not more than 20,
(b) the range is determined in the light of the nature of the work to be carried out under the contract, and
(c) the range is specified in the contract notice.

(7) The number of persons invited to tender shall be sufficient to ensure genuine competition.

(8) The contracting authority shall send invitations to each of the contractors selected to tender and the invitation shall be accompanied by the contract documents, or the invitation shall state the address for requesting them.

(9) The invitation shall be sent in writing simultaneously to each contractor selected to tender.

(10) The following information shall be included in the invitation—

(a) the address to which requests for the contract documents (if not accompanying the invitation) and further information relating to those documents should be sent, the final date for making such a request and the amount and terms of the fee which may be charged for supplying that material;
(b) the final date for the receipt of tenders, the address to which they must be sent and the language or languages in which they must be drawn up;
(c) a reference to the contract notice published in accordance with paragraph (2) above;
(d) an indication of the information to be included with the tender which the contracting authority may require to be provided in accordance with regulations 15, 16 and 17; and
(e) the criteria for the award of the contract if this information was not specified in the contract notice published in accordance with paragraph (2) above.

(11) Subject to paragraphs (12) and (14) below, the date which the contracting authority shall fix as the last date for the receipt by it of tenders made in response to the invitation to tender which shall be specified in the invitation to tender in accordance with paragraph (10)(b) above shall not be less than 40 days from the date of the despatch of the invitation but, if it is necessary that contractors should be given the opportunity to inspect the premises on which the works under the contract are to be carried out or documents

relating to the contract documents, then that minimum period shall be extended to allow for such inspection.

(12) Subject to paragraph (14) below, where the contracting authority has published a notice in accordance with regulation 9 in relation to the public works contract, it may substitute for the period of not less than 40 days in paragraph (11) above a period of not less than 26 days.

(13) Subject to paragraph (14) below, the contracting authority shall supply such further information relating to the contract documents as may reasonably be requested by a contractor selected to tender provided that the request for such information is received in sufficient time to enable the contracting authority to supply it not less than 6 days before the date specified in the invitation to tender as the final date for the receipt of tenders.

(14) Where compliance with the minimum periods referred to in paragraphs (3), (11), (12) and (13) above is rendered impracticable for reasons of urgency, the contracting authority may substitute for the period specified in paragraph (3) a period of not less than 15 days and for the periods specified in (11) and (12) periods of not less than 10 days and for the period specified in paragraph (13) a period of not less than 4 days and, in those circumstances, the contracting authority must send the invitation to tender by the most rapid means possible.

(15) A contracting authority shall not refuse to consider an application to be invited to tender if it is made by letter, telegram, telex, facsimile or telephone provided that, in the last 4 cases, it is confirmed by letter before the date fixed by the contracting authority as the last date for the receipt of requests to be selected to tender.

## The negotiated procedure

**13.**—(1) A contracting authority using the negotiated procedure shall comply with the following provisions of this regulation except that—

(a) a contracting authority using the negotiated procedure pursuant to regulation 10(2)(d), (e), (f), (g) or (h), and

(b) a contracting authority using the negotiated procedure pursuant to regulation 10(2)(a) who invites to negotiate the contract every contractor who submitted a tender following an invitation made during the course of the discontinued open or restricted procedure (not being a tender which was excluded pursuant to regulation 11(7)),

need not comply with paragraphs (2) to (6) below.

(2) The contracting authority shall publicise its intention to seek offers in relation to the public works contract by sending to the Official Journal as soon as possible after forming the intention a notice, in a form substantially corresponding to that set out in Part D of Schedule 2, inviting requests to be selected to negotiate and containing the information therein specified in relation to the contract.

(3) Subject to paragraph (4) below, the date which the contracting authority shall fix as the last date for the receipt by it of requests to be selected to negotiate shall be specified in paragraph 6(a) of the contract notice and shall be not less than 37 days from the date of despatch of the notice.

(4) Where compliance with the minimum period of 37 days in paragraph (3) above is rendered impracticable for reasons of urgency, the contracting authority may substitute a period of not less than 15 days and, in those circumstances, the contracting authority may send the invitation to negotiate the contract by the most rapid means possible.

(5) Where there is a sufficient number of persons who are suitable to be selected to negotiate the contract, the number selected to negotiate shall be not less than 3.

(6) A contracting authority shall not refuse to consider an application to be selected to negotiate if it is made by letter, telegram, telex, facsimile or by telephone provided that, in the last 4 cases, it is confirmed by letter before the date fixed by the contracting authority as the last date for the receipt of requests to be selected to negotiate.

(7) The contracting authority may exclude a contractor from those persons from whom it will make the selection of persons to be invited to negotiate the contract only if the supplier may be treated as ineligible on a ground specified in regulation 14 or if the contractor fails to satisfy the minimum standards of economic and financial standing and technical capacity required of contractors by the contracting authority; for this purpose the contracting authority shall make its evaluation in accordance with regulations 14, 15, 16 and 17.

(8) The contracting authority shall make the selection of the contractors to be invited to negotiate in accordance with regulations 14, 15, 16 and 17; and in making the selection and in issuing the invitations to negotiate the contracting authority shall not discriminate between contractors on the grounds of their nationality or the member State in which they are established.

## PART IV

## SELECTION OF CONTRACTORS

**B–04**   **Criteria for rejection of contractors**

14.—(1) A contracting authority may treat a contractor as ineligible to tender for, or to be included amongst those persons from whom it will make the selection of persons to be invited to tender for or to negotiate a public works contract in accordance with regulations 11(7), 12(4), and 13(7), or decide not to select a contractor to tender for or to negotiate a public works contract in accordance with regulations 12(5) and 13(8) on one of the following grounds, namely that the contractor—

    (a)  being an individual is bankrupt or has had a receiving order or administration order made against him or has made any composition or arrangement with or for the benefit of his creditors or has made any conveyance or assignment for the benefit of his creditors or appears unable to pay, or to have no reasonable prospect of being able to pay, a debt within the meaning of section 268 of the Insolvency Act 1968,[15] or article 242 of the Insolvency (Northern Ireland) Order 1989,[16] or in Scotland has granted a trust deed for creditors or become otherwise apparently insolvent, or is the subject of a petition presented for sequestration of his estate, or is the subject of any similar procedure under the law of any other state;

    (b)  being a partnership constituted under Scots law has granted a trust deed or become otherwise apparently insolvent, or is the subject of a petition presented for sequestration of its estate;

    (c)  being a company has passed a resolution or is the subject of an order by the court for the company's winding up otherwise than for the purposes of bona fide reconstruction or amalgamation, or has had a receiver, manager or administrator on behalf of a creditor appointed in respect of the company's business or any part thereof or is the subject of proceedings for any of the above procedures or is the subject of similar procedures under the law of any other state;

---

[15] 1986 c. 45.
[16] S.I. 1989/2405 (N.I. 19).

(d) has been convicted of a criminal offence relating to the conduct of his business or profession;
(e) has committed an act of grave misconduct in the course of his business or profession;
(f) has not fulfilled obligations relating to the payment of social security contributions under the law of any part of the United Kingdom or of the member State in which the contractor is established;
(g) has not fulfilled obligations relating to the payment of taxes under the law of any part of the United Kingdom;
(h) is guilty of serious misrepresentation in providing any information required of him under this regulation and regulations 15, 16 and 17; or
(i) subject to paragraphs (5) and (6) below, is not registered on the professional or trade register of the member State in which the contractor is established under the conditions laid down by that State.

(2) Subject to regulation 18, the contracting authority may require a contractor to provide such information as it considers it needs to make the evaluation in accordance with paragraph (1) above except that it shall accept as conclusive evidence that a contractor does not fall within the grounds specified in paragraphs (1)(a), (b), (c), (d), (f), or (g) above if that contractor provides to the contracting authority—

(a) in relation to the grounds specified in paragraphs (1)(a), (b), (c) or (d) above,
  (i) an extract from the judicial record, or
  (ii) in a member State which does not maintain such a judicial record, a document issued by the relevant judicial or administrative authority;
(b) in relation to the grounds specified in paragraph (1)(f) or (g) above, a certificate issued by the relevant competent authority;
(c) in a member State where the documentary evidence specified in paragraphs (2)(a) and (b) above is not issued in relation to one of the grounds specified in paragraph (1)(a), (b), (c), (d), (f) or (g) above, a declaration on oath made by the contractor before the relevant judicial, administrative or competent authority or a relevant notary public or commissioner for oaths.

(3) In this regulation, "relevant" in relation to a judicial, administrative or competent authority, notary public or commissioner for oaths means an authority designated by, or a notary public or commissioner for oaths in, the member State in which the contractor is established.

(4) The following are the appropriate professional or trade registers for the purposes of paragraph (1)(i) above—

in Belgium, the registre du commerce/Handelsregister;
in Denmark, the Erhvervs- and Selskabsstyrelsen;
in France, the registre du commerce or the répertoire des métiers;
in Germany, the Handelsregister or the Handwerksrolle;
in Italy, the Registro della Camera di commercio, industria, agricultura e artigianato;
in Luxembourg, the registre aux firmes and the rôle de la Chambre des métiers;
in the Netherlands, the Handelsregister;
in Portugal, the Commissão de Alvarás de Empresas de Obras Públicas e Particulares ("CAEOPP"); and
in Spain, the Registro Oficial de Contratistas de Ministerio de Industria y Energia.

(5) A contractor established in the United Kingdom or Ireland shall be treated as registered on the professional or trade register for the purposes of paragraph (1)(i) above if the contractor—

(a) is established in Ireland and is certified as registered with the Registrar of Friendly Societies, or

(b) is established in either State and is either—

    (i) certified as incorporated by the Registrar of Companies, or

    (ii) is certified as having declared on oath that he is carrying on business in the trade in question in the State in which he is established at a specific place of business and under a specific trading name.

(6) A contractor established in Greece shall be treated as registered on the professional or trade register for the purposes of paragraph (1)(i) if the contractor is certified as having declared on oath before a notary public that he exercises the profession of public works contractor.

## Information as to economic and financial standing

**15.**—(1) Subject to regulation 18 and paragraph (2) below, in assessing whether a contractor meets any minimum standards of economic and financial standing required of contractors by the contracting authority for the purposes of regulations 11(7), 12(4) and 13(7), and in selecting the contractors to be invited to tender for or to negotiate the contract in accordance with regulations 12(5) and 13(8), a contracting authority shall only take into account any of the following information (and it may require a contractor to provide such of that information as it considers it needs to make the assessment or selection)—

(a) appropriate statements from the contractor's bankers;

(b) statement of accounts or extracts therefrom relating to the business of the contractor where publication of the statement is required under the law of the Member State in which the contractor is established;

(c) a statement of the overall turnover of the business of the contractor and the turnover in respect of works in the 3 previous financial years of the contractor.

(2) Where the information specified in paragraph (1) above is not appropriate in a particular case a contracting authority may require a contractor to provide other information to demonstrate the contractor's economic and financial standing.

(3) A contracting authority which requires information to be provided in accordance with paragraphs (1) and (2) above, shall specify in the contract notice or in the invitation to tender the information which the contractor must provide.

(4) Where a contractor is unable for a valid reason to provide the information which the contracting authority has required, the contracting authority shall accept such other information provided by the contractor as the contracting authority considers appropriate.

## Information as to technical capacity

**16.**—(1) Subject to regulation 18, in assessing whether a contractor meets any minimum standards of technical capacity required of contractors by the contracting authority for the purposes of regulations 11(7), 12(4) and 13(7), and in selecting the contractors to be invited to tender for or to negotiate the contract in accordance with regulations 12(5) and 13(8), a contracting authority shall only take into account any of the following information (and it may require a contractor to provide such of that information as it considers it needs to make the assessment or selection)—

(a) a list of the contractor's educational and professional qualifications where the contractor is an individual and a list of such qualifications of the contractor's managerial staff if any and those of the person or persons who would be responsible for carrying out the works under the contract;

(b) a list of works carried out over the past 5 years together with (unless the contracting authority specifies that the following certificates should be submitted direct to the contracting authority by the person certifying) certificates of satisfactory completion for the most important of those works indicating in each case the value of the consideration received, when and where the works were carried out and specifying whether they were carried out according to the rules of the trade or profession and properly completed;

(c) a statement of the tools, plant and technical equipment available to the contractor for carrying out the work under the contract;

(d) a statement of the contractor's average annual manpower and the number of managerial staff over the previous 3 years;

(e) a statement of the technicians or technical services which the contractor may call upon for the carrying out of the work under the contract, whether or not the technicians or persons providing the technical services are independent of the contractor.

(2) The contracting authority shall specify in the contract notice which of the nformation specified in paragraph (1) above it requires to be provided.

## Supplementary information

**17.** Subject to regulation 18, the contracting authority may require a contractor to provide information supplementing the information provided in accordance with regulations 14, 15 and 16 or to clarify that information, provided that the information so required relates to the matters specified in regulations 14, 15 and 16.

## Official lists of recognised contractors

**18.** Where a contractor is registered on the official list of recognised contractors in a Member State which maintains such lists and in which the contractor is established and the contractor submits to the contracting authority a certificate of registration issued by the authority administering the official list which specifies the information submitted to that authority which enabled the contractor to be registered and which states the classification given, the contracting authority, to the extent that the certificate deals with the grounds referred to in regulation 14(1)(a) to (e), (h), and (i), 15(1)(b) and (c) and 16(1)(b) and (d)—

(a) shall accept the certificate as evidence that the contractor does not fall within the grounds specified in regulation 14(1)(a) to (e), (h) and (i) and shall not be entitled to require the contractor to submit such information relating to those grounds as is specified in regulation 14,

(b) shall not be entitled to require the contractor to provide information specified in regulations 15(1)(b) and (c) and 16(1)(b) and (d), and

(c) shall not be entitled to seek any supplementary information in accordance with regulation 17 in relation to the matters specified in paragraphs (a) and (b) above.

## Consortium

**19.**—(1) In this regulation a "consortium" means 2 or more persons, at least one of whom is a contractor, acting jointly for the purpose of being awarded a public works contract.

(2) A contracting authority shall not treat the tender of a consortium as ineligible nor decide not to include a consortium amongst those persons from whom it will make the

133

selection of persons to be invited to tender for or to negotiate a public works contract on the grounds that the consortium has not formed a legal entity for the purposes of tendering for or negotiating the contract; but where a contracting authority awards a public works contract to a consortium it may require the consortium to form a legal entity before entering into, or as a term of, the contract.

(3) In these Regulations references to a contractor or to a concessionaire where the contractor or concessionaire is a consortium includes a reference to each person who is a member of that consortium.

PART V

**THE AWARD OF A PUBLIC WORKS CONTRACT**

**B–05**   **Criteria for the award of a public works contract**

20.—(1) Subject to paragraphs (6) and (7) below, a contracting authority shall award a public works contract on the basis of the offer which—

(a)  offers the lowest price, or
(b)  is the most economically advantageous to the contracting authority.

(2) The criteria which a contracting authority may use to determine that an offer is the most economically advantageous include price, period for completion, running costs, profitability and technical merit.

(3) Where a contracting authority intends to award a public works contract on the basis of the offer which is the most economically advantageous it shall state the criteria on which it intends to base its decision, where possible in descending order of importance, in the contract notice or in the contract documents.

(4) Where a contracting authority awards a public works contract on the basis of the offer which is the most economically advantageous, it may take account of offers which offer variations on the requirements specified in the contract documents if the offer meets the minimum requirements of the contracting authority and it has indicated in the contract notice that offers offering variations will be considered and has stated in the contract documents the minimum requirements which the offer must meet and any specific requirements for the presentation of an offer offering variations.

(5) A contracting authority may not reject a tender on the ground that the technical specifications in the tender have been defined by reference to European specifications (within the meaning of regulation 8(1)) or to the national technical specifications specified in regulation 8(7)(a) and (b).

(6) If an offer for a public works contract is abnormally low the contracting authority may reject that offer but only if it has requested in writing an explanation of the offer or of those parts which it considers contribute to the offer being abnormally low and has—

(a)  if awarding the contract on the basis of the offer which offers the lowest price, examined the details of all the offers made, taking into account any explanation given to it of the abnormally low tender, before awarding the contract, or
(b)  if awarding the contract on the basis of the offer which is the most economically advantageous, taken any such explanation into account in assessing which is the most economically advantageous offer,

and, in considering that explanation, the contracting authority may take into account explanations which justify the offer on objective grounds including the economy of the construction method, the technical solutions suggested by the contractor or the exceptionally favourable conditions available to the contractor for the carrying out of the works or the originality of the works proposed by the contractor.

(7) If a contracting authority which rejects an abnormally low offer is awarding the contract on the basis of the offer which offers the lowest price, it shall send a report justifying the rejection to the Treasury for onward transmission to the Commission.

(8) For the purposes of this regulation an "offer" includes a bid by one part of a contracting authority to carry out work or works for another part of the contracting authority when the former part is invited by the latter part to compete with the offers sought from other persons.

## Contract award notice

**21.**—(1) A contracting authority which has awarded a public works contract shall, no later than 48 days after the award, send to the Official Journal a notice, substantially corresponding to the form set out in Part E of Schedule 2 and, subject to paragraph (2) below, including the information therein specified in relation to the contract.

(2) Any of the information specified in Part E of Schedule 2 to be included in the contract award notice may be omitted in a particular case where to publish such information would impede law enforcement, would otherwise be contrary to the public interest, would prejudice the legitimate commercial interests of any person or might prejudice fair competition between contractors.

## Information about contract award procedures

**22.**—(1) A contracting authority which has awarded a public works contract shall, within 15 days of the date on which it receives a request from any contractor who was unsuccessful (whether pursuant to regulation 11(7), 12(4), 12(5), 13(7), 13(8) or 20), inform that contractor of the reasons why he was unsuccessful and, if the contractor was unsuccessful as a result of the evaluation of offers made in accordance with regulation 20, the name of the person awarded the contract.

(2) A contracting authority shall prepare a record in relation to each public works contract awarded by it specifying—

(a) the name and address of the contracting authority;
(b) the work or works to be carried out under the contract and the value of the consideration to be given under it;
(c) the names of the persons whose offers were evaluated in accordance with regulation 20 and, where the contracting authority has used the restricted or negotiated procedure, the reasons for their selection;
(d) the names of the persons who were unsuccessful pursuant to regulation 11(7), 12(4), 12(5), 13(7) or 13(8);
(e) the name of the person to whom the contract was awarded and the reasons for having awarded the contract to him;
(f) if known to the contracting authority, the works under the contract which the person to whom the contract has been awarded intends to sub-contract to another person;
(g) in the case of a contracting authority which used the negotiated procedure, which of the circumstances specified in regulation 10(2) constituted the grounds for using that procedure.

(3) If the Commission requests a report in relation to a public works contract containing the information specified in paragraph (2) above, the contracting authority shall send a

written report containing that information, or the main features of it, to the Treasury for onward transmission to the Commission.

(4) Where a contracting authority decides not to award a public works contract in respect of which a contract notice was published nor to seek offers in relation to another public works contract for the same purpose it shall inform the Official Journal of that decision and shall, if so requested by any contractor who submitted an offer or who applied to be included amongst the persons to be selected to tender for or negotiate the contract, the reasons for its decision.

PART VI

**MISCELLANEOUS**

B–06    **Subsidised works contracts**

23.—(1) Where a contracting authority undertakes to contribute more than half of the consideration to be or expected to be paid under a contract to which this paragraph applies by virtue of paragraph (2) below which has been or is to be entered into by a person other than another contracting authority (in this paragraph referred to as "the subsidised body"), that contracting authority shall—

(a)  make it a condition of the making of such contribution that the subsidised body complies with the provisions of these Regulations in relation to that contract as if it were a contracting authority, and

(b)  ensure that the subsidised body does so comply or recover the contribution.

(2) Paragraph (1) above applies to a contract which would be a public works contract if the subsidised body were a contracting authority and which is for the carrying out of any of the activities specified in Schedule 1 as are included in Group 502 or for the carrying out of building work for hospitals, facilities intended for sports, recreation and leisure, school and university building or buildings for administrative purposes.

**Public housing scheme works contracts**

24.—(1) For the purpose of seeking offers in relation to a public housing scheme works contract, where the size and complexity of the scheme and the estimated duration of the works involved require that the planning of the scheme be based from the outset on a close collaboration of a team comprising representatives of the contracting authority, experts and the contractor, a contracting authority may, except as indicated in the following paragraphs, depart from the provisions of these Regulations insofar as it is necessary to do so to select the contractor who is most suitable for integration into the team.

(2) The contracting authority shall comply with the provisions of regulation 12(1) to (5).

(3) The contracting authority shall include in the contract notice a job description which is as accurate as possible so as to enable contractors to form a valid idea of the scheme and of the minimum standards relating to the business or professional status, the economic and financial standing and the technical capacity which the person awarded the contract will be expected to fulfil.

**Public works concession contracts**

25.—(1) A contracting authority seeking offers in relation to a public works concession contract shall comply with the following paragraphs of this regulation.

(2) The contracting authority shall publicise its intention to seek offers in relation to the

136

contract by sending to the Official Journal as soon as possible after forming the intention a notice in a form substantially corresponding to that set out in Part F of Schedule 2 and containing the information therein specified in relation to the concession contract.

(3) The date which the contracting authority shall fix as the last date for the receipt by it of tenders or of requests to be selected to tender for or negotiate the contract, as the case may be, shall be specified in paragraph 3(a) of the notice and shall be not less than 52 days from the date of despatch of the notice.

## Sub-contracting the work or works to be carried out under a public works concession contract

**26.**—(1) A contracting authority seeking offers in relation to a public works concession contract shall either—

(a) include in the invitation to tender for, or to apply to be selected to tender for or to negotiate, the concession contract a request that the applicant specify whether he would intend, if awarded the concession contract, to sub-contract to persons who are not affiliated to him any of the work or works to be carried out under the concession contract and, if so, how much as a proportion of the value of such work or works would be so sub-contracted, or

(b) require as a term of the concession contract—

    (i) that the concessionaire sub-contract to persons who are not affiliated to the concessionaire some or all of the work or works to be carried out under the concession contract, and

    (ii) that the amount of the works so sub-contracted be not less than 30%, or such higher percentage as may be specified in the contract at the option of the contracting authority or the concessionaire, of the value of the consideration which the contracting authority would expect to give for the carrying out of the work or works if it did not grant a concession.

(2) Where the concessionaire is a contracting authority that contracting authority shall comply with the provisions of these Regulations in respect of public works contracts it seeks offers in relation to for the purpose of sub-contracting the work or works to be carried out under the public works concession contract.

(3) Where the concessionaire is not a contracting authority the concessionaire shall—

(a) publicise his intention to seek offers in relation to any contract to which this paragraph applies by virtue of paragraph (4) below by sending to the Official Journal as soon as possible after forming the intention a notice in a form substantially corresponding to that set out in Part G of Schedule 2 and containing the information therein specified in relation to the contract;

(b) comply with regulation 30 in relation to that notice as if the concessionaire were a contracting authority;

(c) if that notice invites tenders, fix as the last date for the receipt by the concessionaire of tenders a date of not less than 40 days from the date of the despatch of the notice and specify that date in paragraph 4(a) of the notice; and

(d) if the notice invites applications to be selected to tender for or negotiate the contract—

    (i) fix as the last date for the receipt of such applications a date not less than 37 days from the date of despatch of the notice and specify that date in paragraph 4(a) of the notice; and

    (ii) fix as the last date for the receipt of tenders following selection of the persons to be invited to tender a date not less than 40 days from the date of despatch of the invitation and specify that date in the invitation.

137

(4) Paragraph (3) above applies to a contract—

(a) in relation to which the concessionaire is seeking offers for the purpose of sub-contracting any of the work or works to be carried out under the public works concession contract,

(b) which the concessionaire does not intend to enter into with a person affiliated to him,

(c) which would, if the concessionaire were a contracting authority, be a public works contract other than a public works contract in respect of which a contracting authority would be entitled to use the negotiated procedure pursuant to regulation 10(2)(d) to (h).

(5) For the purposes of this regulation a person is to be treated as affiliated to another person if either exercises, directly or indirectly, a dominant influence over the other or any person exercises, directly or indirectly, a dominant influence over both of them or if they are both members of any consortium formed for the purpose of performing the public works concession contract; and a person shall be taken to exercise a dominant influence over another person—

(a) if he possesses the greater part of the issued share capital of that person or controls the voting power attached to such greater part, or

(b) if he may appoint more than half of the individuals who are ultimately responsible for managing that person's affairs.

(6) A contracting authority shall require applicants for a public works concession contract to submit a list of all persons affiliated to the applicant with the application and to update that list from time to time to take account of any changes in the persons affiliated to the applicant.

## Obligations relating to employment protection and working conditions

**27.** A contracting authority which includes in the contract documents relating to a public works contract information as to where a contractor may obtain information about obligations relating to employment protection and working conditions which will apply to the works to be carried out under the contract, shall request contractors to indicate that they have taken account of those obligations in preparing their tender or in negotiating the contract.

## Statistical and other reports

**28.**—(1) A contracting authority shall, no later than 31st July 1993 and 31st July in each alternate year thereafter, send to the Treasury a report specifying in relation to each public works contract awarded by it during the year preceding the year in which the report is made—

(a) the value (estimated if necessary) of the consideration payable under the contract;

(b) whether the open, restricted or negotiated procedure was used in awarding the contract;

(c) if the negotiated procedure was used, pursuant to which provision of regulation 10(2) that procedure was used;

(d) the principal category of works carried or to be carried out under the contract; and

(e) the nationality of the person to whom the contract was awarded.

(2) A contracting authority shall send to the Treasury a report containing such other information as the Treasury may from time to time require in respect of a particular public works contract (including public works contracts excluded from the application of these Regulations by regulations 6 and 7) for the purpose of informing the Commission.

## Responsibility for obtaining reports

**29.**—(1) Where a contracting authority is not a Minister of the Crown or a government department, that contracting authority shall send any report which it is required in accordance with regulations 8(6), 10(7), 20(7), 22(3) and 28 to send to the Treasury instead to the Minister responsible for that contracting authority and that Minister shall be responsible for sending the report to the Treasury.

(2) The Minister responsible for a contracting authority shall be the Minister of the Crown whose areas of responsibility are most closely connected with the functions of the contracting authority; and any question as to which Minister of the Crown's areas of responsibility are most closely connected with the functions of a contracting authority shall be determined by the Treasury whose determination shall be final.

(3) The requirement on a contracting authority to send any report in accordance with paragraph (1) above to the Minister of the Crown responsible for that contracting authority shall be enforceable, on the application of the Minister responsible, by mandamus or, in Scotland, for an order for specific performance.

(4) Proceedings under paragraph (3) above brought in Scotland shall be brought before the Court of Session.

(5) In the application of this regulation to Northern Ireland references to the Minister shall include references to the head of a Northern Ireland department.

## Publication of notices

**30.**—(1) Any notice required by these Regulations to be sent to the Official Journal shall be sent by the most appropriate means to the Office for Official Publications of the European Communities[17] and where the contracting authority is applying the restricted procedure or the negotiated procedure and, for reasons of urgency, is applying the provisions of regulations 12(14) and 13(4), the notice shall be sent by telex, telegram or telefax.

(2) Any such notice shall not contain more than 650 words.

(3) The contracting authority shall retain evidence of the date of despatch to the Official Journal of each notice.

(4) The contracting authority shall not place a contract notice in the press or like publications in the United Kingdom before the date on which the notice is despatched in accordance with paragraph (1) above and if it does after that date, so place the notice it shall not add to the notice any information in relation to the contract which was not contained in the notice sent to the Official Journal.

PART VII

## APPLICATIONS TO THE COURT

### Enforcement of obligations relating to a public works contract                    B–07

**31.**—(1) The obligation on a contracting authority to comply with the provisions of these Regulations other than regulations 8(6), 10(7), 20(7), 22(3), 28 and 29(1), *and* with any enforceable Community obligation in respect of a public works contract (other than one excluded from the application of these Regulations by regulations 6 and 7), and the

---

[17] The address for the Office for Official Publications of the European Communities is 2 Rue Mercier, 2985, Luxembourg (tel: 499 28–1, telex: 1324 pubof lu, fax: 49 00 03, 49 57 19).

obligation on a concessionaire to comply with the provisions of regulation 26(3) is a duty owed to contractors.

(2) In this regulation and notwithstanding regulation 4, references to a "contractor" *include*, where the duty owed pursuant to paragraph (1) above is the obligation on a concessionaire to comply with regulation 26(3), any person—

(a) who sought, or who seeks, or would have wished, to be the person to whom a contract to which regulation 26(3) applies is awarded, and

(b) who is a national of and established in a member State.

(3) A breach of the duty owed pursuant to paragraph (1) above shall not be a criminal offence but any breach of the duty shall be actionable by any contractor who, in consequence, suffers, or risks suffering, loss or damage.

(4) Proceedings under this regulation shall be brought in England and Wales and in Northern Ireland in the High Court and, in Scotland, before the Court of Session.

(5) Proceedings under this regulation may not be brought *unless*—

(a) the contractor bringing the proceedings has informed the contracting authority or concessionaire, as the case may be, of the breach or apprehended breach of the duty owed to him pursuant to paragraph (1) above by that contracting authority or concessionaire and of his intention to bring proceedings under this regulation in respect of it; and

(b) they are brought promptly and in any event within 3 *months* from the date when grounds for the bringing of the proceedings first arose unless the Court considers that there is good reason for extending the period within which proceedings may be brought.

(6) Subject to paragraph (7) below, but otherwise without prejudice to any other powers of the Court, in proceedings brought under this regulation the Court *may*—

(a) by interim order suspend the procedure leading to the award of the contract in relation to the award of which the breach of the duty owed pursuant to paragraph (1) above is alleged, or suspend the implementation of any decision or action taken by the contracting authority or concessionaire, as the case may be, in the course of following such a procedure; and

(b) if satisfied that a decision or action taken by a contracting authority was in breach of the duty owed pursuant to paragraph (1) above—

(i) order the setting aside of that decision or action or order the contracting authority to amend any document, or

(ii) award damages to a contractor who has suffered loss or damage as a consequence of the breach, or

(iii) do both of those things.

(7) In proceedings under this regulation the Court shall not have power to order any remedy other than an award of damages in respect of a breach of the duty owed pursuant to paragraph (1) above if the contract in relation to which the breach occurred has been entered into.

(8) Notwithstanding sections 21 and 42 of the Crown Proceedings Act 1947,[18] in proceedings brought under this regulation against the Crown the court shall have power to grant an injunction or interdict.

*Irvine Patnick*
*Thomas Sackville*
28th November 1991          Two of the Lords Commissioners of Her Majesty's Treasury

## SCHEDULE 1          Regulation 2(1)          B—09

### ACTIVITIES CONSTITUTING WORKS

| Classes | Groups | Subgroups and items | Descriptions |
|---|---|---|---|
| 50 | | | BUILDING AND CIVIL ENGINEERING |
| | 500 | | General building and civil engineering work (without any particular specialisation) and demolition work |
| | | 500.1 | General building and civil engineering work (without any particular specialisation) |
| | | 500.2 | Demolition work |
| | 501 | | Construction of flats, office blocks, hospitals and other buildings, both residential and non-residential |
| | | 501.1 | General building contractors |
| | | 501.2 | Roofing |
| | | 501.3 | Construction of chimneys, kilns and furnaces |
| | | 501.4 | Waterproofing and damp-proofing |
| | | 501.5 | Restoration and maintenance of outside walls (repainting, cleaning, etc.) |
| | | 501.6 | Erection and dismantlement of scaffolding |
| | | 501.7 | Other specialised activities relating to construction work (including carpentry) |
| | 502 | | Civil engineering: construction of roads, bridges, railways, etc. |
| | | 502.1 | General civil engineering work |
| | | 502.2 | Earth-moving (navvying) |
| | | 502.3 | Construction of bridges, tunnels and shafts, drilling |
| | | 502.4 | Hydraulic engineering (rivers, canals, harbours, flows, locks and dams) |
| | | 502.5 | Road-building (including specialised construction of airports and runways) |
| | | 502.6 | Specialised construction work relating to water (i.e. to irrigation, land drainage, water supply, sewage disposal, sewerage, etc.) |
| | | 502.7 | Specialised activities in other areas of civil engineering |

[18] 1947 c. 44; the Crown Proceedings Act 1947 was extended to Northern Ireland in relation to Her Majesty's Government in the United Kingdom and in Northern Ireland by and with the additions, exceptions and modifications set out in the Crown Proceedings (Northern Ireland) Order 1981, S.I. 1981/233, to which there is an amendment not relevant to these regulations.

| Classes | Groups | Subgroups and items | Descriptions |
|---|---|---|---|
| | 503 | | Installation (fittings and fixtures) |
| | | 503.1 | General installation work |
| | | 503.2 | Gas fitting and plumbing, and the installation of sanitary equipment |
| | | 503.3 | Installation of heating and ventilating apparatus (central heating, air condition, ventilation) |
| | | 503.4 | Sound and heat insulation, insulation against vibration |
| | | 503.5 | Electrical fittings |
| | | 503.6 | Installation of aerials, lightning conductors, telephones etc. |
| | 504 | | Building completion work |
| | | 504.1 | General building completion work |
| | | 504.2 | Plastering |
| | | 504.3 | Joinery, primarily engaged in on the site assembly and/or installation (including the laying of parquet flooring) |
| | | 504.4 | Painting, glazing, paper hanging |
| | | 504.5 | Tiling and otherwise covering floors and walls |
| | | 504.6 | Other building completion work (putting in fireplaces, etc.) |

## SCHEDULE 2

Regulations 9, 11(2), 12(2) 13(2), 25(2), and 26(3

### FORMS OF NOTICES FOR PUBLICATION IN THE OFFICIAL JOURNAL

#### PART A

#### PRIOR INFORMATION NOTICE

1. The name, address, telegraphic address, telephone, telex and facsimile numbers o the contracting authority.

2. (a) The site.
   (b) The nature and extent of the services to be provided and, where relevant, the main characteristics of any lots by reference to the work.
   (c) If available: an estimate of the cost range of the proposed services.

3. (a) Estimated date for initiating the award procedures in respect of the contract o contracts.
   (b) If known: estimated date for the start of the work.
   (c) If known: estimated timetable for completion of the work.

4. If known: terms of financing of the work and of price revision and/or references to the provisions in which these are contained.

5. Other information.

6. Date of despatch of the notice.

#### PART B

#### OPEN PROCEDURE NOTICE

1. The name, address, telephone number, telegraphic address, telex and facsimile numbers of the contracting authority.

2. (a) The award procedure chosen.

(b) Nature of the contract for which tenders are being requested.

3. (a) The site.
   (b) The nature and extent of the services to be provided and general nature of the work.
   (c) If the work or the contract is subdivided into several lots, the size of the different lots and the possibility of tendering for one, for several or for all of the lots.
   (d) Information concerning the purpose of the work or the contract where the latter also involves the drawing up of projects.

4. Any time limit for completion.

5. (a) Name and address of the service from which the contract documents and additional documents may be requested.
   (b) Where applicable, the amount and terms of payment of the sum to be paid to obtain such documents.

6. (a) The final date for receipt of tenders.
   (b) The address to which they must be sent.
   (c) The language or languages in which they must be drawn up.

7. (a) Where applicable, the persons authorised to be present at the opening of tenders.
   (b) The date, hour and place of such opening.

8. Any deposit and guarantees required.

9. Main terms concerning financing, and payment and/or references to the provisions in which these are contained.

10. Where applicable, the legal form to be taken by the grouping of contractors to whom the contract is awarded.

11. Minimum standards of economic and financial standing and technical capacity required of the contractor to whom the contract is awarded.

12. Period during which the tenderer is bound to keep open his tender.

13. The criteria for the award of the contract. Criteria other than that of the lowest price paid shall be mentioned where they do not appear in the contract documents.

14. Where applicable, prohibition on variants.

15. Other information.

16. Date of publication of the prior information notice in the *Official Journal of the European Communities* or references to its non-publication.

17. Date of despatch of the notice.

## Part C

### Restricted Procedure Notice

1. The name, address, telephone number, telex and facsimile numbers of the contracting authority.

2. (a) The award procedure chosen.
   (b) Where applicable, justification for the use of the shorter time limits.[19]

[19] In accordance with regulation 12.

   (c)  Nature of the contract which tenders are being requested.

3. (a) The site.
   (b)  The nature and extent of the services to be provided and general nature of the work.
   (c)  If the work of the contract is subdivided into several lots the size of the different lots and the possibility of tendering for one, for several or for all of the lots.
   (d)  Information concerning the purpose of the work or the contract where the latter also involves the drawing up of projects.

4. Any time limit for completion.

5. Where applicable, the legal form to be taken by the grouping of contractors to whom the contract is awarded.

6. (a) The final date for receipt of requests to participate.
   (b)  The address to which they must be sent.
   (c)  The language or languages in which they must be drawn up.

7. The final date for despatch of invitations to tender.

8. Any deposit and guarantees required.

9. Main terms concerning financing and payment and/or provisions in which these are contained.

10. Information concerning the contractor's personal position and minimum standards of economic and financial standing and technical capacity required of the contractor to whom the contract is awarded.

11. The criteria for the award of the contract where they are not mentioned in the invitation to tender.

12. Where applicable, prohibition on variants.

13. Other information.

14. Date of publication of the prior information notice in the *Official Journal of the European Communities* or reference to its non-publication.

15. Date of despatch of the notice.

PART D

NEGOTIATED PROCEDURE NOTICE

1. The name, address, telegraphic address, telephone, telex and facsimile numbers of the contracting authority.

2. (a) The award procedure chosen.
   (b)  Where applicable, justification for the use of the shorter time limits.[20]
   (c)  Nature of the contract for which tenders are being requested.

3. (a) The site.
   (b)  The nature and extent of the services to be provided and general nature of the work.
   (c)  If the work or the contract is subdivided into several lots, the size of the different lots and the possibility of tendering for one, for several or for all of the lots.

---

[20] In accordance with regulation 13.

(d) Information concerning the purpose of the work or the contract where the latter also involves the drawing up of projects.

4. Any time limit.

5. Where applicable, the legal form to be taken by the grouping of contractors to whom the contract is awarded.

6. (a) Final date for receipt of requests to participate.
   (b) The address to which they must be sent.
   (c) The language or languages in which they must be drawn up.

7. Any deposit and guarantees required.

8. Main terms concerning financing and payment and/or the provisions in which these are contained.

9. Information concerning the contractor's personal position and information and formalities necessary in order to evaluate the minimum standards of economic and financial standing and technical capacity required of the contractor to whom the contract is awarded.

10. Where applicable, prohibition on variants.

11. Where applicable, the names and addresses of suppliers already selected by the awarding authority.

12. Where applicable, date(s) of previous publications in the *Official Journal of the European Communities*.

13. Other information.

14. Date of publication of the prior information notice in the *Official Journal of the European Communities*.

15. Date of despatch of the notice.

PART E

CONTRACT AWARD NOTICE

1. Name and address of contracting authority.

2. Award procedure chosen.

3. Date of award of contract.

4. Criteria for award of contract.

5. Number of offers received.

6. Name and address of successful contractor(s).

7. Nature and extent of the services provided, general characteristics of the finished structure.

8. Price or range of prices (minimum/maximum) paid.

9. Where appropriate, value and proportion of contract likely to be subcontracted to third parties.

10. Other information.

11. Date of publication of the tender notice in the *Official Journal of the European Communities*.

12. Date of despatch of the notice.

145

## Part F

### Public Works Concession Contract Notice

1. The name, address, telegraphic address, telephone, telex and facsimile numbers of the contracting authority.

2. (a) The site.
   (b) The subject of the concession and extent of the services to be provided.

3. (a) Final date for receipt of candidatures.
   (b) The address to which they must be sent.
   (c) The language or languages in which they must be drawn up.

4. Personal, technical and financial conditions to be fulfilled by the candidates.

5. The criteria for the award of the contract.

6. Where applicable, the minimum percentage of the works contracts awarded to third parties.

7. Other information.

8. Date of despatch of the notice.

## Part G

### Notice of Works Contracts Awarded by Concessionaires

1. (a) The site.
   (b) The nature and extent of the service to be provided and the general nature of the work.

2. Any time limit for the completion of the works.

3. Name and address of the service from which the contract documents and additional documents may be requested.

4. (a) The final date for receipt of requests to participate and/or for receipt of tenders.
   (b) The address to which they must be sent.
   (c) The language or languages in which they must be drawn up.

5. Any deposit and guarantees required.

6. The minimum standards of economic and financial standing and technical capacity required of the contractor.

7. The criteria for the award of the contract.

8. Other information.

9. Date of despatch of the notice.

146

# Appendix C

## PROPOSED CONSOLIDATED (AND AMENDED) SUPPLIES DIRECTIVE

**Proposal for a Council Directive coordinating procedures for the award of public supply contracts**

(92/C 277/01)

COM (92) 346 *final*—SYN 442

(*submitted by the Commission on September* 8, 1992)

THE COUNCIL OF THE EUROPEAN COMMUNITIES,

Having regard to the Treaty establishing the European Community, and in particular **C–01** Article 100a thereof,

Having regard to the proposal from the Commission,

In cooperation with the European Parliament,

Having regard to the opinion of the Economic and Social Committee,

Whereas Council Directive 77/62/EEC of 21 December 1976, coordinating procedures for the award of public supply contracts,[1] as last amended by Directive 92/50/EEC,[2] has been amended on a number of occasions; whereas, on the occasion of further amendments, the said Directive should, for reasons of clarity, be redrafted;

Whereas with a view to creating a single coherent body of all procurement rules for public authorities it seems important, in particular, to align the drafting of the present Directive, as far as possible, on the provisions on public procurement as contained in Council Directive 92/.../EEC of ... 1992, concerning the coordination of procedures for the award of public works contracts[3] and Council Directive 92/50/EEC of 18 June 1992, relating to the coordination of procedures on the award of public service contracts[4];

Whereas the alignments to be introduced relate, in particular, to the introduction of the functional definition of contracting authorities, the option to have recourse to the open or restricted procedure, the requirement to justify the refusal of candidates or tenderers, the rules for drawing up reports on the execution of the different award procedures, the conditions for referring to the common rules in the technical field, publication and participation, clarifications, concerning award criteria and the introduction of the Advisory Committee procedure;

Whereas it is also necessary to introduce some editorial changes aimed at improving the clarity of existing provisions;

Whereas the attainment of freedom of movement of goods in respect of public supply contracts awarded in Member States on behalf of the State, or regional or local authorities or other bodies governed by public law entails not only the abolition of restrictions but also the coordination of national procedures for the award of public supply contracts;

---

[1] OJ No L 13, 15.1.1977, p. 1.
[2] OJ No L 209, 24.7.1992, p. 1.
[3] OJ No L ..., (not yet adopted; see common position adopted by the Council with a view to the adoption of a directive concerning the coordination of procedures for the award of public work contracts (6355/92) of 18 June 1992, not published).
[4] OJ No L 209, 24.7.1992, p. 1.

147

Whereas such coordination should take into account as far as possible the procedures and administrative practices in force in each Member State;

Whereas the Council approved on behalf of the European Communities the Agreement on government procurement,[5] hereinafter referred to as "the GATT Agreement";

Whereas Annex I to this Directive sets out the lists of contracting authorities subject to the GATT Agreement; whereas it is necessary to update this Annex in accordance with modifications submitted by the Member States;

Whereas this Directive does not apply to certain supply contracts which are awarded in the water, energy, transport and telecommunication sectors covered by Council Directive 90/531/EEC[6];

Whereas, without prejudice to the application of the threshold set out for supply contracts subject to the GATT Agreement, supply contracts of less than ECU 200 000 may be exempted from competition as provided under this Directive and it is appropriate to provide for their exemption from coordination measures;

Whereas provision must be made for exceptional cases where measures concerning the coordination of procedures may not necessarily be applied, but such cases must be expressly limited;

Whereas the negotiated procedure should be considered to be exceptional and therefore applicable only in limited cases;

Whereas it is necessary to provide common rules in the technical field which take account of the Community policy on standards and specifications;

Whereas, to ensure development of effective competition in the field of public contracts, it is necessary that contract notices drawn up by the contracting authorities of Member States be advertised throughout the Community; whereas the information contained in these notices must enable suppliers established in the Community to determine whether the proposed contracts are of interest to them; whereas, for this purpose, it is appropriate to give them adequate information about the goods to be supplied and the conditions attached thereto; whereas, more particularly, in restricted procedures advertisement is intended to enable suppliers of Member States to express their interest in contracts by seeking from the contracting authorities invitations to tender under the required conditions;

Whereas additional information concerning contracts must, as is customary in Member States, be given in the contract documents for each contract or else in an equivalent document;

Whereas it is necessary to provide common rules for participation in public supply contracts, including both qualitative selection criteria and criteria for the award of the contracts;

Whereas this Directive must not affect the obligations of the Member States concerning the deadlines for transposition into national law and for application indicated in Annex V,

HAS ADOPTED THIS DIRECTIVE:

TITLE I

**GENERAL PROVISIONS**

*Article 1*

**C–02**   For the purpose of this Directive:

(a)  "public supply contracts" are contracts for pecuniary interest concluded in writing

---

[5] OJ No L 71, 17.1.1980, p. 1. OJ No L 345, 9.12.1987, p. 24.
[6] OJ No L 297, 29.10.1990, p. 1.

involving the purchase, lease, rental or hire purchase, with or without option to buy, of products between a supplier (a natural or legal person) and one of the contracting authorities defined in (*b*) below. The delivery of such products may in addition include siting and installation operations;

(*b*) "contracting authorities" shall be the State, regional or local authorities, bodies governed by public law, associations formed by one or several of such authorities or bodies governed by public law.

"body governed by public law" means any body:
 — established for the specific purpose of meeting needs in the general interest, not having an industrial or commercial character, and
 — having legal personality, and
 — financed, for the most part, by the State, or regional or local authorities, or other bodies governed by public law, or subject to management supervision by those bodies, or having an administrative, managerial or supervisory board, more than half of whose members are appointed by the State, regional or local authorities or by other bodies governed by public law.

The lists of bodies or of categories of such bodies governed by public law which fulfil the criteria referred to in the second subparagraph are set out in Annex I to Directive 92/.../EEC. These lists shall be as exhaustive as possible and may be reviewed in accordance with the procedure laid down in Article 35 of Directive 92/.../EEC;

(*c*) — "tenderer" is a supplier who submits a tender,
 — "candidate" is a person who has sought an invitation to take part in a restricted procedure;

(*d*) "open procedures" are those national procedures whereby all interested suppliers may submit tenders;

(*e*) "restricted procedures" are those national procedures whereby only those suppliers invited by the contracting authorities may submit tenders;

(*f*) "negotiated procedures" are those national procedures whereby contracting authorities consult suppliers of their choice and negotiate the terms of the contract with one or more of them.

### Article 2

**1.** This Directive shall not apply to:

(*a*) contracts awarded in the fields referred to in Articles 2, 7, 8 and 9 of Directive 90/531/EEC or fulfilling the conditions of Article 6(2) of that Directive;

(*b*) supply contracts which are declared secret or the execution of which must be accompanied by special security measures in accordance with the laws, regulations or administrative provisions in force in the Member States concerned or when the protection of the basic interests of the Member State's security so requires.

**2.** When a contracting authority within the meaning of Article 1(*b*) grants to a body other than a contracting authority—regardless of its legal status—special or exclusive rights to engage in a public service activity, the instrument granting this right shall stipulate that the body in question must observe the principle of nondiscrimination by nationality when awarding public supply contracts to third parties.

### Article 3

Without prejudice to Articles 2, 4 and 5(1), this Directive shall apply to all products to which Article 1(*a*) relates, including those covered by contracts awarded by contracting authorities in the field of defence, except for the products to which the provisions of Article 223(1)(b) of the Treaty apply.

### Article 4

This Directive shall not apply to public contracts governed by different procedural rules and awarded:

(a) in pursuance of an international agreement, concluded in conformity with the Treaty, between a Member State and one or more non-member countries and covering supplies intended for the joint implementation or exploitation of a project by the signatory States; all agreements shall be communicated to the Commission, which may consult the Advisory Committee for Public Contracts set up by Decision 71/306/EEC[7];

(b) to undertakings in a Member State or a non-member country in pursuance of an international agreement relating to the stationing of troops;

(c) pursuant to the particular procedure of an international organization.

### Article 5

1. (a) Titles II, III and IV and Articles 6 and 7 shall apply to public supply contracts:
   — awarded by the contraction authorities referred to in Article 1(b), including contracts awarded by the contracting authorities in the field of defence listed in Annex I in so far as the products not listed in Annex II are concerned, provided that the estimated value net of VAT is not less than ECU 200 000;
   — awarded by the contracting authorities listed in Annex I and whose estimated value net of VAT is not less than the threshold fixed pursuant to the GATT Agreement; in the case of contracting authorities in the field of defence, this shall apply only to contracts involving products covered by Annex II.

(b) This Directive shall apply to public supply contracts for which the estimated value equals or exceeds the threshold concerned at the time of publication of the notice in accordance with Article 9(2).

(c) The value of the thresholds in national currencies and the threshold of the GATT Agreement expressed in ecu shall in principle be revised every two years with effect from 1 January 1988. The calculation of these values shall be based on the average daily values of the currencies expressed in ecu and of the ecu expressed in SDRs over the 24 months terminating on the last day of August immediately preceding the 1 January revision.

The method of calculation laid down in the present subparagraph shall be reviewed, on the Commission's initiative, by the Advisory Committee for Public Contracts, in principle two years after its initial application.

(d) The thresholds laid down in subparagraph (a) and the value of the thresholds in national currencies and, as regards the threshold fixed by the GATT Agreement its threshold expressed in ECU shall be published in the *Official Journal of the European Communities* at the beginning of the month of November which follows the revision laid down in the first part of subparagraph (c).

2. In the case of contracts for the lease, rental or hire purchase of products, the basis for calculating the estimated contract value shall be:

— in the case of fixed-term contracts, where their term is 12 months or less, the total contract value for its duration, or, where their term exceeds 12 months, its total value including the estimated residual value,

---

[7] OJ No L 185, 16.8.1971, p. 15; amended by Decision 77/63/EEC (OJ No L 13, 15.1.1977, p. 15).

— in the case of contracts for an indefinite period or in cases where there is doubt as to the duration of the contracts, the monthly value multiplied by 48.

**3.** In the case of regular contracts or of contracts which are to be renewed within a given time, the contract value shall be established on the basis of:

— either the accrual aggregate value of similar contracts concluded over the previous fiscal year or 12 months, adjusted, where possible, for anticipated changes in quantity of value over the next 12 months following the initial contract,
— or the estimated aggregate value during the 12 months following the first delivery or during the term of the contract, where this is greater than 12 months.

The selection of the valuation method shall not be used with the intention of avoiding the application of this Directive.

**4.** If a proposed procurement of supplies of the same type may lead to contracts being awarded at the same time in separate parts, the estimated value of the total sum of these parts must be taken as the basis for the application of paragraphs 1 and 2.

**5.** In the cases where a proposed procurement specifies option clauses, the basis for calculating the estimated contract value shall be the highest possible total of the purchase, lease, rental or hire purchase permissible, inclusive of the option clauses.

**6.** No procurement requirement for a given quantity of supplies may be split up with the intention of avoiding the application of this Directive.

*Article 6*

**1.** In awarding public supply contracts the contracting authorities shall apply the procedures defined in Article 1(d), (e) and (f), in the cases set out below.

**2.** The contracting authorities may award their supply contracts by negotiated procedure in the case of irregular tenders in response to an open or restricted procedure or in the case of tenders in response to an open or restricted procedure or in the case of tenders which are unacceptable under national provisions that are in accordance with provisions of Title IV, in so far as the original terms for the contract are not substantially altered. The contracting authorities shall in these cases publish a tender notice unless they include in such negotiated procedures all the enterprises satisfying the criteria of Articles 20 to 24 which, during the prior open or restricted procedure, have submitted tenders in accordance with the formal requirements of the tendering procedure.

**3.** The contracting authorities may award their supply contracts by negotiated procedure without prior publication of a tender notice, in the following cases:

(a) in the absence of tenders in response to an open or restricted procedure in so far as the original terms of the contract are not substantially altered and provided that a report is communicated to the Commission;
(b) when the products involved are manufactured purely for the purpose of research, experiment, study or development, this provision does not extend to quantity production to establish commercial viability or to recover research and development costs;
(c) when, for technical or artistic reasons, or for reasons connected with protection of exclusive rights, the products supplied may be manufactured or delivered only by a particular supplier;
(d) insofar as is strictly necessary when, for reasons of extreme urgency brought about by events unforeseeable by the contracting authorities in question, the time limit laid down for the open restricted or negotiated procedures referred to in paragraph

2 cannot be kept. The circumstances invoked to justify extreme urgency must not in any event be attributable to the contracting authorities;

(e) for additional deliveries by the original supplier which are intended either as a partial replacement of normal supplies or installations or as the extension of existing supplies or installations where a change of supplier would oblige the contracting authority to acquire material having different technical characteristics which would result in incompatibility or disproportionate technical difficulties in operation and maintenance. The length of such contracts as well as that or recurrent contracts may, as a general rule, not exceed three years.

**4.** In all other cases, the contracting authorities shall award their supply contracts by the open procedure or by the restricted procedure.

### Article 7

**1.** The contracting authority shall, within 15 days of the date on which the request is received, inform any eliminated candidate or tenderer who so requests of the reasons of rejection of his application or his tender and, in the case of a tender, the name of the successful tenderer.

**2.** The contracting authority shall inform candidates or tenderers who so request of the grounds on which it decided not to award a contract in respect of which a prior call for competition was made, or to recommense the procedure. It shall also inform the Office for Official Publications of the European Communities of that decision.

**3.** For each contract awarded the contracting authorities shall draw up a written report which shall include at least the following:

— the name and address of the contracting authority, the subject and value of the contract;

— the names of the candidates or tenderers admitted and the reason for their selection;

— the names of the candidates or tenderers rejected and the reasons for their rejection;

— the name of the successful tenderer and the reasons for his tender having been selected and, if known, any share of the contracts the successful tenderer may intend to subcontract to a third party.

— for negotiated procedures, the circumstances referred to in Article 6 which justify the use of these procedures.

This report, or the main features of it, shall be communicated to the Commission at its request.

### TITLE II

### COMMON RULES IN THE TECHNICAL FIELD

### Article 8

**C–03**  **1.** The technical specifications defined in Annex III shall be given in the general or contractual documents relating to each contract.

**2.** Without prejudice to the legally binding national technical rules, in so far as these are compatible with Community law, the technical specifications mentioned in paragraph 1 shall be defined by the contracting authorities by reference to national standards implementing European standards, or by reference to European technical approvals or by reference to common technical specifications.

**3.** A contracting authority may depart from paragraph 2 if:

(a) the standards, European technical approvals or common technical specifications do not include any provision for establishing conformity, or technical means do not exist for establishing satisfactorily the conformity of a product to these standards, European technical approvals or common technical specifications;

(b) the application of paragraph 2 would prejudice the application of Council Directive 86/361/EEC[8] or Council Decision 87/95/EEC[9] or other Community instruments in specific service or product areas;

(c) use of these standards, Europeans technical approvals or common technical specifications would oblige the contracting authority to acquire supplies incompatible with equipment already in use or would entail disproportionate costs or disproportionate technical difficulties, but only as part of a clearly defined and recorded strategy with a view to change-over, within a given period, to European standards, European technical approvals or common technical specifications;

(d) the project concerned is of a genuinely innovative nature for which use of existing European standards, European technical approvals or common technical specifications would not be appropriate.

**4.** Contracting authorities invoking paragraph 3 shall record, wherever possible, the reasons for doing so in the tender notice published in the *Official Journal of the European Communities*, or in the contract documents and in all cases shall record these reasons in their internal documentation and shall supply such information on request to Member States and to the Commission.

**5.** In the absence of European standards or European technical approvals or common technical specifications, the technical specification:

(a) shall be defined by reference to the national technical specifications recognized as complying with the basic requirements listed in the Community directives on technical harmonization, in accordance with the procedures laid down in those directives, and in particular in accordance with the procedures laid down in Council Directive 89/106/EEC[10];

(b) may be defined by reference to national technical specifications relating to design and method of calculation and execution of works and use of materials;

(c) may be defined by reference to other documents.
   In this case, it is appropriate to make reference in order of preference to:
   (i) national standards implementing international standards accepted by the country of the contracting authority;
   (ii) other national standards and national technical approvals of the country of the contracting authority;
   (iii) any other standard.

**6.** Unless such specifications are justified by the subject of the contract, Member States shall prohibit the introduction into the contractual clauses relating to a given contract of technical specifications which mention goods of specific make or source or of a particular process and which therefore favour or eliminate certain suppliers or products. In particular, the indication of trade marks, patents, types or of a specific origin or production shall be prohibited. However, if such indication is accompanied by the words "or equivalent" it shall be authorized in cases where the contracting authorities are unable to give a description of the subject of the contract using specifications which are sufficiently precise and fully intelligible to all parties concerned.

[8] OJ No L 217, 5.8.1986, p. 21.
[9] OJ No L 36, 7.2.1987, p. 31.
[10] OJ No L 40, 11.2.1989, p. 12.

## TITLE III

## COMMON ADVERTISING RULES

*Article 9*

**C–04** **1.** The contracting authorities shall make known, as soon as possible after the beginning of their budgetary year, by means of an indicative notice, the total procurement by product area which they envisage awarding during the subsequent 12 months where the total estimated value, taking into account the provisions of Article 5, is equal to or greater than ECU 750 000.

The product area shall be established by the contracting authorities by means of reference to the nomenclature "Classification of products according to activities (CPA)".[11] The Commission shall determine the conditions of reference in the notice to particular positions of the nomenclature in accordance with the procedure laid down in Article 32(2).

**2.** Contracting authorities who wish to award a public supply contract by open, restricted or negotiated procedure in the cases referred to in Article 6(2), shall make known their intention by means of a notice.

**3.** Contracting authorities who have awarded a contract shall make known the result by means of a notice. However, certain information on the contract award may, in certain cases, not be published where release of such information would impede law enforcement or otherwise be contrary to the public interest would prejudice the legitimate commercial interests of particular enterprises, public or private, or might prejudice fair competition between suppliers.

**4.** The notice shall be drawn up in accordance with the models given in Annex IV and shall specify the information requested in those models. The contracting authorities may not require any conditions other than those specified in Articles 22 and 23 when requesting information concerning the economic and technical standards which they require of suppliers for their selection (section 11 of Annex IV, part B, section 9 of Annex IV, part C and section 8 of Annex IV, part D).

**5.** The contracting authorities shall send the notice as rapidly as possible and by the most appropriate channels to the Office for Official Publications of the European Communities. In the case of the accelerated procedure referred to in Article 12, the notice shall be sent by telex, telegram or telefax.

The notice referred to in paragraph 1 shall be sent as soon as possible after the beginning of each budgetary year.

The notice referred to in paragraph 3 shall be sent, at the latest, 48 days after the award of the contract in question.

**6.** The notices referred to in paragraphs 1 and 3 shall be published in full in the *Official Journal of the European Communities*, and in the TED data bank in the official languages of the Communities, the text in the original language alone being authentic.

**7.** The notices referred to in paragraph 2 shall be published in full in the *Official Journal of the European Communities* and in the TED data bank in their original language. A summary of the important elements of each notice shall be published in the official languages of the Communities, the text in the original language alone being authentic.

**8.** The Office for Official Publications of the European Communities shall publish the notices not later than 12 days after their dispatch. In the case of the accelerated procedure referred to in Article 12, this period shall be reduced to five days.

[11] OJ No L …

**9.** The notices shall not be published in the official journals or in the press of the country of the contracting authority before the date of dispatch to the Office for Official Publications of the European Communities; they shall mention that date. They shall not contain information other than that published in the *Official Journal of the European Communities*.

**10.** The contracting authorities must be able to supply proof of the date of dispatch.

**11.** The cost of publication of the notices in the *Official Journal of the European Communities* shall be borne by the Communities. The length of the notice shall not be greater than one page of the Journal, or approximately 650 words. Each edition of the Journal containing one or more notices shall reproduce the model notice or notices on which the published notice or notices are based.

### Article 10

**1.** In open procedures the time limit for the receipt of tenders, fixed by the contracting authorities shall not be less than 32 days from the date of dispatch of the notice.

**2.** Provided they have been requested in good time, the contract documents and supporting documents must be sent to the suppliers by the contracting authorities or competent departments within six days of receiving their application.

**3.** Provided it has been requested in good time, additional information relating to the contract documents shall be supplied by the contracting authorities not later than six days before the final date fixed for receipt of tenders.

**4.** Where the contract documents, supporting documents or additional information are too bulky to be supplied within the time limits laid down in paragraph 2 or 3 or where tenders can be made only after a visit to the site or after on-the-spot inspection of the documents supporting the contract documents, the time limit laid down in paragraph 1 shall be extended accordingly.

### Article 11

**1.** In restricted procedures and negotiated procedures as described in Article 6(2), the time limit for receipt of requests to participate fixed by the contracting authorities shall not be less than 37 days from the date of dispatch of the notice.

**2.** The contracting authorities shall simultaneously and in writing invite the selected candidates to submit their tenders or negotiate. The letter of invitation shall be accompanied by the contract documents and supporting documents. It shall include at least the following information:

(a) where appropriate, the address of the service from which the contract documents and supporting documents can be requested and the final date for making such a request; also the amount and terms of payment of any sum to be paid for such documents;

(b) the final date for receipt of tenders, the address to which they must be sent and the language or languages in which they must be drawn up;

(c) a reference to the contract notice published;

(d) an indication of any documents to be annexed, either to support the verifiable statements furnished by the candidate in accordance with Article 9(4), or to supplement the information provided for in that Article under the same conditions as those laid down in Articles 22 and 23;

(e) the criteria for the award of the contrary if these are not given in the notice.

**3.** In restricted procedures, the time limit for receipt of tenders fixed by the contracting authorities may not be less than 40 days from the date of dispatch of the written invitation.

**4.** Requests to participate in procedures for the award of contracts may be made by letter, by telegram, telex, telefax or by telephone. If by one of the last four, they must be confirmed by letter dispatched before the end of the period laid down in paragraph 1.

**5.** Provided it has been requested in good time, additional information relating to the contract documents must be supplied by the contracting authorities not later than six days before the final date fixed for receipt of tenders.

**6.** Where tenders can be made only after a visit to the site or after on-the-spot inspection of the documents supporting the contract documents, the time limit laid down in paragraph 3 shall be extended accordingly.

*Article 12*

**1.** In cases where urgency renders impracticable the time limits laid down in Article 11, the contracting authorities may fix the following time limits:

    (*a*)  a time limit for the receipt of requests to participate which shall not be less than 15 days from the date of dispatch of the notice;
    (*b*)  a time limit for the receipt of tenders which shall not be less than 10 days from the date of the invitation to tender.

**2.** Provided it has been requested in good time, additional information relating to the contract documents must be supplied by the contracting authorities not less than four days before the final date fixed for the receipt of tenders.

**3.** Requests for participation in contracts and invitations to tender must be made by the most rapid means of communication possible. When requests to participate are made by telegram, telex, telefax or telephone, they must be confirmed by letter dispatched before the expiry of the time limit referred to in paragraph 1.

*Article 13*

Contracting authorities may arrange for the publication in the *Official Journal of the European Communities* of notices announcing public supply contracts which are not subject to the publication requirement laid down in this Directive.

*Article 14*

The conditions for the drawing up, transmission, receipt, translation, collection and distribution of the notices referred to in Article 9 and of the statistical reports provided for in Article 31 as well as the nomenclature provided for in Article 9 and in Annexes II and IV may be modified in accordance with the procedure laid down in Article 32(2). The conditions for referring in the notices to particular positions in the nomenclature may be determined pursuant to the same procedure.

TITLE IV

**COMMON RULES ON PARTICIPATION**

*Article 15*

**C–05**    **1.** Contracts shall be awarded on the basis of the criteria laid down in Chapter 2 of this Title, taking into account Article 16, after the suitability of the suppliers not excluded under Article 20 has been checked by the contracting authorities in accordance with the criteria of economic and financial standing and of technical capacity referred to in Articles 22, 23 and 24.

**2.** The contracting authorities shall respect fully the confidential nature of any information finished by the suppliers.

### Article 16

**1.** Where the criterion for the award of the contract is that of the most economically advantageous tender, contracting authorities may take account of variants which are submitted by a tenderer and meet the minimum specifications required by the contracting authorities.

The contracting authorities shall state in the contract documents the minimum specifications to be respected by the variants and any specific requirements for their presentation. They shall indicate in the tender notice if variants are not permitted.

Contracting authorities may not reject the submission of a variant on the sole grounds that it has been drawn up with technical specifications defined by reference to national standards transposing European standards, to European technical approvals or to common technical specifications referred to in Article 8(2), or again by reference to national technical specifications referred to in Article 8(5)(a) and (b).

**2.** Contracting authorities which have admitted variants pursuant to paragraph 1 may not reject a variant on the sole grounds that it would lead, if successful, to a service contract rather than a public supply contract within the meaning of this Directive.

### Article 17

In the contract documents, the contracting authority may ask the tenderer to indicate in his tender any share of the contract he may intend to contract to third parties.

This indication shall be without prejudice to the question of the principal supplier's liability.

### Article 18

Tenders may be submitted by groups of suppliers. These groups may not be required to assume a specific legal form in order to submit the tender; however, the group selected may be required to do so when it has been awarded the contract, to the extent that this change is necessary for the satisfactory performance of the contract.

### Article 19

**1.** In restricted and negotiated procedures the contracting authorities shall, on the basis of information given relating to the supplier's personal position as well as to the information and formalities necessary for the evaluation of the minimum conditions of an economic and technical nature to be fulfilled by him, select from among the candidates with the qualifications required by Articles 20 to 24 those whom they will invite to submit a tender or to negotiate.

**2.** Where the contracting authorities award a contract by restricted procedure, they may prescribe the range within which the number of suppliers which they intend to invite will fall. In this case the range shall be indicated in the contract notice. The range shall be determined in the light of the nature of the goods to be supplied. The range must number at least five suppliers and may be up to 20.

In any event, the number of candidates invited to tender shall be sufficient to ensure genuine competition.

157

**3.** Where the contracting authorities award a contract by negotiated procedure as referred to in Article 6(2), the number of candidates admitted to negotiate may not be less than three provided that there is a sufficient number of suitable candidates.

**4.** Each Member State shall ensure that contracting authorities issue invitations without discrimination to those nationals of other Member States who satisfy the necessary requirements and under the same conditions as to its own nationals.

Chapter 1

**Criteria for qualitative selection**

Article 20

**C–06**

**1.** Any supplier may be excluded from participation in the contract who:

(a) is bankrupt or is being wound up, whose affairs are being administered by the court, who has entered into an arrangement with creditors, who has suspended business activities or who is in any analogous situation arising from a similar procedure under national laws and regulations;
(b) is the subject of proceedings for a declaration of bankruptcy, for an order for compulsory winding up or administration by the court or for an arrangement with creditors or of any other similar proceedings under national laws and regulations;
(c) has been convicted of an offence concerning his professional conduct by a judgment which has the force of *res judicata*;
(d) has been guilty of grave professional misconduct proven by any means which the contracting authorities can justify;
(e) has not fulfilled obligations relating to the payment of social security contributions in accordance with the legal provisions of the country in which he is established or with those of the country of the contracting authority;
(f) has not fulfilled obligations relating to the payment of taxes in accordance with the legal provisions of the country in which he is established or those of the country of the contracting authority;
(g) is guilty of serious misrepresentations in supplying the information required under this Chapter.

**2.** Where the contracting authority requires of the supplier proof that none of the cases quoted in (a), (b), (c), (e) or (f) of paragraph 1 applies to him, it shall accept as sufficient evidence:

— for points (a), (b) or (c), the production of an extract from the "judicial record" or, failing this, of an equivalent document issued by a competent judicial or administrative authority in the country of origin or in the country whence that person comes showing that these requirements have been met;
— for points (e) or (f), a certificate issued by the competent authority in the Member State concerned.

**3.** Where the country in question does not issue the documents or certificates referred to in paragraph 2 or where these do not cover all the cases quoted in (a), (b) or (c) of paragraph 1, they may be replaced by a declaration on oath or, in Member States where there is no provision for declarations on oath, by a solemn declaration made by the person concerned before a competent judicial or administrative authority, a notary or a competent professional or trade body, in the country of origin or in the country whence that person comes.

**4.** Member States shall designate the authorities and bodies competent to issue the documents, certificates or declarations referred to in paragraphs 2 and 3 and shall forthwith inform the other Member States and the Commission thereof.

*Article 21*

**1.** Any supplier wishing to take part in a public supply contract may be requested to prove his enrolment, as prescribed in his country of establishment, in one of the professional or trade registers or to provide a declaration on oath or certificate as described in paragraph 2 below.

**2.** The relevant professional and trade registers or declarations or certificates are:

— in Belgium: "registre du commerce/Handelsregister";
— in Denmark: "Aktieselskabs-Registret", "Forenings-Registret' and "Handelsregistret";
— in Germany: "Handelsregister" and "Handwerksrolle";
— in Greece: "Βιοτεχνικό ή Βιομηχανικό ή Εμπορικό Επιμελητήριο";
— in Spain: "Registro Oficial de Contratistas del Ministerio de Industria y Energia";
— in France: "registre du commerce" and "répertoire des métiers";
— in Italy: "registro della camera di commercio, industria, agricoltura e artigianato", and "registro delle commissioni provinciali per l'artigianato";
— in Luxembourg: "registre aux firmes" and "rôle de la chambre des métiers";
— in the Netherlands: "Handelsregister";
— in Portugal: "Registo Nacional das Pessoas Colectivas".
— in the United Kingdom and Ireland, the supplier may be requested to provide a certificate from the Registrar of Companies or the Registrar of Friendly Societies that he is certified as incorporated or registered or, if he is not so certified, a certificate stating that the person concerned has declared on oath that he is engaged in the profession in question in the country in which he is established in a specific place under a given business name and under a specific trading name.

*Article 22*

**1.** Proof of the supplier's financial and economic standing may, as a general rule be furnished by one or more of the following references:

(a) appropriate statements from bankers;
(b) the presentation of the supplier's balance-sheets or extracts from the balance-sheets, where publication of the balance-sheet is required under the law of the country in which the supplier is established;
(c) a statement of the supplier's overall turnover and its turnover in respect of the products to which the contract relates for the three previous financial years.

**2.** The contracting authorities shall specify in the notice or in the invitations to tender which reference or references they have chosen and which references other than those mentioned under paragraph 1 are to be produced.

**3.** If, for any valid reason, the supplier is unable to provide the references requested by the contracting authority, he may prove his economic and financial standing by any other document which the contracting authority considers appropriate.

*Article 23*

**1.** Proof of the supplier's technical capacity may be furnished by one or more of the following means according to the nature, quantity and purpose of the products to be supplied:

(a) a list of the principal deliveries effected in the past three years, with the sums, dates and recipients, public or private, involved:

— where effected to public authorities, evidence to be in the form of certificates issued or countersigned by the competent authority;

— where effected to private purchasers, delivery to be certified by the purchaser or, failing this, simply declared by the supplier to have been effected;

(b) a description of the supplier's technical facilities, its measures for ensuring quality and its study and research facilities;

(c) indication of the technicians or technical bodies involved, whether or not belonging directly to the supplier, especially those responsible for quality control;

(d) samples, description and/or photographs of the products to be supplied, the authenticity of which must be certified if the contracting authority so requests;

(e) certificates drawn up by official quality control institutes or agencies of recognized competence attesting conformity to certain specifications or standards of products clearly identified by references to specifications or standards;

(f) where the products to be supplied are complex or, exceptionally, are required for a special purpose, a check carried out by the contracting authorities or on their behalf by a competent official body of the country in which the supplier is established, subject to that body's agreement, on the production capacities of the supplier and if necessary on his study and research facilities and quality control measures.

**2.** The contracting authority shall specify, in the notice or in the invitation to tender, which references it wishes to receive.

**3.** The extent of the information referred to in Article 22 and in paragraphs 1 and 2 of this Article must be confined to the subject of the contract; contracting authority shall take into consideration the legitimate interests of the suppliers as regards the protection of their technical or trade secrets.

### Article 24

Within the limits of Articles 20 to 23 the contracting authority may invite the suppliers to supplement the certificates and documents submitted or to clarify them.

### Article 25

**1.** Member States who have official lists of recognized suppliers must adapt them to the provisions of points (a) to (d) and (g) of Article 20(1) and of Articles 21, 22 and 23.

**2.** Suppliers registered in the official lists may, for each contract, submit to the contracting authority a certificate of registration issued by the competent authority. This certificate shall state the references which enabled them to be registered in the list and the classification given in that list.

**3.** Certified registration in official lists of suppliers by the competent bodies shall, for the contracting authorities of other Member States, constitute a presumption of suitability corresponding to the suppliers classification only as regards points (a) to (d) and (g) of Article 20(1), Article 21, points (b) and (c) of Article 22(1) and point (a) of Article 23(1).

Information which can be deduced from registration in official lists may not be questioned. However, with regard to the payment of social security contributions, an additional certificate may be required of any registered suppliers whenever a contract is offered.

The contracting authorities of other Member States shall apply the first and second subparagraphs only in favour of suppliers established in the Member State holding the official list.

**4.** For the registration of suppliers of other Member States in an official list, no further proof or statements can be required other than those requested of national suppliers and, in any event, only those provided for under Articles 20 to 23.

**5.** Member States holding an official list shall communicate to other Member States the address of the body to which requests for registration may be made.

Chapter 2

### Criteria for the award of contracts

*Article 26*

**1.** The criteria on which the contracting authority shall base the award of contracts shall    **C–07**
be:

(a)  either the lowest price only;

(b)  or, when the award is made to the most economically advantageous tender, various criteria according to the contract in question: e.g. price, delivery date, running costs, cost-effectiveness, quality, aesthetic and functional characteristics, technical merit, after-sales service and technical assistance.

**2.** In the case referred to in point (b) of paragraph 1, the contracting authority shall state in the contract documents or in the contract notice all the criteria they intend to apply to the award, where possible in descending order of importance.

*Article 27*

If, for a given contract, tenders appear to be abnormally low in relation to the goods to be supplied, the contracting authority shall, before it may reject those tenders, request in writing details of the constituent elements of the tender which it considers relevant and shall verify those constituent elements taking account of the explanations received.

The contracting authority may take into consideration explanations which are justified on objective grounds including the financial aspects of the supply of the products, or the technical solutions chosen, or the exceptionally favourable conditions available to the tenderer for the supply of the goods, or the originality of the supplies proposed by the tenderer.

If the documents relating to the contract provide for its award at the lowest price tendered, the contracting authority must communicate to the Commission the rejection of tenders which it considers to be too low.

TITLE V

### FINAL PROVISION

*Article 28*

For the purposes of the award of public contracts by the contracting authorities referred to in Annex I, and, to the extent that rectifications, modifications or amendments have been made thereto, by their successor authorities, Member States shall apply in their relations conditions as favourable as those which they grant to third countries in implementation of the GATT Agreement, in particular those in Articles V and VI of that Agreement, on the selective procedure, information and review. The Member States shall to this end consult each other within the Advisory Committee for Public Contracts on the measures to be taken pursuant to the Agreement.

*Article 29*

**1.** The Commission shall examine the application of this Directive in consultation with the Advisory Committee for Public Contracts and where appropriate shall submit new proposals to the Council and the aim in particular of harmonizing the measures taken by the Member States for the implementation of this Directive.

**2.** The Commission shall review this Directive and any new measures which may be adopted by virtue of paragraph 1, having regard to the results of the further negotiations provided for in Article IX (6) of the GATT Agreement and shall, if necessary, submit appropriate proposals to the Council.

**3.** The Commission shall update Annex I on the basis of any rectifications, modifications or amendments referred to in Article 28, and shall have the updated version published in the *Official Journal of the European Communities.*

### Article 30

The calculation of time limits shall be made in accordance with Council Regulation (EEC, Euratom) No 1182/71.[12]

### Article 31

**1.** In order to permit assessment of the results of applying this Directive, Member States shall forward to the Commission a statistical report relative to supply contract awards:

(a) not later than 31 October of each year for the preceding year in respect of the contracting authorities listed in Annex I;

(b) not later than 31 October 1991 and for the Hellenic Republic, the Kingdom of Spain and the Portuguese Republic 31 October 1995 and thereafter 31 October of each second year for the preceding year in respect of the other contracting authorities within the meaning of Article 1.

**2.** The statistical report shall detail at least:

(a) the number and value of contracts awarded by each contracting authority above the threshold and, in the case of contracting authorities mentioned in Annex I, the value below the threshold;

(b) the number and value of contracts awarded by each contracting authority above the threshold, subdivided by procedure, product and the nationality of the supplier to whom the contract has been awarded, and in the case of negotiated procedures, subdivided in accordance with Article 6, listing the number and value of the contracts awarded to each member State and to third countries, and in the case of contracting authorities referred to in Annex I, the number and value of the contracts awarded to each signatory to the GATT Agreement.

**3.** The Commission shall determine in accordance with the procedure laid down in Article 32(2) the nature of any additional statistical information, which is required in accordance with this Directive.

### Article 32

**1.** The Commission shall be assisted by the Advisory Committee for Public Contracts set up by Decision 71/306/EEC.

**2.** Where reference is made to the procedure laid down in this paragraph, the representative of the Commission shall submit to the Committee a draft of the measures

[12] OJ No L 124, 8.6.1971, p. 1.

to be taken. The Committee shall deliver its opinion on the draft within a time limit which the chairman may lay down according to the urgency of the matter, if necessary by taking a vote.

The opinion shall be recorded in the minutes; in addition, each Member State shall have the right to ask to have its position recorded in the minutes.

The Commission shall take the utmost account of the opinion delivered by the Committee. It shall inform the Committee of the manner in which its opinion has been taken into account.

**3.** The Committee mentioned in paragraph 1 shall examine, on the initiative of the Commission or at the request of a Member State, any question relating to the application of this Directive.

### Article 33

Directive 77/62/EEC[13] is hereby repealed, without prejudice to the obligation of the Member States concerning the deadlines for transposition into national law and for application indicated in Annex V.

References to the repealed Directives shall be construed as reference to this Directive and should be read in Accordance with the correlation table set out in Annex VI.

### Article 34

**1.** Member States shall bring into force the laws, regulations and administrative provisions necessary to comply with this Directive before.... They shall immediately inform the Commission thereof.

When Member States adopt these provisions, these shall contain a reference to this Directive or shall be accompanied by such reference at the time of their official publication. The procedure for such reference shall be adopted by Member States.

**2.** Member States shall communicate to the Commission the texts of the main provisions of national law which they adopt to comply with this Directive.

### Article 35

This Directive is addressed to the Member States.

---

[13] Including the provisions which amended this Directive, namely:
— Directive 80/767/EEC (OJ No L 215, 18.8.1980, p. 1.),
— Directive 88/295/EEC (OJ No L 127, 20.5.1988, p. 1.),
— Article 35(1) of Directive 90/531/EEC (OJ No L 297, 29.10.1990, p. 1.),
— Article 42(1) of Directive 92/50/EEC (OJ No L 209, 24.7.1992, p. 1.).

# Appendix D

## PUBLIC SUPPLY CONTRACTS REGULATIONS 1991

### (S.I. No. 2679)

#### (In force from December 21, 1991)

#### ARRANGEMENT OF REGULATIONS

#### PART I

##### General

#### PART II

##### Technical Specifications

#### PART III

##### Procedures Leading to the Award of a Public Supply Contract

#### PART IV

##### Selection of Suppliers

#### PART V

##### The Award of a Public Supply Contract

PART VI

*Miscellaneous*

22. Public service bodies
23. Statistical and other reports
24. Responsibility for obtaining reports
25. Publication of notices

PART VII

*Applications to the Court*

26. Enforcement of obligations relating to a public supply contract

## SCHEDULES

**Schedule 1  GATT contracting authorities**
**Schedule 2  Goods for the purposes of the thresholds**
**Schedule 3  Forms of notices for publication in the Official Journal**

The Treasury, being the Minister designated[1] for the purposes of section 2(2) of the European Communities Act 1972[2] in relation to public procurement, in exercise of the powers conferred upon them by the said section 2(2) and of all other powers enabling them in that behalf, hereby make the following Regulations:—

PART I

**GENERAL**

**D–01  Title and commencement**

**1.** These Regulations may be cited as the Public Supply Contracts Regulations 1991 and shall come into force on 21st December 1991.

**Interpretation**

**2.**—(1) In these Regulations—

"to award" means to accept an offer made in relation to a proposed contract;
"the Commission" means the Commission of the Communities;
"contract documents" means the invitation to tender for or negotiate the contract, the proposed conditions of contract, the specifications or description of the goods required by the contracting authority, and all documents supplementary thereto;
"contract notice" means a notice sent to the Official Journal in accordance with regulation 11(2), 12(2) or 13(2);
"contracting authority" has the meaning ascribed to it by regulation 3;
"ECU" means the European Currency Unit as defined in Council Regulation (EEC) No. 3180/78[3];
"established" means the same as it does for the purposes of the Community Treaties;
"financial year" means the period of 12 months ending on 31st March in any year or, in relation to any person whose accounts are prepared in respect of a different 12 month period, that period of 12 months;

[1] S.I. 1991/755.
[2] 1972 c.68.
[3] OJ No. L379, 30.12.78, p.1, as amended by Council Regulation (EEC) No. 2626/84 (OJ No. L247, 16.9.84, p.1).

"a GATT contracting authority" means one of the entities specified in Schedule 1, being entities in respect of which special provision is made by these Regulations in pursuance of the obligations of the Economic Community under the Agreement on Government Procurement between certain parties to the General Agreement on Tariffs and Trade (GATT) signed in Geneva on 12 April 1979[4];

"goods" includes substances, growing crops and things attached to or forming part of the land which are agreed to be severed before purchase or hire under the supply contract and any ship, aircraft or vehicle;

"government department" includes a Northern Ireland department or the head of such department;

"Minister of the Crown" means the holder of any office in Her Majesty's Government in the United Kingdom, and includes the Treasury;

"national of a member State" means, in the case of a person who is not an individual, a person formed in accordance with the laws of a member State and which has its registered office, central administration or principal place of business in a member State;

"negotiated procedure" means a procedure leading to the award of a public supply contract whereby a contracting authority negotiates the terms of the contract with one or more persons selected by it;

"Official Journal" means the Official Journal of the Communities;

"open procedure" means a procedure leading to the award of a public supply contract whereby all interested persons may tender for the contract;

"public supply contract" means a contract in writing for consideration (whatever the nature of the consideration)—

(a) for the purchase of goods by a contracting authority (whether or not the consideration is given in instalments and whether or not the purchase is conditional upon the occurrence of a particular event), or

(b) for the hire of goods by a contracting authority (both where the contracting authority becomes the owner of the goods after the end of the period of hire and where it does not),

and for any siting or installation of those goods, but where under such a contract services are also to be provided, the contract shall only be a public supply contract—

(i) where the value of the consideration attributable to the goods and any siting or installation of the goods is equal to or greater than the value attributable to the services, or

(ii) where the value of the consideration attributable to the services is greater than the value attributable to the goods and of any siting or installation of the goods if the goods could have been provided separately from the services;

"restricted procedure" means a procedure leading to the award of a public supply contract whereby only persons selected by the contracting authority may submit tenders for the contract;

"ship" includes any boat and other description of a vessel used in navigation;

"substance" means any natural or artificial substance, whether in solid, liquid or gaseous form or in the form of a vapour;

"supplier" has the meaning ascribed to it by regulation 4;

"working day" means a day other than a Saturday, Sunday or Bank Holiday (within the meaning of the Banking and Financial Dealings Act 1971[5]); and

"year" means a calendar year.

(2) The value in the currency of any member State of any amount expressed in these Regulations in ECU or of the amount in ECU for the purposes of regulation 7(2) shall be

[4] Cmnd. 7662.
[5] 1971 c.80.

calculated by reference to the exchange rate for the time being applying for the purposes of Council Directive 77/62/EEC[6] as published from time to time in the Official Journal.[7]

(3) Where a thing is required to be done under these Regulations—

(a) within a period after an action is taken, the day on which that action was taken shall not be counted in the calculation of that period;
(b) within a certain period, that period must include two working days;
(c) within a period and the last day of that period is not a working day, the period shall be extended to include the following working day.

(4) References in these Regulations to a regulation are references to a regulation in these Regulations and references to a Schedule are references to a Schedule to these Regulations.

**Contracting Authorities**

**3.**—(1) For the purposes of these Regulations each of the following is a "contracting authority"—

(a) a Minister of the Crown,
(b) a government department,
(c) the House of Commons,
(d) the House of Lords,
(e) the Northern Ireland Assembly,
(f) a local authority,
(g) a fire authority constituted by a combination scheme under the Fire Services Act 1947,[8]
(h) the Fire Authority for Northern Ireland,
(i) a police authority constituted under section 2 of the Police Act 1964[9] or a combined police authority established by an amalgamation scheme under that Act,
(j) the Police Authority for Northern Ireland,
(k) an authority established under section 10 of the Local Government Act 1985,[10]
(l) a joint authority established by Part IV of that Act,
(m) any body established pursuant to an order under section 67 of that Act,
(n) the Broads Authority,
(o) any joint board the constituent members of which consist of any of the bodies specified in paragraphs (f), (g), (i), (k), (l), (m) and (n), above,
(p) a joint or special planning board constituted for a National Park by an order under paragraphs 1 or 3 of Schedule 17 to the Local Government Act 1972,[11]
(q) a joint education board constituted under the provisions of Part I of the first Schedule to the Education Act 1944,[12]
(r) a corporation established, or a group of individuals appointed to act together, for the specific purpose of meeting needs in the general interest through the national

[6] OJ No. L13, 15.1.77, p.1, as amended by Council Directives 80/767/EEC (OJ No. L215, 18.8.80, p.1) and 88/295/EEC (OJ No. L127, 20.5.88, p.1).
[7] The rates are determined for each successive period of two years by calculating the average of the daily exchange rates between each currency and the ECU over a period of 24 months preceding the determination. The exchange rates applying at the time of coming into force of these Regulations are published in OJ No. C18, 25.1.90, p.3.
[8] 1947 c.41.
[9] 1964 c.48.
[10] 1985 c.51.
[11] 1972 c.70.
[12] 1944 c.31.

health service or with respect to education or urban development, not having an industrial or commercial character, and

    (i) financed wholly or mainly by another contracting authority, or

    (ii) subject to management supervision by another contracting authority, or

    (iii) more than half of the board of directors or members of which, or, in the case of a group of individuals, more than half of those individuals, being appointed by another contracting authority,

(s) associations of or formed by one or more of the above, and

(t) to the extent not specified in sub-paragraphs (a) to (q) above, a GATT contracting authority.

(2) In the application of these Regulations to England and Wales, "local authority" in paragraph (1) above means—

(a) a county council, a district council, a London borough council, a parish council, a community council or the Council of the Isles of Scilly;

(b) the Common Council of the City of London in its capacity as local authority or police authority.

(3) In the application of these Regulations to Scotland, "local authority" in paragraph (1) above means a regional, islands or district council or any joint board or joint committee within the meaning of section 235 of the Local Government (Scotland) Act 1973.[13]

(4) In the application of these Regulations to Northern Ireland, "local authority" in paragraph (1) above means a district council within the meaning of the Local Government Act (Northern Ireland) 1972.[14]

(5) Where an entity specified in paragraph (1) above does not have the capacity to enter into a contract, the contracting authority in relation to that entity is a person whose function it is to enter into contracts for that entity.

## Suppliers

**4.**—(1) For the purposes of these Regulations a "supplier" means a person—

(a) who sought, or who seeks, or who would have wished, to be the person to whom a public supply contract is awarded, and

(b) who is a national of and established in a member State.

(2) Where these Regulations apply a contracting authority shall not treat a person who is not a national of and established in a member State more favourably than one who is.

## Application of the Regulations

**5.** These Regulations apply whenever a contracting authority seeks offers in relation to a proposed public supply contract other than a public supply contract excluded from the application of these Regulations by regulations 6 and 7.

## General exclusions

**6.** These Regulations shall not apply to the seeking of offers in relation to a proposed public supply contract—

[(a) for the purpose of carrying out an activity specified in the second column of

[13] 1973 c.65.
[14] 1972 c.9 (N.I.).

169

Schedule 1 to the Utilities Supply and Works Contracts Regulations 1992 other than an activity specified in paragraph 2 or 3 thereof;

(b) when a contracting authority exercises the activity specified in paragraph 1 of Schedule 1 to the Utilities Supply and Works Contracts Regulations 1992 for the purpose of carrying out an activity specified in paragraph 2 or 3 thereof;|*

(d) which is classified as secret or where the delivery of the goods under it must be accompanied by special security measures in accordance with the laws, regulations or administrative provisions of any part of the United Kingdom or when the protection of the basic interests of the security of the United Kingdom requires it;

(e) where goods to be purchased or hired under the contract are goods to which the provisions of Article 223.1(b) of the EEC Treaty apply; or

(f) where different procedures govern the procedures leading to the award of the contract and it is to be entered into—

    (i) pursuant to an international agreement to which the United Kingdom and a State which is not a member State are parties and it relates to goods intended for the joint implementation or exploitation of a project pursuant to that agreement;

    (ii) pursuant to an international agreement relating to the stationing of troops; or

    (iii) in accordance with the contract award procedures of an organisation of which only States are members (an "international organisation") or of which only States or international organisations are members.

**Thresholds**

**7.**—(1) These Regulations shall not apply to the seeking of offers in relation to a proposed public supply contract where the estimated value of the contract (net of value added tax) at the relevant time is less than the relevant threshold.

(2) The relevant threshold for the purposes of paragraph (1) above—

(a) in relation to a public supply contract in relation to which offers are sought by a GATT contracting authority, but in the case of such a contract in relation to which offers are sought by the Secretary of Defence only if it is for the purchase or hire of the goods specified in Schedule 2, is the amount for the time being to be treated as the ECU equivalent of 130,000 special drawing rights for the purposes of Council Directive 77/62/EEC as published from time to time in the Official Journal[15];

(b) in relation to all other public supply contracts, is 200,000 ECU.

(3) Subject to paragraphs (4), (5), (6) and (7) below, the estimated value for the purposes of paragraph (1) above of a public supply contract shall be the value of the consideration which the contracting authority expects to give under the contract.

(4) The estimated value for the purposes of paragraph (1) above of a public supply contract for the hire of goods for an indefinite period, or for a period which is uncertain at the time the contract is entered into, shall be the value of the consideration which the contracting authority expects to give in respect of each month of the hire multiplied by 48.

---

* Publisher's note: Passage in square brackets amended by regulation 32 of the Utilities Supply and Works Contracts Regulations 1992.

[15] The amount is determined for each successive period of 2 years commencing on 1st January 1988 by calculating the average of the daily exchange rate between the ECU and the special drawing right over a period of 24 months preceding the commencement of the revised valuation and adjusting that figure to exclude value added tax at a notional rate of 13 per cent. The amount to be treated as the ECU equivalent of 130,000 special drawing rights for the 2 years from 1st January 1990 is published in OJ No. C18, 25.1.90, p.3 and is 134,000 ECU.

(5) Where a contracting authority proposes to enter into two or more public supply contracts at the same time in order to purchase or hire goods of a particular type, the estimated value for the purposes of paragraph (1) above of each of those contracts shall be the aggregate of the value of the consideration which the contracting authority expects to give under each of those contracts.

(6) Where a contracting authority has a recurrent need to purchase or hire goods of the type to be purchased or hired under the contract and for that purpose enters into separate public supply contracts at different times or into a public supply contract which under its terms is renewable or into a public supply contract for the purchase or hire of goods over an indefinite period, the estimated value for the purposes of paragraph (1) above of the contract shall be the amount calculated by applying one of the following two valuation methods—

(a) by taking the aggregate of the value of the consideration given by the contracting authority under such contracts for the purchase or hire of goods of the type to be purchased or hired under the contract during the last financial year of the contracting authority ending before, or the period of 12 months ending immediately before, the relevant time, and by adjusting that amount to take account of any expected changes in quantity and cost of the goods of that type to be purchased or hired in the period of 12 months commencing with the relevant time, or

(b) by estimating the aggregate of the value of the consideration which the contracting authority expects to give under such contracts for the purchase or hire of goods of the type to be purchased or hired under the contract during the period of 12 months from the first date of delivery of the goods to be purchased or hired under this contract or, where the contract is for a definite term of more than 12 months, during the term of the contract,

except that when the goods to be purchased or hired under the contract are required for the sole purposes of a discrete operational unit within the organisation of the contracting authority and—

(i) the decision whether to purchase or hire goods of that type has been devolved to such a unit; and

(ii) that decision is taken independently of any other part of the contracting authority,

the valuation methods described in sub-paragraphs (a) and (b) above shall be adapted by aggregating only the value of the consideration which the contracting authority has given or expects to give, as the case may be, for goods of the type to be purchased or hired under the contract which were or are required for the sole purposes of that unit.

(7) The estimated value for the purposes of paragraph (1) above of a contract which falls to be treated as a public supply contract by virtue of sub-paragraph (ii) of the definition of a "public supply contract" in regulation 2(1) (public supply contracts under which goods and services are provided and the services have a greater value than, but are separate from, the goods) shall be that proportion of the value of the consideration which the contracting authority expects to give under the contract which is attributable to the purchase or hire of the goods and to any siting or installation of the goods.

(8) Where a public supply contract includes one or more options the estimated value of the contract shall be determined by calculating the highest possible amount which could .be payable under the contract.

(9) The relevant time for the purposes of paragraphs (1) and (6)(a) above means, in relation to a public supply contract, the date on which the contract notice would be sent

171

to the Official Journal if the requirement to send such a notice applied to that contract in accordance with these Regulations.

(10) A contracting authority shall not enter into separate public supply contracts nor select nor exercise a choice under a valuation method in accordance with paragraph (6) above with the intention of avoiding the application of these Regulations to those contracts.

PART II

## TECHNICAL SPECIFICATIONS

**D–02** **Technical specifications in the contract documents**

**8.**—(1) In this regulation—

"common technical specification" means a technical specification drawn up in accordance with a procedure recognised by the member States with a view to uniform application in all Member States and which has been published in the Official Journal;

"European specification" means a common technical specification or a British standard implementing a European standard;

"European standard" means a standard approved by the European Committee for Standardisation ("CEN") or by the European Committee for Electrotechnical Standardisation ("CENELEC") as a "European Standard ("EN") or a "Harmonisation Document" ("HD") according to the Common Rules of those organisations;

"standard" means a technical specification approved by a recognised standardising body for repeated and continuous application, compliance with which is in principle not compulsory; and

"technical specifications" means the technical requirements defining the characteristics required of goods (such as quality, performance, safety or dimensions and requirements in respect of terminology, symbols, tests and testing methods, packaging, marking and labelling) so that the goods are described objectively in a manner which will ensure that they fulfil the use for which they are intended by the contracting authority.

(2) If a contracting authority wishes to lay down technical specifications which the goods to be purchased or hired under a public supply contract must meet it shall specify all such technical specifications in the contract documents.

(3) Subject to paragraph (4) below, the technical specifications in the contract documents relating to a public supply contract shall be defined by reference to any European specifications which are relevant.

(4) A contracting authority may define the technical specifications referred to in paragraph (3) above other than by reference to relevant European specifications if—

(a) the contracting authority is under an obligation to define the technical specifications by reference to technical requirements which are mandatory in the United Kingdom for the goods to be purchased or hired under the contract (but only to the extent that such an obligation is compatible with Community obligations);

(b) the relevant European specifications do not include provision for establishing conformity to, or it is technically impossible to establish satisfactorily that the goods to be purchased or hired under the contract do conform to, the relevant European specifications;

(c) definition by reference to the relevant European specifications would conflict with

172

the application of Council Directive 86/361/EEC on the initial stage of mutual recognition of type approval for telecommunication terminal equipment[16] or Council Decision 87/95/EEC on standardisation in the field of information technology and telecommunications[17] or other Community obligations in specific service or goods areas;

(d) subject to paragraph (5) below, application of the relevant European specifications would oblige the contracting authority to acquire goods incompatible with equipment already in use or would entail disproportionate costs or disproportionate technical difficulties; or

(e) the project for which the goods to be purchased or hired under the contract are required is of a genuinely innovative nature for which use of existing relevant European specifications would be inappropriate.

(5) A contracting authority may only define the technical specifications other than by reference to relevant European specifications on the grounds specified in paragraph (4)(d) above where the contracting authority has a clearly defined and recorded strategy for changing over, within a set period, to European specifications.

(6) A contracting authority shall, unless it is impossible, state in the contract notice relating to the contract which of the circumstances specified in paragraph (4) above was the ground for defining the technical specifications other than by reference to European specifications, and shall in any event keep a record of this information which, if the Commission or any member State requests it, it shall send to the Treasury for onward transmission to the Commission or member State which requested it.

(7) In the absence of European specifications relevant to the goods to be purchased or hired under a public supply contract, the technical specifications in the contract documents may be defined by reference to the following standards (and, if they are so defined, preference shall be given to the following standards in the order in which they are listed)—

(a) British standards implementing international standards;
(b) other British standards; or
(c) any other standards.

(8) Subject to paragraph (10) below, the contract documents relating to a public supply contract shall not include technical specifications which refer to goods of a specific make or source or to a particular process and which have the effect of favouring or eliminating particular goods or suppliers.

(9) Without prejudice to the generality of paragraph (8) above, references to trademarks, patents, types, origin or means of production shall not be incorporated into the technical specifications in the contract documents.

(10) Notwithstanding paragraphs (8) and (9) above, a contracting authority may incorporate the references referred to in paragraphs (8) and (9) above into the technical specifications in the contract documents if—

(a) such references are justified by the subject of the contract, or
(b) the goods to be purchased or hired under the contract cannot otherwise be described by reference to technical specifications which are sufficiently precise and intelligible to all suppliers, provided that the references are accompanied by the words "or equivalent".

[16] OJ No. L217, 5.8.86, p.21.
[17] OJ No. L36, 7.2.87, p.31.

(11) Where the goods to be purchased or hired under a public supply contract are to be the subject of a design competition, or where the supplier is permitted under the terms of the invitation to tender to submit tenders based on different technical specifications, the contracting authority shall not reject a tender on the ground that it has been drawn up by reference to different technical calculations from those used in the United Kingdom if the tender otherwise accords with the terms and conditions of the contract documents and the supplier submits with the tender the evidence necessary for examining the tender and provides such additional explanations as the contracting authority considers necessary.

PART III

## PROCEDURES LEADING TO THE AWARD OF A PUBLIC SUPPLY CONTRACT

**D–03**   **Annual notice of expected public supply contracts**

**9.**—(1) Subject to paragraph (2) below, a GATT contracting authority shall, as soon as possible after the commencement of each of its financial years, send to the Official Journal a notice in a form substantially corresponding to that set out in Part A of Schedule 3 and containing the information therein specified in respect of the public supply contracts in relation to which it expects to seek offers leading to an award during that financial year.

(2) The obligation under paragraph (1) above shall apply only to those public supply contracts which are for the purchase or hire of goods of a type which the contracting authority expects at the date of despatch of the notice to purchase or hire under public supply contracts which have an estimated value (within the meaning of regulation 7) which in aggregate for that type of goods is, or is more than, 750,000 ECU.

**Selection of contract award procedure**

**10.**—(1) For the purposes of seeking offers in relation to a proposed public supply contract a contracting authority shall use the open procedure, the restricted procedure or the negotiated procedure and shall decide which of these procedures to use in accordance with the following paragraphs of this regulation.

(2) A contracting authority may use the restricted procedure when to do so is justified by the circumstances, such as—

(a) when the cost of using the open procedure would be disproportionate to the value of the goods to be purchased or hired under the contract;
(b) the nature of the goods to be purchased or hired under the contract.

(3) A contracting authority may use the negotiated procedure in the following circumstances—

(a) subject to paragraph (4) below, in the event that the procedure leading to the award of a public supply contract by the contracting authority using the open or restricted procedure was *discontinued*—
  (i) because of irregular tenders, or
  (ii) following an evaluation made in accordance with regulation 11(6) or 12(4); and without prejudice to the generality of the meaning of the words "irregular tenders" a tender may be considered irregular if the supplier fails to meet the requirements of, or the tender offers variations on the requirements specified in, the contract documents where this is not permitted under the terms of the invitation to tender, or the goods offered do not meet the technical specifications (within the meaning of regulation 8(1)) of the contracting authority;
(b) subject to paragraph (4), below, in the absence of tenders in response to an

174

invitation to tender by the contracting authority using the open or restricted procedure;

(c) when the goods to be purchased or hired under the contract are to be manufactured purely for the purpose of research, experiment, study or development but not when the goods are |to be purchased or hired| to establish their commercial viability or to recover their research and development costs;

(d) when, for technical or artistic reasons, or for reasons connected with the protection of exclusive rights, the goods to be purchased or hired under the contract may only be manufactured or supplied by a particular person;

(e) when (but only if it is strictly necessary), for reasons of extreme urgency brought about by events unforeseeable by and not attributable to the contracting authority, the time limits specified in regulations 11 and 12 if the open or restricted procedures are used cannot be met; and

(f) subject to paragraph (5) below, when the goods to be purchased or hired under the contract are required by the contracting authority as a partial replacement for, or addition to, existing goods or an installation and when to obtain the goods from a person other than the person who supplied the existing goods or the installation would oblige the contracting authority to acquire goods having different technical characteristics which would result in—

   (i) incompatibility between the existing goods or the installation and the goods to be purchased or hired under the contract, or

   (ii) disproportionate technical difficulties in the operation and maintenance of the existing goods or the installation.

(4) A contracting authority shall not use the negotiated procedure pursuant to paragraphs (3)(a) or (b) above unless the proposed terms of the contract are substantially unaltered from the proposed terms of the contract in relation to which offers were sought using the open or restricted procedure.

(5) A contracting authority shall not use the negotiated procedure pursuant to paragraph (3)(f) above if the term of the proposed contract, or the term of that contract and of any other contract entered into for the same purpose, is more than three years unless there are reasons why it is unavoidable that this period should be exceeded.

(6) In all other circumstances the contracting authority shall use the open procedure.

(7) A contracting authority using the negotiated procedure pursuant to paragraph 3)(b) above shall submit a report recording the fact that it has done so to the Treasury for onward transmission to the Commission.

(8) A contracting authority using the negotiated or restricted procedure shall prepare a record in relation to the contract justifying the use of the procedure applied and specifying—

(a) the name and address of the contracting authority;

(b) the value, quantity and type of the goods to be purchased or hired under the contract;

(c) the number of persons who asked to be selected to tender for or to negotiate the contract;

(d) the number of persons selected to tender for or to negotiate the contract;

(e) the number of persons, if any, who, having sought to be selected to tender or to negotiate, were not so selected and the reasons for not selecting them; and

(f) in the case of a contracting authority using the negotiated procedure, which of the circumstances specified in paragraph (3) above constituted the grounds for using that procedure.

175

(9) If the Commission requests a report justifying the use of the negotiated or restricted procedure, the contracting authority shall send a written report containing the information specified in paragraph (8) above to the Treasury for onward transmission to the Commission.

## The open procedure

**11.**—(1) A contracting authority using the open procedure shall comply with the following paragraphs of this regulation.

(2) The contracting authority shall publicise its intention to seek offers in relation to the public supply contract by sending to the Official Journal as soon as possible after forming the intention a notice, in a form substantially corresponding to that set out in Part B of Schedule 3, inviting tenders and containing the information therein specified in relation to the contract.

(3) The date which the contracting authority shall fix as the last date for the receipt by it of tenders made in response to the contract notice shall be specified in the notice and shall be not less than 52 days from the date of despatch of the notice but, if it is necessary that suppliers be given the opportunity to inspect the premises at which the goods are to be used or documents relating to the contract documents, then that minimum period shall be extended to allow for such inspection.

(4) The contracting authority shall send the contract documents within 4 working days of the receipt of a request from any supplier provided that the documents are requested by the date specified in the contract notice and any fee specified in the notice has accompanied the request.

(5) The contracting authority shall supply such further information relating to the contract documents as may reasonably be requested by a supplier provided that the request is received in sufficient time to enable the contracting authority to supply the information no later than 6 days before the date specified in the contract notice as the final date for the receipt of tenders.

(6) The contracting authority may exclude a tender from the evaluation of offers made in accordance with regulation 20 only if the supplier may be treated as ineligible on a ground specified in regulation 14 or if the supplier fails to satisfy the minimum standards of economic and financial standing and technical capacity required of suppliers by the contracting authority; for this purpose the contracting authority shall make its evaluation in accordance with regulations 14, 15, 16 and 17.

## The restricted procedure

**12.**—(1) A contracting authority using the restricted procedure shall comply with the following paragraphs of this regulation.

(2) The contracting authority shall publicise its intention to seek offers in relation to the public supply contract by sending to the Official Journal as soon as possible after forming the intention a notice, in a form substantially corresponding to that set out in Part C of Schedule 3, inviting requests to be selected to tender and containing the information therein specified in relation to the contract.

(3) Subject to paragraph (9) below, the date which the contracting authority shall fix as the last date for the receipt by it of requests to be selected to tender shall be specified in the contract notice and shall be not less than 37 days from the date of the despatch of the notice.

(4) The contracting authority may exclude a supplier from those persons from whom it

will make the selection of the persons to be invited to tender only if the supplier may be treated as ineligible on a ground specified in regulation 14 or if the supplier fails to satisfy the minimum standards of economic and financial standing and technical capacity required of suppliers by the contracting authority; for this purpose the contracting authority shall make its evaluation in accordance with regulations 14, 15, 16 and 17.

(5) The contracting authority shall make the selection of the suppliers to be invited to tender in accordance with regulations 14, 15, 16 and 17; and in making the selection and in issuing invitations the contracting authority shall not discriminate between suppliers on the grounds of their nationality or the member State in which they are established.

(6) The invitation to tender may be sent by letter, telegram, telex, facsimile or telephone but, in the last 4 cases, it shall be confirmed by letter and the letter of invitation shall be sent simultaneously to each supplier selected to tender together with the contract documents.

(7) Subject to paragraph (9) below, the date which the contracting authority shall fix as the last date for the receipt by it of tenders made in response to the invitation to tender shall be specified in the invitation to tender and shall be not less than 40 days from the despatch of the invitation but, if it is necessary that suppliers be given the opportunity to inspect the premises at which the goods are to be used or documents relating to the contract documents, then that minimum period shall be extended to allow for such inspection.

(8) Subject to paragraph (9) below, the contracting authority shall supply such further information relating to the contract documents as may reasonably be requested by a supplier selected to tender provided that the request for such information is received in sufficient time to enable the contracting authority to supply it not less than 6 days before the date specified in the invitation to tender as the final date for the receipt of tenders.

(9) Where compliance with the minimum periods referred to in paragraphs (3), (7) and (8) above is rendered impracticable for reasons of urgency, the contracting authority may substitute for the periods specified in those paragraphs periods of not less than 15 days, 10 days and 4 days respectively and, in those circumstances, the contracting authority shall send the invitation to tender by the most rapid means possible.

(10) A contracting authority shall not refuse to consider an application to be invited to tender if it is made by letter, telegram, telex or telephone provided that, in the last three cases, it is confirmed by letter without delay.

**The negotiated procedure**

**13.**—(1) A contracting authority using the negotiated procedure shall comply with the following paragraphs of this regulation except that—

(a) a contracting authority using the negotiated procedure pursuant to regulation 10(3)(b), (c), (d), (e) or (f), and

(b) a contracting authority using the negotiated procedure pursuant to regulation 10(3)(a) who invites to negotiate the contract every supplier who submitted a tender following an invitation made during the course of the discontinued open or restricted procedure (not being a tender which was excluded pursuant to regulation 11(6)),

need not comply with paragraphs (2) to (6) below.

(2) The contracting authority shall publicise its intention to seek offers in relation to the public supply contract by sending the Official Journal as soon as possible after forming the intention a notice, in form substantially corresponding to that set out in part D of

Schedule 3, inviting requests to be selected to negotiate and containing the information therein specified in relation to the contract.

(3) Subject to paragraph (4) below, the date which the contracting authority shall fix as the last date for the receipt by it of requests to be selected to negotiate shall be specified in paragraph 6(a) of the contract notice and shall be not less than 37 days from the date of despatch of the notice.

(4) Where compliance with the minimum period of 37 days in paragraph (3) above is rendered impracticable for reasons of urgency, the contracting authority may substitute a period of not less than 15 days and, in those circumstances, the contracting authority must send the invitation to negotiate the contract by the most rapid means possible.

(5) A contracting authority shall not refuse to consider an application to be selected to negotiate if it is made by letter, telegram, telex or telephone provided that, in the last three cases, it is confirmed by letter without delay.

(6) The invitation to negotiate the contract may be sent by letter, telegram, telex, facsimile or telephone but, in the last 4 cases, it shall be confirmed by letter and the letter of invitation shall be sent simultaneously to each supplier selected to negotiate together with the contract documents.

(7) The contracting authority may exclude a supplier from those persons from whom it will make the selection of persons to be invited to negotiate the contract only if the supplier may be treated as ineligible on a ground specified in regulation 14 or if the supplier fails to satisfy the minimum standards of economic and financial standing and technical capacity required of suppliers by the contracting authority; for this purpose the contracting authority shall make its evaluation in accordance with regulations 14, 15, 16 and 17.

(8) The contracting authority may negotiate the terms of the public supply contract with one or more persons and shall make the selection of the suppliers to be invited to negotiate in accordance with regulations 14, 15, 16 and 17; and in making the selection and in issuing the invitation to negotiate the contracting authority shall not discriminate between suppliers on the grounds of their nationality or the member State in which they are established.

PART IV

**SELECTION OF SUPPLIERS**

D–04    **Criteria for rejection of suppliers**

**14.**—(1) A contracting authority may treat a supplier as ineligible to tender for, or to be included amongst those persons from whom it will make the selection of persons to be invited to tender for or negotiate, a public supply contract in accordance with regulations 11(6), 12(4) and 13(7), or decide not to select a supplier to tender for or to negotiate a public supply contract in accordance with regulations 12(5) and 13(8), on one of the following grounds, namely that the supplier—

(a) being an individual is bankrupt or has had a receiving order or administration order made against him or has made any composition or arrangement with or for the benefit of his creditors or has made any conveyance or assignment for the benefit of his creditors or appears unable to pay, or to have no reasonable prospect of being able to pay, a debt within the meaning of section 268 of the Insolvency Act 1986,[18] or article 242 of the Insolvency (Northern Ireland) Order 1989,[19] or in

[18] 1986 c.45.
[19] S.I. 1989/2405 (N.I.19).

Scotland has granted a trust deed for creditors or become otherwise apparently insolvent, or is the subject of a petition presented for sequestration of his estate, or is the subject of any similar procedure under the law of any other State;

(b) being a partnership constituted under Scots law has granted a trust deed or become otherwise apparently insolvent, or is the subject of a petition presented for sequestration of its estate;

(c) being a company has passed a resolution or is the subject of an order by the court for the company's winding up otherwise than for the purposes of bona fide reconstruction or amalgamation, or has had a receiver, manager or administrator on behalf of a creditor appointed in respect of the company's business or any part thereof or is the subject of proceedings for any of the above procedures or is the subject of similar procedures under the law of any other State;

(d) has been convicted of a criminal offence relating to the conduct of his business or profession;

(e) has committed an act of grave misconduct in the course of his business or profession;

(f) has not fulfilled obligations relating to the payment of social security contributions under the law of any part of the United Kingdom or of the member State in which the supplier is established;

(g) has not fulfilled obligations relating to the payment of taxes under the law of any part of the United Kingdom or the member State in which the supplier is established;

(h) is guilty of serious misrepresentation in supplying any information required of him under this regulation and regulations 15, 16 and 17; or

(i) subject to paragraphs (5) and (6) below, is not registered on the professional or trade register of the member State in which the supplier is established under the conditions laid down by that State.

(2) The contracting authority may require a supplier to provide such information as it considers it needs to make the evaluation in accordance with paragraph (1) above except that it shall accept as conclusive evidence that a supplier does not fall within the grounds specified in paragraphs (1)(a), (b), (c), (d), (f) or (g) above if that supplier provides to the contracting authority—

(a) in relation to the grounds specified in paragraphs (1)(a), (b), (c) or (d) above,
   (i) an extract from the judicial record, or
   (ii) in a member State which does not maintain such a judicial record, a document issued by the relevant judicial or administrative authority;

(b) in relation to the grounds specified in paragraph (1)(f) or (g) above, a certificate issued by the relevant competent authority;

(c) in a member State where the documentary evidence specified in paragraphs 2(a) and (b) above is not issued or where it is issued but does not extend to all of the grounds specified in paragraph (1)(a), (b), (c) or (d) above, a declaration on oath, or in a member State which does not provide for a declaration on oath a solemn declaration, made by the supplier before the relevant judicial, administrative or competent authority or a relevant notary public or commissioner for oaths accompanied by a certificate of such relevant authority, notary public or commissioner for oaths attesting the authenticity of the declaration.

(3) In this regulation, "relevant" in relation to a judicial, administrative or competent authority, notary public or commissioner for oaths means such an authority designated by, or a notary public or commissioner of oaths in, the member State in which the supplier is established.

(4) The following are the appropriate professional or trade registers for the purposes of paragraph (1)(i) above—

in Belgium, the registre du commerce/Handelsregister;

in Denmark, the Aktieselskabs-Registeret, Forenings-Registere or Handelsregisteret;

in France, the registre du commerce and répertoire des métiers;

in Germany, the Handelsregister or Handwerksrolle;

in Italy, the registro della camera di commercio, industria, agricoltura e artiginato or registro delle commissioni provinciali per l'artigianato;

in Luxembourg, the registre aux firmes and the rôle de la chambre des métiers;

in the Netherlands, the Handelsregister;

in Portugal, the Registo Nacional das Pessoas Colectivas; and

in Spain, the Registro del Ministerio de Industria y Energia.

(5) A supplier established in the United Kingdom or Ireland shall be treated as registered on the professional or trade register for the purposes of paragraph (1)(i) above if the supplier—

(a) is established in Ireland and is certified as registered with the Registrar of Friendly Societies, or

(b) is established in either State and is either—
  (i) certified as incorporated by the Registrar of Companies, or
  (ii) is certified as having declared on oath that he is carrying on business in the trade in question in the State in which he is established at a specific place of business and under a specific trading name.

(6) A supplier established in Greece shall be treated as registered on the professional or trade register for the purposes of paragraph (1)(i) above if the supplier is certified as having declared on oath before a notary public that he exercises the profession of a supplier.

### Information as to economic and financial standing

**15.**—(1) Subject to paragraph (2) below, in assessing whether a supplier meets any minimum standards of economic and financial standing required of suppliers by the contracting authority for the purposes of regulations 11(6), 12(4) and 13(7), and in selecting the suppliers to be invited to tender for or negotiate the contract in accordance with regulations 12(5) and 13(8), a contracting authority shall only take into account any of the following information (and it may require a supplier to provide such of that information as it considers it needs to make the assessment or selection)—

(a) appropriate statements from the supplier's bankers;

(b) statements of accounts or extracts therefrom relating to the business of the supplier;

(c) a statement of the overall turnover of the business of the supplier and the turnover in respect of goods of a similar type to the goods to be purchased or hired under the public supply contract in the 3 previous financial years of the supplier.

(2) Where the information specified in paragraph (1) above is not appropriate in a particular case, a contracting authority may require a supplier to provide other information to demonstrate the supplier's economic and financial standing.

(3) A contracting authority which requires information to be provided in accordance with paragraphs (1) and (2) above shall specify in the contract notice or in the invitation to tender the information which the supplier must provide.

(4) Where a supplier is unable for a valid reason to provide the information which the contracting authority has required, the contracting authority shall accept such other information provided by the supplier as the contracting authority considers appropriate.

**Information as to technical capacity**

**16.**—(1) In assessing whether a supplier meets any minimum standards of technical capacity required of suppliers by the contracting authority for the purposes of regulations 11(6), 12(4) and 13(7), and in selecting the suppliers to be invited to tender for or to negotiate the contract in accordance with regulations 12(5) and 13(8), a contracting authority shall only take into account any of the following information (and it may require a supplier to provide such of that information as it considers it needs to make the assessment or selection)—

(a) a list of deliveries by the supplier of goods of a similar type to the goods to be purchased or hired under the public supply contract in the past 3 years, specifying in each case the date of delivery, the consideration received and the identity of the purchaser accompanied by a certificate issued or countersigned by the purchaser confirming the details of the sale or, but only where the purchaser was not a contracting authority, a declaration by the supplier attesting the details of the purchase;

(b) a description of the supplier's technical facilities, measures for ensuring quality and study and research facilities in relation to the goods to be purchased or hired under the public supply contract;

(c) an indication of the technicians or technical bodies who would be involved with the production of the goods to be purchased or hired under the public supply contract, particularly those responsible for quality control, whether or not they are independent of the supplier;

(d) samples, descriptions and photographs of the goods to be purchased or hired under the public supply contract and certification of the authenticity of such samples, descriptions or photographs;

(e) certification by official quality control institutes or agencies of recognised competence attesting that the goods to be purchased or hired under the public supply contract conform to standards and technical specifications (within the meaning of regulation 8) identified by the contracting authority;

(f) where the goods to be sold or hired under the public supply contract are complex or are required for a special purpose, a check, carried out by the contracting authority or on its behalf by a competent official body of the member State in which the supplier is established, on the production capacity of the supplier in respect of the goods to be purchased or hired under the contract and, if relevant, on the supplier's study and research facilities and quality control measures.

(2) The contracting authority shall specify in the contract notice which of the information specified in paragraph (1) above it requires to be provided.

**Supplementary information**

**17.** The contracting authority may require a supplier to provide information supplementing the information supplied in accordance with regulations 14, 15 and 16 or to clarify that information, provided that the information so required relates to the matters specified in regulations 14, 15 and 16.

**Confidentiality of information**

**18.** A contracting authority shall comply with such requirements as to the confidentiality of information provided to it by a supplier as the supplier may reasonably request.

181

**Consortia**

**19.**—(1) In this regulation a "consortium" means 2 or more persons, at least one of whom is a supplier, acting jointly for the purpose of being awarded a public supply contract.

(2) A contracting authority shall not treat the tender of a consortium is ineligible nor decide not to include a consortium amongst those persons from whom it will make the selection of persons to be invited to tender for or to negotiate a public supply contract on the grounds that that consortium has not formed a legal entity for the purpose of tendering for or negotiating the contract; but where a contracting authority awards a public supply contract to a consortium it may, if to do so is justified for the satisfactory performance of the contract, require the consortium to form a legal entity before entering into, or as a term of, the contract.

(3) In these Regulations references to a supplier where the supplier is a consortium include a reference to each person who is a member of that consortium.

PART V

**THE AWARD OF A PUBLIC SUPPLY CONTRACT**

D–05 **Criteria for the award of a public supply contract**

**20.**—(1) Subject to paragraphs (4) and (5) below, a contracting authority shall award a public supply contract on the basis of the offer which—

(a)  offers the lowest price, or
(b)  is the most economically advantageous to the contracting authority.

(2) The criteria which a contracting authority may use to determine that an offer is the most economically advantageous include price, delivery date, running costs, cost effectiveness, quality, aesthetic and functional characteristics, technical merit, after sales service and technical assistance.

(3) Where a contracting authority intends to award a public supply contract on the basis of the offer which is the most economically advantageous it shall state the criteria on which it intends to base its decision, where possible in descending order of importance, in the contract notice or in the contract documents.

(4) If an offer for a public supply contract is obviously abnormally low the contracting authority shall request an explanation of the offer, or of those parts which it considers contribute to the offer being abnormally low, and shall—

(a)  if awarding the contract on the basis of the offer which offers the lowest price, examine the details of all the offers made, taking into account any explanation given to it of the abnormally low tender, before awarding the contract, or
(b)  if awarding the contract on the basis of the offer which is the most economically advantageous, take any such explanation into account in assessing which is the most economically advantageous offer.

(5) A contracting authority may, if it is not satisfied with the explanation of any supplier given in respect of an abnormally low offer, reject that offer but, if a contracting authority which rejects an offer for this reason is awarding the contract on the basis of the offer which offers the lowest price, it shall send a report justifying the rejection to the Treasury for onward transmission to the Commission.

(6) For the purposes of this regulation an "offer" includes a bid by one part of a contracting authority to make available to another part of the contracting authority the

goods required by it when the former part is invited by the latter part to compete with the offers sought from other persons.

## Contract award notice

**21.**—(1) A contracting authority which has awarded a public supply contract shall, no later than 48 days after the award, send to the Official Journal a notice, substantially corresponding to the form set out in Part E of Schedule 3, and subject to paragraph (2) below, including the information therein specified in relation to the contract.

(2) Any of the information specified in Part E of Schedule 3 to be included in the contract award notice may be omitted in a particular case where to publish such information would impede law enforcement, would otherwise be contrary to the public interest, would prejudice the legitimate commercial interests of any person or might prejudice fair competition between suppliers.

PART VI

**MISCELLANEOUS**

## Public service bodies

D–06

**22.** Where a contracting authority, other than one which is a contracting authority only by reason of being a GATT contracting authority, grants to a person other than a contracting authority special or exclusive rights to carry on a service for the benefit of the public, it shall impose an express duty on that person not to discriminate in seeking offers in relation to, or in awarding, a contract for the purchase or hire of goods on the grounds of nationality against a person who is a national of and established in a member State or on the grounds that the goods to be supplied under the contract originate in another member State.

## Statistical and other reports

**23.**—(1) A GATT contracting authority shall, no later than 31 July in each year, send to the Treasury a report specifying—

    (a) in relation to each public supply contract awarded by it during the reporting period—
        (i) the value (estimated if necessary) of the consideration given or to be given under the contract;
        (ii) whether the open, restricted or negotiated procedure was used;
        (iii) if the negotiated procedure was used, pursuant to which provision of regulation 10(3) that procedure was used;
        (iv) the type of goods purchased or hired or to be purchased or hired under the contract; and
        (v) the nationality of the person to whom the contract was awarded; and
    (b) the aggregate value (estimated if necessary) of the consideration payable under the public supply contracts excluded from the operation of these Regulations by regulation 7 and awarded by it during the reporting period.

(2) A contracting authority which is not a GATT contracting authority shall, no later than 31 July 1993 and 31 July in each alternate year thereafter, send to the Treasury a report specifying in relation to each public supply contract awarded by it during the reporting period the information specified in paragraphs (1)(a)(i) to (v) above.

(3) A contracting authority shall send to the Treasury a report containing such other information as the Treasury may from time to time require in respect of particular public

supply contract (including public supply contracts excluded from the application of these Regulations by regulations 6 and 7) for the purpose of informing the Commission.

(4) In this regulation "the reporting period" means the year preceding the year in which the reports referred to in paragraphs (1) and (2) above are to be made.

### Responsibility for obtaining reports

**24.**—(1) Where a contracting authority is not a Minister of the Crown or a government department, that contracting authority shall send any report which it is required in accordance with regulations 8(6), 10(7), 10(9), 20(5) and 23 to send to the Treasury instead to the Minister responsible for that contracting authority and that Minister shall be responsible for sending the report to the Treasury.

(2) The Minister responsible for a contracting authority shall be the Minister of the Crown whose areas of responsibility are most closely connected with the functions of the contracting authority; and any question as to which Minister of the Crown's areas of responsibility are most closely connected with the functions of a contracting authority shall be determined by the Treasury whose determination shall be final.

(3) The requirement on a contracting authority to send any report in accordance with paragraph (1) above to the Minister of the Crown responsible for that contracting authority shall be enforceable, on the application of the Minister responsible, by mandamus or, in Scotland, for an order for specific performance.

(4) Proceedings under paragraph (3) above brought in Scotland shall be brought before the Court of Session.

(5) In the application of this regulation to Northern Ireland references to the Minister shall include references to the head of a Northern Ireland department.

### Publication of notices

**25.**—(1) Any notice required by these Regulations to be sent to the Official Journal shall be sent by the most appropriate means to the Office for Official Publications of the European Communities[20] and where the contracting authority is applying the restricted procedure or the negotiated procedure and, for reasons of urgency, is applying the provisions of regulations 12(9) and 13(4), the notice shall be sent by telex, telegram or facsimile.

(2) Any such notice shall not contain more than 650 words.

(3) The contracting authority shall retain evidence of the date of despatch to the Official Journal of each notice.

(4) The contracting authority shall not place a contract notice in the press or like publications in the United Kingdom before the date on which the notice is despatched in accordance with paragraph (1) above and if it does, after that date, so place the notice it shall not add to the notice any information in relation to the public supply contract which was not contained in the notice sent to the Official Journal.

---

[20] The address for the Office for Official Publications of the European Communities is 2 Rue Mercier, 2985, Luxembourg (tel 499 28–1, telex 1324 pubof lu, fax: 49 00 03, 49 57 19).

PART VII

## APPLICATIONS TO THE COURT

**Enforcement of obligations relating to a public supply contract**          **D–07**

**26.**—(1) The obligation on a contracting authority to comply with the provisions of these Regulations other than regulations 8(6), 10(7), 10(9), 20(5), 23 and 24(1), and with any enforceable Community obligation in respect of a public supply contract (other than one excluded from the application of these Regulations by regulations 6 and 7), is a duty owed to suppliers.

(2) A breach of the duty owed pursuant to paragraph (1) above shall not be a criminal offence but any breach of the duty shall be actionably by any supplier who, in consequence, suffers, or risks suffering, loss or damage.

(3) Proceedings under this regulation shall be brought in England and Wales and in Northern Ireland in the High Court and, in Scotland, before the Court of Session.

(4) Proceedings under this regulation may not be brought unless—

(a) the supplier bringing the proceedings has informed the contracting authority of the breach or apprehended breach of the duty owed to him pursuant to paragraph (1) above by that contracting authority and of his intention to bring proceedings under this regulation in respect of it; and

(b) they are brought promptly and in any event within 3 months from the date when grounds for the bringing of the proceedings first arose unless the Court considers that there is good reason for extending the period within which proceedings may be brought.

(5) Subject to paragraph (6) below, but otherwise without prejudice to any other powers of the Court, in proceedings brought under this regulation the Court may—

(a) by interim order suspend the procedure leading to the award of the contract in relation to which the breach of the duty owed pursuant to paragraph (1) above is alleged, or suspend the implementation of any decision or action taken by the contracting authority in the course of following such procedure; and

(b) if satisfied that a decision or action taken by a contracting authority was in breach of a duty owed pursuant to paragraph (1) above—
   (i) order the setting aside of that decision or action or order the contracting authority to amend any document, or
   (ii) award damages to a supplier who has suffered loss or damage as a consequence of the breach, or
   (iii) do both of those things.

(6) In proceedings under this regulation the Court shall not have power to order any remedy other than an award of damages in respect of a breach of the duty owed pursuant to paragraph (1) above if the contract in relation to which the breach occurred has been entered into.

(7) Notwithstanding sections 21 and 42 of the Crown Proceedings Act 1947,[21] in proceedings brought under this regulation against the Crown the court shall have power to grant an injunction or interdict.

*Irvine Patnick*
*Thomas Sackville*

28th November 1991          Two of the Lords Commissioners of Her Majesty's Treasury

---

[21] 1947 c.44; the Crown Proceedings Act 1947 was extended to Northern Ireland in relation to Her Majesty's Government in the United Kingdom and in Northern Ireland by and with the additions, exceptions and modifications set out in the Crown Proceedings (Northern Ireland) Order 1981, to which there is an amemdment not relevant to these regulations.

Regulation 2(1)

GATT CONTRACTING AUTHORITIES

**D–08**  Cabinet Office
　　Civil Service College
　　Civil Service Commission
　　Civil Service Occupational Health Service
　　Office of the Minister for the Civil Service
　　Parliamentary Counsel Office
　Central Office of Information
　Charity Commission
　Crown Estate Commissioners
　Crown Prosecution Service
　Customs and Excise Department
　Department for National Savings
　Department of Education and Science
　　University Grants Committee
　Department of Employment
　　Employment Appeal Tribunal
　　Industrial Tribunals
　　Office of Manpower Economics
　Department of Energy
　Department of Health
　　Central Council for Education and Training in Social Work
　　Dental Estimates Board
　　English National Board for Nursing, Midwifery and Health Visitors
　　Medical Boards and Examining Medical Officers (War Pensions)
　　National Health Service Authorities
　　Prescription Pricing Authority
　　Public Health Laboratory Service Board
　　Regional Medical Service
　　U.K. Central Council for Nursing, Midwifery and Health Visiting
　Department of Social Security
　　Attendance Allowance Board
　　Occupational Pensions Board
　　Social Security Advisory Committee
　　Supplementary Benefits Appeal Tribunals
　Department of the Environment
　　Building Research Establishment
　　Commons Commissioners
　　Countryside Commission
　　Fire Research Station (Boreham Wood)
　　Historic Buildings and Monuments Commission
　　Local Valuation Panels
　　Property Services Agency
　　Rent Assessment Panels
　　Royal Commission on Environmental Pollution
　　Royal Commission on Historical Monuments of England
　　Royal Fine Art Commission (England)
　Department of the Procurator General and Treasury Solicitor
　　Legal Secretariat to the Law Officers
　Department of Trade and Industry
　　Laboratory of the Government Chemist
　　National Engineering Laboratory

National Physical Laboratory
Warren Spring Laboratory
National Weights and Measures Laboratory
Domestic Coal Consumers' Council
Electricity Consultative Councils for England and Wales
Gas Consumers' Council
Transport Users Consultative Committees
Monopolies and Mergers Commission
Patent Office
Department of Transport
Coastguard Services
Transport and Road Research Laboratory
Transport Tribunal
Export Credits Guarantee Department
Foreign and Commonwealth Office
Government Communications Headquarters
Wilton Park Conference Centre
Government Actuary's Department
Home Office
Boundary Commission for England
Gaming Board for Great Britain
Inspectors of Constabulary
Parole Board and Local Review Committees
House of Commons
House of Lords
Inland Revenue, Board of
Intervention Board for Agricultural Produce
Lord Chancellor's Department
Council on Tribunals
County Courts (England and Wales)
Immigration Appellate Authorities
Immigration Adjudicators
Immigration Appeal Tribunal
Judge Advocate General and Judge Advocate of the Fleet
Lands Tribunal
Law Commission
Legal Aid Fund (England and Wales)
Pensions Appeal Tribunals
Public Trustee Office
Office of the Social Security Commissioners
Special Commissioners for Income Tax (England and Wales)
Supreme Court (England and Wales)
Court of Appeal: Civil and Criminal Divisions
Courts Martial Appeal Court
Crown Court
High Court
Value Added Tax Tribunals
Ministry of Agriculture Fisheries and Food
Advisory Services
Agricultural Development and Advisory Service
Agricultural Dwelling House Advisory Committees
Agricultural Land Tribunals
Agricultural Science Laboratories
Agricultural Wages Board and Committees

Cattle Breeding Centre
Plant Variety Rights Office
Royal Botanic Gardens, Kew
Ministry of Defence
Meteorological Office
Procurement Executive
National Audit Office
National Investment Loans Office
Northern Ireland Court Service
Coroners Courts
County Courts
Crown Courts
Enforcement of Judgments Office
Legal Aid Fund
Magistrates Court
Pensions Appeals Tribunals
Supreme Court of Judicature and Courts of Criminal Appeal
Northern Ireland, Department of Agriculture
Northern Ireland, Department for Economic Development
Northern Ireland, Department of Education
Northern Ireland, Department of the Environment
Northern Ireland, Department of Finance and Personnel
Northern Ireland, Department of Health and Social Services
Northern Ireland Office
Crown Solicitor's Office
Department of the Director of Public Prosecutions for Northern Ireland
Northern Ireland Forensic Science Laboratory
Office of Chief Electoral Officer for Northern Ireland
Police Authority for Northern Ireland
Probation Board for Northern Ireland
State Pathologist Service
Office of Arts and Libraries
British Library
British Museum
British Museum (Natural History)
Imperial War Museum
Museums and Galleries Commission
National Gallery
National Maritime Museum
National Portrait Gallery
Science Museum
Tate Gallery
Victoria and Albert Museum
Wallace Collection
Office of Fair Trading
Office of Population Censuses and Surveys
National Health Service Central Register
Office of the Parliamentary Commissioner for Administration and Health Service
Commissioners
Overseas Development Administration
Overseas Development and National Research Institute
Paymaster General's Office
Postal Business of the Post Office
Privy Council Office

Public Record Office
Registry of Friendly Societies
Royal Commission on Historical Manuscripts
Royal Hospital, Chelsea
Royal Mint
Scotland, Crown Office and Procurator Fiscal Service
Scotland, Department of the Registers of Scotland
Scotland, General Register Office
   National Health Service Central Register
Scotland, Lord Advocate's Department
Scotland, Queen's and Lord Treasurer's Remembrancer
Scottish Courts Administration
   Accountant of Court's Office
   Court of Justiciary
   Court of Session
   Lands Tribunal for Scotland
   Pensions Appeal Tribunals
   Scottish Land Court
   Scottish Law Commission
   Sheriff Courts
   Social Security Commissioners' Office
Scottish Office
   Central Services
   Department of Agriculture and Fisheries for Scotland:
      Artificial Insemination Service
      Crofters Commission
      Red Deer Commission
      Royal Botanic Garden, Edinburgh
   Industry Department for Scotland
      Scottish Electricity Consultative Councils
   Scottish Development Department
      Rent Assessment Panel and Committees
      Royal Commission on the Ancient and Historical Monuments of Scotland
      Royal Fine Art Commission for Scotland
   Scottish Education Department
      National Galleries of Scotland
      National Library of Scotland
      National Museums of Scotland
   Scottish Home and Health Departments
      HM Inspectorate of Constabulary
      Local Health Councils
      Mental Welfare Commission for Scotland
      National Board for Nursing, Midwifery and Health Visiting for Scotland
      Parole Board for Scotland and Local Review Committees
      Scottish Antibody Production Unit
      Scottish Council for Postgraduate Medical Education
      Scottish Crime Squad
      Scottish Criminal Record Office
      Scottish Fire Service Training School
      Scottish Health Boards
      Scottish Health Service—Common Services Agency
      Scottish Health Service Planning Council
      Scottish Police College
Scottish Record Office

HM Stationery Office
HM Treasury
   Central Computer and Telecommunications Agency
   Chessington Computer Centre
   Civil Service Catering Organisation
   National Economic Development Council
   Rating of Government Property Department
Welsh Office
   Ancient Monuments (Wales) Commission
   Council for the Education and Training of Health Visitors
   Local Government Boundary Commission for Wales
   Local Valuation Panels and Courts
   National Health Service Authorities
   Rent Control Tribunals and Rent Assessment Panels and Committees

**SCHEDULE 2**          Regulation 7(2)(a)

GOODS FOR THE PURPOSES OF THE THRESHOLDS

**D–09**    The goods for the purposes of regulation 7(2)(a) are those specified in the following chapters of the CCCN (Customs Co-operation Council Nomenclature)

Chapter 25: Salt; sulphur; earths and stone; plastering materials, lime and cement

Chapter 26: Metallic ores, slag and ash

Chapter 27: Mineral fuels, mineral oils and products of their distillation; bituminous substances; mineral waxes
*except*:
ex 27.10: special engine fuels

Chapter 28: Inorganic chemicals; organic and inorganic compounds of precious metals, of rare-earth metals, of radio-active elements and of isotopes
*except*:
ex 28.09: explosives
ex 28.13: explosives
ex 28.14: tear gas
ex 28.28: explosives
ex 28.32: explosives
ex 28.39: explosives
ex 28.50: toxic products
ex 28.51: toxic products
ex 28.54: explosives

Chapter 29: Organic chemicals
*except*:
ex 29.03: explosives
ex 29.04: explosives
ex 29.07: explosives
ex 29.08: explosives
ex 29.11: explosives
ex 29.12: explosives
ex 29.13: toxic products
ex 29.14: toxic products
ex 29.15: toxic products

ex 29.21: toxic products
ex 29.22: toxic products
ex 29.23: toxic products
ex 29.26: explosives
ex 29.27: toxic products
ex 29.29: explosives

Chapter 30: Pharmaceutical products

Chapter 31: Fertilizers

Chapter 32: Tanning and dyeing extracts; tannins and their derivatives; dyes, colours, paints and varnishes; putty, fillers and stoppings; inks

Chapter 33: Essential oils and resinoids; perfumery, cosmetic or toilet preparations

Chapter 34: Soap, organic surface-active agents, washing preparations, lubricating preparations, artificial waxes, prepared waxes, polishing and scouring preparations, candles and similar articles, modelling pastes and "dental waxes"

Chapter 35: Albuminoidal substances; glues; enzymes

Chapter 37: Photographs and cinematographic goods

Chapter 38: Miscellaneous chemical products
*except*:
ex 38.19: toxic products

Chapter 39: Artificial resins and plastic materials, cellulose esters and ethers; articles thereof
*except*:
ex 39.03: explosives

Chapter 40: Rubber, synthetic rubber, factice, and articles thereof
*except*:
ex 40.11: bullet-proof tyres

Chapter 41: Raw hides and skins (other than furskins) and leather

Chapter 42: Articles of leather; saddlery and harness; travel goods, handbags and similar containers; articles of animal gut (other than silk-worm gut)

Chapter 43: Furskins and artificial fur; manufactures thereof

Chapter 44: Wood and articles of wood; wood charcoal

Chapter 45: Cork and articles of cork

Chapter 46: Manufactures of straw of esparto and of other plaiting materials; basketware and wickerwork

Chapter 47: Paper-making material

Chapter 48: Paper and paperboard; articles of paper pulp, of paper or of paperboard

Chapter 49: Printed books, newspapers, pictures and other products of the printing industry; manuscripts, typescripts and plans

Chapter 65: Headgear and parts thereof

Chapter 66: Umbrellas, sunshades, walking-sticks, whips, riding-crops and parts thereof

Chapter 67: Prepared feathers and down and articles made of feathers or of down, artificial flowers; articles of human hair

Chapter 68: Articles of stone, of plaster, of cement, of asbestos, of mica and of similar materials

Chapter 69: Ceramic products

Chapter 70: Glass and glassware

Chapter 71: Pearls, precious and semi-precious stones, precious metals, rolled precious metals, and articles thereof; imitation jewellery

Chapter 73: Iron and steel and articles thereof

Chapter 74: Copper and articles thereof

Chapter 75: Nickel and articles thereof

Chapter 76: Aluminium and articles thereof

Chapter 77: Magnesium and beryllium and articles thereof

Chapter 78: Lead and articles thereof

Chapter 79: Zinc and articles thereof

Chapter 80: Tin and articles thereof

Chapter 81: Other base metals employed in metallurgy and articles thereof

Chapter 82: Tools, implements, cutlery, spoons and forks, of base metal; parts thereof
*except*:
ex 82.05: tools
ex 82.07: tools, parts

Chapter 83: Miscellaneous articles of base metal

Chapter 84: Boilers, machinery and mechanical appliances; parts thereof
*except*:
ex 84.06: engines
ex 84.08: other engines
ex 84.45: machinery
ex 84.53: automatic data-processing machines
ex 84.55: parts of machines under heading No. 84.53
ex 84.59: nuclear reactors

Chapter 85: Electrical machinery and equipment; parts thereof
*except*:
ex 85.13: telecommunication equipment
ex 85.15: transmission apparatus

Chapter 86: Railway and tramway locomotives, rolling-stock and parts thereof; railway and tramway tracks fixtures and fittings; traffic signalling equipment of all kinds (not electrically powered)
*except*:
ex 86.02: armoured locomotives, electric
ex 86.03: other armoured locomotives
ex 86.05: armoured wagons
ex 86.06: repair wagons
ex 86.07: wagons

Chapter 87: Vehicles, other than railway or tramway rolling-stock, and parts thereof
*except*:
ex 87.08: tanks and other armoured vehicles
ex 87.01: tractors
ex 87.02: military vehicles
ex 87.03: breakdown lorries
ex 87.09: motorcycles
ex 87.14: trailers

Chapter 89: Ships, boats and floating structures
*except*:
ex 89.01 A: warships

Chapter 90: Optical, photographic, cinematographic, measuring, checking, precision, medical and surgical instruments and apparatus; parts thereof
*except*:
ex 90.05: binoculars
ex 90.13: miscellaneous instruments, lasers
ex 90.14: telemeters
ex 90.28: electrical and electronic measuring instruments
ex 90.11: microscopes
ex 90.17: medical instruments
ex 90.18: mechano-therapy appliances
ex 90.19: orthopaedic appliances
ex 90.20: X-ray apparatus

Chapter 91: Clocks and watches and parts thereof

Chapter 92: Musical instruments; sound recorders or reproducers; television image and sound recorders or reproducers; parts and accessories of such articles

Chapter 94: Furniture and parts thereof; bedding, mattresses, mattress supports, cushions and similar stuffed furnishings
*except*:
ex 94.01 A: aircraft seats

Chapter 95: Articles and manufactures of carving or moulding material

Chapter 96: Brooms, brushes, powder-puffs and sieves

Chapter 98: Miscellaneous manufactured articles

**SCHEDULE 3**    Regulations 9(1), 11(2), 12(2), 13(2) and 21(1)

FORMS OF NOTICES FOR PUBLICATION IN THE OFFICIAL JOURNAL

PART A

ANNUAL NOTICE OF EXPECTED PUBLIC SUPPLY CONTRACTS

1. Name, address and telephone, telegraphic, telex and facsimile numbers of the contracting authority and of the service from which additional information may be obtained.    **D–10**
2. Nature and quantity or value of the goods to be supplied.
3. Estimated date of the commencement of the procedures leading to the award of the contract(s) (if known).
4. Other information.
5. Date of despatch of the notice.

PART B

OPEN PROCEDURE NOTICE

1. Name, address and telephone, telegraphic, telex and facsimile numbers of the contracting authority.
2. (a) Award procedure chosen;
   (b) form of contract for which offers are invited.
3. (a) Place of delivery;
   (b) nature and quantity of the goods to be supplied;
   (c) indication of whether the suppliers can tender for some and/or all of the goods required;
   (d) derogation from the use of European specifications.[22]
4. Time limit for delivery, if any.
5. (a) Name and address of the service from which the contract documents may be requested;
   (b) final date for making such requests;
   (c) where applicable, the amount and terms of payment of any sum payable for such documents.
6. (a) Final date for receipt of tenders;
   (b) address to which they must be sent;
   (c) language(s) in which they must be drawn up.
7. (a) Persons authorised to be present at the opening of tenders;
   (b) date, time and place of opening.
8. Where applicable, any deposits and guarantees required.
9. The main terms concerning financing and payment and/or references to the relevant provisions.
10. Where applicable, the legal form to be taken by the grouping of suppliers winning the contract.
11. The information and formalities necessary for an appraisal of the minimum standards of economic and financial standing and technical capacity required of the supplier.
12. Period during which the tenderer is bound to keep open his tender.
13. Criteria for the award of the contract. Criteria other than that of the lowest price shall be mentioned if they do not appear in the contract documents.
14. Other information.
15. Date of despatch of the notice.

PART C

RESTRICTED PROCEDURE NOTICE

1. Name, address and telephone, telegraphic, telex and facsimile numbers of the contracting authority.
2. (a) Award procedure chosen;
   (b) where applicable, justification for use of the shorter time limits[23];
   (c) form of contract for which offers are invited.
3. (a) Place of delivery;
   (b) nature and quantity of goods to be delivered;
   (c) indication of whether the supplier can tender for some and/or all of the goods required;

---

[22] Within the meaning of regulation 8.
[23] In accordance with regulation 12.

(d) derogation from the use of European specifications.[24]
4. Time limit on delivery, if any.
5. Where applicable, the legal form to be assumed by the grouping of suppliers winning the contract.
6. (a) Final date for the receipt of requests to participate;
   (b) address to which they must be sent;
   (c) language(s) in which they must be drawn up.
7. Final date for the despatch of invitations to tender.
8. Information concerning the supplier's own position, and the information and formalities necessary for an appraisal of the minimum standards of economic and financial standing and technical capacity required of him.
9. Criteria for the award of the contract if these are not stated in the invitation to tender.
10. Other information.
11. Date of despatch of the notice.

## Part D

### Negotiated Procedure Notice

1. Name, address and telephone, telegraphic, telex and facsimile number of the contracting authority.
2. (a) Award procedure chosen;
   (b) where applicable, justification for use of the shorter time limits[25];
   (c) where applicable, form of contract for which offers are invited.
3. (a) Place of delivery;
   (b) nature and quantity of goods to be delivered;
   (c) indication of whether the suppliers can tender for some and/or all of the goods required;
   (d) derogation from the use of European specifications.[26]
4. Time limit on delivery, if any.
5. Where applicable, the legal form to be assumed by a grouping of suppliers winning the contract.
6. (a) Final date for the receipt of requests to participate;
   (b) address to which they must be sent;
   (c) language(s) in which they must be drawn up.
7. Information concerning the supplier's own position, and the information and formalities necessary for an appraisal of the minimum standards of economic and financial standing and technical capacity required of him.
8. Where applicable, the names and addresses of suppliers already selected by the awarding authority.
9. Date(s) of previous publications in the *Official Journal of the European Communities*.
10. Other information.
11. Date of despatch of the notice.

## Part E

### Contract Award Notice

1. Name and address of contracting authority.
2. (a) Award procedure chosen;

[24] Within the meaning of regulation 8.
[25] In accordance with regulation 13.
[26] Within the meaning of regulation 8.

195

(b) in respect of GATT contracting authorities, where appropriate, justification for the use of the negotiated procedure.[27]

3. Date of award of contract.
4. Criteria for award of contract.
5. Number of offers received.
6. Name(s) and address(es) of supplier(s).
7. Nature and quantity of goods supplied, where applicable, by supplier.
8. Price or range of prices.
9. Other information.
10. Date of publication of the tender notice in the *Official Journal of the European Communities*.
11. Date of despatch of the notice.

[27] In accordance with regulation 10(3).

# Appendix E

## PART 1

### THE UTILITIES DIRECTIVE

**Council Directive**

**of September 17, 1990**

**on the procurement procedures of entities operating in the water, energy, transport and telecommunications sectors**

(90/531/EEC)

THE COUNCIL OF THE EUROPEAN COMMUNITIES,

Having regard to the Treaty establishing in the European Economic Community and in particular the last sentence of Article 57(2), Article 66, Article 100a and Article 113 thereof,  **E–01**

Having regard to the proposal from the Commission,[1]

In cooperation with the European Parliament,[2]

Having regard to the opinion of the Economic and Social Committee,[3]

Whereas the measures aimed at progressively establishing the internal market, during the period up to 31 December 1992, need to be taken; whereas the internal market consists of an area without internal frontiers in which free movement of goods, persons, services and capital is guaranteed;

Whereas the European Council has drawn conclusions concerning the need to bring about a single internal market;

Whereas restrictions on the free movement of goods and on the freedom to provide services in respect of supply contracts awarded in the water, energy, transport and telecommunications sectors are prohibited by the terms of Articles 30 and 59 of the Treaty;

Whereas Article 97 of the Euratom Treaty prohibits any restrictions based on nationality as regards companies under the jurisdiction of a Member State where they desire to participate in the construction of nuclear installations of a scientific or industrial nature in the Community;

Whereas these objectives also require the coordination of the procurement procedures applied by the entities operating in these sectors;

Whereas the White Paper on the completion of the internal market contains an action programme and a timetable for opening up public procurement markets in sectors which are currently *excluded* from Council Directive 71/305/EEC of 26 July 1971 concerning the coordination of procedures for the award of public works contracts,[4] as last amended by Council Directive 89/440/EEC,[5] and Council Directive 77/62/EEC of 21 December 1976

[1] OJ No C 264, 16.10.1989, p. 22.
[2] OJ No C 158, 26.6.1989, p. 258 and OJ No C 175, 16.7.1990, p. 78.
[3] OJ No C 139, 5.6.1989, pp. 23 and 31.
[4] OJ No L 185, 16.8.1971, p. 5.
[5] OJ No L 210, 21.7.1989, p. 1.

coordinating procedures for the award of public supply contracts,[6] as last amended by Directive 88/295/EEC[7];

Whereas among such excluded sectors are those concerning the provision of water, energy and transport services and, as far as Directive 77/62/EEC is concerned, the telecommunications sector;

Whereas the main reason for their exclusion was that entities providing such services are in some cases governed by public law, in others by private law;

Whereas the need to ensure a real opening-up of the market and a fair balance in the application of procurement rules in these sectors requires that the entities to be covered must be identified on a different basis than by reference to their legal status;

Whereas, in the four sectors concerned, the procurement problems to be solved are of a similar nature, so permitting them to be addressed in one instrument;

Whereas, among the main reasons why entities operating in these sectors do not purchase on the basis of Community-wide competition is the closed nature of the markets in which they operate, due to the existence of special or exclusive rights granted by the national authorities, concerning the supply to, provision or operation of, networks for providing the service concerned, the exploitation of a given geographical area for a particular purpose, the provision or operation of public telecommunication networks or the provision of public telecommunications services;

Whereas the other main reason for the absence of Community-wide competition in these areas results from various ways in which national authorities can influence the behaviour of these entities, including participations in their capital and representation in the entities' administrative, managerial or supervisory bodies;

Whereas the Directive should not extend to activities of those entities which either fall outside the sectors of water, energy and transport services or outside the telecommunications sector, or which fall within those sectors but nevertheless are directly exposed to competitive forces in markets to which entry is unrestricted;

Whereas it is appropriate that these entities apply common procurement procedures in respect of their activities relating to water; whereas certain entities have been covered up to now by the Directives 71/305/EEC and 77/62/EEC in respect of their activities in the field of hydraulic engineering projects, irrigation, land drainage or the disposal and treatment of sewage;

Whereas, however, procurement rules of the type proposed for supplies of goods are inappropriate for purchases of water, given the need to procure water from sources near the area it will be used;

Whereas, when specific conditions are fulfilled, exploitation of a geographical area with the aim of exploring for or extracting oil, gas, coal or other solid fuels may be made subject to alternative arrangements which will enable the same objective of opening up contracts to be achieved; whereas the Commission must ensure that these conditions are complied with by the Member States who implement these alternative arrangements;

Whereas the Commission has announced that it will propose measures to remove obstacles to cross-frontier exchanges of electricity by 1992; whereas procurement rules of the type proposed for supplies of goods would not make it possible to overcome existing obstacles to the purchases of *energy and fuels in the energy sector*; whereas, as a result, it is not appropriate to include such purchases in the scope of this Directive, although it should be borne in mind that this exemption will be re-examined by the Council on the basis of a Commission report and Commission proposals;

Whereas Regulations (EEC) No 3975/87[8] and (EEC) No 3976/87,[9] Directive 87/601/EEC[10]

[6] OJ No L 13, 15.1.1977, p. 1.
[7] OJ No L 127, 20.5.1988, p. 1.
[8] OJ No L 374, 31.12.1987, p. 1.
[9] OJ No L 374, 31.12.1987, p. 9.
[10] OJ No L 374, 31.12.1987, p. 12.

and Decision 87/602/EEC[11] are designed to introduce more competition between the entities offering air transport services to the public and it is therefore not appropriate for the time being to include such entities in the scope of this Directive although the situation ought to be reviewed at a later stage in the light of progress made as regards competition;

Whereas, in view of the competitive position of Community shipping, it would be inappropriate for the greater part of the contracts in this sector to be subject to detailed procedures; whereas the situation of shippers operating sea-going ferries should be kept under review; whereas certain inshore and river ferry services operated by public authorities should no longer be excluded from the scope of Directives 71/305/EEC and 77/62/EEC;

Whereas it is appropriate to facilitate compliance with provisions relating to activities not covered by this Directive;

Whereas this Directive should not apply to procurement contracts which are declared secret or may affect basic State security interests or are concluded according to other rules set up by existing international agreements or international organizations;

Whereas the Community's or the Member States' existing international obligations must not be affected by the rules of this Directive;

Whereas products, works or services must be described by reference to European specifications; whereas, in order to ensure that a product, work or service fulfils the use for which it is intended by the contracting entity, such reference may be complemented by specifications which do not change the nature of the technical solution or solutions set out in the European specification;

Whereas the principles of equivalence and of mutual recognition of national standards, technical specifications and manufacturing methods are applicable in the field of application of this Directive;

Whereas, when the contracting entities define by common accord with tenderers the deadlines for receiving tenders, they shall comply with the principle of non-discrimination, and whereas, if there is no such agreement, it is necessary to lay down suitable provisions;

Whereas it could prove useful to provide for greater transparency as to the requirements regarding the protection and conditions of employment applicable in the Member State in which the works are to be carried out;

Whereas it is appropriate that national provisions for regional development requirements to be taken into consideration in the award of public works contracts should be made to conform to the objectives of the Community and be in keeping with the principles of the Treaty;

Whereas contracting entities must not be able to reject abnormally low tenders before having requested in writing explanations as to the constituent elements of the tender;

Whereas, within certain limits, preference should be given to an offer of Community origin where there are equivalent offers of third country origin;

Whereas this Directive should not prejudice the position of the Community in any current or future international negotiations;

Whereas, based on the results of such international negotiations, this Directive should be extendable to offers of third country origin, pursuant to a Council Decision;

Whereas the rules to be applied by the entities concerned should establish a framework for sound commercial practice and should leave a maximum of flexibility;

Whereas, as a counterpart for such flexibility and in the interest of mutual confidence, a minimum level of transparency must be ensured and appropriate methods adopted for monitoring the application of this Directive;

Whereas it is necessary to adapt Directives 71/305/EEC and 77/62/EEC to establish

[11] OJ No L 374, 31.12.1987, p. 19.

well-defined fields of application; whereas the scope of Directive 71/305/EEC should not be reduced, except as regards contracts in the water and telecommunications sectors; whereas the scope of Directive 77/62/EEC should not be reduced, except as regards certain contracts in the water sector; whereas the scope of Directives 71/305/EEC and 77/62/EEC should not, however, be extended to contracts awarded by carriers by land, air, sea, inshore or inland waterway which, although carrying out economic activities of an industrial or commercial nature, belong to the State administration; whereas, nevertheless, certain contracts awarded by carriers by land, air, sea, inshore or inland waterway which belong to the State administration and are carried out only for reasons of public service should be covered by those Directives;

Whereas this Directive should be re-examined in the light of experience;

Whereas the opening up of contracts, on 1 January 1993, in the sectors covered by this Directive might have an adverse effect upon the economy of the Kingdom of Spain; whereas the economies of the Hellenic Republic and the Portuguese Republic will have to sustain even greater efforts; whereas it is appropriate that these Member States be granted adequate additional periods to implement this Directive,

HAS ADOPTED THIS DIRECTIVE:

TITLE I

**GENERAL PROVISIONS**

*Article 1*

**E–02**     For the purposes of this Directive:

1. "public authorities" shall mean the State, regional or local authorities, bodies governed by public law, or associations formed by one or more of such authorities or bodies governed by public law.

A body is considered to be governed by public law where it:

— is established for the specific purpose of meeting needs in the general interest, not being of a commercial or industrial nature, and
— has legal personality, and
— is financed for the most part by the State, or regional or local authorities, or other bodies governed by public law, or is subject to management supervision by those bodies, or has an administrative, managerial or supervisory board more than half of whose members are appointed by the State, regional or local authorities, or other bodies governed by public law;

2. "public undertaking" shall mean any undertaking over which the public authorities may exercise directly or indirectly a dominant influence by virtue of their ownership of it, their financial participation therein, or the rules which govern it. A dominant influence on the part of the public authorities shall be presumed when these authorities, directly or indirectly, in relation to an undertaking:

— hold the majority of the undertaking's subscribed capital, or
— control the majority of the votes attaching to shares issued by the undertaking, or
— can appoint more than half of the members of the undertaking's administrative, managerial or supervisory body;

3. "supply and works contracts" shall mean contracts for pecuniary interest concluded in writing between one of the contracting entities referred to in Article 2 and a supplier or contractor and which have as their object:

(a) in the case of supply contracts, the purchase, lease, rental or hire-purchase, with or without options to buy, of products *or of software services*. These contracts may in addition cover siting and installation operations.

Software services shall be covered by this definition where they are procured by a contracting entity exercising any activity defined in Article 2(2)(d) and are for use *in the operation of a public telecommunications network* or are intended to be used in a public telecommunications service as such;

(b) in the case of works contracts, either the execution, or both the execution and design or the realization, by whatever means, of building or civil engineering activities referred to in Annex XI. These contracts may, in addition, cover supplies and services necessary for their execution.

Contracts which include the provision of services other than those referred to in (a) and (b) shall be regarded as supply contracts if the total value of supplies, including siting and installation operations necessary for the execution of the contract and of software services within the meaning of subparagraph (a), is greater than the value of the other services covered by the contract;

**4.** "framework agreement" shall mean an agreement between one of the contracting entities defined in Article 2 and one or more suppliers or contractors, the purpose of which is to establish the terms, in particular with regard to the prices and, where appropriate, the quantity envisaged, governing the contracts to be awarded during a given period;

**5.** "tenderer" shall mean a supplier or contractor who submits a tender and "candidate" shall mean a person who has sought an invitation to take part in a restricted or negotiated procedure;

**6.** "open, restricted and negotiated procedures" shall mean the award of procedures applied by contracting entities whereby:

(a) in the case of open procedures, all interested suppliers or contractors may submit tenders;
(b) in the case of the restricted procedures, only candidates invited by the contracting entity may submit tenders;
(c) in the case of negotiated procedures, the contracting entity consults suppliers or contractors of its choice and negotiates the terms of the contract with one or more of them;

**7.** "technical specifications" shall mean the technical requirements contained in particular in the tender documents, defining the characteristics of a set of works, material, product or supply, and enabling a piece of work, a material, a product or a supply to be objectively described in a manner such that it fulfils the use for which it is intended by the contracting entity. These technical prescriptions may include quality, performance, safety or dimensions, as well as requirements applicable to the material, product, or supply as regards quality assurance, terminology, symbols, testing and test methods, packaging, marking or labelling. In the case of works contracts, they may also include rules for the design and costing, the test, inspection and acceptance conditions for works and methods or techniques of construction and all other technical conditions which the contracting entity is in a position to prescribe under general or specific regulations, in relation to the finished works and to the materials or parts which they involve;

**8.** "standard" shall mean a technical specification approved by a recognized standardizing body for repeated and continuous application, compliance with which is in principle not compulsory;

**9.** "European standard" shall mean a standard approved by the European Committee for Standardization (CEN) or by the European Committee for Electrotechnical

Standardization (CENELEC) as a "European Standard (EN)" or "Harmonization Document (HD)", according to the common rules of those organizations, or by the European Telecommunications Standards Institute (ETSI) according to its own rules as a "European Telecommunications Standard (ETS)";

**10.** "common technical specification" shall mean a technical specification drawn up in accordance with a procedure recognized by the Member States with a view to uniform application in all Member States and published in the *Official Journal of the European Communities*;

**11.** "European technical approval" shall mean a favourable technical assessment of the fitness for use of a product for a particular purpose, based on fulfilment of the essential requirements for building works, by means of the inherent characteristics of the product and the defined conditions of application and use, as provided for in Council Directive 89/106/EEC of 21 December 1988 on the approximation of laws, regulations and administrative provisions of the Member States relating to construction products.[12] European technical approval shall be issued by an approval body designated for this purpose by the Member State;

**12.** "European specification" shall mean a common technical specification, a European technical approval or a national standard implementing a European standard;

**13.** "public telecommunications network" shall mean the public telecommunications infrastructure which enables to be conveyed between defined network and termination points by wire, by microwave, by optical means or by other electromagnetic means.
"Network termination point" shall mean all physical connections and their technical access specifications which form part of the public telecommunications network and are necessary for access to, and efficient communication through, that public network;

**14.** "public telecommunications services" shall mean telecommunications services the provision of which the Member States have specifically assigned notably to one or more telecommunications entities.
"Telecommunications services" shall mean services the provision of which consists wholly or partly in the transmission and routing of signals on the public telecommunications network by means of telecommunications processes, with the exception of radio-broadcasting and television.

### Article 2

**1.** This Directive shall apply to contracting entities which:

(a) are public authorities or public undertakings and exercise one of the activities referred to in paragraph 2;
(b) or, when they are not public authorities or public undertakings, have as one of their activities any of those referred to in paragraph 2 or any combination thereof and operate on the basis of special or exclusive rights granted by a competent authority of a Member State.

**2.** Relevant activities for the purposes of this Directive shall be:

(a) the provision or operation of fixed networks intended to provide a service to the public in connection with the production, transport or distribution of:
   (i) drinking water, or
   (ii) electricity, or
   (iii) gas or heat;

---

[12] OJ No L 40, 11.2.1989, p. 12.

or the supply of drinking water, electricity, gas or heat to such networks;
(b)  the exploitation of a geographical area for the purpose of:
    (i)  exploring for or extracting oil, gas, coal or other solid fuels, or
    (ii) the provision of airport, maritime or inland port or other terminal facilities to carriers by air, sea or inland waterway;
(c)  the operation of networks providing a service to the public in the field of transport by railway, automated systems, tramway, trolley bus, bus or cable.
    As regards transport services, a network shall be considered to exist where the service is provided under operating conditions laid down by a competent authority of a Member State, such as conditions on the routes to be served, the capacity to be made available or the frequency of the service;
(d)  the provision or operation of public telecommunications networks or the provision of one or more public telecommunications services.

**3.** For the purpose of applying paragraph 1(b), special or exclusive rights shall mean rights deriving from authorizations granted by a competent authority of the Member State concerned, by law, regulation or administrative action, having as their result the reservation for one or more entities of the exploitation of an activity defined in paragraph 2.

A contracting entity shall be considered to enjoy special or exclusive rights in particular where:

(a)  for the purpose of constructing the networks or facilities referred to in paragraph 2, it may take advantage of a procedure for the expropriation or use of property or may place network equipment on, under or over the public highway;
(b)  in the case of paragraph 2(a), the entity supplies with drinking water, electricity, gas or heat a network which is itself operated by an entity enjoying special or exclusive rights granted by a competent authority of the Member State concerned.

**4.** The provision of bus transport services to the public shall not be considered to be a relevant activity within the meaning of paragraph 2(c) where other entities are free to provide those services, either in general or in a particular geographical area, under the same conditions as the contracting entities.

**5.** The supply of drinking water, electricity, gas or heat, to networks which provide a service to the public, by a contracting entity other than a public authority, shall not be considered as a relevant activity within the meaning of paragraph 2(a) where:

(a)  in the case of drinking water or electricity:
    — the production of drinking water or electricity by the entity concerned takes place because its consumption is necessary for carrying out an activity other than that referred to in paragraph 2, and
    — supply to the public network depends only on the entity's own consumption and has not exceeded 30% of the entity's total production of drinking water or energy, having regard to the average for the preceding three years, including the current year;
(b)  in the case of gas or heat:
    — the production of gas or heat by the entity concerned is the unavoidable consequence of carrying on an activity other than that referred to in paragraph 2, and
    — supply to the public network is aimed only at the economic exploitation of such production and amounts to not more than 20% of the entity's turnover having regard to the average for the preceding years, including the current year.

**6.** The contracting entities listed in Annexes I to X shall fulfil the criteria set out above.

203

In order to ensure that the lists are as exhaustive as possible, Member States shall notify the Commission of amendments to their lists. The Commission shall revise Annexes I to X in accordance with the procedure in Article 32.

*Article 3*

**1.** Member States may request the Commission to provide that exploitation of geographical areas for the purpose of exploring for, or extracting, oil, gas, coal or other solid fuels shall not be considered to be an activity defined in Article 2(2)(*b*)(i) and that entities shall not be considered as operating under special or exclusive rights within the meaning of Article 2(3)(*b*) by virtue of carrying on one or more of these activities, provided that all the following conditions are satisfied with respect to the relevant national provisions concerning such activities:

(*a*)  at the time when authorization to exploit such a geographical area is requested, other entities shall be free to seek authorization for that purpose under the same conditions as the contracting entities;

(*b*)  the technical and financial capacity of entities to engage in particular activities shall be established prior to any evaluation of the merits of competing applications for authorization;

(*c*)  authorization to engage in those activities shall be granted on the basis of objective criteria concerning the way in which it is intended to carry out the exploitation for extraction, which shall be established and published prior to the requests and applied in a non-discriminatory manner;

(*d*)  all conditions and requirements concerning the carrying out or termination of the activity, including provisions on operating obligations, royalties, and participation in the capital or revenue of the entities, shall be established and made available prior to the requests for authorization being made and then applied in a non-discriminatory manner; every change concerning these conditions and requirements shall be applied to all the entities concerned, or else amendments must be made in a non-discriminatory manner; however, operating obligations need not be established until immediately before the authorization is granted; and

(*e*)  contracting entities shall not be required by any law, regulation, administrative requirement, agreement or understanding to provide information on a contracting entity's intended or actual sources of procurement, except at the request of national authorities and exclusively with a view to the objectives mentioned in Article 36 of the Treaty.

**2.** Member States which apply the provisions of paragraph 1 shall ensure, through the conditions of the authorization or other appropriate measures, that any entity:

(*a*)  observes the principles of non-discrimination and competitive procurement in respect of the award of supplies and works contracts, in particular as regards the information that the entity makes available to undertakings concerning its procurement intentions;

(*b*)  communicates to the Commission, under conditions to be defined by the latter in accordance with Article 32, information relating to the award of contracts.

**3.** As regards individual concessions or authorizations granted before the date on which Member States apply this Directive in accordance with Article 37, paragraphs 1 (*a*), (*b*) and (*c*) shall not apply, provided that at that date other entities are free to seek authorization for the exploitation of geographical areas for the purpose of exploring for or extracting oil, gas, coal or other solid fuels, on a non-discriminatory basis and in the light of objective criteria. Paragraph 1 (*d*) shall not apply as regards conditions or requirements established, applied or amended before the date referred to above.

**4.** A Member State which wishes to apply paragraph 1 shall inform the Commission accordingly. In doing so, it shall inform the Commission of any law, regulation or administrative provision, agreement or understanding relating to compliance with the conditions referred to in paragraphs 1 and 2.

The Commission shall take a decision in accordance with the procedure laid down in Article 32(4) to (7). It shall publish its decision, giving its reasons, in the *Official Journal of the European Communities*.

It shall forward to the Council each year a report on the implementation of this Article and review its application in the framework of the report provided for in Article 36.

## Article 4

**1.** When awarding supply or works contracts, the contracting entities shall apply procedures which are adapted to the provisions of this Directive.

**2.** Contracting entities shall ensure that there is no discrimination between different suppliers or contractors.

**3.** In the context of provision of technical specifications to interested suppliers and contractors, of qualification and selection of suppliers or contractors and of award of contracts, contracting entities may impose requirements with a view to protecting the confidential nature of information which they make available.

**4.** The provisions of this Directive shall not limit the right of suppliers or contractors to require a contracting entity, in conformity with national law, to respect the confidential nature of information which they make available.

## Article 5

**1.** Contracting entities may regard a framework agreement as a contract within the meaning of Article 1(3) and award in accordance with this Directive.

**2.** Where contracting entities have awarded a framework agreement in accordance with this Directive, they may avail themselves of Article 15(2)(i) when awarding contracts based on that agreement.

**3.** Where a framework agreement has not been awarded in accordance with this Directive, contracting entities may not avail themselves of Article 15(2)(i).

**4.** Contracting entities may not misuse framework agreements in order to hinder, limit or distort competition.

## Article 6

**1.** This Directive shall not apply to contracts which the contracting entities award for purposes other than the pursuit of their activities as described in Article 2(2) or for the pursuit of such activities in a non-member country, in conditions not involving the physical use of a network or geographical area within the Community.

**2.** However, this Directive shall apply to contracts awarded on behalf of the entities which exercise an activity referred to in Article 2(2)(a)(i) and which:

(a) are connected with hydraulic engineering projects, irrigation or land drainage, provided that the volume of water intended for the supply of drinking water represents more than 20% of the total volume of water made available by these projects or irrigation or drainage installations; or
(b) are connected with the disposal or treatment of sewage.

205

**3.** The contracting entities shall notify the Commission at its request of any activitie they regard as excluded under paragraph 1. The Commission may periodically publisl lists of the categories of activities which it considers to be covered by this exclusion, fo information in the *Official Journal of the European Communities.* In so doing, the Commissio shall respect any sensitive commercial aspects the contracting entities may point ou when forwarding this information.

## Article 7

**1.** The provisions of this Directive shall not apply to contracts awarded for purposes c resale or hire to third parties, provided that the contracting entity enjoys no special o exclusive right to sell or hire the subject of such contracts and other entities are free t sell or hire it under the same conditions as the contracting entity.

**2.** The contracting entities shall notify the Commission at its request of all th categories of products they regard as excluded under paragraph 1. The Commission ma periodically publish lists of the categories of activities which it considers to be covered b this exclusion, for information in the *Official Journal of the European Communities.* In so doing the Commission shall respect any sensitive commercial aspects the contracting entitie may point out when forwarding this information.

## Article 8

**1.** This Directive shall not apply to contracts which contracting entities exercising a activity described in Article 2(2)(d) award for purchases intended exclusively to enabl them to provide one or more telecommunications services where other entities are free t offer the same services in the same geographical area and under substantially the sam conditions.

**2.** The contracting entities shall notify the Commission at its request of any service they regard as covered by the exclusion referred to in paragraph 1. The Commission ma periodically publish the list of services which it considers to be covered by this exclusion for information in the *Official Journal of the European Communities.* In so doing, th Commission shall respect any sensitive commercial aspects the contracting entities ma point out when forwarding this information.

## Article 9

**1.** This Directive shall not apply to:

(a)   contracts which the contracting entities listed in Annex I award for the purchase c water;

(b)   contracts which the contracting entities specified in Annexes II, III, IV and V awarc for the supply of energy or of fuels for the production of energy.

**2.** The Council shall re-examine the provisions of paragraph 1 when it has before it report from the Commission together with appropriate proposals.

## Article 10

This Directive shall not apply to contracts when they are declared to be secret by th Member State, when their execution must be accompanied by special security measure in accordance with the laws, regulations or administrative provisions in force in th Member State concerned or when the protection of the basic security interests of tha State so requires.

Article 11

his Directive shall not apply to contracts governed by different procedural rules and warded:

1.  pursuant to an international agreement concluded in conformity with the Treaty between a Member State and one or more third countries and covering supplies or works intended for the joint implementation or exploitation of a project by the signatory States; every agreement shall be communicated to the Commission, which may consult the Advisory Committee for Public Contracts set up by Council Decision 71/306/EEC,[13] as last amended by Decision 77/63/EEC,[14] or, in the case of agreements governing contracts awarded by entities exercising an activity defined in Article 2(2)(d), the Advisory Committee on Telecommunications Procurement referred to in Article 31;
2.  to undertakings in a Member State or a third country in pursuance of an international agreement relating to the stationing of troops;
3.  pursuant to the particular procedure of an international organization.

Article 12

**1.** This Directive shall apply to contracts whose estimated value, net of VAT, is not less han:

(a) ECU 400 000 in the case of supply contracts awarded by entities exercising an activity defined in Article 2(2)(a), (b) and (c);
(b) ECU 600 000 in the case of supply contracts awarded by entities exercising an activity defined in Article 2(2)(d);
(c) ECU 5 million in the case of works contracts.

**2.** In the case of supply contracts for lease, rental or hire-purchase, the basis for alculating the contract value shall be:

(a) in the case of fixed-term contracts, where their term is 12 months or less, the estimated total value for the contract's duration, or, where their term exceeds 12 months, the contract's total value including the estimated residual value;
(b) in the case of contracts for an indefinite period or in cases where there is doubt as to the duration of the contracts, the anticipated total instalments to be paid in the first four years.

**3.** Where a proposed supply contract expressly specifies option clauses, the basis for alculating the contract value shall be the highest possible total purchase, lease, rental or ire-purchase permissible, inclusive of the option clauses.

**4.** In the case of a procurement of supplies over a given period by means of a series of ontracts to be awarded to one or more suppliers or of contracts which are to be renewed, ae contract value shall be calculated on the basis of:

(a) the total value of contracts which had similar characteristics awarded over the previous fiscal year or 12 months, adjusted where possible for anticipated changes in quantity or value over the subsequent 12 months;
(b) or the aggregate value of contracts to be awarded during the 12 months following the first award or during the whole term of the contract, where this is longer than 12 months.

OJ No L 185, 16.8.1971, p. 15.
OJ No L 13, 15.1.1977, p. 15.

**5.** The basis for calculating the value of a framework agreement shall be the estimate maximum value of all the contracts envisaged for the period in question.

**6.** The basis for calculating the value of a works contract for the purposes of paragraph shall be the total value of the work. "Work" shall mean the building and engineerir activities taken as a whole that are intended to fulfil an economic function by themselve In particular, where a supply or work is the subject of several lots, the value of each l shall be taken into account when assessing the value referred to in paragraph 1. Where th aggregate value of the lots equals or exceeds the value laid down in paragraph 1, th paragraph shall apply to all the lots. However, in the case of works contracts, contractir entities may derogate from paragraph 1 in respect of lots whose estimated value net  VAT is less than ECU 1 million, provided that the aggregate value of those lots does n exceed 20% of the overall value of the lots.

**7.** For the purposes of paragraph 1, contracting entities shall include in the estimate value of a works contract the value of any supplies or services necessary for the executio of the contract which they make available to the contractor.

**8.** The value of supplies which are not necessary for the execution of a particular wor contract may not be added to that of the contract with the result of avoiding application  this Directive to the procurement of those supplies.

**9.** Contracting entities may not circumvent this Directive by splitting contracts or usir special methods of calculating the value of contracts.

TITLE II

**TECHNICAL SPECIFICATIONS AND STANDARDS**

Article 13

**E–03**

**1.** Contracting entities shall include the technical specifications in the gener documents or the contract documents relating to each contract.

**2.** The technical specifications shall be defined by reference to European specificatior where these exist.

**3.** In the absence of European specifications, the technical specifications should as f as possible be defined by reference to other standards having currency within th Community.

**4.** Contracting entities shall define such further requirements as are necessary t complement European specifications or other standards. In doing so, they shall pref specifications that indicate performance requirements rather than design or descriptio characteristics unless the contracting entity has objective reasons for considering th such specifications are inadequate for the purposes of the contract.

**5.** Technical specifications which mention goods of a specific make or source or of particular process, and which have the effect of favouring or eliminating certai undertakings, shall not be used unless such specifications are indispensable for th subject of the contract. In particular, the indication of trade marks, patents, types,  specific origin or production shall be prohibited; however, such an indicatio accompanied by the words "or equivalent" shall be authorized where the subject of th contract cannot otherwise be described by specifications which are sufficiently precis and fully intelligible to all concerned.

**6.** Contracting entities may derogate from paragraph 2 if:

(a) it is technically impossible to establish satisfactorily that a product conforms  the European specifications;

208

(*b*) the application of paragraph 2 would prejudice the application of Council Directive 86/361/EEC of 24 July 1986 on the initial stage of the mutual recognition of type approval for telecommunications terminal equipment,[15] or of Council Decision 87/95/EEC of 22 December 1986 on standardization in the field of information technology and telecommunications[16];

(*c*) in the context of adapting existing practice to take account of European specifications, use of these specifications would oblige the contracting entity to acquire supplies incompatible with equipment already in use or would entail disproportionate cost or disproportionate technical difficulty. Contracting entities which have recourse to this derogation shall do so only as part of a clearly defined and recorded strategy with a view to a change-over to European specifications;

(*d*) the relevant European specification is inappropriate for the particular application or does not take account of technical developments which have come about since its adoption. Contracting entities which have recourse to this derogation shall inform the appropriate standardizing organization, or any other body empowered to review the European specification, of the reasons why they consider the European specification to be inappropriate and shall request its revision;

(*e*) the project is of a genuinely innovative nature for which use of European specifications would not be appropriate.

**7.** Notices published pursuant to Article 16(1)(*a*) shall indicate any recourse to the derogations referred to in paragraph 6.

**8.** This Article shall be without prejudice to compulsory technical rules insofar as these are compatible with Community law.

### Article 14

**1.** Contracting entities shall make available on demand to suppliers or contractors interested in obtaining a contract the technical specifications regularly referred to in their supply or works contracts or the technical specifications which they intend to apply to contracts covered by periodic information notices within the meaning of Article 17.

**2.** Where such technical specifications are based on documents available to interested suppliers or contractors, a reference to those documents shall be sufficient.

### TITLE III

## PROCEDURES FOR THE AWARD OF CONTRACTS

### Article 15

**1.** Contracting entities may choose any of the procedures described in Article 1(6), **E–04** provided, subject to paragraph 2, a call for competition has been made in accordance with Article 16.

**2.** Contracting entities may use a procedure without prior call for competition in the following cases:

(*a*) in the absence of tenders or suitable tenders in response to a procedure with a prior call for competition, provided that the original contract conditions have not been substantially changed;

(*b*) where a contract is purely for the purpose of research, experiment, study or development and not for the purpose of ensuring profit or of recovering research and development costs;

---

[5] OJ No L 217, 5.8.1986, p. 21.
[6] OJ No L 36, 7.2.1987, p. 31.

(c)  when, for technical or artistic reasons, or for reasons connected with protection of exclusive rights, the contract may be executed only by a particular supplier or contractor;

(d)  insofar as is strictly necessary when, for reasons of extreme urgency brought about by events unforeseeable by the contracting entities, the time limits laid down for open and restricted procedures cannot be adhered to;

(e)  in the case of supply contracts for additional deliveries by the original supplier which are intended either as a partial replacement of normal supplies or installations or as the extension of existing supplies or installations, where a change of supplier would oblige the contract entity to acquire material having different technical characteristics which would result in incompatibility or disproportionate technical difficulties in operation and maintenance;

(f)  for additional works not included in the project initially awarded or in the contract first concluded but which have, through unforeseen circumstances, become necessary for the execution of the contract, on condition that the award is made to the contractor executing the original contract:
  — when such additional works cannot be technically or economically separated from the main contract without great inconvenience to the contracting entities,
  — or when such additional works, although separable from the execution of the original contract, are strictly necessary to its later stages;

(g)  in the case of works contracts, for new works consisting of the repetition of similar works entrusted to the contractor to which the same contracting entities awarded on earlier contract, provided that such works conform to a basic project for which a first contract was awarded after a call for competition. As soon as the first project is put up for tender, notice must be given that this procedure might be adopted and the total estimated cost of subsequent works shall be taken into consideration by the contracting entities when they apply the provisions of Article 12;

(h)  for supplies quoted and purchased on a commodity market;

(i)  for contracts to be awarded on the basis of a framework agreement, provided that the condition referred to in Article 5(2) is fulfilled;

(j)  for bargain purchases, where it is possible to procure supplies taking advantage of a particularly advantageous opportunity available for a very short space of time at a price considerably lower than normal market prices;

(k)  for purchases of goods under particularly advantageous conditions either from a supplier definitively winding up his business activities or from the receivers or liquidators of a bankruptcy, an arrangement with creditors or a similar procedure under national laws or regulations.

## Article 16

**1.** A call for competition may be made:

(a)  by means of a notice drawn up in accordance with Annex XII, A, B or C; or

(b)  by means of a periodic indicative notice drawn up in accordance with Annex XIV; or

(c)  by means of a notice on the existence of a qualification system drawn up in accordance with Annex XIII.

**2.** When a call for competition is made by means of a periodic indicative notice:

(a)  the notice must refer specifically to the supplies or works which will be the subject of the contract to be awarded;

(b)  the notice must indicate that the contract will be awarded by restricted or negotiated procedure without further publication of a notice of a call for competition and invite interested undertakings to express their interest in writing

(c) contracting entities shall subsequently invite all candidates to confirm their interest on the basis of detailed information on the contract concerned before beginning the selection of tenderers or participants in negotiations.

**3.** When a call for competition is made by means of a notice on the existence of a qualification system, tenderers in a restricted procedure or participants in a negotiated procedure shall be selected from the qualified candidates in accordance with such a system.

**4.** The notices referred to in this Article shall be published in the *Official Journal of the European Communities*.

### Article 17

**1.** Contracting entities shall make known, at least once a year, by means of a periodic indicative notice:

(a) in the case of supply contracts, the total of the contracts for each product area of which the estimated value, taking into account the provisions of Article 12, is equal to or greater than ECU 750 000, and which they intend to award over the following 12 months;

(b) in the case of works contracts, the essential characteristics of the works contracts which the contracting entities intend to award, the estimated value of which is not less than the threshold laid down in Article 12(1).

**2.** The notice shall be drawn up in accordance with Annex XIV and published in the *Official Journal of the European Communities*.

**3.** Where the notice is used as a means of calling for competition in accordance with Article 16(1)(b), it must have been published not more than 12 months prior to the date on which the invitation referred to in Article 16(2)(c) is sent. Moreover, the contracting entity shall meet the deadlines laid down in Article 20(2).

**4.** Contracting entities may, in particular, publish periodic indicative notices relating to major projects without repeating information previously included in a periodic indicative notice, provided it is clearly stated that such notices are additional notices.

### Article 18

**1.** Contracting entities which have awarded a contract shall communicate to the Commission, within two months of the award of the contract and under conditions to be laid down by the Commission in accordance with the procedure laid down in Article 32, the results of the awarding procedure by means of a notice drawn up in accordance with Annex XV.

**2.** Information provided under Section I of Annex XV shall be published in the *Official Journal of the European Communities*. In this connection the Commission shall respect any sensitive commercial aspects the contracting entities may point out when forwarding this information in connection with points 6 and 9 of Annex XV.

**3.** Information provided under Section II of Annex XV must not be published except, in aggregated form, for statistical purposes.

### Article 19

**1.** The contracting entities must be able to supply proof of the date of dispatch of the notices referred to in Articles 15 to 18.

**2.** The notices shall be published in full in their original language in the *Official Journal of the European Communities* and in the TED data bank. A summary of the important elements of each notice shall be published in the other official languages of the Community, the original text alone being authentic.

**3.** The Office for Official Publications of the European Communities shall publish the notices not later than 12 days after their dispatch. In exceptional cases it shall endeavour to publish the notice referred to in Article 16(1)(a) within five days in response to a request by the contracting entity and provided the notice has been sent to the Office by electronic mail, telex or telefax. Each edition of the *Official Journal of the European Communities* which contains one or more notices shall reproduce the model notice or notices on which the published notice or notices are based.

**4.** The cost of publication of the notices in the *Official Journal of the European Communities* shall be borne by the Communities.

**5.** Contracts in respect of which a notice is published in the *Official Journal of the European Communities* pursuant to Article 16(1) shall not be published in any other way before that notice has been dispatched to the Office for Official Publications of the European Communities. Such publication shall not contain information other than that published in the *Official Journal of the European Communities.*

## Article 20

**1.** In open procedures the time limit for the receipt of tenders shall be fixed by contracting entities at not less than 52 days from the date of dispatch of the notice. This time limit may be shortened to 36 days where contracting entities have published a notice in accordance with Article 17(1).

**2.** In restricted procedures and in negotiated procedures with a prior call for competition, the following arrangements shall apply:

(a) the time limit for receipt of requests to participate, in response to a notice published in accordance with Article 16(1)(a) or in response to an invitation from a contracting entity in accordance with Article 16(2)(c), shall, as a general rule, be at least five weeks from the date of dispatch of the notice and shall in any case not be less than the time limit for publication laid down in Article 19(3) plus 10 days;
(b) the time limit for receipt of tenders may be fixed by mutual agreement between the contracting entity and the selected candidates, provided that all tenderers are given equal time to prepare and submit tenders;
(c) where it is not possible to reach agreement on the time limit for the receipt of tenders, the contracting entity shall fix a time limit which shall, as a general rule, be at least three weeks and shall in any case not be less than 10 days from the date of the invitation to tender; the time allowed shall be sufficiently long to take account in particular of the factors mentioned in Article 22(3).

## Article 21

In the contract documents, the contracting entity may ask the tenderer to indicate in his tender any share of the contract he may intend to subcontract to third parties.

This indication shall be without prejudice to the question of the principal contractor's responsibility.

## Article 22

**1.** Provided they have been requested in good time, the contract documents and supporting documents must be sent to the suppliers or contractors by the contracting entities as a general rule within six days of receipt of the application.

**2.** Provided it has been requested in good time, additional information relating to the contract documents shall be supplied by the contract entities not later than six days before the final date fixed for receipt of tenders.

**3.** Where tenders require the examination of voluminous documentation such as lengthy technical specifications, a visit to the site or an on-the-spot inspection of the documents supporting the contract documents, this shall be taken into account in fixing the appropriate time limits.

**4.** Contracting entities shall invite the selected candidates simultaneously and in writing. The letter of invitation shall be accompanied by the contract documents and supporting documents. It shall include at least the following information:

(a) the address from which any additional documents can be requested, the final date for such requests and the amount and methods of payment of any sum to be paid for such documents;
(b) the final date for receipt of tenders, the address to which they must be sent and the language or languages in which they must be drawn up;
(c) a reference to any tender notice published;
(d) an indication of any document to be annexed;
(e) the criteria for the award of the contract if these are not given in the notice;
(f) any other special condition for participation in the contract.

**5.** Requests for participation in contracts and invitations to tender must be made by the most rapid means of communication possible. When requests to participate are made by telegram, telex, telefax, telephone or any electronic means, they must be confirmed by letter dispatched before the expiry of the time limit referred to in Article 20(1) or of the time limit set by contracting entities pursuant to Article 20(2).

*Article 23*

**1.** The contracting entity may state in the contract documents, or be obliged by a Member State so to do, the authority or authorities from which a tenderer may obtain the appropriate information on the obligations relating to the employment protection provisions and the working conditions which are in force in the Member State, region or locality in which the works are to be executed and which shall be applicable to the works carried out on site during the performance of the contract.

**2.** A contracting entity which supplies the information referred to in paragraph 1 shall request the tenderers or those participating in the contract procedure to indicate that they have taken account, when drawing up their tender, of the obligations relating to employment protection provisions and the working conditions which are in force in the place where the work is to be carried out. This shall be without prejudice to the application of the provisions of Article 27(5) concerning the examination of abnormally low tenders.

TITLE IV

**QUALIFICATION, SELECTION AND AWARD**

*Article 24*

**1.** Contracting entities which so wish may establish and operate a system of **E–05** qualification of suppliers or contractors.

**2.** The system, which may involve different qualification stages, shall operate on the basis of objective rules and criteria to be established by the contracting entity. The contracting entity shall use European standards as a reference where they are appropriate. The rules and criteria may be updated as required.

**3.** The rules and criteria for qualification shall be made available on request to interested suppliers or contractors. The updating of these criteria and rules shall be communicated to the interested suppliers and contractors. Where a contracting entity considers that the qualification or certification system of certain third entities or bodies meets its requirements, it shall communicate to interested suppliers and contractors the names of such third entities or bodies.

**4.** Contracting entities shall inform applicants of their decision as to qualification within a reasonable period. If the decision will take longer than six months from the presentation of an application, the contracting entity shall inform the applicant, within two months of the application, of the reasons justifying a longer period and of the date by which its application will be accepted or refused:

**5.** In reaching their decision as to qualification or when the criteria and rules are being updated, contracting entities may not:

— impose conditions of an administrative, technical or financial nature on some suppliers or contractors that are not imposed on others,
— require tests or proof that duplicate objective evidence already available.

**6.** Applicants whose qualification is refused shall be informed of this decision and the reasons for refusal. The reasons must be based on the criteria for qualification referred to in paragraph 2.

**7.** A written record of qualified suppliers or contractors shall be kept, and it may be divided into categories according to the type of contract for which the qualification is valid.

**8.** Contracting entities may bring the qualification of a supplier or contractor to an end only for reasons based on the criteria referred to in paragraph 2. The intention to bring qualification to an end must be notified in writing to the supplier or contractor beforehand, together with the reason or reasons justifying the proposed action.

**9.** The qualification system shall be the subject of a notice drawn up in accordance with Annex XIII and published in the *Official Journal of the European Communities*, indicating the purpose of the qualification system and the availability of the rules concerning its operation. Where the system is of a duration greater than three years, the notice shall be published annually. Where the system is of a shorter duration, an initial notice shall suffice.

*Article 25*

**1.** Contracting entities which select candidates to tender in restricted procedures or to participate in negotiated procedures shall do so according to objective criteria and rules which they lay down and which they shall make available to interested suppliers or contractors.

**2.** The criteria used may include the criteria for exclusion specified in Article 23 of Directive 71/305/EEC and in Article 20 of Directive 77/62/EEC.

**3.** The criteria may be based on the objective need of the contracting entity to reduce the number of candidates to a level which is justified by the need to balance the particular characteristics of the contract award procedure and the resources required to complete it.

214

The number of candidates selected must, however, take account of the need to ensure adequate competition.

Groupings of suppliers or contractors shall be permitted to tender or negotiate. The conversion of such groupings into a specific legal form shall not be required in order to submit a tender or to negotiate, but the grouping selected may be required so to convert itself once it has been awarded the contract where such conversion is necessary for the proper performance of the contract.

**1.** The criteria on which the contracting entities shall base the award of contracts shall be:

(a) the most economically advantageous tender, involving various criteria depending on the contract in question, such as: delivery or completion date, running costs, cost-effectiveness, quality, aesthetic and functional characteristics, technical merit, after-sales service and technical assistance, commitments with regard to spare parts, security of supplies and price; or

(b) the lowest price only.

**2.** In the case referred to in paragraph 1(a), contracting entities shall state in the contract documents or in the tender notice all the criteria they intend to apply to the award, where possible in descending order of importance.

**3.** Where the criterion for the award of the contract is that of the most economically advantageous tender, contracting entities may take account of variants which are submitted by a tenderer and meet the minimum specifications required by the contracting entities. Contracting entities shall state in the contract documents the minimum specifications to be respected by the variants and any specific requirements for their presentation. Where variants are not permitted, they shall so indicate in the contract documents.

**4.** Contracting entities may not reject the presentation of a variant on the sole ground that it was drawn up on the basis of technical specifications defined with reference to European specifications or to national technical specifications recognized as complying with the essential requirements within the meaning of Directive 89/106/EEC.

**5.** If, for a given contract, tenders appear abnormally low in relation to the services, the contracting entity shall, before it may reject those tenders, request in writing details of the constituent elements of the tender which it considers relevant and shall verify those constituent elements taking account of the explanations received. It may set a reasonable period within which to reply.

The contracting entity may take into consideration explanations which are justified on objective grounds relating to the economy of the construction or production method, or the technical solutions chosen, or the exceptionally favourable conditions available to the tenderer for the execution of the contract, or the originality of the product or the work proposed by the tenderer.

Contracting entities may reject tenders which are abnormally low owing to the receipt of State aid only if they have consulted the tenderer and if the tenderer has not been able to show that the aid in question has been notified to the Commission pursuant to Article 93(3) of the Treaty or has received the Commission's approval. Contracting entities which reject a tender under these circumstances shall inform the Commission thereof.

*Article 28*

**1.** Article 27(1) shall not apply where a Member State bases the award of contracts on other criteria within the framework of rules in force at the time of adoption of this Directive whose aim is to give preference to certain tenderers provided the rules invoked are compatible with the Treaty.

**2.** Without prejudice to paragraph 1, this Directive shall not prevent, until 31 December 1992, the application of national provisions in force on the award of supply or works contracts which have as their objective the reduction of regional disparities and the promotion of job creation in disadvantaged regions or those suffering from industrial decline, provided that the provisions concerned are compatible with the Treaty and with the Community's international obligations.

*Article 29*

**1.** This Article shall apply to tenders comprising products originating in third countries with which the Community has not concluded, multilaterally or bilaterally, an agreement ensuring comparable and effective access for Community undertakings to the markets of those third countries. It shall be without prejudice to the obligations of the Community or its Member States in respect of third countries.

**2.** Any tender made for the award of a supply contract may be rejected where the proportion of the products originating in third countries, as determined in accordance with Council Regulation (EEC) No 802/68 of 27 June 1968 on the common definition of the concept of the origin of goods,[17] as last amended by Regulation (EEC) No 3860/87,[18] exceeds 50% of the total value of the products constituting the tender. For the purposes of this Article, software used in the equipment of telecommunication networks shall be considered as products.

**3.** Subject to paragraph 4, where two or more tenders are equivalent in the light of the award criteria defined in Article 27, preference shall be given to the tenders which may not be rejected pursuant to paragraph 2. The prices of tenders shall be considered equivalent for the purposes of this Article, if the price difference does not exceed 3%.

**4.** However, a tender shall not be preferred to another pursuant to paragraph 3 where its acceptance would oblige the contracting entity to acquire material having technical characteristics different from those of existing material, resulting in incompatibility or technical difficulties in operation and maintenance or disproportionate costs.

**5.** For the purposes, in this Article, of determining the proportion referred to in paragraph 2 of products originating in third countries, those third countries to which the benefit of the provisions of this Directive has been extended by a Council Decision in accordance with paragraph 1 shall not be taken into account.

**6.** The Commission shall submit an annual report to the Council (for the first time in the second half of 1991) on progress made in multilateral or bilateral negotiations regarding access for Community undertakings to the markets of third countries in the fields covered by this Directive, on any result which such negotiations may have achieved, and on the implementation in practice of all the agreements which have been concluded.

The Council, acting by a qualified majority on a proposal from the Commission, may amend the provisions of this Article in the light of such developments.

[17] OJ No L 148, 28.6.1968, p. 1.
[18] OJ No L 363, 23.12.1987, p. 30.

## TITLE V

## **FINAL PROVISIONS**

### Article 30

**1.** The value in national currencies of the thresholds specified in Article 12 shall in **E–06** principle be revised every two years with effect from the date provided for in Directive 77/62/EEC as far as the thresholds for supply and software service contracts are concerned and from the date provided for in Directive 71/305/EEC as far as the threshold for works contracts are concerned. The calculation of such value shall be based on the average daily values of those currencies expressed in ecus over the 24 months terminating on the last day of October preceding the revision with effect from 1 January. The values shall be published in the *Official Journal of the European Communities* at the beginning of November.

**2.** The method of calculation laid down in paragraph 1 shall be examined pursuant to the provisions of Directive 77/62/EEC.

### Article 31

**1.** The Commission shall be assisted, as regards procurement by the contracting entities exercising an activity defined in Article 2(2)(d), by a Committee of an advisory nature which shall be the Advisory Committee on Telecommunications Procurement. The Committee shall be composed of representatives of the Member States and chaired by a representative of the Commission.

**2.** The Commission shall consult this Committee on:

(a) amendments to Annex X;
(b) revision of the currency values of the thresholds;
(c) the rules concerning contracts awarded under international agreements;
(d) the review of the application of this Directive;
(e) the procedures described in Article 32(2) relating to notices and statistical accounts.

### Article 32

**1.** Annexes I to X shall be revised in accordance with the procedure laid down in paragraphs 3 to 7 with a view to ensuring that they fulfil the criteria of Article 2.

**2.** The conditions for the presentation, dispatch, reception, translation, keeping and distribution of the notices referred to in Articles 16, 17 and 18 and of the statistical reports provided for in Article 34 shall be established, for the purposes of simplification, in accordance with the procedure laid down in paragraphs 3 to 7.

**3.** The revised Annexes and the conditions referred to in paragraphs 1 and 2 shall be published in the *Official Journal of the European Communities*.

**4.** The Commission shall be assisted by the Advisory Committee for Public Contracts and, in the case of the revision of Annex X, by the Advisory Committee on Telecommunications Procurement provided for in Article 31 of this Directive.

**5.** The Commission representative shall submit to the Committee a draft of the decisions to be taken. The Committee shall deliver its opinion on the draft within a time limit which the Chairman may lay down according to the urgency of the matter, if necessary by taking a vote.

217

**6.** The opinion shall be recorded in the minutes; in addition, each Member State shall have the right to ask for its position to be recorded in the minutes.

**7.** The Commission shall take the utmost account of the opinion delivered by the Committee. It shall inform the Committee of the manner in which its opinion has been taken into account.

### Article 33

**1.** Contracting entities shall keep appropriate information on each contract which shall be sufficient to permit them at a later date to justify decisions taken in connection with:

(a) the qualification and selection of contractors or suppliers and award of contracts;
(b) recourse to derogations from the use of European specifications in accordance with Article 13(6);
(c) use of procedures without prior call for competition in accordance with Article 15(2);
(d) non-application of Titles II, III and IV in accordance with the derogations provided for in Title I.

**2.** The information shall be kept for at least four years from the date of award of the contract so that the contracting entity will be able, during that period, to provide the necessary information to the Commission if it so requests.

### Article 34

**1.** The Member States shall ensure that each year, in accordance with the arrangements to be laid down under the procedure provided for in Article 32(3) to (7), the Commission receives a statistical report concerning the total value, broken down by Member State and each category of activity to which Annexes I to X refer, of the contracts awarded below the thresholds defined in Article 12 which would, if they were not below those thresholds, be covered by this Directive.

**2.** Arrangements shall be fixed in accordance with the procedure referred to in Article 32 to ensure that:

(a) in the interests of administrative simplification, contracts of lesser value may be excluded, provided that the usefulness of the statistics is not jeopardized;
(b) the confidential nature of the information provided is respected.

### Article 35

**1.** Article 2(2) of Directive 77/62/EEC is hereby replaced by the following:

"2. This Directive shall not apply to:
(a) contracts awarded in the fields referred to in Articles 2, 7, 8 and 9 of Council Directive 90/531/EEC of 17 September 1990 on the procurement procedures of entities operating in the water, energy, transport and telecommunications sectors (*) or fulfilling the conditions in Article 6(2) of the said Directive;
(b) supplies which are declared secret or when their delivery must be accompanied by special security measures in accordance with the laws, regulations or administrative provisions in force in the Member State concerned or when the protection of the basic interests of that State's security so requires.
(*)OJ No L 297, 29.10.1990, p. 1."

**2.** Article 3(4) and (5) of Directive 71/305/EEC is hereby replaced by the following:

"4. This Directive shall not apply to contracts awarded in the fields referred to in Articles

2, 7, 8 and 9 of Council Directive 90/531/EEC of 17 September 1990 on the procurement procedures of entities operating in water, energy, transport and telecommunications sectors (*) or fulfilling the conditions in Article 6(2) of the said Directive.
(*) OJ No L 297, 29.10.1990, p. 1."

## Article 36

Not later than four years after the application of this Directive, the Commission, acting in close cooperation with the Advisory Committee for Public Contracts, shall review the manner in which this Directive has operated and its field of application and, if necessary, make further proposals to adapt it, in the light of developments concerning in particular progress in market opening and the level of competition. In the case of entities exercising an activity defined in Article 2(2)(d), the Commission shall act in close cooperation with the Advisory Committee on Telecommunications Procurement.

## Article 37

**1.** Member States shall adopt the measures necessary to comply with this Directive by 1 July 1992. They shall forthwith inform the Commission thereof.

**2.** Member States may stipulate that the measures referred to in paragraph 1 shall apply only from 1 January 1993.

Nevertheless, in the case of the Kingdom of Spain, 1 January 1993 shall be replaced by 1 January 1996. As regards the Hellenic Republic and the Portuguese Republic, 1 January 1993 shall be replaced by 1 January 1998.

**3.** Council recommendation 84/550/EEC of 12 November 1984 concerning the first phase of opening up access to public telecommunications contracts[19] shall cease to have effect as from the date on which this Directive is applied by the Member States.

## Article 38

Member States shall communicate to the Commission the text of the main provisions of national law, whether laws, regulations or administrative provisions, which they adopt in the field governed by this Directive.

## Article 39

This Directive is addressed to the Member States.

Done at Brussels, 17 September 1990.

For the Council
The President
P. ROMITA

[19] OJ No L 298, 16.11.1984, p. 51.

# PART 2

**Policy Guidelines**

**on**

**"Standards having currency in the Community"**

Directive 90/531, Article 13 Paragraph 3

(*Utilities*)

(*This document was favourably considered by the Advisory Committee on the opening-up Public Procurement at its 36th meeting on October 14, 1992 and by the Advisory Committee on Public Procurement at its 68th meeting on October 21, 1992.*)

**E–23**    If a European standard relevant to the need of the purchasing entity is available, then the entity has the obligation to refer to that European standard. Other standards or documents may only be used in the technical specifications if they are complementary to the European standard, and subject to what follows.

If there is no European standard relevant to the need of the purchaser then "other standards having currency in the Community" should as far as possible be used in this specification. The term "other standard" means that the document concerned should have the status of a standard and not simply be a specification. According to the definitions in the public procurement Directives, a standard is a technical specification that has been approved by a recognized standardizing body. Such recognized standardizing bodies within the European communities are listed in the annex to Directive 83/189. Other recognized standardizing bodies could also be taken into account, for example the International Standardization Bodies (ISO, IEC and CCITT), the American National Standards Institute (ANSI), etc. Other standards-making bodies associated to the recognized standardizing bodies also produce specifications. If these specifications have been through the appropriate consultation procedure and obtained the necessary approvals, they are to be regarded as "standards". Such bodies may issue other specifications which do not necessarily qualify as "standards".

The meaning of "having currency" is best illustrated with examples.

For instance, a DIN standard in use in Germany has currency in the Community. It does not mean it has currency in all Community Member States. In reality it may have currency in some countries which do not have a national standard. It is therefore reasonable to expect that the purchasing entities in those countries where the standard in question has currency (on a pragmatic base) prescribe that standard in their specifications.

If at the same time in the absence of the European standard there is another national standard, for example an AFNOR or BSI standard, which has currency at least in their countries of origin (in this case France and UK) it is reasonable that the entities in the country in question prescribe that standard in their specifications.

The case could also arise where the national standard of a non-Community country is widely used internationally and within the Community. This is the case, for example, in the oil and gas extraction industry for a number of standards developed by the American Petroleum Institute (API). Insofar as these standards have been developed in coordination with a recognized standardization body, they would also fall into the category of "standards having currency".

220

**Draft Policy Guidelines**

**on**

**defining the term "Product Area" in Periodic Indicative Notices for Directive 90/531/EEC**

*This is a working document which does not reflect the official position of the Commission.*

**Background**

**1.** Article 17 of the Utilities Directive, like Article 9 of the Supplies Directive, requires  **E–24**
contracting entities to announce at least once a year their planned procurement by
product area" of supplies where the total value of that planned procurement in the year
exceeds 750 000 Ecu. The Directive does not define, nor does it give guidance on, the
meaning of "product area" in this context. In the context of the Supplies Directive,
relatively few of these "periodic indicative/information notices" (PINs) have been issued
by contracting entities. Several entities have sought guidance on the interpretation of
product area". The purpose of this note is to give guidelines for putting this notion into
effect.

**The purpose of the PIN**

**2.** The PIN is intended to inform potential suppliers that there is likely to be
procurement, possibly involving contracts below the threshold value, in classes of goods
they are able to supply. Suppliers may then make their interest known to the contracting
entity and seek to establish their status and capabilities in advance of any specific
invitation to tender. In the case of the utilities, the PIN can also itself form a call for
competition if the contracting entity so chooses.
To provide information which is either so disaggregated as to conceal the real market
potential for closely related products, or which is so aggregated as to give little or no
useful information to would-be suppliers, would be to distort the aims of the Directive.

**Relevant nomenclatures**

**3.** The use of product nomenclatures is relevant to this problem but, unfortunately,
does not entirely resolve it. The reasons for this are explained below.

**4.** Within the European Community, types of economic activity are currently classified
by reference to NACE Rev. 1. This nomenclature has a most detailed level defined by a
4–digit code number. Businesses engaged in closely similar activities, like manufacturing
computers, are classified to the same 4–digit heading, in this instance 30.02.

**5.** Closely related to NACE is the new nomenclature "classification of Products
according to Activities" (CPA), which allocates narrowly defined classes of goods and
services to headings with a 6–digit code. The first 4 digits of this code are the same as the 4
digits of the NACE Rev. 1 code for the sector of industry which produces that product.
For example, code 30.02.12 relates to:
Digital data-processing machines with input and output units.
While 30.02.13 relates to:
Digital processing units, with storage, input or output units
It is planned that the CPA will form the basis of a Community Procurement Vocabulary
(CPV) which will enable suppliers to identify notices of interest in the Official Journal or
TED, and also facilitate the automatic translation of those notices. The requirements of
this vocabulary are thus that it should be quite specific to individual products. Between

221

the 4–digit level corresponding to NACE Rev 1 and the 8–digit level of the planned CPV this hierarchy provides a number of intermediate levels of product grouping.

**6.** While the CPA and CPV provide a useful framework for grouping related product together, however, the remains a problem of deciding at what level that grouping should be undertaken for the purposes of PINs.

### Policy guidelines

**7.** A typical supplier will have a range of related products. For example, a compute manufacturer may well sell mainframe, mini and personal computers and a range c storage, input and output devices. The business could be interested in a procuremen covering a variety of those products, even if the value of any individual product in tha procurement plan were below the threshold for publication of a tender notice. Thus ir order for the PIN to serve the intended purpose of alerting appropriate suppliers th "product area" should aggregate products to the level at which they are likely to fall withir the range of a hopeful supplier. The grouping of products should not, however, include products which are most unlikely to be in one supplier's product range. This would ris misleading suppliers, attracting many who were incapable of fulfilling the requirements wasting the time and resources of both purchasers and suppliers.

**8.** At the other extreme, it would be technically possible for an uncooperative purchase to define his "product area" so narrowly that it fell below the threshold for the issue of a PIN, with the intention of avoiding the effort involved or of deliberately restricting hi procurement to known suppliers. This would constitute an abuse of the Directive.

**9.** Unfortunately it cannot be guaranteed that a specific number of digits of the CPA classification will always divide suppliers into meaningful groups in the context of public procurement. Although it can in general be recommended that aggregation be done tc the 4–digit level of the CPA, there are a number of areas where the 4–digit level c aggregation is either rather high or rather low to be ideal. Purchasing entities canno escape their responsibility of adopting the level of aggregation, on the basis of thei knowledge of the markets concerned, with a view to ensuring that the informatior provided meets, as far as possible, the Directive's aim of providing information that i. useful to potential suppliers.

**10.** It can be added that, in particular in cases where the PIN also forms a call fo competition there is nothing to prevent entities, within a single PIN, from providing more specific details for particular parts of a given product range.

### Policy Guidelines

#### on

#### contracts awarded by separate units of a contracting entity under Directive 90/531/EEC (Utilities)

(Draft)

*This is a working document which does not reflect the official position of the Commission.*

### The issue

**1.** This note deals with the calculation of thresholds for the purposes of complying with Council Directive 90/531/EEC of 17 September 1990 on the procurement procedures o entities operating in the water, energy, transport and telecommunications sectors (the

Utilities Directive), where separate operational units of one and the same contracting entity purchase products.

## The description of the problem

**2.** Several utilities throughout the Community have devolved their procurement operations on to individual operational units which have a large amount of autonomy in procurement. In certain cases, such individual units even constitute geographical subdivisions of the contracting entity. Such delegation of responsibility has inter alia been done in order to contribute to reducing the entity's overhead costs, to increase efficiency and to improve accountability at the business unit. Experience has confirmed that, in many circumstances, this can be a commercially efficient way of organizing procurement in a large organization.

**3.** The utilities in question have sought guidance on how the estimated value of a proposed procurement of supplies should be calculated for the purpose of determining whether it exceeds the threshold laid down by the Directive when that procurement is carried out by such individual operational units by means of separate contracts. In particular, the utilities have inquired whether it is acceptable to take as a basis only the value of the procurement of each unit and not, therefore, made by all units as the Directive might be considered, on the face of it, to require.

## The approach of the Directive

**4.** Article 12(4) of the Directive provides that:

"In the case of a procurement of supplies over a given period by means of a series of contracts to be awarded to one or more suppliers or of contracts which are to be renewed, the contract value shall be calculated on the basis of:
   (a)  the total value of contracts which had similar characteristics awarded over the previous fiscal year or 12 months, adjusted where possible for anticipated changes in quantity or value over the subsequent 12 months;
   (b)  or the aggregate value of contracts to be awarded during the 12 months following the first award or during the whole term of the contract, where this is longer than 12 months."

Further, Article 12(9) provides that:

"Contracting entities may not circumvent this Directive by splitting contracts or using special methods of calculating the value of contracts."

Article 17(1) provides that a periodic information notice shall be published where:

"(a) in the case of supply contracts, the total of the contracts for each product area of which the estimated value, taking into account the provisions of Article 12, is equal to or greater than ECU 750 000, and which they intend to award over the following 12 months;
(b) in the case of works contracts, the essential characteristics of the works contracts which the contracting entities intend to award, the estimated value of which is not less than the threshold laid down in Article 12(1)."

**5.** In the 32nd and 33rd "whereas" clauses of the Directive it is laid down that:

"...the rules to be applied by the entities concerned should establish a framework for sound commercial practice and should leave a maximum of flexibility" and
"...as a counterpart for such flexibility and in the interest of mutual confidence, a minimum level of transparency must be ensured and appropriate methods adopted for monitoring the application of this Directive."

This approach is therefore concerned to balance sound commercial practice with transparency and monitoring.

**Policy guidelines**

**6.** In deciding whether or not certain units could be treated as separate operational units, a case-by-case assessment is required. The crucial consideration in this analysis i whether the procuring entity is really organizing its purchase on a devolved basis. Thi would require its units to carry out their purchases independently and autonomously a separate businesses, not accountable to the head office at least as regards the categorie of products for which the unit is considered to be responsible.

**7.** If the units of a contracting entity constitute discrete units, which have full capacit to award contracts within the meaning of the utilities directive, then the contracting entit must take into consideration the totality of the requirements of all of its units, whe estimating the value of a contract.

**8.** In assessing whether or not the Directive could be applied at the level of the separate operational unit, due consideration needs to be given to whether or not:

— procurement responsibilities have been devolved to the effect that the unit in question can independently run the procedure for the award of contracts and ultimately, make the buying decision, independently of any other part of the contracting entity;
— such delegation of procurement responsibility is also reflected in the separation of budgets; whether this encompasses the actual conclusion of a contract by the individual unit and its financing from its own budget;
— the procurement is intended to satisfy a demand of that individual unit or whether such procurement is rather intended to satisfy a demand of more units or of the contracting entity as a whole, the procurement of which is merely organized in a decentralized way;
— the contracting entity, while delegating the procurement responsibility to an individual unit, is in fact still trying to exploit its overall position as a major purchaser in its discussions with tenderers with a view to obtaining more favourable terms.

# Appendix F

## UTILITIES SUPPLY AND WORKS CONTRACTS REGULATIONS 1992

(S.I. No. 3279)

*(In force from January 13, 1993)*

**ARRANGEMENT OF REGULATIONS**

225

PART VI

*Miscellaneous*

PART VII

*Applications to the Court and Conciliation*

PART VIII

*Amendments*

## SCHEDULES

The Treasury, being the Minister designated[1] for the purposes of section 2(2) of the European Communities Act 1972[2] in relation to public procurement, in exercise of the powers conferred upon them by the said section 2(2) and of all other powers enabling them in that behalf, hereby make the following Regulations:—

PART I

## GENERAL

### Title and commencement

**F–01**  **1.** These Regulations may be cited as the Utilities Supply and Works Contracts Regulations 1992 and shall come into force on 13th January 1993.

### Interpretation

**2.**—(1) In these Regulations—

"to award" means to accept an offer made in relation to a proposed contract;
"carrying out" in relation to a work or works means the construction or the design and construction of that work or those works;
"the Commission" means the Commission of the Communities;
"contract documents" means the invitation to tender for or to negotiate the contract,

---

[1] S.I. 1991/755.
[2] 1972 c.68.

the proposed conditions of contract, the specifications or descriptions of the goods, services, work or works required by the utility and all documents supplementary thereto;

"contract notice" means a notice sent to the Official Journal in accordance with regulation 14(2)(b);

"contractor" has the meaning ascribed to it by regulation 4;

"ECU" means the European Currency Unit as defined in Council Regulation (EEC) No. 3180/78[3];

"established" means the same as it does for the purposes of the Community Treaties;

"financial year" means the period of 12 months ending on the date in any year in respect of which the accounts of a utility are prepared;

"framework agreement" means a contract or other arrangement which is not in itself a supply or a works contract but which establishes the terms (in particular the terms as to price and, where appropriate, quantity) under which the supplier or contractor will enter into supply or works contracts with a utility in the period during which the framework agreement applies;

"goods" includes substances, growing crops and things attached to or forming part of the land which are agreed to be severed before the purchase or hire under a supply contract, any ship, aircraft or vehicle, and, when the utility is an entity specified in Part T of Schedule 1, is deemed to include telecommunications software services;

"Minister" has the meaning ascribed to it by regulation 27;

"Minister of the Crown" means the holder of an office in Her Majesty's Government in the United Kingdom, and includes the Treasury;

"national of a member State" means, in the case of a person who is not an individual, a person formed in accordance with the laws of a Member State and which has its registered office, central administration or principal place of business in a member State;

"negotiated procedure" means a procedure leading to the award of a contract whereby the utility negotiates the terms of the contract with one or more persons selected by it;

"Official Journal" means the Official Journal of the Communities;

"open procedure" means a procedure leading to the award of a contract whereby all interested persons may tender for the contract;

"periodic indicative notice" means a notice sent to the Official Journal in accordance with regulation 13;

"public telecommunications network" means an infrastructure for the use of the public which enables signals to be conveyed by wire, microwave, optical means or other electromagnetic means between physical connections which are necessary for access to and efficient communication through the network;

"public telecommunications services" means services which consist in whole or in part in the transmission and routing of signals on a public telecommunications network by means of telecommunications processes other than radio broadcasting and television;

"restricted procedure" means a procedure leading to the award of a contract whereby only persons selected by the utility may submit tenders for the contract;

"ship" includes any boat and any other description of a vessel used in navigation;

"software services" means the design or adaptation of software;

"substance" means any natural or artificial substance, whether in solid, liquid or gaseous form or in the form of a vapour;

"supplier" has the meaning ascribed to it by regulation 4;

---

[3] OJ No. L 379, 30.12.78, p.1, as amended by Council Regulation (EEC) No. 2626/84 (OJ No. L 247), 16.9.84, p.1) and Council Regulation (EEC) No. 1971/89 (OJ No. L 189, 4.7.89, p.1).

"supply contract" means a contract in writing for consideration (whatever the nature of the consideration)—

    (a) for the purchase of goods by a utility (whether or not the consideration is given in instalments and whether or not the purchase is conditional upon the occurrence of a particular event), or

    (b) for the hire of goods by a utility (both where the utility becomes the owner of the goods after the end of the period of hire and where it does not),

and for any siting and installation of those goods, but where, under such a contract services are also to be provided, the contract shall only be a supply contract if the value of the consideration attributable to the goods and to any siting or installation of the goods is greater than the value attributable to the services;

"telecommunications software services" means software services for use in the operation of a public telecommunications network or which are intended to be used in a public telecommunications service as such;

"utility" has the meaning ascribed to it by regulation 3;

"work" means the outcome of any works which is sufficient of itself to fulfil an economic function;

"working day" means a day other than a Saturday, Sunday or Bank Holiday within the meaning of the Banking and Financial Dealings Act 1971[4];

"works" means any of the activities specified in Schedule 3, being activities contained in the general industrial classification of economic activities within the Communities;

"works contract" means a contract in writing for consideration (whatever the nature of the consideration)—

    (a) for the carrying out of a work or works for a utility, or

    (b) under which a utility engages a person to procure by any means the carrying out for the utility of a work corresponding to specified requirements;

and

"year" means a calendar year.

(2) The value in the currency of any Member State of any amount expressed in these Regulations in ECU shall be determined by reference to the rate for the time being applying for the purposes of Council Directive 90/531/EEC[5] as published from time to time in the Official Journal.[6]

(3) Where a thing is required to be done under these Regulations—

    (a) within a period after an action is taken, the day on which that action was taken shall not be counted in the calculation of that period;

    (b) within a certain period, that period must include 2 working days;

    (c) within a period and the last day of that period is not a working day, the period shall be extended to include the following working day.

(4) References in these Regulations to a regulation are references to a regulation in these Regulations and references to a Schedule are references to a Schedule to these Regulations.

## Utilities

**3.** For the purposes of these Regulations a utility is a person specified in the first column of Schedule 1.

---

[4] 1971 c.80.

[5] OJ No. L 297, 29.10.90, p.1.

[6] The rates are determined for each successive period of two years by calculating the average of the daily exchange rates between each currency and the ECU in a period of 24 months preceding the determination.

## Suppliers and Contractors

**4.**—(1) For the purposes of these Regulations a "supplier" means a person who sought, or who seeks, or would have wished, to be the person to whom a supply contract is awarded, and a "contractor" means a person who sought, or who seeks, or would have wished, to be the person to whom a works contract is awarded, and in either case means a person who is a national of and established in a Member State.

(2) When these Regulations apply a utility shall not treat a person who is not a national of and established in a Member State more favourably than one who is.

## Application of the Regulations

**5.** These Regulations apply whenever a utility seeks offers in relation to a proposed supply contract or a proposed works contract other than contracts excluded from the operation of these Regulations by regulations 6, 7 and 9 below.

## General exclusions

**6.** These Regulations shall not apply to the seeking of offers in relation to a contract—

(a) other than for the purpose of carrying out an activity specified in the Part of Schedule 1 in which the utility is specified;
(b) for the purpose of carrying out any activity outside the territory of the Communities but only if the carrying out of that activity does not involve the physical use of a network or geographical area within the Communities;
(c) for the purpose of acquiring goods or works in order to sell or hire them to another person unless the utility has a special or exclusive right to sell or hire them under the same conditions;
(d) which is classified as secret by the Minister or where the performance of the contract must be accompanied by special security measures in accordance with the laws, regulations or administrative provisions of any part of the United Kingdom or when the protection of the basic interests of the security of the United Kingdom require it;
(e) where different procedures govern the procedures leading to the award of the contract and it is to be entered into—
  (i) pursuant to an international agreement to which the United Kingdom and a State which is not a Member State are parties and it relates to goods or provides for the carrying out of works intended for the joint implementation or exploitation of a project pursuant to that agreement;
  (ii) pursuant to an international agreement relating to the stationing of troops; or
  (iii) in accordance with the contract award procedures of an organisation of which only States are members (an "international organisation") or of which only States or international organisations are members.
(f) by a utility which engages in an activity specified in Part A, B or C of Schedule 1 for the purchase of water; and
(g) by a utility which engages in an activity specified in Parts D to N of Schedule 1 for the purchase of energy or of fuel for the production of energy;

## Exclusion in respect of certain contracts awarded by utilities operating in the telecommunications sector

**7.**—(1) These Regulations shall not apply to the seeking of offers in relation to a contract by a utility specified in Schedule 2 for the exclusive purpose of enabling it to provide one or more of the public telecommunications services specified in the Part of Schedule 2 in which the utility is specified.

(2) A utility specified in Schedule 2 when requested shall send a report to the Minister for onward transmission to the Commission describing the public telecommunications services provided by it which it considers are services specified in the Part of Schedule 2 in which the utility is specified.

(3) A utility may indicate that any of the information included in the report referred to in paragraph (2) above is of a sensitive commercial nature and request that it not be published.

**Exemption in respect of certain utilities operating in the energy sector**

**8.**—(1) Where the Commission has decided that an activity specified in Parts M or N of Schedule 1 to these Regulations is not to be considered an activity defined in article 2(2)(b)(i) of Council Directive 90/531/EEC[7] and that entities undertaking that activity shall not be considered as operating under special or exclusive rights by virtue of article 2(3)(b) of that Directive, a utility need not comply with Parts II to V of these Regulations and regulations 23, 24, 25, 26 other than paragraph 2(a), and 28 below in seeking offers in relation to a contract to be awarded for the purpose of carrying out any activity referred to in that decision.

(2) A utility which relies on the exemption in paragraph (1) above shall observe the principles of non-discrimination and competitive procurement, and in particular shall—

(a) hold a competition unless it can objectively justify not doing so; and
(b) in making information about its procurement intentions available to suppliers and contractors, in specifying its requirements to them, in establishing and using a qualification system, in selecting suppliers or contractors to tender for or to negotiate the contract and in awarding the contract, make decisions objectively on the basis of relevant criteria.

**Thresholds**

**9.**—(1) These Regulations shall not apply to the seeking of offers in relation to a proposed contract where the estimated value of the contract (net of value added tax) at the relevant time is less than the relevant threshold.

(2) The relevant threshold for the purposes of paragraph (1) above—

(a) in relation to a supply contract to be awarded by a utility other than one specified in Part T of Schedule 1, is 400,000 ECU;
(b) in relation to a supply contract to be awarded by a utility specified in Part T of Schedule 1, is 600,000 ECU; and
(c) in relation to a works contract, is 5,000,000 ECU.

(3) Subject to paragraphs (4), (5), (6), (9), (14) and (15) below in the case of a supply contract, and subject to paragraphs (10), (11), (12), (13), (14) and (15) below in the case of a works contract, the estimated value of a contract for the purposes of paragraph (1) above shall be the value of the consideration which the utility expects to give under the contract.

(4) The estimated value for the purposes of paragraph (1) above of a supply contract for the hire of goods for an indefinite period, or for a period which is uncertain at the time the contract is entered into, shall be the value of the consideration which the utility expects to give in respect of the first four years of the hire.

[7] OJ No. L 297, 29.10.90, p.1.

(5) Subject to paragraph (8) below where a utility proposes to enter into two or more supply contracts at the same time in order to purchase or hire goods of a particular type, the estimated value for the purposes of paragraph (1) above of each of those contracts shall be the aggregate of the value of the consideration which the utility expects to give under each of those contracts.

(6) Subject to paragraph (8) below where a utility has a requirement over a period to purchase or hire goods of the type to be purchased or hired under the contract and for that purpose enters into—

(a) a series of supply contracts,
(b) a supply contract which under its terms is renewable, or
(c) a supply contract which is for the purchase of goods over an indefinite period,

the estimated value for the purposes of paragraph (1) above of the supply contract shall be the amount calculated under paragraph (7) below.

(7) The utility shall calculate the amount referred to in paragraph (6) above either—

(a) by taking the aggregate of the value of the consideration given by the utility under supply contracts which have similar characteristics, and which are for the purchase or hire of goods of the type to be purchased or hired under the contract, during the last financial year of the utility ending before, or the period of 12 months ending immediately before, the relevant time, and by adjusting that amount to take account of any expected changes in quantity and cost of the goods to be purchased or hired in the period of 12 months commencing with the relevant time, or

(b) by estimating the aggregate of the value of the consideration which the utility expects to give under supply contracts which have similar characteristics, and which are for the purchase or hire of goods of the type to be purchased or hired under the contract, during the period of 12 months from the first date of delivery of the goods to be purchased or hired under the contract or, where the contract is for a definite term of more than 12 months, during the term of the contract.

(8) Notwithstanding paragraphs (5) and (6) above when the goods to be purchased or hired under the contract are required for the sole purposes of a discrete operational unit within the organisation of a utility and—

(a) the decision whether to purchase or hire goods of that type has been devolved to such a unit, and
(b) that decision is taken independently of any other part of the utility,

the valuation methods described in paragraphs (5) and (7) above shall be adapted by aggregating only the value of the consideration which the utility has given or expects to give, as the case may be, under contracts for the purchase or hire of goods which were or are required for the sole purposes of that unit.

(9) Where a supply contract includes one or more options the estimated value of the contract shall be determined by calculating the highest possible amount which could be payable under the contract.

(10) Subject to paragraphs (11) and (12) below, the estimated value for the purposes of paragraph (1) above of a works contract which is one of a number of contracts entered or to be entered into for the carrying out of a work shall be the aggregate of the value of the consideration which the utility has given or expects to give under all the contracts for the carrying out of the work.

(11) Paragraph (10) above shall not apply to any works contract (unless the utility chooses to apply that paragraph to that contract) if that contract has an estimated value

(calculated in accordance with paragraph 3 above) of less than 1,000,000 ECU, and the aggregate value of that contract and of any other works contract for the carrying out of the work in respect of which the utility takes advantage of the disapplication of paragraph (10) above by virtue of this paragraph is less than 20 per cent of the aggregate of the value of the consideration which the utility has given or expects to give under all the contracts for the carrying out of the work.

(12) Where a utility intends to provide any goods or services to the person awarded a works contract for the purpose of carrying out that contract, the value of the consideration for the purposes of paragraphs (3) and (10) above shall be taken to include the estimated value at the relevant time of those goods and services.

(13) Where the estimated value of a works contract estimated in accordance with paragraph (3) above is less than the relevant threshold and where goods which are not necessary for its execution are to be purchased or hired under it the estimated value of the contract for the purposes of paragraph (1) above shall be the value of the consideration which the utility expects to give for the goods and the relevant threshold shall be determined in accordance with paragraph (2) above as if the works contract were a supply contract.

(14) The estimated value of a framework agreement shall be the aggregate of the values estimated in accordance with this regulation of all the contracts which could be entered into under the framework agreement.

(15) A utility shall not enter into separate contracts nor select nor exercise a choice under a valuation method in accordance with paragraph (7) above with the intention of avoiding the application of these Regulations to those contracts.

(16) The relevant time for the purposes of paragraphs (1), (7) and (12) above means—

(a) if the utility selects suppliers or contractors to tender for or to negotiate the contract in accordance with a qualification system established in accordance with regulation 17 below, the date on which the selection commences, or

(b) if the utility satisfies the requirement that there be a call for competition by indicating the intention to award the contract in a periodic indicative notice in accordance with regulation 14(2)(a)(i) below, the date on which the notice is sent to the Official Journal; or

(c) in any other case, the date on which a contract notice would be sent to the Official Journal if the requirement that there be a call for competition applied and the utility decided to satisfy that requirement by sending such a notice.

**Framework agreements**

10.—(1) A utility which is proposing to enter into a framework agreement may choose to treat that agreement as a contract to which these Regulations apply; and, accordingly, in respect of such an agreement references in these Regulations to a contract shall include a reference to such a framework agreement.

(2) A utility which chooses to treat a framework agreement as a contract under paragraph (1) above shall not use the framework agreement to hinder, limit or distort competition.

232

PART II

## TECHNICAL SPECIFICATIONS

### Technical specifications in the contract documents

11.—(1) In this regulation—

F–02

"common technical specification" means a technical specification drawn up in accordance with a procedure recognised by the Member States with a view to uniform application in all member States and which has been published in the Official Journal;

"European specification" means a common technical specification, a British standard implementing a European standard or a European technical approval;

"European standard" means a standard approved by the European Committee for Standardisation ("CEN") or by the European Committee for Electrotechnical Standardisation ("CENELEC") as a "European Standard ('EN')" or a "Harmonisation Document ('HD')" according to the Common Rules of those organisations or by the European Telecommunications Standards Institute ("ETSI") according to its own rules as a "European Telecommunications Standard ('ETS')";

"European technical approval" means an approval of the fitness of a product for a particular use, issued by an approval body designated for the purpose by a member State, following a technical assessment of whether the product fulfils the essential requirements for building works, having regard to the inherent characteristics of the product and the defined conditions of application and use as provided for in Council Directive 89/106/EEC on the approximation of laws, regulations and administrative procedures in the Member States relating to construction projects[8];

"standard" means a technical specification approved by a recognised standardising body for repeated and continuous application, compliance with which is in principle not compulsory;

"technical specifications" means the technical requirements defining the characteristics required of the work or works, materials or goods (such as quality, performance, safety or dimensions) so that the works, work, materials or goods are described objectively in a manner which will ensure the use for which they are intended by the utility. In relation to materials and goods, "technical specifications" include requirements in respect of quality assurance, terminology, symbols, test and testing methods, packaging, marking and labelling. In relation to a work or works, they include requirements relating to design and costing, the testing, inspection and acceptance of the work or works, the methods or techniques of construction and all other technical conditions.

(2) If a utility wishes to lay down technical specifications which the goods to be purchased or hired under a supply contract or the work or works to be carried out under a works contract and which the materials and goods used in or for a works contract must meet, it shall specify all such technical specifications in the contract documents.

(3) Subject to paragraph (4) below, the technical specifications in the contract documents shall be defined by reference to any European specifications which are relevant.

(4) A utility may define the technical specifications referred to in paragraph (3) above other than by reference to relevant European specifications if—

(a)  the utility is under an obligation to define the technical specifications by reference

---

[8] OJ No. L 40, 11.2.89, p.12.

to technical requirements which are mandatory in the United Kingdom (but only to the extent that such an obligation is compatible with Community obligations);

(b) it is technically impossible to establish satisfactorily that the goods, materials, work or works do conform to the relevant European specifications;

(c) definition by reference to European specifications would conflict with the application of Council Directive 91/263/EEC on the initial stage of the mutual recognition of type approval for telecommunications terminal equipment[9] or Council Decision 87/95/EEC on standardisation in the field of information technology and telecommunications[10];

(d) subject to paragraph (5) below, application of European specifications would oblige the utility to acquire a work, works or goods incompatible with equipment already in use or would entail disproportionate costs or disproportionate technical difficulties;

(e) subject to paragraph (6) below, the relevant European specification is inappropriate for the particular purpose or it does not take account of technical developments which have come about since its adoption;

(f) the project for which the contract is to be entered into is of a genuinely innovative nature for which use of existing relevant European specifications would be inappropriate.

(5) A utility may only define the technical specifications other than by reference to European specifications on the grounds specified in paragraph (4)(d) above where the utility has a clearly defined and recorded strategy for changing over to European specifications.

(6) A utility relying on the derogation in paragraph (4)(e) above shall inform the appropriate standardising organisation or other body empowered to review the European specification, of the reasons why it considers the European specification to be inappropriate and shall request its revision.

(7) A utility shall state in any contract notice or periodic indicative notice sent pursuant to regulation 14(2)(a)(i) below which of the circumstances specified in paragraph (4) above was the ground for defining the technical specifications other than by reference to European specifications.

(8) In the absence of European specifications which relate to the matter in respect of which the utility wishes to lay down technical specifications, the technical specifications in the contract documents shall be defined, as far as possible, by reference to other standards which are in common use within the Community.

(9) If it is necessary to lay down further technical specifications to complement European specifications or other standards included in the contract documents the utility shall, if possible, lay down technical specifications that indicate performance requirements rather than design or description characteristics unless they would be inadequate.

(10) Subject to paragraph (12) below, the contract documents shall not include technical specifications which refer to goods of a specific make or source or to a particular process and which have the effect of favouring or eliminating particular suppliers or contractors.

(11) Without prejudice to the generality of paragraph (10) above, references to

---

[9] OJ No. L 128, 23.5.91, p.1.
[10] OJ No. L 36, 7.2.87, p.31.

trademarks, patents, types, origin or means of production shall not be incorporated into the technical specifications in the contract documents.

(12) Notwithstanding paragraph (10) and (11) above, a utility may incorporate the references referred to in paragraph (10) and (11) above into the technical specifications in the contract documents if—

(a) the subject of the contract makes the use of such references indispensable, or
(b) the subject of the contract cannot otherwise be described by reference to technical specifications which are sufficiently precise and intelligible to all suppliers or contractors, provided that the references are accompanied by the words "or equivalent".

(13) Subject to paragraph (14) below, the utility shall provide to any supplier or contractor who requests it a copy of the technical specifications which are regularly laid down as terms of the supply and works contracts which it awards or which it intends to lay down as terms of a contract which has been indicated in a periodic indicative notice sent to the Official Journal in accordance with regulation 13 below.

(14) Where the technical specifications referred to in paragraph (13) above are based on documents which are available to suppliers and contractors the obligation in paragraph (13) shall be satisfied by informing any supplier or contractor who requests it of the documents which include those technical specifications.

PART III

## PROCEDURES LEADING TO THE AWARD OF A CONTRACT

### The Open, Restricted and Negotiated Procedures

**12.** For the purposes of seeking offers in relation to a proposed contract a utility shall use the open, the restricted or the negotiated procedure.    **F–03**

### Periodic indicative notices

**13.**—(1) Subject to paragraphs (2) and (3) below, a utility shall, at least once every 12 months, send to the Official Journal a notice, in a form substantially corresponding to that set out in Part A of Schedule 4 and containing the information therein specified, in respect of—

(a) the supply contracts which the utility expects to award during the period of 12 months beginning with the date of the notice; and
(b) the works contracts which the utility expects to award.

(2) The obligation under paragraph (1)(a) above shall apply only to those supply contracts whose estimated value (within the meaning of regulation 9 above) at the date of despatch of the notice is not less than the relevant threshold specified in regulation 9(2) above and which are for the purchase or hire of goods of a type which the utility expects at the date of despatch of the notice to purchase or hire under supply contracts which have an estimated value (within the meaning of regulation 9(3), (9) and (14) above) which in aggregate for that type of goods is, or is more than, 750,000 ECU.

(3) The obligation under paragraph 1(b) above shall apply only to those works contracts whose estimated value at the date of despatch of the notice is not less than the relevant threshold specified in Regulation 9(2) above.

(4) A notice sent to the Official Journal in accordance with paragraph (1) above need not

repeat information about contracts included in a previous periodic indicative notice, provided that the notice clearly states that it is an additional notice.

## Call for competition

**14.**—(1) Subject to regulation 15, for the purposes of seeking offers in relation to a proposed contract a utility shall make a call for competition.

(2) The requirement under paragraph (1) above to make a call for competition shall be satisfied—

(a) in the case of a contract to be awarded using the restricted or negotiated procedure—
  (i) if the intention to award the contract has been indicated in a periodic indicative notice and the requirements referred to in paragraph (3) below are satisfied in relation to the contract; or
  (ii) if a notice indicating the existence of a qualification system for suppliers or contractors has been sent to the Official Journal in accordance with regulation 17(12) below and the requirement referred to in paragraph (4) below is satisfied; or
(b) in any case by sending to the Official Journal a contract notice in a form substantially corresponding to that set out in—
  (i) Part B of Schedule 4, in the case of a contract to be awarded using the open procedure,
  (ii) Part C of Schedule 4, in the case of a contract to be awarded using the restricted procedure, and
  (iii) Part D of Schedule 4, in the case of a contract to be awarded using the negotiated procedure,
  and containing the information specified in the relevant Part in respect of the contract.

(3) The requirements referred to in paragraph (2)(a)(i) above are that—

(a) the periodic indicative notice refers specifically to the goods or works which are to be the subject of the proposed contract,
(b) the notice states that offers are to be sought using the restricted or negotiated procedure without further publication of a notice calling for competition and invites suppliers or contractors to express their interest in writing,
(c) the utility sends to all suppliers or contractors who express such an interest detailed information on the contract concerned and before beginning the selection of suppliers or contractors invites them to confirm their wish to be selected to tender for or to negotiate the contract, and
(d) the notice was not published more than 12 months before the date on which the invitation sent in accordance with sub-paragraph (c) above is sent.

(4) The requirement referred to in paragraph (2)(a)(ii) above is that the suppliers or contractors selected to tender for or to negotiate the contract are selected from the candidates who qualify in accordance with the system.

## Award without a call for competition

**15.**—(1) A utility may seek offers in relation to a proposed contract without a call for competition in the following circumstances—

(a) in the absence of tenders or suitable tenders in response to a procedure with a call for competition but only if the original terms of the proposed contract have not been substantially altered;

(b)  when the contract is to be awarded purely for the purposes of research, experiment, study or development but not where it has the purpose of ensuring profit or of recovering research and development costs;

(c)  when for technical or artistic reasons, or for reasons connected with the protection of exclusive rights, the contract may only be performed by a particular person;

(d)  when (but only if it is strictly necessary) for reasons of extreme urgency brought about by events unforeseeable by the utility, the time limits specified in regulation 16(1) to (4) below cannot be met;

(e)  when the contract to be awarded is a supply contract and the goods to be purchased or hired under the contract are required by the utility as a partial replacement for, or addition to, existing goods or an installation when to obtain the goods from a person other than the person who supplied the existing goods or the installation would oblige the utility to acquire goods having different technical characteristics which would result in—

 (i)  incompatibility between the existing goods or installation and the goods to be purchased or hired under the contract, or

 (ii)  disproportionate technical difficulties in the operation and maintenance of the goods or installation;

(f)  when the contract to be awarded is a works contract and the utility wants a person who has entered into a works contract with the utility to carry out additional works which through unforeseen circumstances were not included in the project initially considered or in the original works contract and—

 (i)  such works cannot for technical or economic reasons be carried out separately from the works carried out under the original works contract without great inconvenience to the utility, or

 (ii)  such works can be carried out separately from the works carried out under the original works contract but are strictly necessary to the later stages of that contract;

(g)  subject to paragraph (2) below when the contract to be awarded is a works contract and the utility wishes a person who has entered into a works contract with it following a call for competition which satisfies the requirement of regulation 14(1) above to carry out new works which are a repetition of works carried out under the original contract and which are in accordance with the project for the purpose of which the first contract was entered into;

(h)  in respect of a supply contract for the purchase or hire of goods quoted and purchased on a commodity market;

(i)  when the contract to be awarded is to be awarded under a framework agreement which has been awarded in accordance with these Regulations and to which the provisions of regulation 10 apply;

(j)  when the contract to be awarded is a supply contract, to take advantage of a particularly advantageous bargain available for a very short period of time at a price considerably lower than normal market prices; and

(k)  when the contract to be awarded is a supply contract, to take advantage of particularly advantageous conditions for the purchase of goods in a closing down sale or in a sale brought about by insolvency.

(2) A utility shall not seek offers without a call for competition pursuant to paragraph 1)(g) above unless—

(a)  the original contract was awarded after a call for competition,

(b)  when the utility invited contractors to tender for or to negotiate the contract it gave notice that a works contract for new works which would be a repetition of the works carried out under the original contract might be awarded without a call for competition pursuant to paragraph (1)(g) above, and

(c) in determining the estimated value of the original contract for the purposes of regulation 9 above the utility took into account the value of the consideration which it expected to pay for the new works.

## Time Limits

**16.**—(1) Subject to paragraph (2) below, the date which a utility using the open procedure shall fix as the last date for the receipt by it of tenders made in response to the contract notice shall be specified in the notice and shall be not less than 52 days from the date of dispatch of the notice.

(2) When the utility has published a periodic indicative notice in accordance with regulation 13(1) above it may substitute for the period of not less than 52 days specified in paragraph (1) above a period of not less than 36 days.

(3) The date which a utility using the restricted or the negotiated procedure with a call for competition shall fix as the last date for the receipt by it of requests to be selected to tender for or to negotiate the contract shall be specified in the contract notice or, where the call for competition is made by means of a periodic indicative notice, in the invitation to suppliers or contractors made in accordance with regulation 14(3)(c), and shall in general be at least five weeks from the date of the dispatch of the notice or invitation and shall in any case be not less than 22 days from that date.

(4) The date which shall be the last date for the receipt of tenders made in response to an invitation to tender by a utility using the restricted or the negotiated procedure with a call for competition shall be agreed between the utility and the suppliers or contractors invited to tender and shall be the same date for all suppliers or contractors or, in the absence of agreement as to the date, shall be fixed by the utility and shall be as a general rule at least 3 weeks and in any event not less than 10 days from the date of despatch of the invitation to tender.

(5) In fixing the time limits referred to in paragraphs (1), (2) and (4) above a utility shall take into account the time required to allow for any examination of voluminous documentation such as lengthy technical specifications, or any inspection of the site or documents relating to the contract documents, which is necessary.

(6) A utility using the open procedure shall send the contract documents as a general rule within 6 days of the receipt of a request from any supplier or contractor provided that the documents are requested in good time and any fee specified in the contract notice has accompanied the request.

(7) A utility using the restricted or the negotiated procedure with or without a call for competition shall send invitations in writing and simultaneously to each of the suppliers or contractors selected to tender for or to negotiate the contract and the invitation shall be accompanied by the contract documents.

(8) The following information shall be included in the invitation—

(a) the address to which requests for any further information should be sent, the final date for making such a request and the amount and method of payment of any fee which may be charged for supplying that information;
(b) the final date for the receipt of tenders, the address to which they must be sent and the language or languages in which they must be drawn up;
(c) a reference to any contract notice;
(d) an indication of the information to be included with the tender;
(e) the criteria for the award of the contract if this information was not specified in the contract notice; and

(f)  any other special contract condition.

(9) A utility using the open, the restricted or the negotiated procedure with or without a call for competition shall provide not less than 6 days before the final date for the receipt of tenders such further information relating to the contract documents as may reasonably be requested by a supplier or contractor provided the information is requested in good time and any fee specified in the contract notice or in the invitation to tender has accompanied the request.

(10) A utility shall not refuse to consider an application to be invited to tender for or to negotiate the contract if it is made by letter, telegram, telex, facsimile, telephone or any electronic means provided that, in the last 5 cases, it is confirmed by letter dispatched before the date fixed by the utility as the last date for the receipt of applications to be invited to tender for or negotiate the contract.

PART IV

## QUALIFICATION AND SELECTION OF SUPPLIERS AND CONTRACTORS

### Qualification system for suppliers or contractors

**17.**—(1) A utility may establish and operate a system of qualification of suppliers or **F—04**
contractors if that system complies with the following paragraphs of this regulation.

(2) The system may involve different stages of qualification and shall be based on objective rules and criteria as determined from time to time by the utility using European standards as a reference when they are appropriate.

(3) The rules and criteria shall be made available on request to suppliers or contractors and if so requested any amendment of those rules and criteria shall be sent to them as the amendment is incorporated into the system.

(4) A utility may establish a system of qualification pursuant to which a supplier or contractor may qualify under the system of, or be certified by, another person, and in those circumstances the utility shall inform suppliers and contractors who apply to qualify of the name of that other person.

(5) The utility shall inform applicants for qualification of the success or failure of their application within a reasonable period and, if the decision will take longer than 6 months from the presentation of an application, the utility shall inform the applicant, within 2 months of the application, of the reasons justifying a longer period and of the date by which his application will be accepted or refused.

(6) In determining what rules and criteria are to be met by applicants to qualify under the system and in determining whether a particular applicant does qualify under the system a utility shall not impose conditions of an administrative, technical or financial nature on some suppliers or contractors which are not imposed upon others and shall not require the application of tests or the submission of evidence which duplicates objective evidence already available.

(7) A utility shall inform any applicant whose application to qualify is refused of the decision and the reasons for refusal.

(8) An application may only be refused if the applicant fails to meet the requirements for qualification laid down in accordance with paragraph (2) above.

(9) The utility shall keep a written record of qualified suppliers and contractors which may be divided into categories according to the type of contract for which the qualification is valid.

(10) The utility may cancel the qualification of a supplier or contractor who ha qualified under the qualification system only if he does not continue to meet the rule and criteria laid down in accordance with paragraph (2) above.

(11) The utility may not cancel a qualification unless it notifies the supplier ( contractor in writing beforehand of its intention and of the reason or reasons justifyir the proposed cancellation.

(12) The utility shall send a notice substantially corresponding to the form set out Part E of Schedule 4 and containing the information relating to the qualification syste therein specified to the Official Journal when the system is first established and, if th utility expects to operate the system for more than three years, or if it has operated th system for more than three years, it shall send additional notices annually.

## Selection of suppliers and contractors in the restricted or negotiated procedures

**18.**—(1) A utility using the restricted or the negotiated procedure, with or without a ca for competition, shall make the selection of the suppliers or contractors to be invited t tender for or to negotiate the contract on the basis of objective criteria and rules which determines and which it makes available to suppliers or contractors who request ther

(2) The criteria which a utility uses for deciding not to select a supplier or contract( may include the following, namely that the supplier or contractor—

(a) being an individual is bankrupt or has had a receiving order or administration orde made against him or has made any composition or arrangement with or for th benefit of his creditors or has made any conveyance or assignment for the benef of his creditors or appears unable to pay, or to have no reasonable prospect ( being able to pay, a debt within the meaning of section 268 of the Insolvency A( 1986,[11] or Article 242 of the Insolvency (Northern Ireland) Order 1989,[12] or i Scotland has granted a trust deed for creditors or become otherwise apparent insolvent, or is the subject of a petition presented for sequestration of his estate, ( is the subject of any similar procedure under the law of any other state;

(b) being a partnership constituted under Scots law has granted a trust deed c become otherwise apparently insolvent, or is the subject of a petition presented fc sequestration of its estate;

(c) being a company has passed a resolution or is the subject of an order by the cou for the company's winding up otherwise than for the purposes of bona fid reconstruction or amalgamation, or has had a receiver, manager or administrat( on behalf of a creditor appointed in respect of the company's business or any pa thereof or is the subject of proceedings for any of the above procedures or is th subject of similar procedures under the law of any other state;

(d) has been convicted of a criminal offence relating to the conduct of his business ( profession;

(e) has committed an act of grave misconduct in the course of his business c profession;

(f) has not fulfilled obligations relating to the payment of social securit contributions under the law of any part of the United Kingdom or of the membe State in which the supplier or contractor is established;

(g) has not fulfilled obligations relating to the payment of taxes under the law of an part of the United Kingdom or of the Member State in which the supplier c contractor is established; or

[11] 1986, c.45.
[12] S.I. 1989/2405 (N.I.19).

(h)  is guilty of serious misrepresentation in providing information to the utility.

(3) Without prejudice to the generality of paragraph (1) above the criteria may be based on the need of the utility to reduce the number of suppliers or contractors selected to tender for or to negotiate the contract to a level which is justified by the characteristics of the award procedure and the resources required to complete it.

(4) The utility shall take account of the need to ensure adequate competition in determining the number of persons selected to tender for or to negotiate the contract.

## Consortia

**19.**—(1) In this regulation a "consortium" means two or more persons, at least one of whom is a supplier or contractor, acting jointly for the purpose of being awarded a contract.

(2) A utility shall not treat the tender of a consortium as ineligible nor decide not to include a consortium amongst those persons from whom it will make the selection of persons to be invited to tender for or to negotiate a contract on the grounds that the consortium has not formed a legal entity for the purpose of tendering for or negotiating the contract; but where a utility awards a contract to a consortium it may, if to do so is justified for the satisfactory performance of the contract, require the consortium to form a legal entity before entering into, or as a term of, the contract.

(3) In these Regulations references to a supplier or contractor where the supplier or contractor is a consortium includes a reference to each person who is a member of that consortium.

## PART V

## THE AWARD OF A CONTRACT

### Criteria for the award of a contract

**20.**—(1) Subject to regulation 21 below, a utility shall award a contract on the basis of the offer which—

  **F—05**

(a)  offers the lowest price, or
(b)  is the most economically advantageous to the utility.

(2) The criteria which a utility may use to determine that an offer is the most economically advantageous include price, delivery date or period for completion, running costs, cost effectiveness, quality, aesthetic and functional characteristics, technical merit, after sales service and technical assistance, commitments with regard to spare parts and security of supply.

(3) Where a utility intends to award a contract on the basis of the offer which is the most economically advantageous it shall state the criteria on which it intends to base its decision, where possible in descending order of importance, in any contract notice or in the contract documents.

(4) Where a utility awards a contract on the basis of the offer which is the most economically advantageous, it may take account of offers which offer variations on the requirements specified in the contract documents if the offer meets the minimum requirements of the utility and it has stated those minimum requirements and any specific requirements for the presentation of an offer offering variations in the contract documents; but if the utility will not take account of offers which offer such variations it shall state that fact in the contract documents.

(5) A utility may not reject a tender on the ground that the tender is based on, or the technical specifications in the tender have been defined by reference to, European specifications (within the meaning of regulation 11(1) above) or to national technical specifications recognised as complying with the essential requirements of Council Directive 89/106/EEC on the approximation of laws, regulations and administrative procedures in the Member States relating to construction products.[13]

(6) If an offer for a contract is abnormally low the utility may reject that offer but only if it has requested in writing an explanation of the offer or of those parts which it considers contribute to the offer being abnormally low, which request may set a reasonable period for reply, and has—

(a) if awarding the contract on the basis of the offer which offers the lowest price examined the details of all the offers made, taking into account any explanation given to it of the abnormally low offer, before awarding the contract, or
(b) if awarding the contract on the basis of the offer which is the most economically advantageous, taken any such explanation into account in assessing which is the most economically advantageous offer,

and, in considering that explanation, the utility may take into account explanations which justify the offer on objective grounds including the economy of the construction or production method, the technical solutions suggested by the supplier or contractor or the exceptionally favourable conditions available to the supplier or contractor for the performance of the contract or the originality of the goods or works proposed by the supplier or contractor.

(7) A utility may reject a tender for a contract which is abnormally low owing to the receipt of a state aid within the meaning of article 92 of the Treaty but only if it has consulted the supplier or contractor and the supplier or contractor has not been able to show that the aid in question has been notified to the Commission pursuant to article 93(3) of the Treaty or has received the Commission's approval.

(8) A utility which rejects a tender in accordance with paragraph (7) above shall send a report to the Minister for onward transmission to the Commission.

(9) For the purposes of this regulation "offer" includes a bid by one part of a utility to supply goods or to carry out a work or works for another part of the utility when the former part is invited by the latter part to compete with the offers sought from other persons.

### Rejection of third country offers

**21.**—(1) In this regulation an offer of third country origin is an offer to enter a supply contract under which more than 50% of the value of the goods offered originate, as determined in accordance with Council Regulation (EEC) No. 802/68,[14] in States with which the Communities have not concluded, multilaterally or bilaterally, an agreement ensuring comparable and effective access for undertakings in Member States to the markets of those States or in States to which the benefit of the provisions of Council Directive 90/531/EEC[15] has not been extended.

(2) Notwithstanding regulation 20, a utility need not accept an offer of third country origin.

[13] OJ No. L 40, 11.2.89, p.12.
[14] OJ No. L 148, 28.6.68, p.1, as amended by Council Regulation (EEC) No. 3860/87 (OJ No. L 363 23.12.87, p.30).
[15] OJ No. L 297, 29.10.90, p.1.

(3) Notwithstanding regulation 20, where an offer of third country origin is equivalent to an offer which is not of third country origin a utility shall not accept the offer of third country origin unless not to accept that offer would oblige the utility to acquire goods having technical characteristics different from those of existing goods or an installation resulting in incompatibility, technical difficulties in operation and maintenance or disproportionate costs.

(4) In the case of a contract to be awarded on the basis of the offer which offers the lowest price offers are equivalent for the purposes of paragraph (3) above if their prices are to be treated as equivalent in accordance with paragraph (6) below.

(5) In the case of a contract to be awarded on the basis of the offer which is the most economically advantageous to the utility offers are equivalent for the purposes of paragraph (3) above if their prices are to be treated as equivalent in accordance with paragraph (6) below and if disregarding any difference in price the offer which is not of third country origin is at least as economically advantageous to the utility as the offer of third country origin.

(6) The prices of offers are to be treated as equivalent for the purposes of paragraphs (4) and (5) above if the price of the offer which is not of third country origin is the same as or is not more than 3% greater than the offer of third country origin.

## Contract award notice

**22.**—(1) A utility which has awarded a supply or a works contract (other than one excluded from the application of these Regulations by regulations 6 to 9 above) shall no later than two months after the award, send to the Official Journal a notice, substantially corresponding to the form set out in Part F of Schedule 4 and including the information therein specified.

(2) The utility may indicate that any of the information included in paragraphs 6 and 9 of the notice is of a sensitive commercial nature, and request that it not be published.

PART VI

## MISCELLANEOUS

## Obligations relating to employment protection and working conditions

**23.** A utility which includes in the contract documents relating to a works contract **F–06** information as to where a contractor may obtain information about the obligations relating to employment protection and working conditions which will apply to the works to be carried out under the contract, shall request contractors to indicate that they have taken account of those obligations in preparing their tender or in negotiating the contract.

## Sub-contracting

**24.** A utility may require a supplier or contractor to indicate in his tender what part of the contract if any he intends to sub-contract to another person.

## Preservation of records

**25.**—(1) When these Regulations apply to the seeking of offers in relation to a contract a utility shall keep appropriate information on each such contract sufficient to justify decisions taken in connection with—

(a) the qualification and selection of suppliers or contractors and the award of contracts;

(b) the recourse to derogations from the requirement that European specifications be referred to pursuant to regulation 11(4) above; and

(c) the use of a procedure without a call for competition pursuant to regulation 15 above.

(2) When a utility decides not to apply these Regulations to the seeking of offers in relation to a contract in accordance with regulations 6, 7 and 9 above it shall keep appropriate information on such a contract sufficient to justify that decision.

(3) The information referred to in paragraphs (1) and (2) above shall be preserved for at least four years from the date of the award of the contract.

### Statistical and other reports

**26.**—(1) A utility shall each year by the date notified to it by the Minister send to the Minister a report specifying the aggregate value (estimated if necessary) of the consideration payable under the contracts awarded in the previous year and excluded from the operation of these Regulations by regulation 9 above for each of the following categories of activity—

(a) the production, transport or distribution of drinking water, hydraulic engineering, irrigation, land drainage or the disposal or treatment of sewage;

(b) the production, transport or distribution of electricity;

(c) the transport or distribution of gas or heat;

(d) the exploration for and extraction of oil or gas;

(e) the exploration for and extraction of coal or other solid fuels;

(f) railway services;

(g) urban railway, tramway, trolleybus or bus services;

(h) the provision of airport facilities;

(i) the provision of maritime or inland port or other terminal facilities; and

(j) the operation of telecommunications networks or the provision of telecommunications services.

(2) A utility when requested shall send to the Minister a report for the purpose of informing the Commission—

(a) containing such information as the Minister may from time to time require in respect of a particular supply or works contract (including contracts excluded from the application of these Regulations by regulations 6 to 9 above);

(b) specifying which of its activities it considers are not activities specified in the Part of Schedule 1 in which the utility is specified, or are activities outside the territory of the Communities not involving the physical use of a network or geographical area within the Communities; and

(c) specifying the categories of goods or works it considers comprise the goods and works which it acquires in order to sell or to hire them to another person, but which it does not have a special or exclusive right to sell or hire and which other persons are free to sell or hire under the same conditions.

(3) A utility may indicate that any of the information included in a report sent to the Minister pursuant to paragraph 2(c) above is of a sensitive commercial nature, and request that it not be published.

### The Responsible Minister

**27.**—(1) Any reference to the Minister in these Regulations shall be deemed to be a reference to the Minister responsible for that utility.

(2) The Minister responsible for a utility shall be the Minister of the Crown whose areas of responsibility are most closely connected with the functions of the utility; and any question as to which Minister of the Crown's areas of responsibility are most closely connected with the functions of a utility shall be determined by the Treasury whose determination shall be final.

(3) The requirement on a utility to send any report in accordance with regulations 7(2), 20(8) and 26 to the Minister shall be enforceable, on the application of the Minister responsible, by mandamus, or in Scotland, for an order for specific performance.

(4) Proceedings under paragraph (3) above brought in Scotland shall be brought before the Court of Session.

(5) In the application of this regulation to Northern Ireland references to the Minister shall include references to the head of a Northern Ireland department.

(6) The Minister to whom a report is sent in accordance with regulations 7(2), 20(8) and 26 shall send the report to the Treasury for onward transmission to the Commission.

## Official Journal notices

**28.**—(1) Any notice required by these Regulations to be sent to the Official Journal shall be sent by the most appropriate means to the Official Publications of the European Communities.[16]

(2) The utility shall retain evidence of the date of dispatch to the Official Journal of each notice.

(3) The utility may in exceptional cases request that a contract notice be published within 5 days of the date of despatch, provided that it is sent by electronic mail, telex or facsimile.[17]

(4) The utility may publish the information contained in a contract notice in such other way as it thinks fit but it shall not do so until the notice has been dispatched in accordance with paragraph (1) above and shall not publish any information other than that contained in the notice.

## Confidentiality of Information

**29.** A utility which makes information available to a supplier or contractor pursuant to these Regulations may impose requirements on him for the purpose of protecting the confidentiality of that information.

PART VII

**APPLICATIONS TO THE COURT AND CONCILIATION**

## Enforcement of obligations

**30.**—(1) The obligation on a utility to comply with the provisions of these Regulations other than regulations 7(2), 20(8) and 26, and with any enforceable Community obligation      **F–07**

---

[16] The address for the Office for Official Publications of the European Communities is 2 rue Mercier, L-2985, Luxembourg, tel 499 28–1, telex 1324 PUBOF LU, fax 49 00 03, 49 57 19.
[17] The Office for the Official Publications is required by article 19(3) of Council Directive 90/531/EEC (OJ No. L 297, 29.10.90, p.1) to publish notices within 12 days of the date of despatch, and to endeavour to publish contract notices within 5 days of the date of despatch in response to a request pursuant to this paragraph.

in respect of a supply or a works contract (other than one excluded from the application of these Regulations by regulations 6, 7 or 9 above), is a duty owed to suppliers and contractors.

(2) A breach of the duty owed pursuant to paragraph (1) shall not be a criminal offence but any breach of the duty shall be actionable by any supplier or contractor who, in consequence, suffers, or risks suffering, loss or damage.

(3) Proceedings under this regulation shall be brought in England and Wales and in Northern Ireland in the High Court and, in Scotland, before the Court of Session.

(4) Proceedings under this regulation may not be brought unless—

(a) the supplier or contractor bringing the proceedings has informed the utility of the breach or apprehended breach of the duty owed to him pursuant to paragraph (1) above by that utility and of his intention to bring proceedings under this regulation in respect of it; and

(b) they are brought promptly, and in any event within 3 months from the date when grounds for the bringing of the proceedings first arose unless the Court considers that there is good reason for extending the period within which proceedings may be brought.

(5) Subject to paragraph (6) below, but otherwise without prejudice to any other powers of the Court, in proceedings brought under this regulation the Court may—

(a) by interim order suspend the procedure leading to the award of the contract in relation to which the breach of the duty owed pursuant to paragraph (1) above is alleged, or suspend the implementation of any decision or action taken by the utility in the course of following such a procedure; and

(b) if satisfied that a decision or action taken by a utility was in breach of the duty owed pursuant to paragraph (1) above—
   (i) order the setting aside of that decision or action or order the utility to amend any document, or
   (ii) award damages to a supplier or contractor who has suffered loss or damage as a consequence of the breach, or
   (iii) do both of those things.

(6) In proceedings under this regulation the Court shall not have power to order any remedy other than an award of damages in respect of a breach of the duty owed pursuant to paragraph (1) above if the contract in relation to which the breach occurred has been entered into.

(7) Where in proceedings under this regulation the Court is satisfied that a supplier or contractor would have had a real chance of being awarded a contract if that chance had not been adversely affected by a breach of the duty owed to him by the utility pursuant to paragraph (1) above the supplier or contractor shall be entitled to damages amounting to his costs in preparing his tender and in participating in the procedure leading to the award of the contract.

(8) Paragraph (7) above shall not affect a claim by a supplier or contractor that he has suffered other loss or damage or that he is entitled to relief other than damages and is without prejudice to the matters on which a supplier or contractor may be required to satisfy the Court in respect of any other such claim.

(9) Notwithstanding sections 21 and 42 of the Crown Proceedings Act 1947,[18] in proceedings brought under this regulation against the Crown the Court shall have power to grant an injunction or interdict.

## Conciliation

**31.**—(1) A supplier or contractor who considers that—

(a) a utility has breached or may breach the duty referred to in regulation 30(1) above, and

(b) in consequence he has suffered, or risks suffering, loss or damage

and who wishes to use the conciliation procedure provided for in articles 10 and 11 of Council Directive 92/13/EEC[19] shall send a request for the application of the procedure to the Treasury for onward transmission to the Commission.

(2) Neither the request for nor any action taken pursuant to the conciliation procedure referred to in paragraph (1) above shall affect the rights or liabilities of the supplier or contractor requesting it, of the utility in respect of which the request is made, or of any other person.

PART VIII

**AMENDMENTS**

## Amendment of the Public Works Contracts Regulations and the Public Supply Contracts Regulations

**32.**—(1) The Public Works Contracts Regulations 1991[20] shall be amended by substituting—
**F–08**

(a) for paragraphs (a), (b) and (c) of regulation 6 the following paragraphs:
"(a) for the purpose of carrying out an activity specified in the second column of Schedule 1 to the Utilities Supply and Works Contracts Regulations 1992, other than an activity specified in paragraphs 2 or 3 thereof;
(b) when a contracting authority exercises the activity specified in paragraph 1 of Schedule 1 to the Utilities Supply and Works Contracts Regulations 1992, for the purpose of carrying out an activity specified in paragraph 2 or 3 thereof;";

(b) in regulation 10(2)—
(i) in subparagraph (a) where it first appears "(3)" for "(4)" and "restricted" for "negotiated";
(ii) in subparagraph (d) "(3)" for "(4)";
(iii) in subparagraph (g) "(4)" for "(5)";
(iv) in subparagraph (h) "(5)" for "(6)";

(c) in regulation 12(4) "contractor" for "supplier";

(d) in regulation 13—
(i) in paragraph (1)(b) "11(7)" for "11(6)";
(ii) in paragraph (2) "2" for "3";

(e) in regulation 18 "16(1)(b)" for "17(1)(b)";

(f) in regulation 31(6) "paragraph (7)" for "paragraph (6)"; and

---

[18] 1947 c.44; the Crown Proceedings Act 1947 was extended to Northern Ireland in relation to Her Majesty's Government in the United Kingdom and in Northern Ireland by and with the additions, exceptions and modifications set out in the Crown Proceedings (Northern Ireland) Order 1981, to which there is an amendment not relevant to these Regulations.

[19] OJ No. L 76, 23.3.92, p.14.

[20] S.I. 1991/2680.

(g) in paragraph 6(a) of Part D of Schedule 2 "requests to participate" for "tenders".

(2) The Public Supply Contracts Regulations 1991[21] shall be amended—

(a) by substituting for paragraphs (a), (b) and (c) of regulation 6 the following paragraphs:
  "(a) for the purpose of carrying out an activity specified in the second column of Schedule 1 to the Utilities Supply and Works Contracts Regulations 1992 other than an activity specified in paragraph 2 or 3 thereof;
   (b) when a contracting authority exercises the activity specified in paragraph 1 of Schedule 1 to the Utilities Supply and Works Contracts Regulations 1992 for the purpose of carrying out an activity specified in paragraph 2 or 3 thereof;"
(b) by inserting in regulation 10(3)(e), "and not attributable to", after the words "unforeseeable by"; and
(c) by substituting in regulation 26(6) "has" for "had".

*Norman Lamont*
*Tim Wood*
23rd December 1992         Two of the Lords Commissioners of Her Majesty's Treasury

**SCHEDULE 1**                    Regulation 6

UTILITIES AND ACTIVITIES

| Utility | Activity |
|---|---|
| **PART A** ||
| A company holding an appointment as a water undertaker under the Water Industry Act 1991. | 1. The provision or operation of a fixed network which provides or will provide a service to the public in connection with the production, transport or distribution of drinking water. |
| A water authority as defined in section 3(1) of the Water (Scotland) Act 1980. | |
| The Department of the Environment for Northern Ireland. | 2. Hydraulic engineering, irrigation or land drainage, but only if more than 20% of the total volume of water made available by such activity is intended for the supply of drinking water. |
| | 3. The disposal or treatment of sewage. |
| **PART B** ||
| A relevant person not specified in Part C. | 4. The supply of drinking water to a network referred to in paragraph 1 above. |
| Any other person not specified in Part C who supplies drinking water to a network which is referred to in paragraph 1 above and which is provided or operated by a person specified in Part A. | |

F–09

[21] S.I. 1991/2679.

| Utility | Activity |
| --- | --- |

## PART C

A relevant person other than a public authority who produces drinking water because its consumption is necessary for the purpose of carrying out an activity not specified in the second column of this Schedule and who supplies only the excess to a network which is referred to in paragraph 1 above.

5. The supply of drinking water to a network referred to in paragraph 1 above but only if the drinking water supplied in the period of 36 months ending at the relevant time as defined in regulation 9(16) above has exceeded 30% of the total produced by the utility in that period.

Any other person who is not a public authority, who produces drinking water because its consumption is necessary for the purpose of carrying out an activity not specified in the second column of this Schedule and who supplies only the excess to a network which is referred to in paragraph 1 above and which is provided or operated by a person specified in Part A.

## PART D

A person licensed under section 6 of the Electricity Act 1989.

A person licensed under article 10(1) of the Electricity (Northern Ireland) Order 1992.

6. The provision or operation of a fixed network which provides or will provide a service to the public in connection with the production, transport or distribution of electricity.

## PART E

A relevant person not specified in Part F.

Any other person not specified in Part F who supplies electricity to a network which is referred to in paragraph 6 above and which is provided or operated by a person specified in Part D.

7. The supply of electricity to a network referred to in paragraph 6 above.

## PART F

A relevant person other than a public authority who produces electricity because its use is necessary for the purpose of carrying out an activity not specified in the second column of this Schedule and who supplies only the excess to a network referred to in paragraph 6 above.

8. The supply of electricity to a network referred to in paragraph 6 above but only if the electricity supplied in the period of 36 months ending at the relevant time as defined in regulation 9(16) above has exceeded 30% of the total produced by the utility in that period.

Any other person who is not a public authority, who produces electricity because its use is necessary for the purpose of carrying out an activity not specified in the second column of this Schedule and who supplies only the excess to a network which is referred to in paragraph 6 above and which is provided or operated by a person specified in Part D.

## PART G

A public gas supplier as defined in section 7(1) of the Gas Act 1986.

A person declared to be an undertaker for the supply of gas under article 14(1) of the Gas (Northern Ireland) Order 1977.

9. The provision or operation of a fixed network which provides or will provide a service to the public in connection with the production, transport or distribution of gas.

249

| Utility | Activity |
|---|---|

### PART H

A relevant person not specified in Part I.

Any other person not specified in Part I who supplies gas to a network which is referred to in paragraph 9 above and which is provided or operated by a person specified in Part G.

10. The supply of gas to a network referred to in paragraph 9 above.

### PART I

A relevant person other than a public authority who produces gas only as the unavoidable consequence of carrying out an activity not specified in the second column of this Schedule and who supplies gas for the sole purpose of the economic exploitation of the production to a network referred to in paragraph 9 above.

Any other person who is not a public authority, who produces gas only as the unavoidable consequence of carrying out an activity not specified in the second column of this Schedule and who supplies gas for the sole purpose of the economic exploitation of the production to a network which is referred to in paragraph 9 above and which is provided or operated by a person specified in Part G.

11. The supply of gas to a network referred to in paragraph 9 above but only if the total consideration payable in the period of 36 months ending at the relevant time as defined in regulation 9(16) above on account of such supply has exceeded 20% of the total turnover of the utility in that period.

### PART J

A local authority.

A person licensed under section 6(1)(a) of the Electricity Act 1989 whose licence includes the provisions referred to in section 10(3) of that Act.

The Northern Ireland Housing Executive.

12. The provision or operation of a fixed network which provides or will provide a service to the public in connection with the production, transport or distribution of heat.

### PART K

A relevant person not specified in Part L.

Any other person not specified in Part L who supplies heat to a network which is referred to in paragraph 12 above and which is provided or operated by a person specified in Part J.

13. The supply of heat to a network referred to in paragraph 12 above.

### PART L

A relevant person other than a public authority who produces heat as the unavoidable consequence of carrying out an activity not specified in the second column of this Schedule and who supplies heat for the sole purpose of the economic exploitation of the production to a network referred to in paragraph 12 above.

Any other person who is not a public authority, who produces heat only as the unavoidable consequence of carrying out an activity not specified in the second column of this Schedule

14. The supply of heat to a network referred to in paragraph 12 above but only if the total consideration payable in the 36 months ending at the relevant time as defined in regulation 9(16) above on account of such supply has exceeded 20% of the total turnover of the utility in that period.

| Utility | Activity |
| --- | --- |

and who supplies heat for the sole purpose of the economic exploitation of the production to a network which is referred to in paragraph 12 above and which is provided or operated by a person specified in Part J.

### PART M

| | |
| --- | --- |
| A person licensd under the Petroleum (Production) Act 1934. | 15. The exploitation of a geographical area for the purpose of exploring for or extracting oil or gas. |
| A person licensed under the Petroleum (Production) Act (Northern Ireland) 1964. | |

### PART N

| | |
| --- | --- |
| The British Coal Corporation. | 16. The exploitation of a geographical area for the purposes of exploring for or extracting coal or other solid fuels. |
| A person licensed by the British Coal Corporation under the Coal Industry (Nationalisation) Act 1946. | |
| The Department of Economic Development (Northern Ireland). | |
| A person who holds a prospecting licence, a mining lease, a mining licence or a mining permission as defined by section 57(1) of the Mineral Development Act (Northern Ireland) 1969. | |

### PART O

| | |
| --- | --- |
| A local authority. | 17. The exploitation of a geographical area for the purpose of providing airport or other terminal facilities to carriers by air. |
| An airport operator within the meaning of the Airports Act 1986 who has the management of an airport subject to economic regulation under Part IV of that Act. | |
| Highland and Islands Airports Limited. | |
| A subsidiary of the Northern Ireland Transport Holding Company within the meaning of the Aerodromes Act (Northern Ireland) 1971. | |
| An aerodrome undertaking within the meaning of the Aerodromes Act (Northern Ireland) 1971. | |
| Any other relevant person. | |

### PART P

| | |
| --- | --- |
| A harbour authority within the meaning of section 57 of the Harbours Act 1964. | 18. The exploitation of a geographical area for the purpose of providing maritime or inland port or other terminal facilities to carriers by sea or inland waterway. |
| British Waterways Board. | |
| A local authority. | |
| A harbour authority as defined by section 38(1) of the Harbours Act (Northern Ireland) 1970. | |
| Any other relevant person. | |

251

| Utility | Activity |
|---|---|

PART Q

British Railways Board.

A subsidiary of British Railways Board within the meaning of section 25 of the Transport Act 1962.

19. The operation of a network providing a service to the public in the field of transport by railway.

Eurotunnel plc.

Northern Ireland Transport Holding Company.

Northern Ireland Railways Company Limited.

London Regional Transport.

London Underground Limited.

Docklands Light Railway Limited.

Strathclyde Passenger Transport Executive.

Greater Manchester Passenger Transport Executive.

Greater Manchester Metro Limited.

Tyne and Wear Passenger Transport Executive.

Brighton Borough Council.

South Yorkshire Passenger Transport Executive.

South Yorkshire Supertram (No. 2) Limited.

Any other relevant person.

PART R

Greater Manchester Passenger Transport Executive.

Greater Manchester Metro Limited.

20. The operation of a network providing a service to the public in the field of transport by automated systems, tramway, trolleybus, or cable.

Blackpool Transport Services Limited.

Aberconwy Borough Council.

South Yorkshire Passenger Transport Executive.

South Yorkshire Supertram (No. 2) Limited.

Any other relevant person.

PART S

London Regional Transport.

A subsidiary of London Regional Transport within the meaning of section 36 of the Transport Act 1985.

21. The operation of a network providing a service to the public in the field of transport by bus in a geographical area in which other persons are not free to provide the service under the same conditions as the utility.

A person who provides a London bus service as defined in section 34(2)(b) of the Transport Act 1985 in pursuance of an agreement entered into by London Regional Transport by virtue of section 3(2) of the London Regional Transport Act 1984.

Northern Ireland Tranport Holding Company.

| Utility | Activity |
|---|---|
| A person who holds a road service licence under section 4(1) of the Transport Act (Northern Ireland) 1967 which authorises him to provide a regular service within the meaning of that licence. | |
| Any other relevant person. | |

PART T

| A public telecommunications operator under the Telecommunications Act 1984. | 22. The provision or operation of a public telecommunications network. |
|---|---|
| | 23. The provision of one or more public telecommunications services. |

In this Schedule—

"local authority" means an authority in England and Wales, in Scotland or in Northern Ireland referred to in paragraphs (2) to (4) respectively or regulation 3 of the Public Works Contracts Regulations 1991(a);

"network", in relation to a service in the field of transport, means a system operated in accordance with conditions laid down by or under the law in any part of the United Kingdom including such conditions as the routes to be served, the capacity to be made available and the frequency of the service;

"public authority" means a contracting authority within the meaning of regulation 3(1) of the Public Works Contracts Regulations 1991;[22]

"public telecommunications network" has the meaning ascribed to it by regulation 2(1);

"public telecommunications services" has the meaning ascribed to it by regulation 2(1);

"public undertaking" means a person over whom one or more public authorities are able to exercise directly or indirectly a dominant influence by virtue of—

(a) their ownership of it,

(b) their financial participation in it, or

(c) the rights accorded to them by the rules which govern it;

and in particular a public authority shall be considered to be able to exercise a dominant influence over a person when it directly or indirectly—

(d) possesses the majority of the issued share capital of that person or controls the voting power attached to such majority, or

(e) may appoint more than half of the individuals who are ultimately responsible for managing that person's affairs, more than half its members or, in the case of a group of individuals, more than half of those individuals;

"relevant person" means a person who is—

(a) a public authority,

(b) a public undertaking, or

(c) not a public authority or a public undertaking and has as one of its activities an activity specified in the second column of this Schedule other than an activity specified in paragraphs 2 or 3 thereof and carries out that activity on the basis of a special or exclusive right; and

"special or exclusive right" means a right deriving from authorisations granted by a competent authority when the requirement for the authorisation has the effect of reserving for one or more persons the exploitation of an activity specified to in the

[22] S.I. 1991/2680.

second column of this Schedule, and in particular a person shall be considered to enjoy a special or exclusive right where for the purpose of constructing a network or facilities referred to in the second column of this Schedule it may take advantage of a procedure for the expropriation or use of property or may place network equipment on, under or over a highway.

**SCHEDULE 2**    Regulation 7

EXCLUDED PUBLIC TELECOMMUNICATIONS SERVICES

| Utility | Activity |
|---|---|
| **PART A** | |
| Public telecommunications operators under the Telecommunications Act 1984 other than British Telecommunications plc and Kingston Communications (Hull) plc. | 1. All public telecommunications services. |
| **PART B** | |
| British Telecommunications plc. Kingston Communications (Hull) plc. | 2. All public telecommunications services, other than the following services when they are provided within the geographical area for which the provider is licensed as a public telecommunications operator: basic voice telephony services, basic data transmission services, the provision of private leased circuits and maritime services. |

**F–10**

In this Schedule—

"basic data transmission services" means telecommunications services consisting of the conveyance of messages other than two-way live speech telephone calls, including only such switching, processing, data storage or protocol conversion as is necessary for the conveyance of those messages in real time;

"basic voice telephony services" means telecommunications services consisting of the conveyance of messages in the form of two-way live speech telephone calls, including only such switching, processing, data storage or protocol conversion as is necessary for the conveyance of those messages in real time;

"maritime services" means two-way telecommunications services including voice telephony and data transmission services consisting of the transmission and reception of messages conveyed between seagoing vessels and hovercraft;

"private leased circuit" means a communication facility which is—

(a) provided by one or more public telecommunications networks,

(b) for the conveyance of messages between points, all of which are points of connection between public telecommunications networks and other telecommunications networks,

(c) made available to a particular person or particular persons,

(d) such that all of the messages transmitted at any of the points referred to in subparagraph (b) above are received at every other such point, and

(e) such that the points mentioned in subparagraph (a) above are fixed by the way in which the facility is installed and cannot otherwise be selected by persons or telecommunications apparatus sending messages by means of the facility;

"public telecommunications networks" and "public telecommunications services" have the meanings ascribed to them by regulation 2(1); and

"public telecommunications operator" has the meaning given by section 9(3) of the Telecommunications Act 1984.

254

**SCHEDULE 3**                                   Regulation 2(1)

ACTIVITIES CONSTITUTING WORKS

| Classes | Groups | Subgroups and items | Descriptions |
|---------|--------|---------------------|--------------|
| 50 | | | BUILDING AND CIVIL ENGINEERING |
| | 500 | | General building and civil engineering work (without any particular specialisation) and demolition work |
| | | 500.1 | General building and civil engineering work (without any particular specialisation) |
| | | 500.2 | Demolition work |
| | 501 | | Construction of flats, office blocks, hospitals and other buildings, both residential and non-residential |
| | | 501.1 | General building contractors |
| | | 501.2 | Roofing |
| | | 501.3 | Construction of chimneys, kilns and furnaces |
| | | 501.4 | Waterproofing and damp-proofing |
| | | 501.5 | Restoration and maintenance of outside walls (repainting, cleaning, etc.) |
| | | 501.6 | Erection and dismantlement of scaffolding |
| | | 501.7 | Other specialised activities relating to construction work (including carpentry) |
| | 502 | | Civil engineering: construction of roads, bridges, railways, etc. |
| | | 502.1 | General civil engineering work |
| | | 502.2 | Earth-moving (navvying) |
| | | 502.3 | Construction of bridges, tunnels and shafts, drilling |
| | | 502.4 | Hydraulic engineering (rivers, canals, harbours, flows, locks and dams) |
| | | 502.5 | Road-building (including specialised construction of airports and runways) |
| | | 502.6 | Specialised construction work relating to water (i.e. to irrigation, land drainage, water supply, sewage disposal, sewerage, etc.) |
| | | 502.7 | Specialised activities in other areas of civil engineering |
| | 503 | | Installation (fittings and fixtures) |
| | | 503.1 | General installation work |
| | | 503.2 | Gas fitting and plumbing, and the installation of sanitary equipment |
| | | 503.3 | Installation of heating and ventilating apparatus (central heating, air condition, ventilation) |
| | | 503.4 | Sound and heat insulation, insulation against vibration |
| | | 503.5 | Electrical fittings |
| | | 503.6 | Installation of aerials, lightning conductors, telephones, etc. |
| | 504 | | Building completion work |
| | | 504.1 | General building completion work |
| | | 504.2 | Plastering |
| | | 504.3 | Joinery, primarily engaged in on the site assembly and/or installation (including the laying of parquet flooring) |
| | | 504.4 | Painting, glazing, paper hanging |
| | | 504.5 | Tiling and otherwise covering floors and walls |
| | | 504.6 | Other building completion work (putting in fireplaces, etc.) |

## SCHEDULE 4

Regulations 13(1), 14(2)(b), 17(12) and 22(1)

FORMS OF NOTICES FOR PUBLICATION IN THE OFFICIAL JOURNAL

PART A

PERIODIC INDICATIVE NOTICE

**A. For supply contracts:**

**F–12**

1. The name, address and telephone, telegraphic, telex and facsimile numbers of the utility and of the service from which additional information may be obtained.

2. For each type of goods or services the total quantity or value to be supplied under the contract(s).

3. (a) Estimated date of the commencement of the procedures leading to the award of the contract(s) (if known).
   (b) Type of award procedure to be used.

4. Other information (for example, indicate if a call for competition will be published later).

5. Date of despatch of the notice.

**B. For works contracts**

1. The name, address and telephone, telegraphic, telex and facsimile numbers of the utility.

2. (a) The site.
   (b) The nature and extent of the services to be provided, the main characteristics of the work or where relevant of any lots of reference to the work.
   (c) An estimate of the cost of the service to be provided.

3. (a) Type of award procedure to be used.
   (b) Estimated date for initiating the award procedures in respect of the contract or contracts.
   (c) Estimated date for the start of the work.
   (d) Estimated time-table for completion of the work.

4. Terms of financing of the work and of price revision.

5. Other information (for example, indicate if a call for competition will be published later).

6. Date of despatch of the notice.

PART B

OPEN PROCEDURES NOTICE

1. The name, address and telephone, telegraphic, telex and facsimile numbers of the utility.

2. Nature of the contract (supply or works; where applicable, state if it is a framework agreement[23]).

[23] In accordance with regulation 10.

256

3. (a) Place of delivery, or site.
   (b) Nature and quantity of the goods to be supplied; or the nature and extent of the services to be provided and general nature of the work.
   (c) Indication of whether the suppliers can tender for some and/or all of the goods required. If, for works contracts, the work or the contract is subdivided into several lots, the size of the different lots and the possibility of tendering for one, for several or for all of the lots.
   (d) Authorisation to submit variants.
   (e) For works contracts: information concerning the purpose of the work or the contract where the latter also involves the drawing up of projects.

4. Derogation from the use of European specifications, in accordance with regulation 11(4).

5. Time limits for delivery or completion.

6. (a) Name and address from which the contract documents and additional documents may be requested.
   (b) Where applicable, the amount and terms of payment of the sum to be paid to obtain such documents.

7. (a) the final date for receipt of tenders.
   (b) The address to which they must be sent.
   (c) the language or languages in which they must be drawn up.

8. (a) Where applicable, the persons authorised to be present at the opening of tenders.
   (b) The date, hour and place of such opening.

9. Any deposits and guarantees required.

10. Main terms concerning financing and payment and/or reference to the provisions in which these are contained.

11. Where applicable, the legal form to be taken by the grouping of suppliers or contractors to whom the contract is awarded.

12. Minimum standards of economic and financial standing and technical capacity required of the supplier or contractor to whom the contract is awarded.

13. Period during which the tenderer is bound to keep open his tender.

14. The criteria for the award of the contract. Criteria other than that of the lowest price shall be mentioned where they do not appear in the contract documents.

15. Other information.

16. Where applicable, the date of publication in the Official Journal of the European Communities of the periodic indicative notice which refers to the contract.

17. Date of dispatch of the notice.

## Part C

### Restricted Procedures Notice

1. The name, address and telephone, telegraphic, telex and facsimile numbers of the utility.

2. Nature of the contract (supply or works; where applicable, state if it is a framework agreement[24]).

3. (a) Place of delivery, or site.
   (b) Nature and quantity of the goods to be supplied; or the nature and extent of the services to be provided and general nature of the work.
   (c) Indication of whether the suppliers can tender for some and/or all of the goods required. If, for works contracts, the work or the contract is subdivided into several lots, the size of the different lots and the possibility of tendering for one, for several or for all of the lots.
   (d) Authorisation to submit variants.
   (e) For works contracts: information concerning the purpose of the work or the contract where the latter also involves the drawing up of projects.

4. Derogation from the use of European specifications, in accordance with regulation 11(4).

5. Time limits for delivery or completion.

6. Where applicable, the legal form to be taken by the grouping of suppliers or contractors to whom the contract is awarded.

7. (a) The final date for receipt of requests to participate.
   (b) The address to which they must be sent.
   (c) The language or languages in which they must be drawn up.

8. The final date for despatch of invitations to tender.

9. Any deposits and guarantees required.

10. Main terms concerning financing and payment and/or reference to the provisions in which these are contained.

11. Information concerning the supplier's or contractor's personal position and minimum standards of economic and financial standing and technical capacity required of the supplier or contractor to whom the contract is awarded.

12. The criteria for the award of the contract where they are not mentioned in the invitation to tender.

13. Other information.

14. Where applicable, the date of publication in the Official Journal of the European Communities of the periodic indicative notice which refers to the contract.

15. Date of despatch of the notice.

PART D

NEGOTIATED PROCEDURES NOTICE

1. The name, address and telephone, telegraphic, telex and facsimile numbers of the utility.

2. Nature of the contract (supply or works; where applicable, state if it is a framework agreement[25]).

---

[24] In accordance with regulation 10.
[25] In accordance with regulation 10.

3. (a) Place of delivery, or site.
   (b) Nature and quantity of the goods to be supplied; or the nature and extent of the services to be provided and general nature of the work.
   (c) Indication of whether the suppliers can tender for some and/or all of the goods required. If, for works contracts, the work or the contract is subdivided into several lots, the size of the different lots and the possibility of tendering for one, for several or for all of the lots.
   (d) For works contracts: information concerning the purpose of the work or the contract where the latter also involves the drawing up of projects.

4. Derogation from the use of European specifications, in accordance with Regulation 11(4).

5. Time limit for delivery or completion.

6. Where applicable, the legal form to be taken by the grouping of suppliers or contractors to whom the contract is awarded.

7. (a) The final date for receipt of requests to participate.
   (b) The address to which they must be sent.
   (c) The language or languages in which they must be drawn up.

8. Any deposits and guarantees required.

9. Main terms concerning financing and payment and/or references to the provisions in which these are contained.

10. Information concerning the supplier's or contractor's personal position and minimum standards of economic and financial standing and technical capacity required of the supplier or contractor to whom the contract is awarded.

11. Where applicable, the names and addresses of suppliers or contractors already selected by the utility.

12. Where applicable, date(s) of previous publications in the Official Journal of the European Communities.

13. Other information.

14. Where applicable, the date of publication in the Official Journal of the European Communities of the periodic indicative notice which refers to the contract.

15. Date of despatch of the notice.

## Part E

### Notice on the Existence of a Qualification System

1. The name, address and telephone, telegraphic, telex and facsimile numbers of the utility.

2. Purpose of the qualification system.

3. Address where the rules concerning the qualification system can be obtained (if different from the address mentioned under 1.)

4. Where applicable, duration of the qualification system.

PART F

CONTRACT AWARD NOTICE

## I. Information for publication in the Official Journal of the European Communities

1. Name and address of the utility.

2. Nature of the contract (supply or works; where applicable, state if it is a framework agreement[26]).

3. At least a summary indication of the nature of the goods, works or services provided.

4. (a) Form of the call for competition (notice on the existence of a qualification procedure; periodic indicative notice; contract notice).
   (b) Date of publication of the notice in the Official Journal of the European Communities.

   (c) In the case of contracts awarded without a prior call for competition, indication of the relevant sub-paragraph of regulation 15(1) relied upon.

5. Award procedure (open, restricted or negotiated).

6. Number of tenders received.

7. Date of award of the contract.

8. Price paid for bargain purchases under regulation 15(1)(j).

9. Name and address of successful supplier(s) or contractor(s).

10. State, where applicable, whether the contract has been, or may be, sub-contracted.

11. Optional information:
    — value and share of the contract which may be sub-contracted to third parties,
    — award criteria,
    — price paid (or range of prices).

## II. Information not intended for publication

12. Number of contracts awarded (where an award has been split between more than one supplier).

13. Value of each contract awarded.

14. Country of origin of the product or services (EEC origin or non-EEC origin; if the latter, broken down by third country).

15. Was recourse made to the exceptions to the use of European specifications provided for under regulation 11(4). If so, which?

16. Which award criteria was used (most economically advantageous; lowest price)?

17. Was the contract awarded to a bidder who submitted a variant, in accordance with regulation 20(4)?

18. Were any tenders excluded on the grounds that they were abnormally low, in accordance with regulation 20(6) and (7).

19. Date of dispatch of the notice.

[26] In accordance with regulation 10.

# Appendix G

## REMEDIES DIRECTIVES

### Council Directive

### of December 21, 1989

**on the coordination of the laws, regulations and administrative provisions relating to the application of review procedures to the award of public supply and public works contracts**

(89/665/EEC)

THE COUNCIL OF THE EUROPEAN COMMUNITIES,

Having regard to the Treaty establishing the European Economic Community, and in particular Article 100a thereof, **G–01**

Having regard to the proposal from the Commission[1];

In cooperation with the European Parliament,[2]

Having regard to the opinion of the Economic and Social Committee,[3]

Whereas Community Directives on public procurement, in particular Council Directive 71/305/EEC of 26 July 1971 concerning the coordination of procedures for the award of public works contracts,[4] as last amended by Directive 89/440/EEC,[5] and Council Directive 77/62/EEC of 21 December 1976 coordinating procedures for the award of public supply contracts,[6] as last amended by Directive 88/295/EEC,[7] do not contain any specific provisions ensuring their effective application;

Whereas the existing arrangements at both national and Community levels for ensuring their application are not always adequate to ensure compliance with the relevant Community provisions particularly at a stage when infringements can be corrected;

Whereas the opening-up of public procurement to Community competition necessitates a substantial increase in the guarantees of transparency and non-discrimination; whereas, for it to have tangible effects, effective and rapid remedies must be available in the case of infringements of Community law in the field of public procurement or national rules implementing that law;

Whereas in certain Member States the absence of effective remedies or inadequacy of existing remedies deter Community undertakings from submitting tenders in the Member State in which the contracting authority is established; whereas, therefore, the Member States concerned must remedy this situation;

Whereas, since procedures for the award of public contracts are of such short duration, competent review bodies must, among other things, be authorized to take interim measures aimed at suspending such a procedure or the implementation of any decisions which may be taken by the contracting authority; whereas the short duration of the procedures means that the aforementioned infringements need to be dealt with urgently;

---

[1] OJ No C 230, 28.8.1987, p. 6 and OJ No C 15, 19.1.1989, p. 8.
[2] OJ No C 167, 27.6.1988, p. 77 and OJ No C 323, 27.12.1989.
[3] OJ No C 347, 22.12.1987, p. 23.
[4] OJ No L 185, 16.8.1971, p. 5.
[5] OJ No L 210, 21.7.1989, p. 1.
[6] OJ No L 13, 15.1.1977, p. 1.
[7] OJ No L 127, 20.5.1988, p. 1.

Whereas it is necessary to ensure that adequate procedures exist in all the Member States to permit the setting aside of decisions taken unlawfully and compensation of persons harmed by an infringement;

Whereas, when undertakings do not seek review, certain infringements may not be corrected unless a specific mechanism is put in place;

Whereas, accordingly, the Commission, when it considers that a clear and manifest infringement has been committed during a contract award procedure, should be able to bring it to the attention of the competent authorities of the Member State and of the contracting authority concerned so that appropriate steps are taken for the rapid correction of any alleged infringement;

Whereas the application in practice of the provisions of this Directive should be re-examined within a period of four years of its implementation on the basis of information to be supplied by the Member States concerning the functioning of the national review procedures,

HAS ADOPTED THIS DIRECTIVE:

*Article 1*

**G–02**  **1.** The Member States shall take the measures necessary to ensure that, as regards contract award procedures falling within the scope of Directives 71/305/EEC and 77/62/EEC, decisions taken by the contracting authorities may be reviewed effectively and, in particular, as rapidly as possible in accordance with the conditions set out in the following Articles, and, in particular, Article 2(7) on the grounds that such decisions have infringed Community law in the field of public procurement or national rules implementing that law.

**2.** Member States shall ensure that there is no discrimination between undertakings claiming injury in the context of a procedure for the award of a contract as a result of the distinction made by this Directive between national rules implementing Community law and other national rules.

**3.** The Member States shall ensure that the review procedures are available, under detailed rules which the Member States may establish, at least to any person having or having had an interest in obtaining a particular public supply or public works contract and who has been or risks being harmed by an alleged infringement. In particular, the Member States may require that the person seeking the review must have previously notified the contracting authority of the alleged infringement and of his intention to seek review.

*Article 2*

**1.** The Member States shall ensure that the measures taken concerning the review procedures specified in Article 1 include provision for the powers to:

(a) take, at the earliest opportunity and by way of interlocutory procedures, interim measures with the aim of correcting the alleged infringement or preventing further damage to the interests concerned, including measures to suspend or to ensure the suspension of the procedure for the award of a public contract or the implementation of any decision taken by the contracting authority;

(b) either set aside or ensure the setting aside of decisions taken unlawfully, including the removal of discriminatory technical, economic or financial specifications in the invitation to tender, the contract documents or in any other document relating to the contract award procedure;

(c) award damages to persons harmed by an infringement.

**2.** The powers specified in paragraph 1 may be conferred on separate bodies responsible for different aspects of the review procedure.

**3.** Review procedures need not in themselves have an automatic suspensive effect on the contract award procedures to which they relate.

**4.** The Member States may provide that when considering whether to order interim measures the body responsible may take into account the probable consequences of the measures for all interests likely to be harmed, as well as the public interest, and may decide not to grant such measures where their negative consequences could exceed their benefits. A decision not to grant interim measures shall not prejudice any other claim of the person seeking these measures.

**5.** The Member States may provide that where damages are claimed on the grounds that a decision was taken unlawfully, the contested decision must first be set aside by a body having the necessary powers.

**6.** The effects of the exercise of the powers referred to in paragraph 1 on a contract concluded subsequent to its award shall be determined by national law.

Furthermore, except where a decision must be set aside prior to the award of damages, a Member State may provide that, after the conclusion of a contract following its award, the powers of the body responsible for the review procedures shall be limited to awarding damages to any person harmed by an infringement.

**7.** The Member States shall ensure that decisions taken by bodies responsible for review procedures can be effectively enforced.

**8.** Where bodies responsible for review procedures are not judicial in character, written reasons for their decisions shall always be given. Furthermore, in such a case, provision must be made to guarantee procedures whereby any allegedly illegal measure taken by the review body or any alleged defect in the exercise of the powers conferred on it can be the subject of judicial review or review by another body which is a court or tribunal within the meaning of Article 177 of the EEC Treaty and independent of both the contracting authority and the review body.

The members of such an independent body shall be appointed and leave office under the same conditions as members of the judiciary as regards the authority responsible for their appointment, their period of office, and their removal. At least the President of this independent body shall have the same legal and professional qualifications as members of the judiciary. The independent body shall take its decisions following a procedure in which both sides are heard, and these decisions shall, by means determined by each Member State, be legally binding.

### Article 3

**1.** The Commission may invoke the procedure for which this Article provides when, prior to a contract being concluded, it considers that a clear and manifest infringement of Community provisions in the field of public procurement has been committed during a contract award procedure falling within the scope of Directives 71/305/EEC and 77/62/EEC.

**2.** The Commission shall notify the Member State and the contracting authority concerned of the reasons which have led it to conclude that a clear and manifest infringement has been committed and request its correction.

**3.** Within 21 days of receipt of the notification referred to in paragraph 2, the Member State concerned shall communicate to the Commission:

(a) its confirmation that the infringement has been corrected; or
(b) a reasoned submission as to why no correction has been made; or
(c) a notice to the effect that the contract award procedure has been suspended either

by the contracting authority on its own initiative or on the basis of the powers specified in Article 2(1)(a).

**4.** A reasoned submission in accordance with paragraph 3(b) may rely among other matters on the fact that the alleged infringement is already the subject of judicial or other review proceedings or of a review as referred to in Article 2(8). In such a case, the Member State shall inform the Commission of the result of those proceedings as soon as it becomes known.

**5.** Where notice has been given that a contract award procedure has been suspended in accordance with paragraph 3(c), the Member State shall notify the Commission when the suspension is lifted or another contract procedure relating in whole or in part to the same subject matter is begun. That notification shall confirm that the alleged infringement has been corrected or include a reasoned submission as to why no correction has been made.

### Article 4

**1.** Not later than four years after the implementation of this Directive, the Commission, in consultation with the Advisory Committee for Public Contracts, shall review the manner in which the provisions of this Directive have been implemented and, if necessary, make proposals for amendments.

**2.** By 1 March each year the Member States shall communicate to the Commission information on the operation of their national review procedures during the preceding calendar year. The nature of the information shall be determined by the Commission in consultation with the Advisory Committee for Public Contracts.

### Article 5

Member States shall bring into force, before 1 December 1991, the measures necessary to comply with this Directive. They shall communicate to the Commission the texts of the main national laws, regulations and administrative provisions which they adopt in the field governed by this Directive.

### Article 6

This Directive is addressed to the Member States.

Done at Brussels, 21 December 1989.

*For the Council*
*The President*
É. CRESSON

## Council Directive

## of February 25, 1992

**coordinating the laws, regulations and administrative provisions relating to the application of Community rules on the procurement procedures of entities operating in the water, energy, transport and telecommunications sectors**

(92/13/EEC)

THE COUNCIL OF THE EUROPEAN COMMUNITIES,

Having regard to the Treaty establishing the European Economic Community, and in particular Article 100a thereof,

**G–03**

Having regard to the proposal from the Commission,[1]

In cooperation with the European Parliament,[2]

Having regard to the opinion of the Economic and Social Committee,[3]

Whereas Council Directive 90/531/EEC of 17 September 1990 on the procurement procedures of entities operating in the water, energy, transport and telecommunications sectors[4] lays down rules for procurement procedures to ensure that potential suppliers and contractors have a fair opportunity to secure the award of contracts, but does not contain any specific provisions ensuring its effective application;

Whereas the existing arrangements at both national and Community levels for ensuring its application are not always adequate;

Whereas the absence of effective remedies or the inadequacy of existing remedies could deter Community undertakings from submitting tenders; whereas, therefore, the Member States must remedy this situation;

Whereas Council Directive 89/665/EEC of 21 December 1989 on the coordination of the laws, regulations and administrative provisions relating to the application of review procedures to the award of public supply and public works contracts[5] is limited to contract award procedures within the scope of Council Directive 71/305/EEC of 26 July 1971 concerning the coordination of procedures for the award of public works contracts,[6] as last amended by Directive 90/531/EEC, and Council Directive 77/62/EEC of 21 December 1976 coordinating procedures for the award of public supply contracts,[7] as last amended by Directive 90/531/EEC;

Whereas the opening-up of procurement in the sectors concerned to Community competition implies that provisions must be adopted to ensure that appropriate review procedures are made available to suppliers or contractors in the event of infringement of the relevant Community law or national rules implementing that law;

Whereas it is necessary to provide for a substantial increase in the guarantees of transparency and non-discrimination and whereas, for it to have tangible effects, effective and rapid remedies must be available;

Whereas account must be taken of the specific nature of certain legal orders by authorizing the Member States to choose between the introduction of different powers for the review bodies which have equivalent effects;

Whereas one of these options includes the power to intervene directly in the

[1] OJ No C 216, 31.8.1990, p. 8; and OJ No C 179, 10.7.1991, p. 18.
[2] OJ No C 106, 22.4.1991, p. 82 and OJ No C 39, 17.2.1992.
[3] OJ No C 60, 8.3.1991, p. 16.
[4] OJ No L 297, 29.10.1990, p. 1.
[5] OJ No L 395, 30.12.1989, p. 33.
[6] OJ No L 185, 16.8.1971, p. 5.
[7] OJ No L 13, 15.1.1977, p. 1.

contracting entities' procurement procedures such as by suspending them, or by setting aside decisions or discriminatory clauses in documents or publications;

Whereas the other option provides for the power to exert effective indirect pressure on the contracting entities in order to make them correct any infringements or prevent them from committing infringements, and to prevent injury from occurring;

Whereas claims for damages must always be possible;

Whereas, where a claim is made for damages representing the costs of preparing a bid or of participating in an award procedure, the person making the claim is not be required, in order to obtain the reimbursement of his costs, to prove that the contract would have been awarded to him in the absence of such infringement;

Whereas the contracting entities which comply with the procurement rules may make this known through appropriate means; whereas this requires an examination, by independent persons, of procurement procedures and practices applied by those entities;

Whereas for this purpose an attestation system, allowing for a declaration on the correct application of the procurement rules, to be made in notices published in the *Official Journal of the European Communities*, is appropriate;

Whereas the contracting entities should have the opportunity of having recourse to the attestation system if they so wish; whereas the Member States must offer them the possibility of doing so; whereas they can do so either by setting up the system themselves or by allowing the contracting entities to have recourse to the attestation system established by another Member State; whereas they may confer the task of carrying out the examination under the attestation system to persons, professions or staff of institutions;

Whereas the necessary flexibility in the introduction of such a system is guaranteed by laying down the essential requirements for it in this Directive; whereas operational details should be provided in European Standards to which this Directive refers;

Whereas the Member States may need to determine operational details prior to, or in addition to, the rules contained in European Standards;

Whereas, when undertakings do not seek review, certain infringements may not be corrected unless a specific mechanism is put in place;

Whereas, accordingly, the Commission, when it considers that a clear and manifest infringement has been committed during a contract award procedure, should be able to bring it to the attention of the competent authorities of the Member State and of the contracting entity concerned so that appropriate steps are taken for the rapid correction of that infringement;

Whereas it is necessary to provide for the possibility of conciliation at Community level to enable disputes to be settled amicably;

Whereas the application in practice of this Directive should be reviewed at the same time as that of Directive 90/531/EEC on the basis of information to be supplied by the Member States concerning the functioning of the national review procedures;

Whereas this Directive must be brought into effect at the same time as Directive 90/531/EEC;

Whereas it is appropriate that the Kingdom of Spain, the Hellenic Republic and the Portuguese Republic are granted adequate additional periods to transpose this Directive, taking account of the dates of application of Directive 90/531/EEC in those countries,

HAS ADOPTED THIS DIRECTIVE:

Chapter I

## Remedies at national level

*Article 1*

**G–04**  1. The Member States shall take the measures necessary to ensure that decisions taken by contracting entities may be reviewed effectively and, in particular, as rapidly as possible in accordance with the conditions set out in the following Articles and, in particular, Article 2(8), on the grounds that such decisions have infringed *Community law* in the field or procurement or national rules implementing that law as regards:

(a) contract award procedures falling within the scope of Council Directive 90/531/EEC; and
(b) compliance with Article 3(2)(a) of that Directive in the case of the contracting entities to which that provision applies.

**2.** Member States shall ensure that there is no discrimination between undertakings likely to make a claim for injury in the context of a procedure for the award of a contract as a result of the distinction made by this Directive between national rules implementing Community law and other national rules.

**3.** The Member States shall ensure that the review procedures are available, under detailed rules which the Member States may establish, at least to any person having or having had an interest in obtaining a particular contract and who has been or risks being harmed by an alleged infringement. In particular, the Member States may require that the person seeking the review must have previously notified the contracting entity of the alleged infringement and of his intention to seek review.

### Article 2

**1.** The Member States shall ensure that the measures taken concerning the review procedures specified in Article 1 include provision for the powers:

either

(a) to take, at the earliest opportunity and by way of interlocutory procedure, interim measures with the aim of correcting the alleged infringement or preventing further injury to the interests concerned, including measures to suspend or to ensure the suspension of the procedure for the award of a contract or the implementation of any decision taken by the contracting entity; and
(b) to set aside or ensure the setting aside of decisions taken unlawfully, including the removal of discriminatory technical, economic or financial specifications in the notice of contract, the periodic indicative notice, the notice on the existence of a system of qualification, the invitation to tender, the contract documents or in any other document relating to the contract award procedure in question;

or

(c) to take, at the earliest opportunity, if possible by way of interlocutory procedures and if necessary by a final procedure on the substance, measures other than those provided for in points (a) and (b) with the aim of correcting any identified infringement and preventing injury to the interests concerned; in particular, making an order for the payment of a particular sum, in cases where the infringement has not been corrected or prevented.

Member States may take this choice either for all contracting entities or for categories of entities defined on the basis of objective criteria, in any event preserving the effectiveness of the measures laid down in order to prevent injury being caused to the interests concerned;
(d) and, in both the above cases, to award damages to persons injured by the infringement.

Where damages are claimed on the grounds that a decision has been taken unlawfully, Member States may, where their system of internal law so requires and provides bodies having the necessary powers for that purpose, provide that the contested decision must first be set aside or declared illegal.

**2.** The powers referred to in paragraph 1 may be conferred on separate bodies responsible for different aspects of the review procedure.

**3.** Review procedures need not in themselves have an automatic suspensive effect on the contract award procedures to which they relate.

**4.** The Member States may provide that, when considering whether to order interim measures, the body responsible may take into account the probable consequences of the measures for all interests likely to be harmed, as well as the public interest, and may decide not to grant such measures where their negative consequences could exceed their benefits. A decision not to grant interim measures shall not prejudice any other claim of the person seeking these measures.

**5.** The sum to be paid in accordance with paragraph 1 (c) must be set at a level high enough to dissuade the contracting entity from committing or persisting in an infringement. The payment of that sum may be made to depend upon a final decision that the infringement has in fact taken place.

**6.** The effects of the exercise of the powers referred to in paragraph 1 on a contract concluded subsequent to its award shall be determined by national law. Furthermore, except where a decision must be set aside prior to the award of damages, a Member State may provide that, after the conclusion of a contract following its award, the powers of the body responsible for the review procedures shall be limited to awarding damages to any person harmed by an infringement.

**7.** Where a claim is made for damages representing the costs of preparing a bid or of participating in an award procedure, the person making the claim shall be required only to prove an infringement of Community law in the field of procurement or national rules implementing that law and that he would have had a real chance of winning the contract and that, as a consequence of that infringement, that chance was adversely affected.

**8.** The Member States shall ensure that decisions taken by bodies responsible for review procedures can be effectively enforced.

**9.** Whereas bodies responsible for review procedures are not judicial in character, written reasons for their decisions shall always be given. Furthermore, in such a case, provision must be made to guarantee procedures whereby any allegedly illegal measures taken by the review body or any alleged defect in the exercise of the powers conferred on it can be the subject of judicial review or review by another body which is a court or tribunal within the meaning of Article 177 of the Treaty and independent of both the contracting entity and the review body.

The members of the independent body referred to in the first paragraph shall be appointed and leave office under the same conditions as members of the judiciary as regards the authority responsible for their appointment, their period of office, and their removal. At least the President of this independent body shall have the same legal and professional qualifications as members of the judiciary. The independent body shall take its decisions following a procedure in which both sides are heard, and these decisions shall, by means determined by each Member State, be legally binding.

## Chapter 2

### **Attestation**

#### Article 3

The Member States shall give contracting entities the possibility of having recourse to an attestation system in accordance with Articles 4 to 7.

#### Article 4

Contracting entities may have their contract award procedures and practices which fall within the scope of Directive 90/531/EEC examined periodically with a view to obtaining an attestation that, at that time, those procedures and practices are in conformity with Community law concerning the award of contracts and the national rules implementing the law.

#### Article 5

**1.** Attestors shall report to the contracting entity, in writing, on the results of their examination. They shall satisfy themselves, before delivering to the contracting entity the attestation referred to in Article 4, that any irregularities identified in the contracting entity's award procedures and practices have been corrected and measures have been taken to ensure that those irregularities are not repeated.

**2.** Contracting entities having obtained that attestation may include the following statement in notice published in the *Official Journal of the European Communities* pursuant to Articles 16 to 18 of Directive 90/531/EEC:

"The contracting entity has obtained an attestation in accordance with Council Directive 92/13/EEC that, on ..., its contract award procedures and practices were in conformity with Community law and the national rules implementing that law."

#### Article 6

**1.** Attestors shall be independent of the contracting entities and must be completely objective in carrying out their duties. They shall offer appropriate guarantees of relevant professional qualifications and experience.

**2.** Member States may identify any persons, professions or institutions whose staff, called upon to act as attestors, they regard as fulfilling the requirements of paragraph 1. For these purposes, Member States may require professional qualifications, at least at the level of a higher education diploma within the meaning of Directive 89/48/EEC,[8] which they regard as relevant, or provide that particular examinations of professional competence organized or recognized by the State offer such guarantees.

#### Article 7

The provisions of Articles 4, 5 and 6 shall be considered as essential requirements for the development of European standards on attestation.

[8] OJ No L 19, 24.1.1989, p. 16.

Chapter 3

**Corrective mechanism**

*Article 8*

**G–06**    **1.** The Commission may invoke the procedures for which this Article provides when, prior to a contract being concluded, it considers that a clear and manifest infringement of Community provisions in the field of procurement has been committed during a contract award procedure falling within the scope of Directive 90/531/EEC or in relation to Article 3(2)(a) of that Directive in the case of the contracting entities to which that provision applies.

**2.** The Commission shall notify the Member State and the contracting entity concerned of the reasons which have led it to conclude that a clear and manifest infringement has been committed and request its correction by appropriate means.

**3.** Within 30 days of receipt of the notification referred to in paragraph 2, the Member State concerned shall communicate to the Commission:

(a)  its confirmation that the infringement has been corrected; or
(b)  a reasoned submission as to why no correction has been made; or
(c)  a notice to the effect that the contract award procedure has been suspended either by the contracting entity on its own initiative or on the basis of the powers specified in Article 2(1)(a).

**4.** A reasoned submission in accordance with paragraph 3(b) may rely among other matters on the fact that the alleged infringement is already the subject of judicial review proceedings or of a review as referred to in Article 2(9). In such a case, the Member State shall inform the Commission of the result of those proceedings as soon as it becomes known.

**5.** Where notice has been given that a contract award procedure has been suspended in accordance with paragraph 3(c), the Member State concerned shall notify the Commission when the suspension is lifted or another contract procedure relating in whole or in part to the same subject matter is begun. That new notification shall confirm that the alleged infringement has been corrected or include a reasoned submission as to why no correction has been made.

Chapter 4

**Conciliation**

*Article 9*

**G–07**    **1.** Any person having or having had an interest in obtaining a particular contract falling within the scope of Directive 90/531/EEC and who, in relation to the procedure for the award of that contract, considers that he has been or risks being harmed by an alleged infringement of Community law in the field of procurement or national rules implementing that law may request the application of the conciliation procedure provided for in Articles 10 and 11.

**2.** The request referred to in paragraph 1 shall be addressed in writing to the Commission or to the national authorities listed in the Annex. These authorities shall forward requests to the Commission as quickly as possible.

*Article 10*

**1.** Where the Commission considers, on the basis of the request referred to in Article 9, that the dispute concerns the correct application of Community law, it shall ask the contracting entity to state whether it is willing to take part in the conciliation procedure. If the contracting entity declines to take part, the Commission shall inform the person who made the request that the procedure cannot be initiated. If the contracting entity agrees, paragraphs 2 to 7 shall apply.

**2.** The Commission shall propose, as quickly as possible, a conciliator drawn from a list of independent persons accredited for this purpose. This list shall be drawn up by the Commission, following consultation of the Advisory Committee for Public Contracts or, in the case of contracting entities the activities of which are defined in Article 2(2)(d) of Directive 90/531/EEC, following consultation of the Advisory Committee on Telecommunications Procurement.

Each party to the conciliation procedure shall declare whether it accepts the conciliator, and shall designate an additional conciliator. The conciliators may invite not more than two other persons as experts to advise them in their work. The parties to the conciliation procedure and the Commission may reject any expert invited by the conciliators.

**3.** The conciliators shall give the person requesting the application of the conciliation procedure, the contracting entity and any other candidate or tenderer participating in the relevant contract award procedure the opportunity to make representations on the matter either orally or in writing.

**4.** The conciliators shall endeavour as quickly as possible to reach an agreement between the parties which is in accordance with Community law.

**5.** The conciliators shall report to the Commission on their findings and on any result achieved.

**6.** The person requesting the application of the conciliation procedure and the contracting entity shall have the right to terminate the procedure at any time.

**7.** Unless the parties decide otherwise, the person requesting the application of the conciliation procedure and the contracting entity shall be responsible for their own costs. In addition, they shall each bear half of the costs of the procedure, excluding the costs of intervening parties.

*Article 11*

**1.** Where, in relation to a particular contract award procedure, an interested person within the meaning of Article 9, other than the person requesting the conciliation procedure, is pursuing judicial review proceedings or other proceedings for review within the meaning of this Directive, the contracting entity shall inform the conciliators. These shall inform that person that a request has been made to apply the conciliation procedure and shall invite that person to indicate within a given time limit whether he agrees to participate in that procedure. If that person refuses to participate, the conciliators may decide, acting if necessary by a majority, to terminate the conciliation procedure if they consider that the participation of this person is necessary to resolve the dispute. They shall notify their decision to the Committee and give the reasons for it.

**2.** Action taken pursuant to this Chapter shall be without prejudice to:

(a) any action that the Commission or any Member State might take pursuant to Articles 169 or 170 of the Treaty or pursuant to Chapter 3 of this Directive;

(b) the rights of the persons requesting the conciliation procedure, of the contracting entity or of any other person.

## Chapter 5

### Final provisions

#### Article 12

**G—08** **1.** Not later than four years after the application of this Directive, the Commission, in consultation with the Advisory Committee for Public Contracts, shall review the manner in which the provisions of this Directive have been implemented and, in particular, the use of the European Standards and, if necessary, make proposals for amendments.

**2.** Before 1 March each year the Member States shall communicate to the Commission information on the operation of their national review procedures during the preceding calendar year. The nature of the information shall be determined by the Commission in consultation with the Advisory Committee for Public Contracts.

**3.** In the case of matters relating to contracting entities the activities of which are defined in Article 2(2)(d) of Directive 90/531/EEC, the Commission shall also consult the Advisory Committee on Telecommunications Procurement.

#### Article 13

**1.** Member States shall take, before 1 January 1993, the measures necessary to comply with this Directive. The Kingdom of Spain shall take these measures not later than 30 June 1995. The Hellenic Republic and the Portuguese Republic shall take these measures not later than 30 June 1997. They shall forthwith inform the Commission thereof.

When Member States adopt these measures, they shall contain a reference to this Directive or shall be accompanied by such reference on the occasion of their official publication. The methods of making such a reference shall be laid down by the Member States.

**2.** Member States shall bring into force the measures referred to in paragraph 1 on the same dates as those laid down in Directive 90/531/EEC.

**3.** Member States shall communicate to the Commission the texts of the main provisions of domestic law which they adopt in the field governed by this Directive.

#### Article 14

This Directive is addressed to the Member States.

Done at Brussels, 25 February 1992.

*For the Council*
*The President*
VITOR MARTINS

# *Appendix* H

## SERVICES DIRECTIVE

**Council Directive**

**of June 18, 1992**

**relating to the coordination of procedures for the award of public service contracts**

(92/50/EEC)

THE COUNCIL OF THE EUROPEAN COMMUNITIES,

Having regard to the Treaty establishing the European Economic Community, and in particular the last sentence of Article 57(2) and Article 66 thereof,

**H–01**

Having regard to the proposal from the Commission,[1]

In cooperation with the European Parliament,[2]

Having regard to the opinion of the Economic and Social Committee,[3]

Whereas the European Council has drawn conclusions on the need to complete the internal market;

Whereas measures aimed at progressively establishing the internal market during the period up to 31 December 1992 need to be taken; whereas the internal market is an area without internal frontiers in which the free movement of goods, persons, services and capital is ensured;

Whereas these objectives require the coordination of the procurement procedures for the award of public service contracts;

Whereas the White Paper on the completion of the internal market contains an action programme and a timetable for opening up public procurement, including in the field of services insofar as this is not already covered by Council Directive 71/305/EEC of 26 July 1971 concerning the coordination of procedures for the award of public works contracts[4] and Council Directive 77/62/EEC of 21 December 1976 coordinating procedures for the award of public supply contracts[5];

Whereas this Directive should be applied by all contracting authorities within the meaning of Directive 71/305/EEC;

Whereas obstacles to the free movement of services need to be avoided; whereas, therefore, service providers may be either natural or legal persons; whereas this Directive shall not, however, prejudice the application, at national level, of rules concerning the conditions for the pursuit of an activity or a profession provided that they are compatible with Community law;

Whereas the field of services is best described, for the purpose of application of procedural rules and for monitoring purposes, by subdividing it into categories corresponding to particular positions of a common classification; whereas Annexes IA

---

[1] OJ No C 23, 31.1.1991, p. 1, and OJ No C 250, 25.9.1991, p. 4.

[2] OJ No C 158, 17.6.1991, p. 90, and OJ No C 150, 15.6.1992.

[3] OJ No C 191, 22.7.1991, p. 41.

[4] OJ No L 185, 16.8.1971, p. 5. Directive last amended by Directive 90/531/EEC (OJ No L 297, 29.10.1990, p. 1).

[5] OJ No L 13, 15.1.1977, p. 1. Directive last amended by Directive 90/531/EEC (OJ No L 297, 29.10.1990, p. 1).

273

and IB of this Directive refer to the CPC nomenclature (common product classification) o the United Nations; whereas that nomenclature is likely to be replaced in the future by Community nomenclature; whereas provision should be made for adapting the CPC nomenclature in Annexes IA and B in consequence;

Whereas the provision of services is covered by this Directive only in so far as it is based on contracts; whereas the provision of services on other bases, such as law or regulations or employment contracts, is not covered;

Whereas, in accordance with Article 130f of the Treaty, the encouragement of research and development is a means to strengthen the scientific and technological basis o European industry and the opening up of public contracts will contribute to this end whereas contributions to the financing of research programmes should not be subject to this Directive; whereas research and development service contracts other than those where the benefits accrue exclusively to the contracting authority for its use in the conduct of its own affairs, on condition that the service provided is wholly remunerated by the contracting authority, are not therefore covered by this Directive;

Whereas contracts relating to the acquisition or rental of immovable property or to rights thereon have particular characteristics, which make the application of procurement rules inappropriate;

Whereas the award of contracts for certain audiovisual services in the broadcasting field is governed by considerations which make the application of procurement rules inappropriate;

Whereas arbitration and conciliation services are usually provided by bodies or individuals which are agreed on, or selected, in a manner which cannot be governed by procurement rules;

Whereas for the purposes of this Directive financial services do not include the instruments of monetary, exchange rate, public debt, reserve management, and other policies involving transactions in securities and other financial instruments; whereas therefore, contracts in connection with the issue, sale, purchase or transfer of securities and other financial instruments are not covered by this Directive; whereas central bank services are also excluded;

Whereas, in the field of services, the same derogations as in Directives 71/305/EEC and 77/62/EEC should apply as regards State security or secrecy and the priority of other procurement rules such as those pursuant to international agreements, those concerning the stationing of troops, or the rules of international organizations;

Whereas this Directive does not prejudice the application of, in particular, Articles 55, 56 and 66 of the Treaty;

Whereas public service contracts, particularly in the field of property management, may from time to time include some works; whereas it results from Directive 71/305/EEC that, for a contract to be a public works contract, its object must be the achievement of a work; whereas, in so far as these works are incidental rather than the object of the contract, they do not justify treating the contract as a public works contract;

Whereas the rules concerning service contracts as contained in Council Directive 90/531/EEC of 17 September 1990 on the procurement procedures of entities operating in the water, energy, transport and telecommunications sectors[6] should remain unaffected by this Directive;

Whereas contracts with a designated single source of supply may, under certain conditions, be fully or partly exempted from this Directive;

Whereas this Directive should not apply to small contracts below a certain threshold in order to avoid unnecessary formalities; whereas this threshold may in principle be the same as that for public supply contracts; whereas the calculation of the contract value, the publication and the method of adaptation of the thresholds should be the same as in the other Community procurement directives;

[6] OJ No L 297, 29.10.1990, p. 1.

Whereas, to eliminate practices that restrict competition in general and participation in contracts by other Member States' nationals in particular, it is necessary to improve the access of service providers to procedures for the award of contracts;

Whereas full application of this Directive must be limited, for a transitional period, to contracts for those services where its provisions will enable the full potential for increased cross-frontier trade to be realized; whereas contracts for other services need to be monitored for a certain period before a decision is taken on the full application of this Directive; whereas the mechanism for such monitoring needs to be defined; whereas this mechanism should at the same time enable those interested to share the relevant information;

Whereas the rules for the award of public service contracts should be as close as possible to those concerning public supply contracts and public works contracts;

Whereas the procurement rules contained in Directives 71/305/EEC and 77/62/EEC can be appropriate, with necessary adaptations so as to take into account special aspects of procurement of services such as the choice of the negotiated procedure, design contests, variants, the legal form under which the service providers operate, the reservation of certain activities to certain professions, registration and quality assurance;

Whereas use may be made of the negotiated procedure with prior publication of a notice when the service to be provided cannot be specified with sufficient precision, particularly in the field of intellectual services, with the result that such a contract cannot be awarded by selection of the best tender in accordance with the rules governing the open and restricted procedures;

Whereas the relevant Community rules on mutual recognition of diplomas, certificates or other evidence of formal qualifications apply when evidence of a particular qualification is required for participation in an award procedure or a design contest;

Whereas the objectives of this Directive do not require any changes in the current situation at national level as regards price competition between service providers of certain services;

Whereas the operation of this Directive should be reviewed at the latest three years after the date set for procurement rules to be transposed into national law; whereas the review should extend in particular to the possibility of making the Directive fully applicable to a wider range of service contracts,

HAS ADOPTED THIS DIRECTIVE:

## TITLE I

### GENERAL PROVISIONS

*Article 1*

For the purposes of this Directive:

H–02

(a) *public service contracts* shall mean contracts for pecuniary interest concluded in writing between a service provider and a contracting authority, to the exclusion of:
  (i) public supply contracts within the meaning of Article 1 (a) of Directive 77/62/EEC or public works contracts within the meaning of Article 1 (a) of Directive 71/305/EEC;
  (ii) contracts awarded in the fields referred to in Articles 2, 7, 8 and 9 of Directive 90/531/EEC or fulfilling the conditions in Article 6(2) of the same Directive;
  (iii) contracts for the acquisition or rental, by whatever financial means, of land, existing buildings, or other immovable property or concerning rights thereon; nevertheless, financial service contracts concluded at the same time as, before or after the contract of acquisition or rental, in whatever form, shall be subject to this Directive;
  (iv) contracts for the acquisition, development, production or co-production of programme material by broadcasters and contracts for broadcasting time;

275

     (v)  contracts for voice telephony, telex, radiotelephony, paging and satellite services;

    (vi)  contracts for arbitration and conciliation services;

   (vii)  contracts for financial services in connection with the issue, sale, purchase or transfer of securities or other financial instruments, and central bank services

 (viii)  employment contracts;

    (ix)  research and development service contracts other than those where the benefits accrue exclusively to the contracting authority for its use in the conduct of its own affairs, on condition that the service provided is wholly remunerated by the contracting authority;

(b)  *contracting authorities* shall mean the State, regional or local authorities, bodies governed by public law, associations formed by one or more of such authorities or bodies governed by public law.

    *Body governed by public law* means any body:

    — established for the specific purpose of meeting needs in the general interest not having an industrial or commercial character, and

    — having legal personality and

    — financed, for the most part, by the State, or regional or local authorities, or other bodies governed by public law; or subject to management supervision by those bodies; or having an administrative, managerial or supervisory board, more than half of whose members are appointed by the State, regional or local authorities or by other bodies governed by public law.

    The lists of bodies or of categories of such bodies governed by public law which fulfil the criteria referred to in the second subparagraph of this point are set out in Annex I to Directive 71/305/EEC. These lists shall be as exhaustive as possible and may be reviewed in accordance with the procedure laid down in Article 30b of that Directive;

(c)  *service provider* shall mean any natural or legal person, including a public body, which offers services. A service provider who submits a tender shall be designated by the term *tenderer* and one who has sought an invitation to take part in a restricted or negotiated procedure by the term *candidate*;

(d)  *open procedures* shall mean those national procedures whereby all interested service providers may submit a tender;

(e)  *restricted procedures* shall mean those national procedures whereby only those service providers invited by the authority may submit a tender;

(f)  *negotiated procedures* shall mean those national procedures whereby authorities consult service providers of their choice and negotiate the terms of the contract with one or more of them;

(g)  *design contests* shall mean those national procedures which enable the contracting authority to acquire, mainly in the fields of area planning, town planning, architecture and civil engineering, or data processing, a plan or design selected by a jury after being put out to competition with or without the award of prizes.

## Article 2

If a public contract is intended to cover both products within the meaning of Directive 77/62/EEC and services within the meaning of Annexes IA and IB to this Directive, it shall fall within the scope of this Directive if the value of the services in question exceeds that of the products covered by the contract.

## Article 3

**1.** In awarding public service contracts or in organizing design contests, contracting authorities shall apply procedures adapted to the provisions of this Directive.

276

**2.** Contracting authorities shall ensure that there is no discrimination between different service providers.

**3.** Member States shall take the necessary measures to ensure that the contracting authorities comply or ensure compliance with this Directive where they subsidize directly by more than 50% a service contract awarded by an entity other than themselves in connection with a works contract within the meaning of Article 1a(2) of Directive 71/305/EEC.

### Article 4

**1.** This Directive shall apply to public service contracts awarded by contracting authorities in the field of defence, except for contracts to which the provisions of Article 223 of the Treaty apply.

**2.** This Directive shall not apply to services which are declared secret or the execution of which must be accompanied by special security measures in accordance with the laws, regulations or administrative provisions in force in the Member State concerned or when the protection of the basic interests of that State's security so requires.

### Article 5

This Directive shall not apply to public contracts governed by different procedural rules and awarded:

(a) in pursuance of an international agreement concluded between a Member State and one or more third countries and covering services intended for the joint implementation or exploitation of a project by the signatory States; any agreement shall be communicated to the Commission, which may consult the Advisory Committee for Public Contracts set up by Council Decision 71/306/EEC[7];

(b) to undertakings in a Member State or a third country in pursuance of an international agreement relating to the stationing of troops;

(c) pursuant to the particular procedure of an international organization.

### Article 6

This Directive shall not apply to public service contracts awarded to an entity which is itself a contracting authority within the meaning of Article 1 (b) on the basis of an exclusive right which it enjoys pursuant to a published law, regulation or administrative provision which is compatible with the Treaty.

### Article 7

**1.** This Directive shall apply to public service contracts, the estimated value of which, net of VAT, is not less than ECU 200 000.

**2.** For the purposes of calculating the estimated value of the contract, the contracting authority shall include the estimated total remuneration of the service provider, taking account of the provisions of paragraphs 3 to 8.

**3.** The selection of the valuation method shall not be used with the intention of avoiding the application of this Directive, nor shall any procurement requirement for a given amount of services be split up with the intention of avoiding the application of this Article.

---

[7] OJ No L 185, 16.8.1971, p. 15. Decision amended by Decision 77/63/EEC (OJ No L 13, 15.1.1977, p. 15).

**4.** For the purposes of calculating the estimated contract value for the following types of services, account shall be taken, where appropriate:

— as regards insurance services, of the premium payable,
— as regards banking and other financial services, of fees, commissions and interest as well as other types of remuneration,
— as regards contracts which involve design, of the fee or commission payable.

Where the services are subdivided into several lots, each one the subject of a contract, the value of each lot must be taken into account for the purpose of calculating the amount referred to above.

Where the value of the lots is not less than this amount, the provisions of this Directive shall apply to all lots. Contracting authorities may waive application of paragraph 1 for any lot which has an estimated value net of VAT of less than ECU 80 000, provided that the total value of such lots does not exceed 20% of the total value of all the lots.

**5.** In the case of contracts which do not specify a total price, the basis for calculating the estimated contract value shall be:

— in the case of fixed-term contracts, where their term is 48 months or less, the total contract value for its duration;
— in the case of contracts of indefinite duration or with a term of more than 48 months, the monthly instalment multiplied by 48.

**6.** In the case of regular contracts or of contracts which are to be renewed within a given time, the contract value may be established on the basis of:

— either the actual aggregate cost of similar contracts for the same categories of services awarded over the previous fiscal year or 12 months, adjusted, where possible, for anticipated changes in quantity or value over the 12 months following the initial contract,
— or the estimated aggregate cost during the 12 months following the first service performed or during the term of the contract, where this is greater than 12 months.

**7.** Where a proposed contract provides for options, the basis for calculating the contract value shall be the maximum permitted total including use of the option clauses.

**8.** The value of the thresholds in national currencies shall be revised every two years with effect from 1 January 1994. The calculation of these values shall be based on the average daily values of those currencies expressed in ecus over the 24 months terminating on the last day of August immediately preceding the 1 January revision. The values shall be published in the *Official Journal of the European Communities* at the beginning of November.

The method of calculation referred to in the preceding subparagraph shall be examined, on the Commission's initiative, within the Advisory Committee for Public Contracts in principle two years after its initial application.

TITLE II

**TWO-TIER APPLICATION**

*Article 8*

**H–03**    Contracts which have as their object services listed in Annex I A shall be awarded in accordance with the provisions of Titles III to VI.

*Article 9*

Contracts which have as their object services listed in Annex I B shall be awarded in accordance with Articles 14 and 16.

*Article 10*

Contracts which have as their object services listed in both Annexes I A and I B shall be awarded in accordance with the provisions of Titles III to VI where the value of the services listed in Annex I A is greater than the value of the services listed in Annex I B. Where this is not the case, they shall be awarded in accordance with Articles 14 and 16.

TITLE III

## CHOICE OF AWARD PROCEDURES AND RULES GOVERNING DESIGN CONTESTS

*Article 11*

**1.** In awarding public service contracts, contracting authorities shall apply the **H–04** procedures defined in Article 1(*d*), (*e*) and (*f*), adapted for the purposes of this Directive.

**2.** Contracting authorities may award their public service contracts by negotiated procedure, with prior publication of a contract notice in the following cases:

(*a*) in the event of irregular tenders in response to an open or restricted procedure or in the event of tenders which are unacceptable under national provisions that are in accordance with Articles 23 to 28, insofar as the original terms of the contract are not substantially altered. Contracting authorities may in such cases refrain from publishing a contract notice where they include in the negotiated procedure all the tenderers who satisfy the criteria of Articles 29 to 35 and who, during the prior open or restricted procedure, have submitted tenders in accordance with the formal requirements of the tendering procedure;

(*b*) in exceptional cases, when the nature of the services or the risks involved do not permit prior overall pricing;

(*c*) when the nature of the services to be procured, in particular in the case of intellectual services and services falling within category 6 of Annex I A, is such that contract specifications cannot be established with sufficient precision to permit the award of the contract by selecting the best tender according to the rules governing open or restricted procedures.

**3.** Contracting authorities may award public service contracts by negotiated procedure without prior publication of a contract notice in the following cases:

(*a*) in the absence of tenders or of appropriate tenders in response to an open or restricted procedure provided that the original terms of the contract are not substantially altered and that a report is communicated to the Commission at its request;

(*b*) when, for technical or artistic reasons, or for reasons connected with the protection of exclusive rights, the services may be provided only by a particular service provider;

(*c*) where the contract concerned follows a design contest and must, under the rules applying, be awarded to the successful candidate or to one of the successful candidates. In the latter case, all successful candidates shall be invited to participate in the negotiations;

(*d*) in so far as is strictly necessary when, for reasons of extreme urgency brought about by events unforeseeable by the contracting authorities in question, the time limit for the open, restricted or negotiated procedures referred to in Articles 17 and 20 cannot be kept. The circumstances invoked to justify extreme urgency must not in any event be attributable to the contracting authorities;

(e) for additional services not included in the project initially considered or in the contract first concluded but which have, through unforeseen circumstances, become necessary for the performance of the service described therein, on condition that the award is made to the service provider carrying out such service:

— when such additional services cannot be technically or economically separated from the main contract without great inconvenience to the contracting authorities, or

— when such services, although separable from the performance of the original contract, are strictly necessary for its completion.

However, the aggregate estimated value of contracts awarded for additional services may not exceed 50% of the amount of the main contract;

(f) for new services consisting in the repetition of similar services entrusted to the service provider to which the same contracting authorities awarded an earlier contract, provided that such services conform to a basic project for which a first contract was awarded according to the procedures referred to in paragraph 4. As soon as the first project is put up for tender, notice must be given that the negotiated procedure might be adopted and the total estimated cost of subsequent services shall be taken into consideration by the contracting authorities when they apply the provisions of Article 7. This procedure may be applied solely during the three years following the conclusion of the original contract.

**4.** In all other cases, the contracting authorities shall award their public service contracts by the open procedure or by the restricted procedure.

*Article 12*

**1.** The contracting authority shall, within fifteen days of the date on which the request is received, inform any eliminated candidate or tenderer who so requests in writing of the reasons for rejection of his application or his tender, and, in the case of a tender, the name of the successful tenderer.

**2.** The contracting authority shall inform candidates or tenderers who so request in writing of the grounds on which it decided not to award a contract in respect of which a prior call for competition was made, or to recommence the procedure. It shall also inform the Office for Official Publications of the European Communities of that decision.

**3.** For each contract awarded, the contracting authorities shall draw up a written report which shall include at least the following:

— the name and address of the contracting authority, the subject and value of the contract,

— the names of the candidates or tenderers admitted and the reasons for their selection,

— the names of the candidates or tenderers rejected and the reasons for their rejection,

— the name of the successful tenderer and the reasons why his tender was selected and, if known, the part of the contract which the successful tenderer intends to subcontract to third parties,

— for negotiated procedures, the circumstances referred to in Article 11 which justify the use of these procedures.

This report, or the main features of it, shall be communicated to the Commission at its request.

*Article 13*

**1.** This Article shall apply to design contests organized as part of a procedure leading to the award of a service contract whose estimated value net of VAT is not less than the value referred to in Article 7(1).

**2.** This Article shall apply to all design contests where the total amount of contest prizes and payments to participants is not less than ECU 200 000.

**3.** The rules for the organization of a design contest shall be in conformity with the requirements of this Article and shall be communicated to those interested in participating in the contest.

**4.** The admission of participants to design contests shall not be limited:

— by reference to the territory or part of the territory of a Member State,
— on the grounds that, under the law of the Member State in which the contest is organized, they would have been required to be either natural or legal persons.

**5.** Where design contests are restricted to a limited number of participants, the contracting authorities shall lay down clear and non-discriminatory selection criteria. In any event, the number of candidates invited to participate shall be sufficient to ensure genuine competition.

**6.** The jury shall be composed exclusively of natural persons who are independent of participants in the contest. Where a particular professional qualification is required from participants in a contest, at least a third of its members must have the same qualification or its equivalent.

The jury shall be autonomous in its decisions or opinions. These shall be reached on the basis of projects submitted anonymously and solely on the grounds of the criteria indicated in the notice within the meaning of Article 15(3).

## TITLE IV

## COMMON RULES IN THE TECHNICAL FIELD

*Article 14*

**1.** The technical specifications defined in Annex II shall be given in the general documents or the contractual documents relating to each contract.

**H–05**

**2.** Without prejudice to the legally binding national technical rules and insofar as these are compatible with Community law, such technical specifications shall be defined by the contracting authorities by reference to national standards implementing European standards or by reference to European technical approvals or by reference to common technical specifications.

**3.** A contracting authority may depart from paragraph 2 if:

(*a*) the standards, European technical approvals or common technical specifications do not include any provisions for establishing conformity, or technical means do not exist for establishing satisfactorily the conformity of a product with these standards, European technical approvals or common technical specifications;

(*b*) the application of paragraph 2 would prejudice the application of Council Directive 86/361/EEC of 24 July 1986 on the initial stage of the mutual recognition of type approval for telecommunications terminal equipment,[8] or Council Decision 87/95/EEC of 22 December 1986 on standardization in the field of information

---

[8] OJ No L 217, 5.8.1986, p. 21. Amended by Directive 91/263/EEC (OJ No L 128, 23.5.1991, p. 1).

technology and telecommunications[9] or other Community instruments in specific service or product areas;

(c) these standards, European technical approvals or common technical specifications would oblige the contracting authority to use products or materials incompatible with equipment already in use or would entail disproportionate costs or disproportionate technical difficulties, but only as part of a clearly defined and recorded strategy with a view to the transition, within a given period, to European standards, European technical approvals or common technical specifications;

(d) the project concerned is of a genuinely innovative nature for which use of existing European standards, European technical approvals or common technical specifications would not be appropriate.

**4.** Contracting authorities invoking paragraph 3 shall record, wherever possible, the reasons for doing so in the contract notice published in the *Official Journal of the European Communities* or in the contract documents and in all cases shall record these reasons in their internal documentation and shall supply such information on request to Member States and to the Commission.

**5.** In the absence of European standards or European technical approvals or common technical specifications, the technical specifications:

(a) shall be defined by reference to the national technical specifications recognized as complying with the basic requirements listed in the Community directives on technical harmonization, in accordance with the procedures laid down in those directives, and in particular in accordance with the procedures laid down in Directive 89/106/EEC[10];

(b) may be defined by reference to national technical specifications relating to design and method of calculation and execution of works and use of materials;

(c) may be defined by reference to other documents.
   In this case, it is appropriate to make reference in order of preference to:
      (i) national standards implementing international standards accepted by the country of the contracting authority;
      (ii) other national standards and national technical approvals of the country of the contracting authority;
      (iii) any other standard.

**6.** Unless it is justified by the subject of the contract, Member States shall prohibit the introduction into the contractual clauses relating to a given contract of technical specifications which mention products of a specific make or source or of a particular process and which therefore favour or eliminate certain service providers. In particular, the indication of trade marks, patents, types, or of specific origin or production shall be prohibited. However, if such indication is accompanied by the words "or equivalent", it shall be authorized in cases where the contracting authorities are unable to give a description of the subject of the contract using specifications which are sufficiently precise and intelligible to all parties concerned.

TITLE V

**COMMON ADVERTISING RULES**

Article 15

**H–06**    **1.** Contracting authorities shall make known, by means of an indicative notice to be

[9] OJ No L 36, 7.2.1987, p. 31.
[10] OJ No L 40, 11.2.1989, p. 12.

published as soon as possible after the beginning of their budgetary year, the intended total procurement in each of the service categories listed in Annex I A which they envisage awarding during the subsequent 12 months where the total estimated value, taking account of the provisions of Article 7, is not less than ECU 750 000.

**2.** Contracting authorities who wish to award a public service contract by open, restricted or, under the conditions laid down in Article 11, negotiated procedure, shall make known their intention by means of a notice.

**3.** Contracting authorities who wish to carry out a design contest shall make known their intention by means of a notice.

### Article 16

**1.** Contracting authorities who have awarded a public contract or have held a design contest shall send a notice of the results of the award procedure to the Office for Official Publications of the European Communities.

**2.** The notices shall be published:

— in the case of public contracts for services listed in Annex I A, in accordance with Articles 17 to 20,
— in the case of design contests, in accordance with Article 17.

**3.** In the case of public contracts for services listed in Annex I B, the contracting authorities shall indicate in the notice whether they agree on its publication.

**4.** The Commission shall draw up the rules for establishing regular reports on the basis of the notices referred to in paragraph 3, and for the publication of such reports in accordance with the procedure laid down in Article 40(3).

**5.** Where the release of information on the contract award would impede law enforcement or otherwise be contrary to the public interest or would prejudice the legitimate commercial interests of a particular enterprise, public or private, or might prejudice fair competition between service providers, such information need not be published.

### Article 17

**1.** The notices shall be drawn up in accordance with the models set out in Annexes III and IV and shall specify the information requested in those models. The contracting authorities may not require any conditions other than those specified in Articles 31 and 32 when requesting information concerning the economic and technical standards which they require of service providers for their selection (section 13 of Annex III B, section 13 of Annex III C, and section 12 of Annex III D).

**2.** The contracting authorities shall send the notices as rapidly as possible and by the most appropriate channels to the Office for Official Publications of the European Communities. In the case of the accelerated procedure referred to in Article 20, the notice shall be sent by telex, telegram or fax.

The notice referred to in Article 15(1) shall be sent as soon as possible after the beginning of each budgetary year.

The notice referred to in Article 16(1) shall be sent at the latest 48 days after the award of the contract in question or the closure of the design contest in question.

**3.** The notices referred to in Articles 15(1) and 16(1) shall be published in full in the *Official Journal of the European Communities* and in the TED data bank in the official languages of the Communities, the text in the original language alone being authentic.

**4.** The notices referred to in Article 15(2) and (3) shall be published in full in the *Official Journal of the European Communities* and in the TED data bank in their original language. A summary of the important elements of each notice shall be published in the official languages of the Communities, the text in the original language alone being authentic.

**5.** The Office for Official Publications of the European Communities shall publish the notices not later than 12 days after their dispatch. In the case of the accelerated procedure referred to in Article 20, this period shall be reduced to five days.

**6.** The notices shall not be published in the official journals or in the press of the country of the contracting authority before the date of dispatch to the Office for Official Publications of the European Communities; they shall mention that date. They shall not contain information other than that published in the *Official Journal of the European Communities.*

**7.** The contracting authorities must be able to supply proof of the date of dispatch.

**8.** The cost of publication of the notices in the *Official Journal of the European Communities* shall be borne by the Communities. The length of the notice shall not be greater than one page of the Official Journal, or approximately 650 words. Each edition of the Official Journal containing one or more notices shall reproduce the model notice or notices on which the published notice or notices are based.

### Article 18

**1.** In open procedures the time limit for the receipt of tenders shall be fixed by the contracting authorities at not less than 52 days from the date of dispatch of the notice.

**2.** The time limit for the receipt of tenders provided for in paragraph 1 may be reduced to 36 days where the contracting authorities have published the contract notice, drafted in accordance with the model in Annex III A provided for in Article 15(1), in the *Official Journal of the European Communities.*

**3.** Provided that they have been requested in good time, the contract documents and supporting documents shall be sent to the service providers by the contracting authorities or competent departments within six days of receipt of their application.

**4.** Provided that it has been requested in good time, additional information relating to the contract documents shall be supplied by the contracting authorities not later than six days before the final date fixed for receipt of tenders.

**5.** Where the contract documents, supporting documents or additional information are too bulky to be supplied within the time limits laid down in paragraph 3 or 4 or where the tenders can be made only after a visit to the site or after on-the-spot inspection of the documents supporting the contract documents, the time limits laid down in paragraph 1 and 2 shall be extended accordingly.

### Article 19

**1.** In restricted procedures and negotiated procedures within the meaning of Article 11(2), the time limit for receipt of requests to participate fixed by the contracting authorities shall be not less than 37 days from the date of dispatch of the notice.

**2.** The contracting authorities shall simultaneously and in writing invite the selected candidates to submit their tenders. The letter of invitation shall be accompanied by the contract documents and supporting documents. It shall include at least the following information:

(a) where appropriate, the address of the service from which the contract documents and supporting documents can be requested and the final date for making such a request; also the amount and terms of payment of any sum to be paid for such documents;

(b) the final date for receipt of tenders, the address to which they must be sent and the language or languages in which they must be drawn up;

(c) a reference to the contract notice published;

(d) an indication of any documents to be annexed, either to support the verifiable statements furnished by the candidate in accordance with Article 17(1), or to supplement the information provided for in that Article under the same conditions as those laid down in Articles 31 and 32;

(e) the criteria for the award of the contract if these are not given in the notice.

**3.** In restricted procedures, the time limit for receipt of tenders fixed by the contracting authorities may not be less than 40 days from the date of dispatch of the written invitation.

**4.** The time limit for receipt of tenders laid down in paragraph 3 may be reduced to 26 days where the contracting authorities have published the contract notice, drafted according to the model in Annex III A provided for in Article 15(1), in the *Official Journal of the European Communities.*

**5.** Requests to participate in procedures for the award of contracts may be made by letter, telegram, telex, fax or telephone. If by one of the last four, they must be confirmed by letter dispatched before the end of the period laid down in paragraph 1.

**6.** Provided it has been requested in good time, additional information relating to the contract documents must be supplied by the contracting authorities not later than six days before the final date fixed for the receipt of tenders.

**7.** Where tenders can be made only after a visit to the site or after on-the-spot inspection of the documents supporting the contract documents, the time limit laid down in paragraphs 3 and 4 shall be extended accordingly.

### Article 20

**1.** In cases where urgency renders impracticable the time limits laid down in Article 19, the contracting authorities may fix the following time limits:

(a) a time limit for receipt of requests to participate which shall be not less than 15 days from the date of dispatch of the notice;

(b) a time limit for the receipt of tenders which shall be not less than 10 days from the date of the invitation to tender.

**2.** Provided it has been requested in good time, additional information relating to the contract documents must be supplied by the contracting authorities not later than four days before the final date fixed for the receipt of tenders.

**3.** Requests for participation in contracts and invitations to tender must be made by the most rapid means of communication possible. When requests to participate are made by telegram, telex, fax or telephone, they must be confirmed by letter dispatched before the expiry of the time limit referred to in paragraph 1.

### Article 21

Contracting authorities may arrange for the publication in the *Official Journal of the European Communities* of notices announcing public service contracts which are not subject to the publication requirement laid down in this Directive.

*Article* 22

The conditions for the drawing up, transmission, receipt, translation, collection and distribution of the notices referred to in Articles 15, 16 and 17 and of the statistical reports provided for in Articles 16(4) and 39 and the nomenclature provided for in Annexes I A and B together with the reference in the notices to particular positions of the nomenclature within the categories of services listed in those Annexes may be modified in accordance with the procedure laid down in Article 40(3).

TITLE VI

Chapter 1

**Common rules on participation**

*Article* 23

**H–07**  Contracts shall be awarded on the basis of the criteria laid down in Chapter 3, taking into account Article 24, after the suitability of the service providers not excluded under Article 29 has been checked by the contracting authorities in accordance with the criteria referred to in Articles 31 and 32.

*Article* 24

**1.** Where the criterion for the award of the contract is that of the economically most advantageous tender, contracting authorities may take account of variants which are submitted by a tenderer and meet the minimum specifications required by such contracting authorities. The contracting authorities shall state in the contract documents the minimum specifications to be respected by the variants and any specific requirements for their presentation. They shall indicate in the contract notice if variants are not authorized.

Contracting authorities may not reject the submission of a variant on the sole grounds that it has been drawn up with technical specifications defined by reference to national standards transposing European standards, to European technical approvals or to common technical specifications referred to in Article 14(2) or even by reference to national technical specifications referred to in Article 14(5)(*a*) and (*b*).

**2.** Contracting authorities which have admitted variants pursuant to paragraph 1 may not reject a variant on the sole grounds that it would lead, if successful, to a supply contract rather than a public service contract within the meaning of this Directive.

*Article* 25

In the contract documents, the contracting authority may ask the tenderer to indicate in his tender any share of the contract he may intend to subcontract to third parties.

This indication shall be without prejudice to the question of the principal service provider's liability.

*Article* 26

**1.** Tenders may be submitted by groups of service providers. These groups may not be required to assume a specific legal form in order to submit the tender; however, the group selected may be required to do so when it has been awarded the contract.

**2.** Candidates or tenderers who, under the law of the Member State in which they are established, are entitled to carry out the relevant service activity, shall not be rejected solely on the grounds that, under the law of the Member State in which the contract is awarded, they would have been required to be either natural or legal persons.

**3.** Legal persons may be required to indicate in the tender or the request for participation the names and relevant professional qualifications of the staff to be responsible for the performance of the service.

### Article 27

**1.** In restricted and negotiated procedures the contracting authorities shall, on the basis of information given relating to the service provider's position as well as to the information and formalities necessary for the evaluation of the minimum conditions of an economic and technical nature to be fulfilled by him, select from among the candidates with the qualifications required by Articles 29 to 35 those whom they will invite to submit a tender or to negotiate.

**2.** Where the contracting authorities award a contract by restricted procedure, they may prescribe the range within which the number of service providers which they intend to invite will fall. In this case the range shall be indicated in the contract notice. The range shall be determined in the light of the nature of the service to be provided. The range must number at least five service providers and may be up to 20.

In any event, the number of candidates invited to tender shall be sufficient to ensure genuine competition.

**3.** Where the contracting authorities award a contract by negotiated procedure as referred to in Article 11(2), the number of candidates admitted to negotiate may not be less than three, provided that there is a sufficient number of suitable candidates.

**4.** Each Member State shall ensure that contracting authorities issue invitations without discrimination to those nationals of other Member States who satisfy the necessary requirements and under the same conditions as to its own nationals.

### Article 28

**1.** The contracting authority may state in the contract documents, or be obliged by a Member State to do so, the authority or authorities from which a tenderer may obtain the appropriate information on the obligations relating to the employment protection provisions and the working conditions which are in force in the Member State, region or locality in which the services are to be performed and which shall be applicable to the services provided on site during the performance of the contract.

**2.** The contracting authority which supplies the information referred to in paragraph 1 shall request the tenderers or those participating in the contract award procedure to indicate that they have taken account, when drawing up their tender, of the obligations relating to employment protection provisions and the working conditions which are in force in the place where the service is to be carried out. This shall be without prejudice to the application of the provisions of Article 37 concerning the examination of abnormally low tenders.

### Chapter 2

#### Criteria for qualitative selection

### Article 29

Any service provider may be excluded from participation in a contract who:     **H—08**

   (a) is bankrupt or is being wound up, whose affairs are being administered by the court, who has entered into an arrangement with creditors, who has suspended business activities or who is in any analogous situation arising from a similar procedure under national laws and regulations;

(b) is the subject of proceedings for a declaration of bankruptcy, for an order for compulsory winding-up or administration by the court or for an arrangement with creditors or of any other similar proceedings under national laws or regulations;

(c) has been convicted of an offence concerning his professional conduct by a judgment which has the force of *res judicata*;

(d) has been guilty of grave professional misconduct proven by any means which the contracting authorities can justify;

(e) has not fulfilled obligations relating to the payment of social security contributions in accordance with the legal provisions of the country in which he is established or with those of the country of the contracting authority;

(f) has not fulfilled obligations relating to the payment of taxes in accordance with the legal provisions of the country of the contracting authority;

(g) is guilty of serious misrepresentation in supplying or failing to supply the information that may be required under this Chapter.

Where the contracting authority requires of the service provider proof that none of the cases quoted in (a), (b), (c), (e), or (f) applies to him, it shall accept as sufficient evidence:

— for (a), (b) or (c), the production of an extract from the "judicial record" or, failing this, of an equivalent document issued by a competent judicial or administrative authority in the country of origin or in the country whence that person comes showing that these requirements have been met,

— for (e) or (f), a certificate issued by the competent authority in the Member State concerned.

Where the country concerned does not issue such documents or certificates, they may be replaced by a declaration on oath made by the person concerned before a judicial or administrative authority, a notary or a competent professional or trade body, in the country of origin or in the country whence that person comes.

Member States shall, within the time limit referred to in Article 44, designate the authorities and bodies competent to issue such documents or certificates and shall forthwith inform the other Member States and the Commission thereof.


### Article 30

**1.** In so far as candidates for a public contract or tenderers have to possess a particular authorization or to be members of a particular organization in their home country in order to be able to perform the service concerned, the contracting authority may require them to prove that they hold such authorization or membership.

**2.** Any candidate or tenderer may be requested to prove his enrolment, as prescribed in his country of establishment, in one of the professional or trade registers or to provide a declaration or certificate as described in paragraph 3 below.

**3.** The relevant professional and trade registers or declarations or certificates are:

— in Belgium, the "registre du commerce—Handelsregister" and the "ordres professionels—Beroepsorden",

— in Denmark, the "Erhvervs- og Selskabstyrelsen",

— in Germany, the "Handelsregister", the "Handwerksrolle' and the "Vereinsregister",

— in Greece, the service provider may be asked to provide a declaration on the exercise of the profession concerned made on oath before a notary; in the cases provided for by existing national legislation, for the provision of research services as mentioned in Annex I A, the professional register 'Μητρώο Μελετητών' ανδ 'Μητρώο Γραφείων Μελετών',

— in Spain, the "Registro Central de Empresas Consultoras y de Servicios del Ministerio de Economía y Hacienda",
— in France, the "registre du commerce" and the "répertoire des métiers",
— in Italy, the "Registro della Camera di commercio, industria, agricoltura e artigianato", the "Registro delle commissioni provinciali per l'artigianato" or the "Consiglio nazionale degli ordini professionali",
— in Luxembourg, the "registre aux firmes" and the "rôle de la Chambre des métiers",
— in the Netherlands, the "Handelsregister",
— in Portugal, the "Registro nacional das Pessoas Colectivas",
— in the United Kingdom and Ireland, the service provider may be requested to provide a certificate from the Registrar of Companies or the Registrar of Friendly Societies or, if he is not so certified, a certificate stating that the person concerned has declared on oath that he is engaged in the profession in question in the country in which he is established in a specific place under a given business name.

### Article 31

**1.** Proof of the service provider's financial and economic standing may, as a general rule, be furnished by one or more of the following references:

(a) appropriate statements from banks or evidence of relevant professional risk indemnity insurance;
(b) the presentation of the service provider's balance sheets or extracts therefrom, where publication of the balance sheets is required under company law in the country in which the service provider is established;
(c) a statement of the undertaking's overall turnover and its turnover in respect of the services to which the contract relates for the previous three financial years.

**2.** The contracting authorities shall specify in the contract notice or in the invitation to tender which reference or references mentioned in paragraph 1 they have chosen and which other references are to be produced.

**3.** If, for any valid reason, the service provider is unable to provide the references requested by the contracting authority, he may prove his economic and financial standing by any other document which the contracting authority considers appropriate.

### Article 32

**1.** The ability of service providers to perform services may be evaluated in particular with regard to their skills, efficiency, experience and reliability.

**2.** Evidence of the service provider's technical capability may be furnished by one or more of the following means according to the nature, quantity and purpose of the services to be provided:

(a) the service provider's educational and professional qualifications and/or those of the firm's managerial staff and, in particular, those of the person or persons responsible for providing the services;
(b) a list of the principal services provided in the past three years, with the sums, dates and recipients, public or private, of the services provided;
    — where provided to contracting authorities, evidence to be in the form of certificates issued or countersigned by the competent authority,
    — where provided to private purchasers, delivery to be certified by the purchaser or, failing this, simply declared by the service provider to have been effected;
(c) an indication of the technicians or technical bodies involved, whether or not

belonging directly to the service provider, especially those responsible for quality control;

(d) a statement of the service provider's average annual manpower and the number of managerial staff for the last three years;

(e) a statement of the tool, plant or technical equipment available to the service provider for carrying out the services;

(f) a description of the service provider's measures for ensuring quality and his study and research facilities;

(g) where the services to be provided are complex or, exceptionally, are required for a special purpose, a check carried out by the contracting authority or on its behalf by a competent official body of the country in which the service provider is established, subject to that body's agreement, on the technical capacities of the service provider and, if necessary, on his study and research facilities and quality control measures;

(h) an indication of the proportion of the contract which the service provider may intend to sub-contract.

**3.** The contracting authority shall specify, in the notice or in the invitation to tender, which references it wishes to receive.

**4.** The extent of the information referred to in Article 31 and in paragraphs 1, 2 and 3 of this Article must be confined to the subject of the contract; contracting authorities shall take into consideration the legitimate interests of the service providers as regards the protection of their technical or trade secrets.

*Article 33*

Where contracting authorities require the production of certificates drawn up by independent bodies for attesting conformity of the service with certain quality assurance standards, they shall refer to quality assurance systems based on the relevant EN 29 000 European standards series certified by bodies conforming to the EN 45 000 European standards series. They shall recognize equivalent certificates from bodies established in other Member States. They shall also accept other evidence of equivalent quality assurance measures from service providers who have no access to such certificates, or no possibility of obtaining them within the relevant time limits.

*Article 34*

Within the limits of Articles 29 to 32, contracting authorities may invite the service providers to supplement the certificates and documents submitted or to clarify them.

*Article 35*

**1.** Member States who have official lists of recognized service providers must adapt them to the provisions of Articles 29(a) to (d) and (g) and of Articles 30, 31 and 32.

**2.** Service providers registered in the official lists may, for each contract, submit to the contracting authority a certificate of registration issued by the competent authority. This certificate shall state the reference which enabled them to be registered in the list and the classification given in this list.

**3.** Certified registration in official lists of service providers by the competent bodies shall, for the contracting authorities of other Member States, constitute a presumption of suitability corresponding to the service provider's classification only as regards Article 29(a) to (d) and (g), Article 30, Article 31(b) and (c) and Article 32(a).

Information which can be deduced from registration in official lists may not be questioned. However, with regard to the payment of social security contributions, an additional certificate may be required of any registered service provider whenever a contract is offered.

The contracting authorities of other Member States shall apply the above provisions only in favour of service providers established in the Member State holding the official list.

**4.** When registering service providers from other Member States in a official list, no proof or statement can be required in addition to those required of national service providers and, in any case, none in addition to those required in Articles 29 to 33.

**5.** Member States which have official lists shall be obliged to inform the other Member States of the address of the body to which applications for registration should be sent.

### Chapter 3

**Criteria for the award of contracts**

*Article 36*

**1.** Without prejudice to national laws, regulations or administrative provisions on the remuneration of certain services, the criteria on which the contracting authority shall base the award of contracts may be: **H–09**

(a) where the award is made to the economically most advantageous tender, various criteria relating to the contract: for example, quality, technical merit, aesthetic and functional characteristics, technical assistance and after-sales service, delivery date, delivery period or period of completion, price; or

(b) the lowest price only.

**2.** Where the contract is to be awarded to the economically most advantageous tender, the contracting authority shall state in the contract documents or in the tender notice the award criteria which it intends to apply, where possible in descending order of importance.

*Article 37*

If, for a given contract, tenders appear to be abnormally low in relation to the service to be provided, the contracting authority shall, before it may reject those tenders, request in writing details of the constituent elements of the tender which it considers relevant and shall verify those constituent elements taking account of the explanations received.

The contracting authority may take into consideration explanations which are justified on objective grounds including the economy of the method by which the service is provided, or the technical solutions chosen, or the exceptionally favourable conditions available to the tenderer for the provision of the service, or the originality of the service proposed by the tenderer.

If the documents relating to the contract provide for its award at the lowest price tendered, the contracting authority must communicate to the Commission the rejection of tenders which it considers to be too low.

### TITLE VII

**FINAL PROVISIONS**

*Article 38*

The calculation of time limits shall be made in accordance with Council Regulation (EEC, Euratom) No 1182/71 of 3 June 1971 determining the rules applicable to periods, dates and time limits.[11] **H–10**

[11] OJ No L 124, 8.6.1971, p. 1.

### Article 39

**1.** In order to permit assessment of the results of applying the Directive, Member States shall, by 31 October 1995 at the latest for the preceding year and thereafter by 31 October of every second year, forward to the Commission a statistical report on the service contracts awarded by contracting authorities.

**2.** This report shall detail at least the number and value of contracts awarded by each contracting authority or category of contracting authority above the threshold, subdivided as far as possible by procedure, category of service and the nationality of the service provider to whom the contract has been awarded and, in the case of negotiated procedures, subdivided in accordance with Article 11, listing the number and value of the contracts awarded to each Member State and to third countries.

**3.** The Commission shall determine in accordance with the procedure laid down in Article 40(3) the nature of any statistical information which is required in accordance with this Directive.

### Article 40

**1.** The Commission shall be assisted by the Advisory Committee for Public Contracts set up by Decision 71/306/EEC.

**2.** As regards telecommunications services falling within category 5 of Annex I A, the Commission shall also be assisted by the Advisory Committee on Telecommunications Procurement set up by Directive 90/531/EEC.

**3.** Where reference is made to the procedure laid down in this paragraph, the representative of the Commission shall submit to the Committee a draft of the measures to be taken. The Committee shall deliver its opinion on the draft within a time limit which the chairman may lay down according to the urgency of the matter, if necessary by taking a vote.
The opinion shall be recorded in the minutes; in addition, each Member State shall have the right to ask to have its position recorded in the minutes.
The Commission shall take the utmost account of the opinion delivered by the Committee. It shall inform the Committee of the manner in which its opinion has been taken into account.

**4.** The Committees mentioned in paragraphs 1 and 2 shall examine, on the initiative of the Commission or at the request of a Member State, any question relating to the application of the Directive.

### Article 41

Article 1(1) of Council Directive 89/665/EEC of 21 December 1989 on the coordination of the laws, regulations and administrative provisions relating to the application of review procedures to the award of public supply and public works contracts[12] shall be replaced by the following:

"1. The Member States shall take the measures necessary to ensure that, as regards contract award procedures falling within the scope of Directives 71/305/EEC, 77/62/EE, and 92/50/EEC (*), decisions taken by the contracting authorities may be reviewed effectively and, in particular, as rapidly as possible in accordance with the conditions set out in the following Articles and, in particular, Article 2(7) on the grounds that such

[12] OJ No L 395, 30.12.1989, p. 33.

decisions have infringed Community law in the field of public procurement or national rules implementing that law.
(\*) OJ No L 209, 24.7.1992, p. 1."

## Article 42

**1.** Article 5(1)(c) of Directive 77/62/EEC shall be replaced by the following:

"(c) the value of the thresholds in national currencies and the threshold of the GATT Agreement expressed in ecus shall in principle be revised every two years with effect from 1 January 1988. The calculation of these values shall be based on the average daily values of these currencies expressed in ecus and of the ecu expressed in SDRs over the 24 months terminating on the last day of August immediately preceding the 1 January revision. These values shall be published in the *Official Journal of the European Communities* at the beginning of November."

**2.** Article 4a(2) of Directive 71/305/EEC shall be replaced by the following:

"2. (a) The value of the threshold in national currencies shall normally be revised every two years with effect from 1 January 1992. The calculation of this value shall be based on the average daily values of these currencies expressed in ecus over the 24 months terminating on the last day of August immediately preceding the 1 January revision. These values shall be published in the *Official Journal of the European Communities* at the beginning of November.
(b) The method of calculation laid down in subparagraph (a) shall be reviewed, on a proposal from the Commission, by the Advisory Committee for Public Contracts in principle two years after its initial application."

## Article 43

Not later than three years after the time limit for compliance with this Directive, the Commission, acting in close cooperation with the Committees referred to in Article 40(1) and (2), shall review the manner in which this Directive has operated, including the effects of the application of the Directive to procurement of the services listed in Annex I A and the provisions concerning technical standards. It shall evaluate, in particular, the prospects for the full application of the Directive to procurement of the other services listed in Annex I B, and the effects of in-house performance of services on the effective opening-up procurement in this area. It shall make the necessary proposals to adapt the Directive accordingly.

## Article 44

**1.** Member States shall bring into force the laws, regulations and administrative provisions necessary to comply with this Directive before 1 July 1993. They shall forthwith inform the Commission thereof.
When Member States adopt these provisions, they shall contain a reference to this Directive or shall be accompanied by such reference on the occasion of their official publication. The methods of making such a reference shall be laid down by the Member States.

**2.** Member States shall communicate to the Commission the texts of the main provisions of national law which they adopt in the field governed by this Directive.

Article 45

This Directive is addressed to the Member States.

Done at Luxembourg, 18 June 1992.

For the Council
The President
VITOR MARTINS

## ANNEX I A

## SERVICES WITHIN THE MEANING OF ARTICLE 8

| Category No | Subject | CPC Reference No |
|---|---|---|
| 1. | Maintenance and repair services | 6112, 6122, 633, 886 |
| 2. | Land transport services,[13] including armoured car services, and courier services, except transport of mail | 712 (except 71235), 7512, 87304 |
| 3. | Air transport services of passengers and freight, except transport of mail | 73 (except 7321) |
| 4. | Transport of mail byu land[13] and by air | 71235, 7321 |
| 5. | Telecommunications services[14] | 752 |
| 6. | Financial services<br><br>(a) Insurance services<br>(b) Banking and investment services[15] | ex 81<br>812, 814 |
| 7. | Computer and related services | 84 |
| 8. | R&D services[16] | 85 |
| 9. | Accounting, auditing and book-keeping services | 862 |
| 10. | Market research and public opinion polling services | 864 |
| 11. | Management consultant services[17] and related services | 865, 866 |
| 12. | Architectural services; engineering services and integrated engineering services; urban planning and landscape architectural services; related scientific and technical consulting services; technical testing and analysis services | 867 |
| 13. | Advertising services | 871 |
| 14. | Building-cleaning services and property management services | 874<br>82201 to 82206 |
| 15. | Publishing and printing services on a fee or contract basis | 88442 |
| 16. | Sewage and refuse disposal services; sanitation and similar services | 94 |

[13] Except for rail transport services covered by Category 18.
[14] Except voice telephony, telex, radiotelephony, paging and satellite services.
[15] Except contracts for financial services in connection with the issue, sale, purchase or transfer of securities or other financial instruments, and central bank services.
[16] Except research and development service contracts other than those where the benefits accrue exclusively to the contracting authority for its use in the conduct of its own affairs on condition that the service provided is wholly remunerated by the contracting authority.
[17] Except arbitration and conciliation services.

## ANNEX I B

## SERVICES WITHIN THE MEANING OF ARTICLE 9

**H–12**

| Category No | Subject | CPC Reference No |
|---|---|---|
| 17. | Hotel and restaurant services | 64 |
| 18. | Rail transport services | 711 |
| 19. | Water transport services | 72 |
| 20. | Supporting and auxiliary transport services | 74 |
| 21. | Legal services | 861 |
| 22. | Personnel placement and supply services | 872 |
| 23. | Investigation and security services, except armoured car services | 873 (except 87304) |
| 24. | Education and vocational education services | 92 |
| 25. | Health and social services | 93 |
| 26. | Recreational, cultural and sporting services | 96 |
| 27. | Other services | |

## ANNEX II

## DEFINITION OF CERTAIN TECHNICAL SPECIFICATIONS

**H–13**    For the purpose of this Directive the following terms shall be defined as follows:

1. *Technical specifications*: the totality of the technical prescriptions contained in particular in the tender documents, defining the characteristics required of a work, material, product or supply, which permits a work, a material, a product or a supply to be described in a manner such that it fulfils the use for which it is intended by the contracting authority. These technical prescriptions shall include levels of quality, performance, safety or dimensions, including the requirements applicable to the material, the product or to the supply as regards quality assurance, terminology, symbols, testing and test methods, packaging, marking or labelling. They shall also include rules relating to design and costing, the test, inspection and acceptance conditions for works and methods or techniques of construction and all other technical conditions which the contracting authority is in a position to prescribe, under general or specific regulations, in relation to the finished works and to the materials or parts which they involve.

2. *Standard*: a technical specification approved by a recognized standardizing body for repeated and continuous application, compliance with which is in principle not compulsory.

3. *European standard*: a standard approved by the European Committee for Standardization (CEN) or by the European Committee for Electrotechnical Standardization (Cenelec) as "European Standards (EN)" or "Harmonization documents (HD)" according to the common rules of these organizations or by the European Telecommunications Standards Institute (ETSI) as a "European Telecommunications Standard" (ETS).

4. *European technical approval*: a favourable technical assessment of the fitness for use of a product, based on fulfilment of the essential requirements for building works, by means of the inherent characteristics of the product and the defined conditions of

applications and use. European approval shall be issued by an approval body designated for this purpose by the Member State;

5. *Common technical specification*: a technical specification laid down in accordance with a procedure recognized by the Member States to ensure uniform application in all Member States which has been published in the *Official Journal of the European Communities*.

6. *Essential requirements*: requirements regarding safety, health and certain other aspects in the general interest, that the construction works can meet.

## ANNEX III

## MODEL CONTRACT NOTICES

### A. *Prior information*

1. Name, address, telegraphic address, telephone, telex and fax numbers of the contracting authority, and, if different, of the service from which additional information may be obtained.
2. Intended total procurement in each of the service categories listed in Annex I A.
3. Estimated date for initiating the award procedures, per category.
4. Other information.
5. Date of dispatch of the notice.
6. Date of receipt of the notice by the Office for Official Publications of the European Communities.

**H–14**

### B. *Open procedure*

1. Name, address, telegraphic address, telephone, telex and fax numbers of the contracting authority.
2. Category of service and description. CPC reference number.
3. Place of delivery.
4. (a) Indication of whether the execution of the service is reserved by law, regulation or administrative provision to a particular profession.
   (b) Reference of the law, regulation or administrative provision.
   (c) Indication of whether legal persons should indicate the names and professional qualifications of the staff to be responsible for the execution of the service.
5. Indication of whether service providers can tender for a part of the services concerned.
6. Where applicable, non-acceptance of variants.
7. Duration of contract or time limit for completion of the service.
8. (a) Name and address of the service from which the necessary documents may be requested.
   (b) Final date for making such requests.
   (c) Where applicable, the amount and terms of payment of any sum payable for such documents.
9. (a) Persons authorized to be present at the opening of tenders.
   (b) Date, time and place of the opening.
10. Where applicable, any deposits and guarantees required.
11. Main terms concerning financing and payment and/or references to the relevant provisions.
12. Where applicable, the legal form to be taken by the grouping of service providers winning the contract.
13. Information concerning the service provider's own position, and information and

297

formalities necessary for an appraisal of the minimum economic and technical standards required of him.

14. Period during which the tenderer is bound to keep open his tender.
15. Criteria for the award of the contract and, if possible, their order of importance. Criteria other than that of the lowest price shall be mentioned if they do not appear in the contract documents.
16. Other information.
17. Date of dispatch of the notice.
18. Date of receipt of the notice by the Office for Official Publications of the European Communities.

## C. Restricted procedure

1. Name, address, telegraphic address, telephone, telex and fax number of the contracting authority.
2. Category of service and description. CPC reference number.
3. Place of delivery.
4. (a) Indication of whether the execution of the service is reserved by law, regulation or administrative provision to a particular profession.
   (b) Reference of the law, regulation or administrative provision.
   (c) Indication whether legal persons should indicate the names and professional qualifications of the staff to be responsible for the execution of the service.
5. Indication of whether the service provider can tender for a part of the services concerned.
6. Envisaged number or range of service providers which will be invited to tender.
7. Where applicable, non-acceptance of variants.
8. Duration of contract, or time limit for completion of the service.
9. Where applicable, the legal form to be assumed by the grouping of service providers winning the contract.
10. (a) Where applicable, justification for the use of the accelerated procedure.
    (b) Final date for the receipt of requests to participate.
    (c) Language(s) in which they must be drawn up.
11. Final date for the dispatch of invitations to tender.
12. Where applicable, any deposits and guarantees required.
13. Information concerning the service provider's own position, and the information and formalities necessary for an appraisal of the minimum economic and technical standards required of him.
14. Criteria for the award of the contract and, if possible, their order of importance if these are not stated in the invitation to tender.
15. Other information.
16. Date of dispatch of the notice.
17. Date of receipt of the notice by the Office of Official Publications of the European Communities.

## D. Negotiated procedure

1. Name, address, telegraphic address, telephone, telex and fax number of the contracting authority.
2. Category of service and description. CPC reference number.
3. Place of delivery.
4. (a) Indication of whether the execution of the service is reserved by law, regulation or administrative provision to a particular profession.
   (b) Reference of the law, regulation or administrative provision.
   (c) Indication of whether legal persons should indicate the names and

professional qualifications of the staff to be responsible for the execution of the service.
5. Indication of whether the service provider can tender for a part of the services concerned.
6. Envisaged number or range of service providers which will be invited to tender.
7. Where applicable, non-acceptance of variants.
8. Duration of contract, or time limit for completion of the service.
9. Where applicable, the legal form to be assumed by the grouping of service providers winning the contract.
10. (a) Where applicable, justification for the use of the accelerated procedure.
    (b) Final date for the receipt of requests to participate.
    (c) Address to which they must be sent.
    (d) Language(s) in which they must be drawn up.
11. Where applicable, any deposits and guarantees required.
12. Information concerning the service provider's own position, and the information and formalities necessary for an appraisal of the minimum economic and technical standards required of him.
13. Where applicable, the names and addresses of service providers already selected by the contracting authority.
14. Other information.
15. Date of dispatch of the notice.
16. Date of receipt of the notice by the Office for Official Publications of the European Communities.
17. Previous date(s) of publication in the *Official Journal of the European Communities.*

## E. *Contract award notice*

1. Name and address of the contracting authority.
2. Award procedure chosen. In the case of the negotiated procedure without prior publication of a tender notice, justification (Article 11(3)).
3. Category of service and description. CPC reference number.
4. Date of award of the contract.
5. Criteria for award of the contract.
6. Number of tenders received.
7. Name and address of service provider(s).
8. Price or range of prices (minimum/maximum) paid.
9. Where appropriate, value and proportion of the contract which may be subcontracted to third parties.
10. Other information.
11. Date of publication of the contract notice in the Official Journal of the European Communities.
12. Date of dispatch of the notice.
13. Date of receipt of the notice by the Office for Official Publications of the European Communities.
14. In the case of contracts for services listed in Annex I B, agreement by the contracting authority to publication of the notice (Article 16(3)).

## ANNEX IV

### A. *Design contest notice*

1. Name, address, telegraphic address, telephone, telex and fax numbers of the contracting authority and of the service from which additional documents may be obtained.   **H–15**
2. Project description.

299

**3.** Nature of the contest: open or restricted.

**4.** In the case of open contests: final date for receipt of projects.

**5.** In the case of restricted contests:
  (a) the number of participants envisaged;
  (b) where applicable, names of participants already selected;
  (c) criteria for the selection of participants;
  (d) final date for receipt of requests to participate.

**6.** Where applicable, indication of whether participation is reserved to a particular profession.

**7.** Criteria to be applied in the evaluation of projects.

**8.** Where applicable, names of the selected members of the jury.

**9.** Indication of whether the decision of the jury is binding on the contracting authority.

**10.** Where applicable, number and value of prizes.

**11.** Where applicable, details of payments to all participants.

**12.** Indication of whether the prize-winners are permitted any follow-up contracts.

**13.** Other information.

**14.** Date of dispatch of the notice.

**15.** Date of receipt of the notice by the Office for Official Publications of the European Communities.

B. Results of design contest

**1.** Name, address, telegraphic address, telephone, telex and fax numbers of the contracting authority.

**2.** Project description.

**3.** Total number of participants.

**4.** Number of foreign participants.

**5.** Winner(s) of the contest.

**6.** Where applicable, the prize(s).

**7.** Other information.

**8.** Reference of the design contest notice.

**9.** Date of dispatch of the notice.

**10.** Date of receipt of the notice by the Office for Official Publications of the European Communities.

# Appendix I

## THRESHOLD VALUES

**Values of thresholds in the field of public procurement applicable as from January 1,  I–01
1992 to December 31, 1993**

(91/C 321/07)

### 1. Values of thresholds under the directives on public procurement

The values of the thresholds applicable as of 1 January 1992 regarding:
— public works contracts, pursuant to Council Directive 71/305/EEC,[1] as amended by
  Directive 89/440/EEC,[2]
— public supply contracts, pursuant to Council Directive 77/62/EEC,[3] as amended by
  Directive 88/295/EEC.[4]
are as follows:

| | Public supply contracts | | Public works contracts |
|---|---|---|---|
| | ECU 200 000 | ECU 750 000 | ECU 5 000 000* |
| Belgian franc/ | | | |
| Luxembourg franc | 8 496 820 | 31 863 075 | 212 420 500 |
| Danish krone | 1 578 412 | 5 919 045 | 39 460 300 |
| German mark | 410 532 | 1 539 495 | 10 263 300 |
| Greek drachma | 41 110 400 | 154 164 000 | 1 027 760 000 |
| French franc | 1 388 660 | 5 207 475 | 34 716 500 |
| Dutch guilder | 462 696 | 1 735 110 | 11 567 400 |
| Irish pound | 153 818 | 576 819 | 3 845 460 |
| Italian lira | 304 442 000 | 1 141 657 500 | 7 611 050 000 |
| Pound sterling | 141 431 | 530 366 | 3 535 775 |
| Spanish peseta | 25 834 400 | 96 879 000 | 645 860 000 |
| Portuguese escudo | 35 917 400 | 134 690 250 | 897 935 000 |

* In the case of the Hellenic Republic, the previous threshold of ECU 1 000 000 for public works
contracts shall apply until 1 March 1992 which is the deadline for the bringing into force of the
necessary measures to comply with Directive 89/440/EEC. The value of this threshold in national
currency, effective from 1 January 1992, is Dr 205 552 000.

### 2. Value of thresholds under the GATT Agreement on Government Procurement

Pursuant to the second indent of Article 5(1)(a) of Directive 77/62/EEC, as amended by
Directive 88/295/EEC, and by the Agreement on Government Procurement concluded
within the framework of the GATT, as amended by the Protocol of 2 February 1987 and
approved by Council Decision 87/565/EEC,[5] the value of the threshold applicable as of 1
January 1992 to public contracts covered by the GATT Agreement is ECU 125 576.

[1] OJ No L 185, 16.8.1971, p. 5.
[2] OJ No L 210, 21.7.1989, p. 1.
[3] OJ No L 13, 15.1.1977, p. 1.
[4] OJ No L 127, 20.5.1988, p. 1.
[5] OJ No L 345, 9.12.1987, p. 24.

**I–02** **Threshold values in the field of public procurement (Council Directive 90/531/EEC) applicable as of 1.1.1993/31.12.1993**

(92/C 301/09)

The threshold values applicable as of 1.1.93 regarding supplies and works contracts, pursuant to Council Directive 90/531/EEC[6] are as follows:

|  | Supplies contracts | | | Works contracts |
|---|---|---|---|---|
|  | ECU 400 000 | ECU 600 000 | ECU 750 000 | ECU 5 000 000 |
| Belgian franc/ Luxembourg franc | 16 993 640 | 25 490 460 | 31 863 075 | 212 420 500 |
| Danish krone | 3 156 824 | 4 735 236 | 5 919 045 | 39 460 300 |
| German mark | 821 064 | 1 231 596 | 1 539 495 | 10 263 300 |
| Greek drachma | 82 220 800 | 123 331 200 | 154 164 000 | 1 027 760 000 |
| French franc | 2 777 320 | 4 165 980 | 5 207 475 | 34 716 500 |
| Dutch guilder | 925 392 | 1 388 088 | 1 735 110 | 11 567 400 |
| Irish pound | 307 637 | 461 455 | 576 819 | 3 845 460 |
| Italian lira | 608 884 000 | 913 326 000 | 1 141 657 500 | 7 611 050 000 |
| Pound sterling | 282 862 | 424 293 | 530 366 | 3 535 775 |
| Spanish peseta | 51 668 800 | 77 503 200 | 96 879 000 | 645 860 000 |
| Portuguese escudo | 71 834 800 | 107 752 200 | 134 690 250 | 897 935 000 |

[6] OJ No L 297, 29.10.1990, p. 1.

# INDEX

303